MASSACHUSETTS AVENUE ARCHITECTURE
Volume I
Northwest Washington, District of Columbia

Issued by

THE COMMISSION OF FINE ARTS

708 Jackson Place, N.W.
Washington, D.C. 20006

Charles H. Atherton
Secretary

Donald B. Myer
Assistant Secretary

Jeffrey R. Carson
Architectural Historian

Lynda L. Smith
Historian

J.L. Sibley Jennings, Jr.
Architect

1973

For sale by the Superintendent of Documents, U.S. Government Printing Office
Washington, D.C. 20402 - Price $5.20
Stock No. 010-000-00006-8

THE COMMISSION OF FINE ARTS
Established by Congress
17 May 1910

Hon. J. Carter Brown, Chairman

Hon. Nicolas Arroyo   Hon. Edward D. Stone, Jr.
Hon. Jane O. Dart   Hon. Chloethiel W. Smith
Hon. E. Kevin Roche   Hon. George A. Weymouth

FOREWORD

This volume is the seventh in a series of studies of historic architecture conducted by the Commission of Fine Arts. In the first six, attention was focused on the Georgetown area, with emphasis on a representative sampling of building forms and styles, especially in those areas subject to development. Areas on the waterfront and adjacent to the Georgetown University campus are obvious examples.

The purpose behind a study on Massachusetts Avenue is essentially the same - to preserve and record a unique collection of architecture threatened by development and change. These forces represent a formidable menace since the area does not yet enjoy the status of an historic district that would automatically insure some measure of protection, such as the case in Georgetown. This study seeks partial compensation for the lack of historic district legislation by identifying a number of notable structures and by providing information through the Joint Committee on Landmarks necessary for nomination to the National Register.

Such action, however, is no guarantee against the destruction of a building, no matter how important or unique it may be. Already large sections of the avenue have been demolished. What is needed is wide public concern and recognition of the particular value this section of the city has to the whole Capital.

It is the hope of those who have worked on this study that the avenue can be given formal status as an historic district. By this means, together with a concerned public awareness, perhaps the recent trend of demolishing these structures can be halted.

C.H.A.

PREFACE

Until recently the study of American architectural history centered about early domestic construction. As a result, there has been a lack of information regarding later and equally formative eras. For example, during the years between 1890 and 1930, American society was greatly influenced by the École des Beaux Arts in Paris. This influence produced a period that was rich, diversified and flamboyant.

Northwest Massachusetts Avenue in Washington, D.C. represents a style of life that fused the grand scheme of the Nation's Capital with the building aspirations of many of its more affluent inhabitants. This survey by the Commission of Fine Arts' staff records a selection of beaux-arts buildings which typify a portion of the avenue's rich and varied architectural heritage.

The depth and scale of this study are sufficient in scope for the understanding of both the individuality of the architecture and its builders. For many structures, the permits, illustrations and technical descriptions (which include a detailed analysis of exteriors, interiors and landscaping) supply a practical knowledge basic enough for reconstruction or restoration. The documentation of deeds, biographies, and physical and social histories are structured to give the tools by which one may grasp the personality of the owners and the character of their era.

We have attempted to create a repository of information, the sources of which (due to the destruction of the buildings themselves or to data pertinent to them) might not be readily available in the near future. In so doing we hope to impress upon the public the architectural wealth and historical interest of Washington and the value of protecting its impressive physical and residential qualities.

J.R.C.

ACKNOWLEDGEMENTS

The staff of the Commission of Fine Arts would like to express its gratitude to the many individuals, societies, and the District of Columbia and Federal agencies whose cooperation has aided in the completion of this book.

Personal thanks are extended to Jay R.L. de Sibour of Sagenaw, Michigan for the loan of his grandfather's portfolio, "Selections From the Work of J.H. de Sibour, Architect, Washington, D.C."; Mrs. Alice Trout, Assistant Chief of Circulation and Collection Maintenance Branch of the Interior Department Library; Mrs. Elden Billings, (former) Librarian of the Columbia Historical Society; Robert A. Truax, Librarian and Assistant Curator for the Columbia Historical Society; Miss Virginia Daiker of the Prints and Photographs Division, Library of Congress; the staff of the American Archives Association, Washington, D.C.; the staff of the Washingtoniana Room at the Martin Luther King Library; the staff of the Columbia Real Estate Title Insurance Company; the staff of the National Archives and Records Service at Suitland, Maryland, particularly Jack Bumgarner, Reference Branch Chief, and Lawrence Byrd and George Ellis, Archives Technicians; and the Commission of Fine Arts temporary staff historians: Thomas Paine and Dr. Daniel D. Reiff (for their initial research during the summer of 1970); and Dr. Philip A. Noffsinger (for his advice during the summer of 1971).

This survey would not have been possible without the understanding and approval of the foreign governments and private citizens whose properties are included in this study. We are grateful to:

The Embassy of Australia, formerly at 1700 Massachusetts Avenue, N.W.
    His Excellency Sir James Plimsoll, C.B.E.
        Ambassador Extraordinary and Plenipotentiary
    Mr. Bernard McCabe, Second Secretary (Administration)

The Embassy of the United Republic of Cameroon, 2349 Massachusetts Avenue, N.W.
    His Excellency Francois-Xavier Tchoungui,
        Ambassador Extraordinary and Plenipotentiary

The Embassy of Canada, 1746 Massachusetts Avenue, N.W.
    His Excellency Marcel Cadieux,
        Ambassador Extraordinary and Plenipotentiary
    Mr. Lawrence L. Banville, Second Secretary and Consul
    Mr. Glenn Bullard, Maintenance Supervisor

The Embassy of (Nationalist) China, 2311 Massachusetts Avenue, N.W.
    His Excellency James C.H. Shen,
        Ambassador Extraordinary and Plenipotentiary
    His Excellency Chow Shu-Kai, former
        Ambassador Extraordinary and Plenipotentiary
    Mr. Martin Wong, Minister (Special Assistant to the Ambassador)
    Mr. Kuan-hua Tuanmu, First Secretary

The Embassy of the Czechoslovak Socialist Republic, formerly at
    2349 Massachusetts Avenue, N.W.
    His Excellency Dr. Dušan Spáčil,
        Ambassador Extraordinary and Plenipotentiary
    His Excellency Ivan Rohal, former
        Ambassador Extraordinary and Plenipotentiary
    Mr. Emil Lansky, Attaché

The Embassy of India: Egyptian Interests Section, 2301 Massachusetts Avenue, N.W.
    Mr. Ahmed Tawfik Khalil,
        Minister Plenipotentiary
    Dr. Ashref Abdel Ghorbal, former
        Minister Plenipotentiary
    Mrs. Jamie Fish, personal secretary to the Minister

The Embassy of the Republic of Indonesia, 2020 Massachusetts Avenue, N.W.
    His Excellency Sjarif Thajeb,
        Ambassador Extraordinary and Plenipotentiary
    His Excellency R. Mangundiningrat Soedjatmoko, former
        Ambassador Extraordinary and Plenipotentiary
    Mr. Herqutanto Sosronegoro, Secretary

The Embassy of Ireland, 2234 Massachusetts Avenue, N.W.
    His Excellency William Warnok,
        Ambassador Extraordinary and Plenipotentiary
    Mr. Jerome Craig, Third Secretary

The Embassy of Japan, 2516 Massachusetts Avenue, N.W.
    His Excellency Nobuhiko Ushiba,
        Ambassador Extraordinary and Plenipotentiary
    Mr. Sho Watanabe, First Secretary (Construction)
    Mr. Masato Akazawa, Third Secretary

The Embassy of Luxembourg, 2200 Massachusetts Avenue, N.W.
    His Excellency Jean Wagner,
        Ambassador Extraordinary and Plenipotentiary

The Embassy of Pakistan, 2315 Massachusetts Avenue, N.W.
    His Excellency Sultan M. Khan, S.Pk., S.Q.A., P.F.S.
        Ambassador Extraordinary and Plenipotentiary

The Embassy of Peru, 1700 Massachusetts Avenue, N.W.
    His Excellency Fernando Berckmeyer,
        Ambassador Extraordinary and Plenipotentiary
    Mr. Luis Chavez, Attaché

The Embassy of the Philippines, 2253 R Street, N.W.
    His Excellency Eduardo Z. Romualdez,
        Ambassador Extraordinary and Plenipotentiary
    His Excellency Ernesto V. Lagdameo, former
        Ambassador Extraordinary and Plenipotentiary
    Miss V. Menciano, Assistant Cultural Officer

The Embassy of the Republic of Turkey, 1606 23rd Street, N.W.
   His Excellency Melih Esenbel,
      Ambassador Extraordinary and Plenipotentiary
   Mr. Erdinc Karasapan, Counselor

1746 Massachusetts Avenue, N.W.
   Mr. George H. Swift, Jr., Chicago

1785 Massachusetts Avenue, N.W.
   Mr. Thomas Rosser, Business Manager for Brookings Institution

1801 Massachusetts Avenue, N.W., The Sulgrave Club
   Mrs. William Anderson, President
   Mrs. James F. Lynn, former President
   Miss Marie Knapp, Manager

15 Dupont Circle, The Washington Club
   Mrs. Ruth Edmond Clark, President
   Mrs. J. Leslie Robinson, Chairman of the Fine Arts Committee
   Mr. Wilson Duprey, The New York Historical Society

2020 Massachusetts Avenue, N.W.
   Mr. Alan Burnham, Executive Director of the New York Landmarks
      Preservation Commission

2118 Massachusetts Avenue, N.W., The Society of the Cincinnati
   Mr. Herman Weissberger, Director Emeritus

2121 Massachusetts Avenue, N.W., The Cosmos Club
   Dr. George Crossette, member and Historian for the Cosmos Club
   Mr. E. Gunthar Skole, former Manager

2201 Massachusetts Avenue, N.W., Argyle Terrace
   Mr. George H. Bechtel
   The late Mrs. Christina Hull, resident manager
   Mr. John Hays, resident manager

2230 Massachusetts Avenue, N.W., private residence
   Mr. and Mrs. Edward T. Hines

2306 Massachusetts Avenue, N.W., Studio House
   Mr. Andrew Michaels, Director of the Buildings Management Department
      for the Smithsonian Institution
   Mr. Donald R. McClelland, Coordinator of the Lending Program for the
      National Collection of Fine Arts

2370 Massachusetts Avenue, N.W., private residence
   The Reverend and late Mrs. James B. Davis

CONTENTS

        page

Foreword i
Preface iii
Acknowledgements v
Map x

1700 Massachusetts Avenue, N.W. 3
1746 Massachusetts Avenue, N.W. 31
1785 Massachusetts Avenue, N.W. 61
1801 Massachusetts Avenue, N.W. 83
15 Dupont Circle, N.W. 93
2020 Massachusetts Avenue, N.W. 117
2118 Massachusetts Avenue, N.W. 149
2121 Massachusetts Avenue, N.W. 189
2200 Massachusetts Avenue, N.W. 241
2201 Massachusetts Avenue, N.W. 259
2230 Massachusetts Avenue, N.W. 285
2234 Massachusetts Avenue, N.W. 291
1606 23rd Street, N.W. 319
2253 R Street, N.W. 349
2301 Massachusetts Avenue, N.W. 355
2306 Massachusetts Avenue, N.W. 381
2311 Massachusetts Avenue, N.W. 391
2315 Massachusetts Avenue, N.W. 411
2349 Massachusetts Avenue, N.W. 421
2370 Massachusetts Avenue, N.W. 447
2516 Massachusetts Avenue, N.W. 453

Bibliography 457
Glossary 461

        The organization of the material in this publication is adapted from the standard Historic American Building Survey form. The original text and negatives for the illustrations are on file at the Prints and Photographs Division of the Library of Congress.

        Photographs for the survey were taken by Jack E. Boucher, Linwood, New Jersey; J. Alexander, Wheaton, Maryland; and the staff of the Commission of Fine Arts.

MOSQUE
BELMONT
KALORAMA
WYOMING
AVE
TRACY
PL
MASSACHUSETTS
AVE
CALIFORNIA
24TH
ST
BANCROFT
23RD
POOL
OAK HILL CEMETERY
Rock
Creek
2516
2349
2315
2311
2301
2253
2370
2306
1606
2234
2236
SHERIDAN
POTOMAC
PARKWAY
R
ST
Q
MILL RD
EAST ST
GARDEN
30TH
29TH
28TH
BRIDGE PL
P
POPLAR ST
O
TENNIS COURTS
DUMBARTON
FRANCIS J H S
PARKING

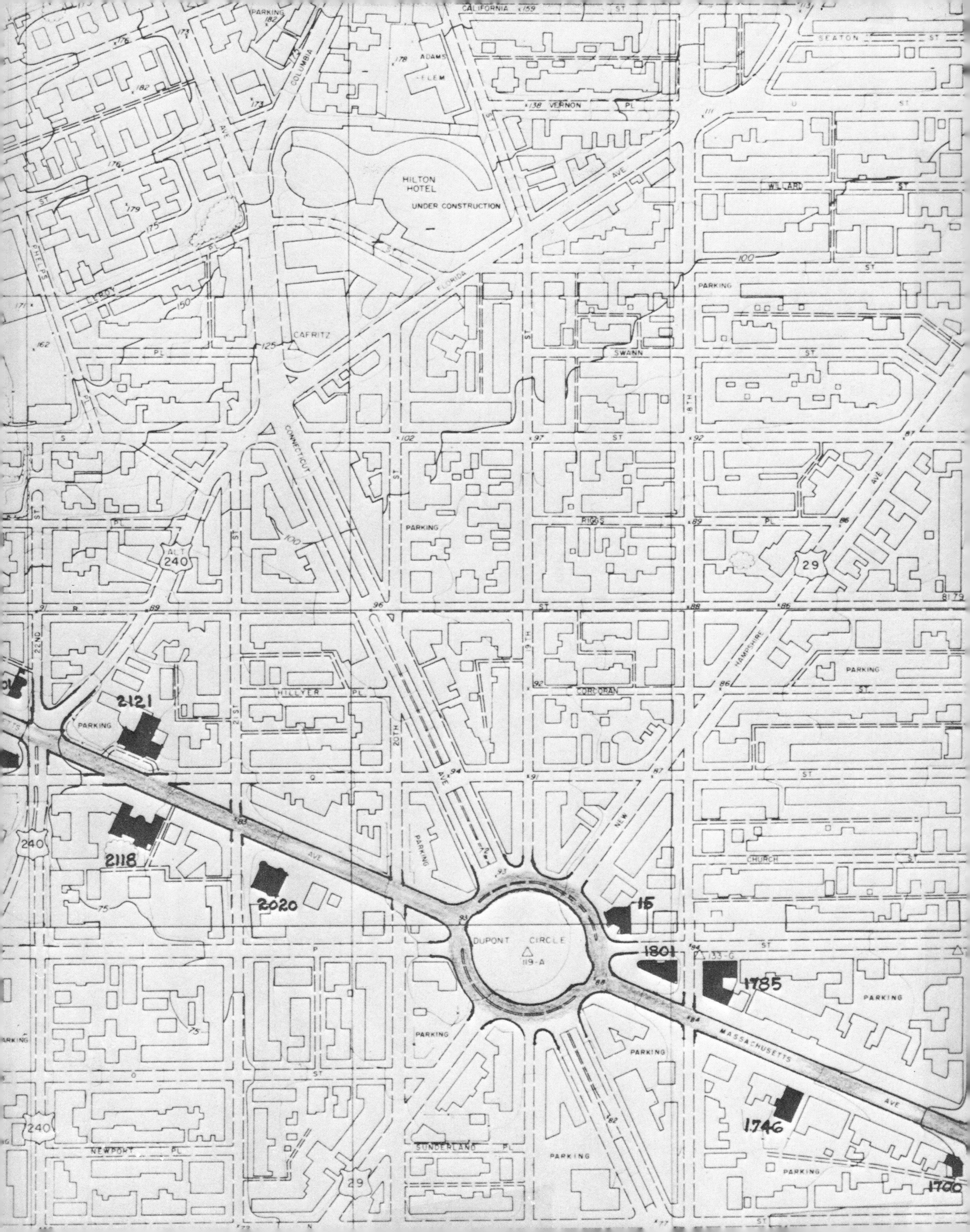

CALIFORNIA
ST
SEATON
PARKING
ADAMS
FLEM
COLUMBIA
AVE
VERNON
PL
U
HILTON
HOTEL
UNDER CONSTRUCTION
WILLARD
FLORIDA
T
LEROY
PHELPS
CAFRITZ
SWANN
18TH
S
CONNECTICUT
RIGGS
PARKING
ALT 240
29
R
HAMPSHIRE
19TH
HILLYER
CORCORAN
21 ST
20TH
22ND
2121
Q
NEW
CHURCH
240
2118
2020
15
DUPONT CIRCLE
119-A
1801
133-G
1785
P
MASSACHUSETTS
O
1746
NEWPORT
SUNDERLAND
1700
N

1700 MASSACHUSETTS AVENUE, N.W., WASHINGTON, D.C.

CFA photo
Boucher 1970

Location: 1700 Massachusetts Avenue, N.W., Washington, D.C.;
                       on the southwest corner of Massachusetts Avenue and
                       17th Street.

Present Owner: Republic of Peru

Present Occupant: Republic of Peru

Present Use: Chancery

Statement of   Originally a private residence, this semidetached build-
Significance: ing, subtly designed in the 16th century manner of Italian
                       classicism, is related to the intersection of 17th Street
                       and Massachusetts Avenue by an entrance facade set diago-
                       nally to the two principal street elevations. Special
                       attention is drawn to interior details, such as on the
                       stair, paneling and doors, which are similar to those used
                       at 2200 Massachusetts Avenue.

PART I. HISTORICAL INFORMATION

   A. Lot and Square:

   The building is located in Square 157, lot 72 (formerly lots 34
   through 37 which were subdivided from original lot 1. Original lot
   1 was subdivided into lots 23 through 37 in 1859.)

   B. Original and Subsequent Owners:

   The following chain of title to the property shows the owners of the
   present structure and of any known preceding structures on the site:

   1873   Deed June 9, 1873, recorded July 2, 1873 in
          Liber 721 folio 334

          Hallet Kilbourn
               To
          Timothy Gannon

          Lot 37 in Square 158.

   1882   Deed March 18, 1882, recorded April 18, 1882 in
          Liber 1004 folio 105

          John H. Pilling et ux,
          Elizabeth C.
               To
          Timothy Gannon

1700 Massachusetts Avenue, N.W.

"...for and in consideration of the sum of twelve hundred and fifty (1250) Dollars, ...Lot...(34) in Spalding and Wilson's subdivision of original lot...(1) in Square ...(158)..."

1885   Deed March 23, 1885, recorded April 3, 1885 in
Liber 1119 folio 115

Michael C. McDonough et ux,
Marcia
    To
Timothy Gannon

"...for and in consideration of the sum of Five thousand and two hundred and fifty dollars ($5250)...Lots...(35) and...(36) in Spalding and Wilson's subdivision of original lot...(1) in square ...(158)..."

1895   Deed June 26, 1895, recorded June 26, 1895 in
Liber 2034 folio 136

Timothy Gannon et ux,
Annie A.
    To
Michael Shea

Lot 37 in Square 158

1896   Deed September 16, 1896, recorded September 17, 1896 in
Liber 2151 folio 279

Michael Shea et ux,
Mary C.
    To
Timothy Gannon et ux,
Annie A.

Lot 37 in Square 158.

1902   Deed June 5, 1902, recorded June 5, 1902 in
Liber 2659 folio 187

Timothy Gannon et ux,
Annie A.
    To
Arthur D. Addison

"...Lots...(34),...(35),...(36), and...(37) in William E. Spalding and John C. Wilson's subdivision of Original lot...(1) in Square...(158)... said subdivision is recorded in the

1700 Massachusetts Avenue, N.W.

Office of the Surveyor of the District of Columbia in Book
B, page 182...

Subject to a certain deed of trust recorded among the Land
Records of the District of Columbia in Liber 2490 folio 305
securing an indebtedness of Sixteen thousand dollars. The
payment of which is assumed by said party of the second part..."

1902   Deed December 30, 1902, recorded December 30, 1902 in
Liber 2703 folio 228

Arthur D. Addison et ux,
Caroline H.
    To
James B. Oliver

"This Deed,...Witnesseth that Arthur D. Addison and Caroline
H. Addison, his wife of the District of Columbia, parties
hereto of the first part,...James B. Oliver, of Pittsburgh,
Pennsylvania, party hereto of the second part...Subject to an
indebtedness of Sixteen thousand Dollars ($16,000) secured by
Deed of Trust dated June 18th 1900, and recorded in Liber No.
2490 folio 305..."

Lots 34 through 37, Square 158.

1908   Deed July 2, 1908, recorded July 9, 1908 in
Liber 3157 folio 91

Amelia N. S. Oliver
George T. Oliver
    To
Emily J. Wilkins

"This Deed, made...by and between Amelia N. S. Oliver, George
T. Oliver and the Union Trust Company, of Pittsburgh, Pa.
Executors and Trustees, under the last will and Testament of
James B. Oliver, deceased...parties hereto of the first part;
...and Emily J. Wilkins, of the District of Columbia, party
hereto of the second part...Lots...(34) to...(37), both inclusive, in William E. Spalding and John C. Wilson's Subdivision..."

NOTE: April 10, 1909 Emily J. Wilkins and John F. Wilkins
combined lots 34 to 37, Square 158, into lot 72.
Recorded in Subdivisions Liber 35, folio 113, Office
of the Surveyor, District of Columbia.

Will of Emily J. Wilkins was recorded January 11, 1911
in Will Book No. 70, page 179, Registrar of Wills,
District of Columbia:

1700 Massachusetts Avenue, N.W.

"I, Emily Jane Wilkins, of Washington City, District of Columbia...give, devise and bequeath all of my property, both real and personal, and wheresoever situated,...unto my children John F. Wilkins and Robert C. Wilkins,...I give, devise and bequeath to my son, John F. Wilkins, the house known as No. 1700 Massachusetts Avenue, Northwest, in which I now reside, and being at the Southwest corner of 17th Street and Massachusetts Avenue,...in the City of Washington, District of Columbia, and all of the land which I now own in Square...(158)...I also give and bequeath to my said son, John F. Wilkins, all of the household furniture and other articles of personal property which I own and are contained in said house..."

Will of John F. Wilkins, Sr. was recorded January 5, 1942 in Will Book No. 296, page No. 427, Registrar of Wills, District of Columbia:

"...I do give, devise and bequeath all the rest and residue of the estate, real, personal, or mixed...to my wife Jula C. Wilkins, and the American Security and Trust Company, of Washington, D.C.... The said Trustees shall, in the event that I predecease my wife, with her consent, sell my town house at 1700 Massachusetts Avenue, Northwest, Washington, D.C., and my farm in Montgomery County, Maryland and the proceeds of said sales to become a part of the corpus of this trust fund..."

son: John F. Wilkins, Jr.
daughter: Katherine Wilkins Newbold

1942   Deed March 3, 1942, recorded March 12, 1942 in
Liber 7732 folio 61

American Security and Trust Co. and
Jula C. Wilkins, Trustees
    To
The M.R. Corporation

Lot 72 in Emily J. Wilkins' subdivision in Square 158. "...for and in consideration of the sum of Seventy-Five Thousand Dollars ($75,000)..."

1942   Deed July 27, 1942, recorded July 28, 1942 in
Liber 7777 folio 147

The M.R. Corporation
    To
Doris C. Lowe

1700 Massachusetts Avenue, N.W.

1942   Deed July 27, 1942, recorded July 28, 1942 in
Liber 7777 folio 149

Doris C. Lowe
     To
M.R. Corporation
Anna Taetle
Leona B. Gerber

Lot 72 in Square 158 and lots 31, 32, and 33 in William E. Spalding and John C. Wilson's subdivision of part of Square 158. "...Unto the M.R. Corporation ...an undivided one-half interest. Unto Anna Taetle an undivided one-fourth interest. Unto Leona B. Gerber an undivided one-fourth interest..."

1946   Deed December 5, 1946, recorded December 11, 1946 in
Liber 8387 folio 478

The M.R. Corporation
     To
Morris Rodman
Gertrude Rodman

Lot 72 in Square 158 and lots 31, 32, and 33 in Square 158. "Unto Morris Rodman an undivided one fourth interest. Unto Gertrude Rodman an undivided one fourth interest." (Note: Rodman was president and Gertrude Rodman was Secretary of the M.R. Corporation.)

1947   Deed January 10, 1947, recorded January 10, 1947 in
Liber 8402 folio 135

Anne Taetle et vir, Max
Leona B. Gerber et vir, Karl
Morris Rodman
Gertrude Rodman
     To
His Majesty George VI, in right of the
Commonwealth of Australia

Lot 72 in Square 158.

1973   Deed January 31, 1973, recorded February 23, 1973
Liber 13452 folio 558

The Government of Australia
     To
The Republic of Peru

Source: Recorder of Deeds, Washington, D.C.

1700 Massachusetts Avenue, N.W.

C. Date of Erection:

The building was begun in the spring of 1909 and completed in June 1910.

D. Building Permits:

The applications for the following building permits were filed by the architect, contractor or owner's agent and provide significant data:

No. 3852, April 16, 1909
Permit to build dwelling
    Owner: Emily J. Wilkins
    Architect: J. H. de Sibour
    Builder: William P. Lipscomb
    Estimated cost: $75,000.

Filed with No. 3852, April 16, 1909
Application for Projection beyond Building Line, February 6, 1909
    Owner: Mrs. Beriah Wilkins
    "Bay windows", 2'11" x 6'4"
    "One on Massachusetts Avenue and one on 17th Street."
    ("Bay windows" are corners of entrance facade.)

No. 5089, June 29, 1909
Permit for hoisting engine
    "Smokestack to be well braced and carried up so as to emit the smoke above neighboring buildings."

No. 766, August 5, 1909
Permit for office or storage shed

No. 292628, February 28, 1947
Permit to Repair or Reconstruct Building
    Owner: The Government of the Commonwealth of Australia
    "Close-up with solid brick masonry the party wall openings, between this building and 1708 Massachusetts Avenue, N.W., now existing on the 1st, 3rd and 4th floors."

Source: D.C. Government: Department of Economic Development, Bureau of Licenses and Permits, Central Files.

E. Alterations and Additions:

At the time of our survey in 1971, the reception room on the ground floor, and library and drawing room on the first floor were partitioned for offices. (Purchased by Peru on January 31, 1973, the building is being renovated at the time of this writing.)

The blueprint of the front elevation filed with Permit No. 3852, April 16, 1909 does not indicate a roof balustrade. However, a photograph in a private publication of about 1924, <u>Selections from the Work of J. H. de Sibour, Architect, Washington, D.C.</u>, does show a roof balustrade which has since been removed. (See photographs and front elevation drawing.)

F. Architect: J. H. de Sibour, New York and Washington, D.C.

Jules Henri de Sibour (1872-1938), the son of Vicomte Gabriel de Sibour and the former Mary Louisa Johnson of Belfast, Maine, was born in France. "Through his father he was descended from King Louis XVI of France." (<u>The Evening Star</u>, 11-4-38) When a young boy, de Sibour was brought to America where he attended St. Paul's School in New Hampshire and Yale University. In 1898, he married Margaret Marie Clagett, daughter of Mr. and Mrs. William H. Clagett, of Washington, D.C. They were to have three sons: Henri Louis, Jacques Blaise, and Jean Raymond.

In 1899, de Sibour went to Paris to study architecture at the École des Beaux Arts. One year later, he returned to the United States and began practice in New York City. He was taken into a partnership in 1902 or 1903 with Bruce Price, noted New York architect. About seven years later, he moved to Washington, D.C.

The following city directories list "Bruce Price & de Sibour" from 1903 through 1909. However, Bruce Price died May 28, 1903, about a year after de Sibour became a partner in the firm. From 1909 through 1911, de Sibour continued the New York practice under his own name and also maintained an office in Washington, D.C.

<u>Trow's New York City Business Directory</u>

1898-1902 Bruce Price, architect
           1133 Broadway

1901-1902 Jules de Sibour, architect
           1133 Broadway

1903-1906 Bruce Price & de Sibour
           1133 Broadway

1908   Bruce Price & de Sibour
           527 5th Avenue

1909-1911 Jules H. de Sibour
           527 5th Avenue

<u>Boyd's City Directory, District of Columbia</u>

1908-1909 Bruce Price & de Sibour, Hibbs Bldg.

1910-1922 J. H. de Sibour
           Hibbs Bldg.

1923-1924 J. H. de Sibour
           Edmonds Bldg.

1700 Massachusetts Avenue, N.W.

1925-1928 J. H. de Sibour
            Investment Bldg.

Jules Henri de Sibour was one of the National Capital's most successful and prolific architects during his 30 years of practice here. His designs in Washington, D.C., include the Wilkins, Hibbs, F. H. Smith, and Investment office buildings; the Chevy Chase Club; the University Club; and the Riggs Theatre and Office Building. He also designed the French Embassy (2221 Kalorama Road, N.W.); the Wilkins Residence (Peruvian Chancery, 1700 Massachusetts Avenue, N.W.); the Moore Residence (Canadian Chancery, 1746 Massachusetts Avenue, N.W.); and the Stewart Residence (Embassy of Luxembourg, 2200 Massachusetts Avenue, N.W.). The most outstanding example of his work surveyed to date is 1746 Massachusetts Avenue, N.W.

Sources: Alfred Johnson, <u>History and Genealogy of One Line of Descent from Captain Edward Johnson together with His English Ancestry: 1500-1914</u>, Boston: The Stanhope Press, 1930, p. 126.

Henry F. Withey and Elsie R. Withey, <u>Biographical Dictionary of American Architects (Deceased)</u>, Los Angeles: New Age Publishing Co., 1956.

<u>The Evening Star</u>, 11-4-38, 1:3 (obituary).

G. Known Plans, Drawings, Elevations, etc.:

Front Elevation. Blueprint. Scale 1/4" = 1'
Filed with Permit No. 3852, April 16, 1909
    "Residence for Mrs. Beriah Wilkins, Washington, D.C.
     J. H. de Sibour, Architect
     527 Fifth Avenue, New York
     February 2, 1909"
(see reproduction)

Plan for projections on Massachusetts Avenue Ink on linen.
Scale 1/8" = 1'
Filed with Permit No. 3852, April 16, 1909
    "Residence for Mrs. Beriah Wilkins, Washington, D.C.
     J. H. de Sibour, Architect
     527 Fifth Avenue, New York
     Hibbs Building, Washington, D.C.
     January 18, 1909"

H. Important Old Views:

Exterior photograph showing roof balustrade.
<u>Selections from the Work of J. H. de Sibour, Architect, Washington,</u>

1700 Massachusetts Avenue, N.W.

D.C., Edward F. Gruver Co., Washington, D.C.: bookbinder.
Private publication: property of Mr. Jay R. L. de Sibour, grandson
of J. H. de Sibour. (see reproduction)

I. Residents:

1. City and telephone directories list the following tenants:

   1911-1924   John F. Wilkins
   1925-1927   Finnish Legation
   1928   Catherine and John F. Wilkins
   1929   Vacant
   1930   John F. Wilkins
   1931   Vacant
   1932-1941   John F. Wilkins
   1942   Julia C. Wilkins (Jula?)
   1943-1946   Australian War Supplies
   1947-1969   Australian Embassy - Chancery
   1970-1972   Vacant

2. Biographies of the residents:

   Beriah Wilkins was born in Union County, Ohio, in 1846 and
   married in 1870 to Emily J. Robinson, also of Ohio. After
   serving in the Ohio State Senate, Wilkins was elected to the
   U.S. Congress in 1883 and subsequently re-elected for two more
   terms. In Congress, Wilkins was Chairman of the Committee on
   Banking and Currency. In 1894 he acquired an interest in The
   Washington Post and in 1899 became its majority share-holder.
   Wilkins worked as editor and publisher until his death in 1905.

   The Will of Beriah Wilkins (recorded June 22, 1905, in Will Book
   No. 60, page No. 253, Registrar of Wills, District of Columbia)
   stated: "...my stock in the incorporation known as the Washington
   Post Co. shall be equally divided between my beloved wife Emily
   J. Wilkins, and my two sons John F. and Robert C. share and share
   alike..."

   Sources: American Biographical Directories, District of
   Columbia, 1908-1909, Washington, D.C.: The Potomac
   Press, 1908.

   The New York Times, 2-8-05, 9:7 (obituary).

   Mrs. Emily J. Wilkins, widow of Beriah, bought the property for
   1700 Massachusetts Avenue in 1908 and applied for a building
   permit in 1909. She died the year of its completion, leaving
   the residence and its furnishings to her son John F. Wilkins.

   John F. Wilkins, Sr., born in 1872, was the son of Beriah and

Emily J. Wilkins. After his graduation from Princeton in 1894, Wilkins worked on The Washington Post as reporter, "sports editor, assistant city editor, manager of the now defunct Weekly Post, secretary of the Post Publishing Co., and, from 1903 to 1905, as co-publisher of the daily Post with his brother, Robert C. Wilkins." (The Washington Post, 12-16-41) In October 1905 John R. McLean bought the controlling interest of the Post.

Wilkins then involved himself in other business enterprises, becoming president of the Randolph Hotel Co.; president of Potomac Realty Co.; director of National Metropolitan Bank; and a member of the Washington Stock Exchange. During World War I, he was Director of the War Industries Bureau under Bernard Baruch. At the time of his death, he was director of American Security and Trust Co., Washington, D.C.

Socially prominent, Wilkins was the president of the Chevy Chase Club from 1914 to 1918 and member of the Board of Governors of the Metropolitan Club from 1914 to 1919. He died at his Massachusetts Avenue home in 1941, leaving his wife, Jula; son John F. Wilkins, Jr.; and daughter, Catherine Wilkins Newbold.

Sources: The Evening Star, 1-1-42, B9:5.
The New York Times, 12-16-41, 28:2 (obituary).
The Washington Post, 12-16-41, 33:6 (obituary).

Stanley H. Williamson (ed.), Who's Who in the Nation's Capital, 1938-1939, Washington, D.C.: Ransdell Incorporated.

Jula C. Wilkins (1876-1957), the former Jula Crittenden Harris of Richmond, Virginia, married John F. Wilkins, Sr. in 1905 and became "one of the best known hostesses in Washington".

Source: The New York Times, 2-27-57, 27:1 (obituary).

J. Previous Structure on the Site:

City directories and building permits indicate that a grocery store with the address 1700 Massachusetts Avenue, N.W. was located on lot 37, Square 158.

Deeds to the property show that Timothy Gannon acquired lot 37 in 1873, lot 34 in 1882, and lots 35 and 36 in 1885. Timothy Gannon, grocer, was listed at 1700 Massachusetts Avenue in both business and residential directories between 1873 and 1899. From 1900 through 1901 only his residence was listed at this address. By 1903 he had moved to 1451 N Street, N.W.

1700 Massachusetts Avenue, N.W.

Three building permits show that Gannon maintained a store and residence on the site. Permit No. 1075, dated August 17, 1878, was issued to Timothy Gannon for a brick, private stable measuring 19'-0" by 29'-0" and costing $400. A permit was issued to the same owner March 30, 1885, to repair the sill of a store. "Two show windows - each projecting 3 feet" were added to the store on lot 37 in November 1893. Although the owner was listed as John A. Hughes, Timothy Gannon was actually the owner according to the deeds.

Typical Stair Hall Bracket
CFA photo
Boucher 1970

Detail Mantle Frieze
Ground Floor Reception Room
CFA photo 1973

RESIDENCE FOR JOHN F. WILKINS, ESQ., WASHINGTON, D. C.

Wm. P. Lipscomb Co., Inc., *Builders*

J. H. de Sibour, *Architect*

Photo prior to 1925
Courtesy of Jay R.L. de Sibour

Detail Plaster Console
CFA photo 1973

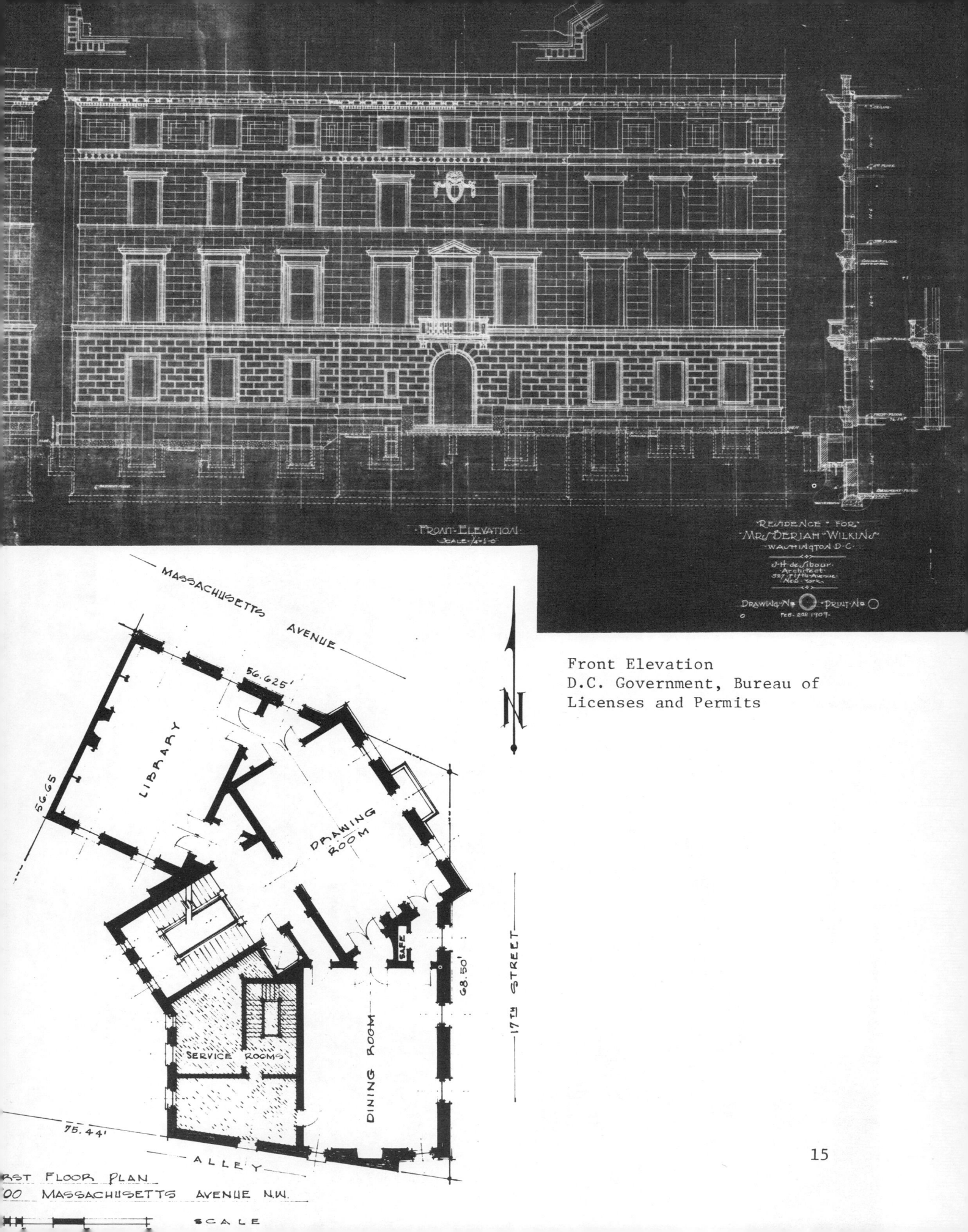

Front Elevation
D.C. Government, Bureau of
Licenses and Permits

Typical door panel
Stair Hall
CFA photo 1973

Stair detail
Ground floor
CFA photo
Boucher 1970

Stair Hall at first floor
CFA photo
Boucher 1970

Typical Balustrade Panel
CFA photo 1973

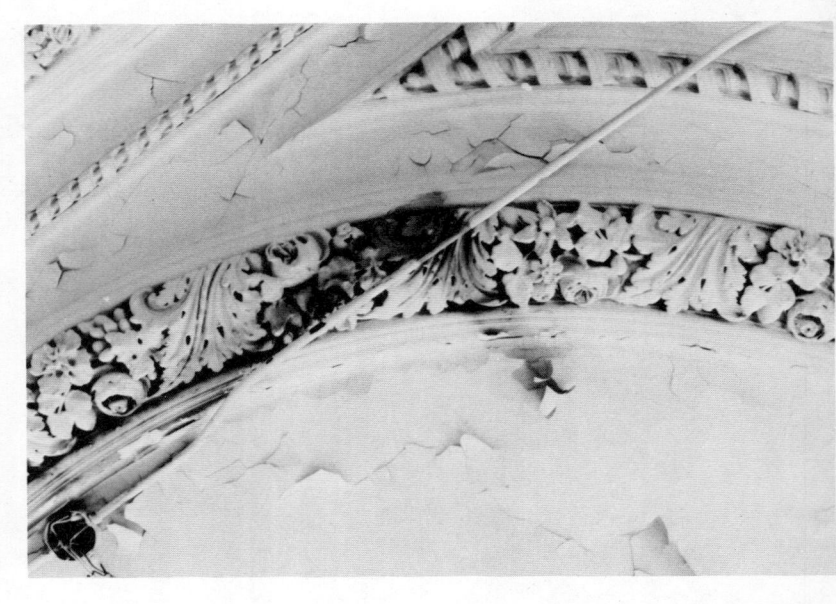

Above
Detail Cornice and Ceiling
Drawing Room
CFA photo 1973

Upper Right
Detail Ceiling
Drawing Room
CFA photo 1973

Right
Drawing Room
CFA photo
Boucher 1970

18

Dining Room
CFA photo
Boucher 1970

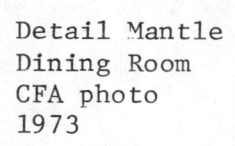

Detail Mantle
Dining Room
CFA photo
1973

Typical linen fold panel
CFA photo 1973

Library
CFA photo
Boucher 1970

1700 Massachusetts Avenue, N.W.

PART II. ARCHITECTURAL INFORMATION

    A. General Statement:

        1. Architectural character: This semidetached residence, with a mid - 16th century Italianate exterior, has 17th century English interior details.

        2. Condition: The exterior is preserved, the interior partitioned for offices (unoccupied).

    B. Exterior Description:

        1. Overall dimensions: The four story plus basement structure measures 59'-6" from sidewalk to cornice cap. The three bay, 39'-2" wide, entrance facade breaks forward diagonally to the three bay, 43'-0" east elevation (17th Street) and the three bay, 24'-6" north elevation (Massachusetts Avenue). The building depth from the entrance facade is approximately 56'-0".

        2. Foundations: concrete footings and slab.

        3. Wall construction: The limestone-faced basement has a torus water table which supports a plain frieze and moulded cap. The horizontally rusticated ground floor is separated from the smoothly dressed first and second floors by a frieze, corona and cyma string course. A cyma string course acts as second floor window sill. The third floor, with alternating windows and incised panels, rests on an omega frieze and cyma string course. The south and west elevations are exposed brick.

        4. Structure: brick bearing walls.

        5. Mechanical: The building is heated by an oil-burning, hot air furnace (the manufacturer, unknown). The passenger elevator is by Otis; the lighting is electric.

        6. Porches, stoops, bulkheads, etc.: The entrance stoop has three limestone risers flanked by block balustrades. The bay above the entrance has a turned-baluster balcony supported by consoles. An areaway gives access to the basement entrance at the rear (southwest) elevation.

        7. Chimneys: An exterior brick chimney rises above the south wall; all others are concealed behind the roof balustrade base.

        8. Openings:

             a. Doorways and doors: The glazed, double door with transom and side lights is recessed into a semicircular-arched, limestone architrave with a scroll keystone.

  b. Windows: All windows are double-hung and set within limestone, fascia and cyma architraves. Each first floor window architrave has consoles supporting a cornice. The central first floor bay, which opens onto the balcony above the entrance, has consoles and pedimented cornice. The second floor architraves each have a cornice. The south elevation bays have three-header brick courses forming segmental arches.

9. Roof:

  a. Shape, covering: built-up flat roofing.

  b. Cornice, eaves: The Corinthian entablature has a talon architrave, plain frieze, and dentil and modillion cornice, above which is the base for a panelled limestone balustrade with balusters centered over each bay (now removed).

  c. Dormers, cupolas, towers: none.

C. Interior Description:

1. Floor plans: The obtuse-angled plan is formed by the street elevations flanking the diagonal entrance facade which faces the street intersection. On axis with the ground floor vestibule is the central entrance hall and main stair. Immediately upon entering the entrance hall are flanking north and south lounges contained within the triangles formed by the reception room to the northwest and the serving rooms to the south. Each lounge has a lavatory and closet. A trapezoidal antehall gives access from the entrance hall to the northwest reception room. At the southwest is an elevator, and the service rooms and stair.

Over the ground floor entrance hall, and on axis with the main stair, is the first floor central foyer and drawing room. From the foyer, a trapezoidal antehall leads into the north library and a corridor leads to the southeast dining room and the southwest service area. Triangular areas are left between the three main spaces. The triangular areas are designed as an anteroom connecting the drawing room and library, and an antehall and room-with-safe connecting the drawing and dining rooms.
(See plan.)

Principal bedrooms and baths are on the second floor where a plain staircase over the drawing room continues to the third floor servants' quarters.

1700 Massachusetts Avenue, N.W.

2. Spaces:

Entrance hall:

a. Flooring: carpeted.

b. Baseboard: 6", wood.

c. Wainscot: 7'-0" high. There are three rows of flat, oak panels capped by a bracket and cyma cornice and broken by the Tudor arch of the reception room antehall.

d. Walls: plaster painted white.

e. Cornice: cyma.

f. Ceiling: 11'-0" high, plaster painted white; square panels within bound leaf ribs with crossing bosses.

g. Doorways and doors: The double door to the vestibule is plate glass with cast iron balusters and scrolls. The doors to the lounges, the service area and the elevator are panelled as the wainscot. The reception room antehall is set within a Tudor archway.

h. Hardware: oval, brass door knobs.

i. Lighting: There are four, two-light, gilded plaster, baroque sconces.

Lounges:

a. Flooring: oak, herringbone parquetry (beneath modern linoleum).

b. Baseboard: 6", wood with cyma cap.

c. Chairrail: 2'-6" high, wood, fascia.

d. Walls: The plaster and damask-panelled walls have been painted grey. Below the windows are applied mouldings.

e. Cornice: cyma and ogee mouldings below a beaded cove.

f. Ceiling: 10'-0" high, plaster painted white.

g. Doorways and doors: raised panels; fascia architrave.

h. Windows: fascia architrave to floor.

i. Lavatories: hexagonal ceramic tile floor; 6'-0" high square ceramic tile dado; plaster walls and ceiling.

1700 Massachusetts Avenue, N.W.

Reception room:

a. Flooring: oak, herringbone parquetry (beneath modern linoleum).

b. Baseboard: 7", wood with cyma cap.

c. Walls: The papered, plaster walls are painted over. There are applied, gilded mouldings.

d. Ceiling: 11'-0" high, plaster painted white. Bisecting circles form quatrefoil with bosses and rosettes in the late Tudor manner.

e. Doorways and doors: doors removed.

f. Lighting: There are three, two-light, brass and black enamel, Georgian revival sconces.

g. Heating: The north wall chimney has a black marble hearth. The plaster and wood mantle, in the Georgian manner, has flanking panels of leaves and fruit below consoles supporting a sunburst mask frieze, and an egg and dart shelf.

Main stair:

The reverse turn stair ascends west thirteen risers to the mid-landing and east thirteen risers to the first floor. The closed stringer soffit is plaster painted white, having square panels within bound leaf ribs with crossing bosses. The stringer, treads, risers and balustrade are oak. The candelabra-panelled newel is buttressed by a scrolled console, and the balustrade is pierced by panels of carved dolphins, nuts, fruit and flowers. A tripartite window and a gilded wood, baroque chandelier light the stair well. (See photographs.)

Foyer: (see photographs)

a. Flooring: carpeted.

b. Baseboard: 6", wood.

c. Wainscot: 8'-6" high. There are five rows of flat, oak panels below a bracket and cyma cornice. The wainscot is recessed for the drawing room door and continued into the library antehall.

d. Walls: plaster painted white. There are four-centered archways to the library antehall and the south corridor. A plaster-panelled, four-centered arch caps the recessed drawing room door.

e. Cornice: cyma.

1700 Massachusetts Avenue, N.W.

f. Ceiling: 13'-0" high, plaster painted white; square panels within bound leaf ribs with crossing bosses.

g. Doorways and doors: The double doors to the drawing room and library are of wainscot height. Each leaf has raised panels with a central acanthus leaf diamond panel. The wainscot cornice is continued over the doors.

h. Hardware: decorative, oval, brass door knobs.

i. Lighting: There are two, three-light, acanthus leaf, gilded plaster, baroque sconces.

Drawing room: (partitioned for offices. See photographs.)

a. Flooring: walnut, herringbone parquetry.

b. Baseboard: 6", wood painted black with bead cap.

c. Dado: raised wood panels in cyma mouldings.

d. Chairrail: 2'-6" high, wood with bead, plain frieze and fascia between cyma.

e. Walls: Flat plaster panels in applied cyma and fascia mouldings.

f. Cornice: plaster and wood with talon, fascia, egg and dart, acanthus modillions, talon and cyma below a cove.

g. Ceiling: 13'-0" high, plaster painted white. The cove is bordered by oak leaf pulvination followed by three, concentric, decorative mouldings which surround a pulvinated central oval.

h. Doorways and doors: There are 8'-0" high double doors to the foyer, library, and flanking the south chimney, to the anterooms and dining room. The doors have cornucopia lock-rails between raised panels within egg and dart mouldings, and fascia and ogee architraves.

i. Hardware: decorative, oval, brass door knobs.

j. Heating: The south wall chimney has a marble hearth with panel inlays, and a cast iron firebox and surround in the lattice motif. The white marble mantle, 4'-0" high, has floral pendant consoles, with corner rosette side panels, and a rosette guilloche frieze broken back over either console and centered by a floral swag key. The overmantle panel, its brocade painted over, has an egg and dart moulding with a feather and flower cap which interrupts the room cornice.

Library: (oak-panelled. Jacobean manner. See photographs.)

a. Flooring: walnut, herringbone parquetry.

b. Walls: There are six rows of stylized linen fold panels. Flanking the north wall chimney are pairs of bookshelves over cabinets, separated by decorative panelled pedestals and fluted pilasters, with rosette, and egg and dart capitals.

c. Cornice: denticulated.

d. Ceiling: 13'-0" high, plaster painted white. Leaf and rosette mouldings, which form repetitive Greek cross quatrefoil, are connected to square and diamond panels.

e. Doorways and doors: The 8'-0" high, double doors to the hall and anteroom each have two rows of acanthus leaf diamond panels within concentric rectangles.

f. Hardware: decorative, oval, brass door knobs.

g. Lighting: There are seven, three-light, brass sconces with strap work scroll bases.

h. Heating: The north wall chimney hearth is marble and the firebox is closed. The purple, grey and white-veined marble mantle, 6'-0" high, has a fascia and bolection surround, a plain frieze with scroll terminals and a cyma reversa, corona and cyma shelf. (See photograph.)

Dining room: (oak-panelled. Jacobean manner. See photographs.)

a. Flooring: walnut, basket weave parquetry.

b. Baseboard: 4", with bead cap.

c. Walls: Between fluted composite pilasters on panelled pedestals are four rows of paired, diamond-within-square, panels. The pilasters also flank the south chimney, and the windows and double door.

d. Cornice: The full entablature has a fascia and bead architrave, a strap work frieze interrupted by acanthus consoles over each pilaster, and a cyma cornice.

e. Ceiling: 13'-0" high, plaster painted white. The slightly coved ceiling has hexagonal and octagonal panels.

f. Doorways and doors: The north wall double door to the antehall (and drawing room) has raised panels (centered by an acanthus leaf diamond panel) and a cyma architrave. Flank-

1700 Massachusetts Avenue, N.W.

ing the double door are single doors with raised panels, one to the corridor and the other to the room-with-safe.

g. Hardware: decorative, oval, brass door knobs.

h. Lighting: There are four, three-light, escutcheon and arm, brass sconces.

i. Heating: The south wall chimney hearth is stone and the firebox is herringbone brick. The grey limestone mantle (6'-0" wide by 7'-0" high) has guilloche-panelled pilasters with egg and dart capitals which support guilloche consoles that flank a plain frieze. The consoles support a bead, fascia and talon architrave, a ribbon frieze, centered by an escutcheon and broken forward over either console, and a talon, corona, bead, and cyma shelf. (See photographs.)

D. Site:

1. Setting and orientation: The building faces northeast across the intersection of 17th Street and Massachusetts Avenue on a lot measuring 56'-8" on the north (Massachusetts Avenue), 68'-6" on the east (17th Street), 75'-5" on the south (public alley), 27'-4" on the southwest and 55'-3" on the northwest.

2. Enclosures: none.

3. Outbuildings: none.

4. Walks: There is a brick-paved alley at the south and a curved concrete entrance drive connecting Massachusetts Avenue and 17th Street.

5. Landscaping: The oval section formed by the drive and the areas abutting the east and west building walls are planted with oak, silver beech, blue spruce, hemlock and Virginia creeper.

1746 MASSACHUSETTS AVENUE, N.W., WASHINGTON, D.C.

RESIDENCE FOR CLARENCE MOORE, ESQ., WASHINGTON, D. C.

J. H. de Sibour, *Architect*

1746 Massachusetts Avenue, N.W. prior to 1925
Courtesy of Jay R. L. de Sibour

Location: 1746 Massachusetts Avenue, N.W., Washington, D.C.;
                    on the south side of Massachusetts Avenue between
                    17th and 18th Streets.

Present Owner: Canada

Present Occupant: Canada

Present Use: Chancery

Statement of   Originally a private residence, this structure was
Significance: designed in the Louis XV manner and, as built, was one
                    of the largest and most costly on the avenue. The simple,
                    logical progression of interior spaces and the sequence
                    of their stylistic changes exhibit a quality in both
                    design and craftmanship. Special attention is drawn to
                    the particularly fine wood carving, plaster and iron
                    work, and the remarkable hardware and lighting fixtures
                    used throughout.

PART I.   HISTORICAL INFORMATION

   A. Lot and Square:

   The building is located in Square 158, original lot 17. Parts of
   original lots 15 and 16, Square 158 are also included in the
   property.

   B. Original and Subsequent Owners:

   The following chain of title to the property shows the owners of
   the present structure and of any known preceding structures on the
   site:

   1901   Deed July 5, 1901, recorded July 16, 1901 in
          Liber 2561 folio 257

          Edward J. Stellwagen et ux et al.
                       To
          Mabelle Swift Moore

          "This Deed...Witnesseth that Edward J. Stellwagen and
          Charlotte M. Stellwagen his wife and said Edward J. Stell-
          wagen as Trustee under a certain Deed in trust from Francis
          G. Newlands and others, dated January 16th, 1901 and duly
          recorded in Liber No. 2569 folio 18 et seq. of the Land
          Records of the District of Columbia, parties hereto of the
          first part, for and in consideration of Thirty-seven thou-

1746 Massachusetts Avenue, N.W.

sand, four hundred and twenty-two dollars...to them paid by Mabelle Swift Moore, of said District of Columbia, party hereto of the second part...convey...All of Original Lot... (17) in Square...(158)..."

1907 Deed August 1, 1907, recorded September 30, 1907 in Liber 3099 folio 293

Arthur Herbert et al., Trustees
    To
Mabelle Swift Moore

"This Deed made...by and between Arthur Herbert, Julian T. Burke and Richard D. Roszelle, Trustees under the last Will and Testament of H. Grafton Dulany, deceased, by virtue of a Deed to them from Guy Fairfax Whiting and others, recorded November 1, 1892 in Liber No. 1752 folio 9 of the Land Records of the District of Columbia; - parties hereto of the first part, and Mabelle Swift Moore, of the District of Columbia, party hereto of the second part...for and in consideration of the sum of Ten thousand Dollars...Parts of Original Lots Fifteen (15) and Sixteen (16) in Square... (158), contained within the following metes and bounds; ...Beginning for the same on the Easterly line of said Lot ...(16), at a point distant...120 feet from Massachusetts Avenue, and running thence in a Southwesterly direction on said Easterly line,...42 feet to the southeast corner of said Lot...(16); thence west...62 feet to the southwest corner of said Lot...(16); thence north...63 feet to the northeast corner of original Lot...(14) in said Square; thence in a northwesterly direction to the southeast corner of the...10 feet wide alley...;thence in a northeasterly direction along the rear of said alley,...10 feet; and thence in a southeasterly direction...190.14 feet, more or less, to the point of beginning..."

1927 Deed May 28, 1927, recorded June 2, 1927 in Liber 6093 folio 357

Mabelle Swift Wichfeld
    To
His Majesty George V

"This Deed...between Mabelle Swift Wichfeld (formerly Moore)...and His Majesty George V, in Right of Canada, represented herein by the Minister of Public Works of Canada...Parts of Original Lots...(15) and...(16) in Square...(158)...Also all of Original Lot...(17) in said Square...(158)..."

Source: Recorder of Deeds, Washington, D.C.

1746 Massachusetts Avenue, N.W.

C. Date of Erection:

The building was begun in September 1906 and completed in 1909.

D. Building Permits:

The applications for the following building permits were filed by the architect, contractor or owner's agent and provide significant data:

No. 825, September 12, 1906
Permit to build dwelling
    Owner: Clarence Moore
    Architect: Bruce Price & de Sibour
    Builder: George A. Fuller & Company
    Address: 1748 Massachusetts Avenue, N.W. (later 1746)
    Location: Lot 17, Square 158
    Estimated cost: $200,000.

Filed with No. 825, September 12, 1906
Application for Projections beyond Building Line, No. 61267
    Total of six balconies on 2nd and 3rd floors.
    Steps to main entrance.

No. 3852, June 3, 1907
Permit to install electric passenger elevator and electric dumbwaiter
    Owner: Clarence Moore
    Mechanic: Otis Elevator Company
    Estimated cost: $5500, including dumbwaiter

No. 2322, December 19, 1908
Permit to erect marquise
    Owner: Clarence Moore
    Architect: Bruce Price & de Sibour
    Contractor: George A. Fuller & Company
    Dimensions: 7'-6" projection, 11'-0" width
    Estimated cost: $2500.

No. 586, July 28, 1909
Permit to Repair or Reconstruct
    "Build cellar in rear yard, connected to rear area."

No. 3780, December 15, 1909
Permit to erect freight elevator (electric)
    Owner: Mrs. Clarence Moore
    Contractor: G. W. Forsberg
    Use: Ashes, freight, etc.

Location: Rear of building
Dimensions: 5' x 4'
Estimated cost: $1000.

No. 5116, June 8, 1915
Permit to Repair or Reconstruct Building
    Owner: Mrs. Mabelle Wichfeld
    Architect: J. H. de Sibour
    Estimated cost: $2420.
    "Remodeling of interior of 3 rooms on third floor front and building scaffold on exterior of building for access to work."

No. 565, August, 24, 1917
Permit to Repair or Reconstruct Building
    Owner: Mrs. Aksel Wichfeld
    Architect: J. H. de Sibour
    Contractor: D. K. Nichol
    Estimated cost: $15,000.
    "It is proposed to construct a four story and basement addition on the west of present building, complete with heating, plumbing, and electric systems."

Source: D.C. Government: Department of Economic Development, Bureau of Licenses and Permits, Central Files.

E. Alterations and Additions:

A four story and basement addition containing small service rooms was built on the west elevation in 1917. Minor partitioning was added to the north drawing room and the west parlor on the first floor. Otherwise, there have been no major alterations to the main rooms on the ground and first floors.

F. Architect: J. H. de Sibour (Bruce Price & de Sibour, New York City)

See biography of J. H. de Sibour under 1700 Massachusetts Avenue.

G. Known Plans, Drawings, Elevations, etc.:

Front elevation. Ink on linen. Scale 1/4" = 1'
Filed with Permit No. 825, September 12, 1906
    "Residence for Clarence Moore, Esq., Washington, D.C.
    Bruce Price & de Sibour, Architects
    1133 Broadway, New York
    June 20, 1906"
(see reproduction)

1746 Massachusetts Avenue, N.W.

Elevation, plan and section. Three blueprints. Scale 3/4" = 1'
Filed with Permit No. 2322, December 19, 1908
    "Marquise - Residence for Clarence Moore, Esq.
    Bruce Price & de Sibour, Architects.
    1133 Broadway, New York
    December 16, 1907. Revised January 29, 1908"
(see reproduction)

Plan of projections beyond building line. Ink on linen.
Filed with Permit No. 825, September 12, 1906

Plan of elevator. Blueprint. Scale 1/2" = 1'
Filed with Permit No. 3780, December 15, 1909
    "Standard Electric Power Cellar Elevator
    G. W. Foresberg, Elevator Builders and Erectors"

H. Important Old Views:

Exterior photograph showing marquise. "Residence for Clarence Moore, Esq."
<u>Selections from the Work of J. H. de Sibour, Architect, Washington, D. C.</u> Edward F. Gruver Co., Washington, D.C.: Bookbinder.
Private publication: property of Mr. Jay R. L. de Sibour, grandson of J. H. de Sibour. (see reproduction)

I. Residents:

1. City and telephone directories list the following tenants:

    1909-1914   Clarence Moore
    1915   Mrs. Clarence Moore
    1916-1927   Aksel Wichfeld
    1928-1943   Canadian Legation and Chancery
    1944-1946   Canadian Embassy and Chancery
    1947-1972   Canadian Chancery

2. Biographies of the residents:

<u>Clarence Moore</u> perished on the Titanic, which sank April 15, 1912 after colliding with an iceberg. Moore, who was born in Clarksburg, West Virginia March 1, 1865, had been interested in developing West Virginia coal mining, oil and timber properties. In 1890 he came to Washington where he became associated with W. B. Hibbs & Co., which became one of Washington's more successful banking and brokerage firms. Through Hibbs & Co., Moore engaged in many large real estate transactions.

Moore's first wife, Alice McLaughlin, daughter of Frank McLaughlin who was once the owner of the <u>Philadelphia Times</u>, died in 1897. In 1900 Moore married the former Mabelle Swift of

Chicago. Six years after their marriage, the Moores began building their residence at 1746 Massachusetts Avenue, N.W.

A newspaper article at the time of the Titanic disaster reported:

> Mr. Clarence Moore has been identified with smart Washington circles for the last fifteen years. He was a noted horseman and he exhibited both in this country and in Europe. He was for some years master of the hounds of the Chevy Chase Club.[1888-1911] His residence, 1748 Massachusetts Avenue, [now 1746] completed about three years ago, is one of the handsomest in the city, and is a constant scene of hospitality. (The Washington Post, 4-16-12)

Moore left Washington on March 16, 1912 to vacation in England and to purchase foxhounds. A Night to Remember by Walter Lord mentions that "Clarence Moore of Washington...had been dog-shopping, but the 50 pairs of English foxhounds he bought for the Loudoun Hunt weren't making the trip." Clarence Moore was lost with 1513 others on the Titanic.

Sources: Walter Lord, A Night to Remember, New York: Holt, 1955, p. 13.

The Sunday Star, 4-28-12, 1:8.
The Washington Post, 4-16-12, 1:8.

Mabelle Swift Moore Wichfeld, Clarence Moore's second wife, was born March 28, 1878 and died February 1, 1933. Mabelle Swift was daughter of Edwin Carlton Swift of the Chicago meat packing family and therefore an heiress to the Swift fortune when her father died in 1901.

After her first husband's death, Mrs. Moore married Aksel C. P. Wichfeld in 1915. Aksel Wichfeld had come to the United States from his native Denmark in 1910. He engaged in banking and the operation of taxicab companies in New York City before being appointed as an attaché of the Danish Legation in 1916. At the time of his marriage to Mrs. Moore, Wichfeld was a guest of his uncle, the Danish Minister Constantin Brun, in Washington, D.C.

The Wichfelds maintained residences in New York, Paris, Washington, D.C., and Swiftmoor at Prides Crossing, Massachusetts. The Sunday Star, April 17, 1927, when reporting the sale of the Wichfeld's Washington residence to the Canadian government, indicated that "while the Wichfelds have lived abroad chiefly for some years, their home here in recent times was the scene of many fashionable gatherings of diplomatic and social circles."

1746 Massachusetts Avenue, N.W.

Mr. and Mrs. Wichfeld were divorced in 1932. Mr. Wichfeld later married Josephine (Fifi) Widener, daughter of Joseph E. Widener, art collector and capitalist. Mrs. Wichfeld died in 1933 while visiting friends in England, leaving three sons: Jaspar, Clarence and Lloyd Moore.

Sources: The Sunday Star, 4-17-27, 3:1.

    The Evening Star, 2-3-33, 3:1 (Mabelle Swift Moore Wichfeld, obituary).

    The New York Times, 9-12-56, 37:2 (Aksel C. P. Wichfeld obituary).

    The New York Times, 4-5-06, 9:3 (Edwin C. Swift, obituary).

    The Washington Post, 2-4-33, 3:4 (Mabelle Swift Moore Wichfeld, obituary).

Canada's first diplomatic post in the United States was established when Vincent Massey presented his credentials as Minister Plentipotentiary to President Coolidge on February 18, 1927. Before this time, Canada's representation in America and other foreign countries was controlled by the British government. In 1943 the legation was raised to Embassy status, and Leighton McCarthy was appointed Ambassador.

On May 28, 1927 Canada bought the residence at 1746 Massachusetts Avenue from Mabelle Wichfeld for $375,000. A portion of its furnishings were also acquired for an additional $100,000.

The Assistant Chief Architect of the Department of Public Works of Canada reported to the Privy Council in 1927:

> The whole building is of the very best and most expensive type of construction, and is at present in very excellent state of repair. The interior finish, while most elaborate and expensive, is in good taste, dignified and in keeping with the interior requirements of any embassy... [From] what could be ascertained, backed by the opinion of one of the prominent architects of Washington, the building is considered one of the best built residences in the City.

From 1927 until 1946, the building served as combined chancery and residence for the Minister and later the Ambassador. Since 1946, when the original Wichfeld furnishings were moved to the present embassy residence at 2825 Rock Creek Drive, it has been used solely for offices.

The heads of the mission since its inception have been:

37

1746 Massachusetts Avenue, N.W.

The Honorable Vincent Massey	1927-1930
The Honorable W. D. Herridge	1931-1935
Sir Herbert Marler	1936-1939
The Honorable Loring Christie	1939-1941
The Honorable Leighton McCarthy	1941-1944
The Honorable L. B. Pearson	1944-1946
The Honorable H. H. Wrong	1946-1953
The Honorable A. D. P. Heeney	1953-1957
The Honorable Norman Robertson	1957-1958
The Honorable A. D. P. Heeney	1959-1962
The Honorable C. S. A. Ritchie	1962-1966
The Honorable A. E. Ritchie	1966-1970
The Honorable Marcel Cadieux	1970-

Sources: <u>The Canadian Embassy in Washington</u> (pamphlet provided by the Canadian Embassy).

Minutes of a Meeting of the Privy Council, April 14, 1927. "Report from the Minister of Public Works concerning proposed Canadian Legation in Washington" (records of the Canadian Embassy).

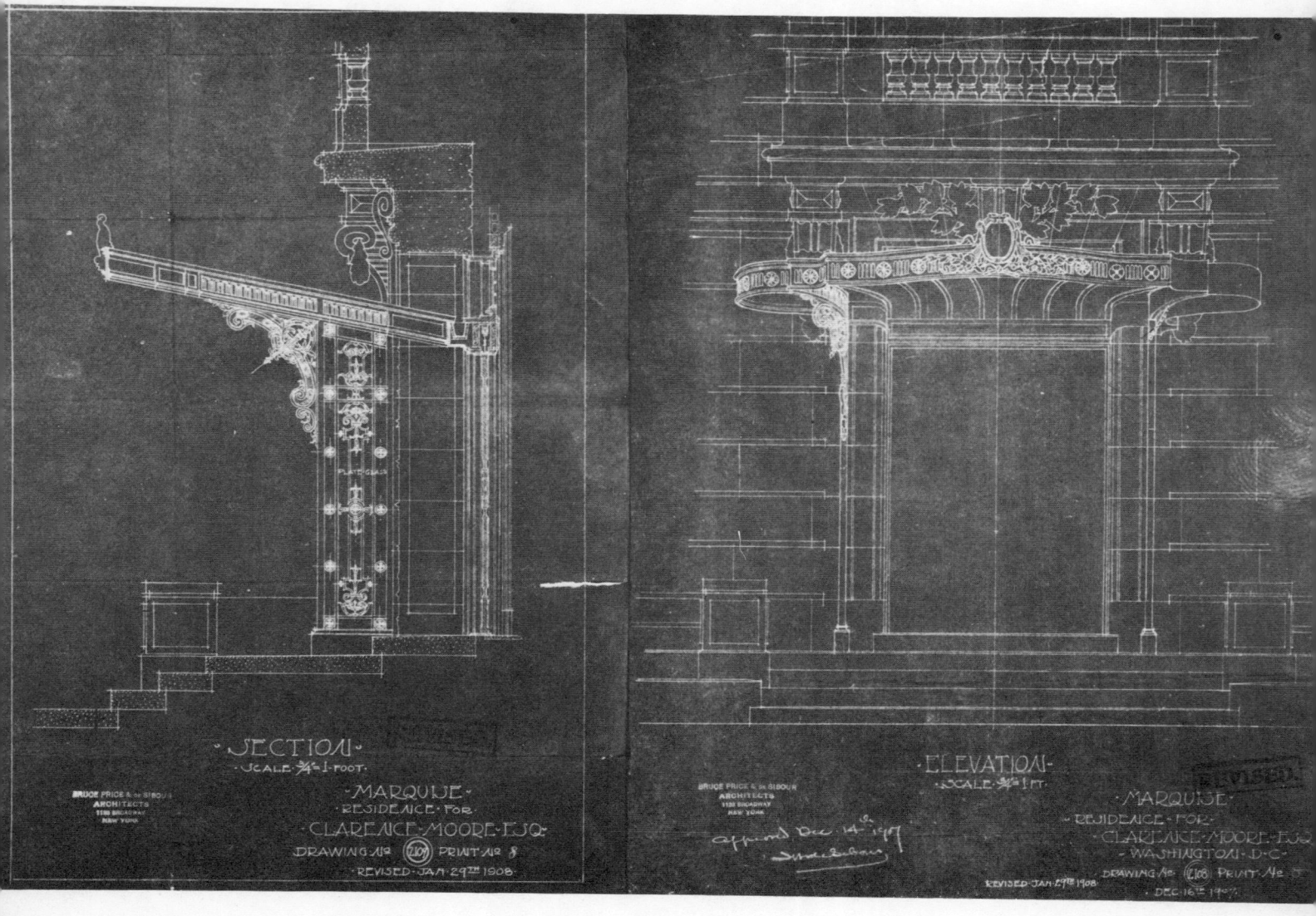

Marquise Drawings, D.C. Government, Bureau of Licenses and Permits

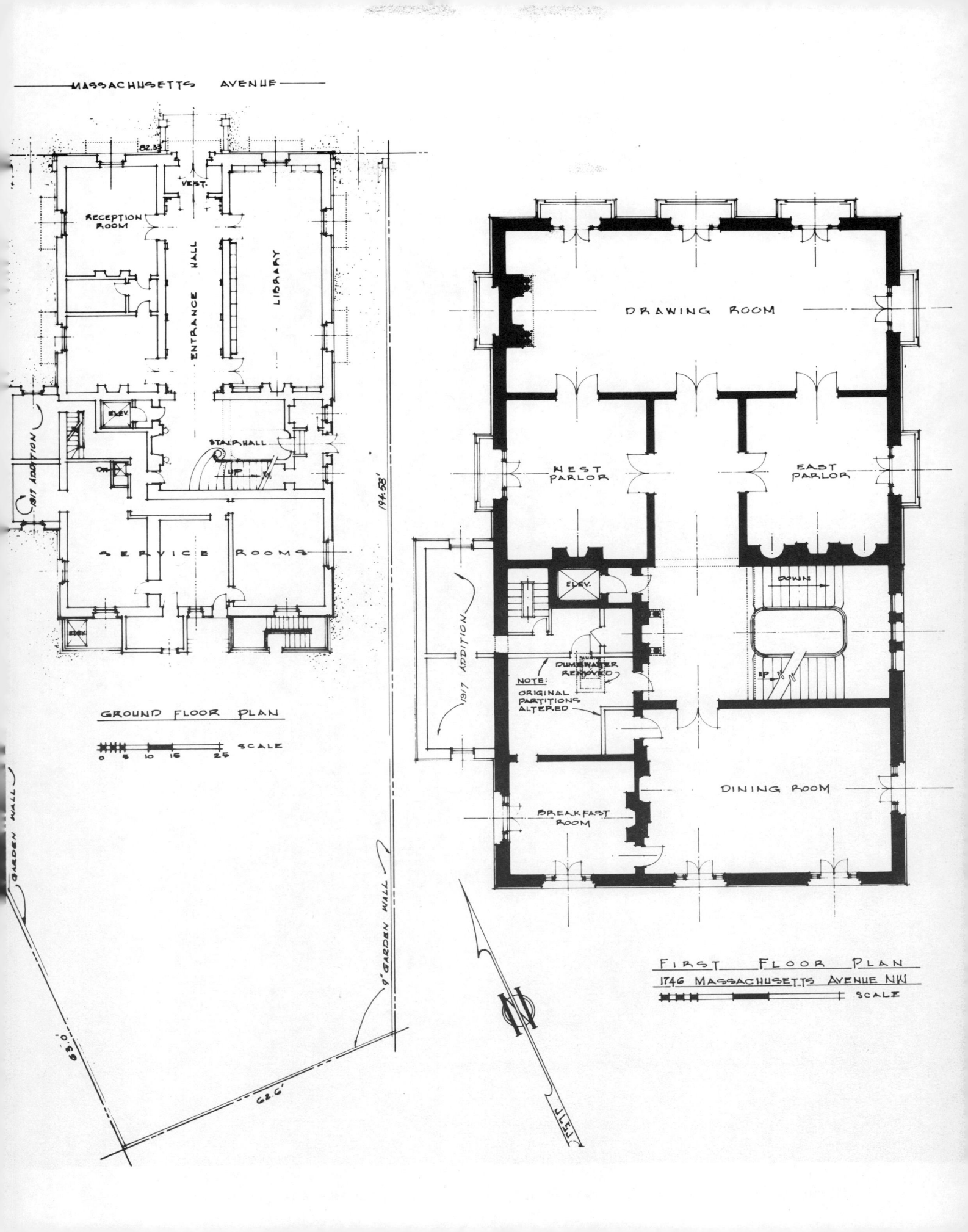

GROUND FLOOR PLAN

- RECEPTION ROOM
- VEST.
- ENTRANCE HALL
- LIBRARY
- ELEV.
- STAIR HALL
- SERVICE ROOMS
- 1917 ADDITION

FIRST FLOOR PLAN
1746 MASSACHUSETTS AVENUE NW

- DRAWING ROOM
- WEST PARLOR
- EAST PARLOR
- ELEV.
- DUMBWAITER REMOVED
- NOTE: ORIGINAL PARTITIONS ALTERED
- DOWN
- BREAKFAST ROOM
- DINING ROOM
- 1917 ADDITION

MASSACHUSETTS AVENUE

8' GARDEN WALL

17TH ST

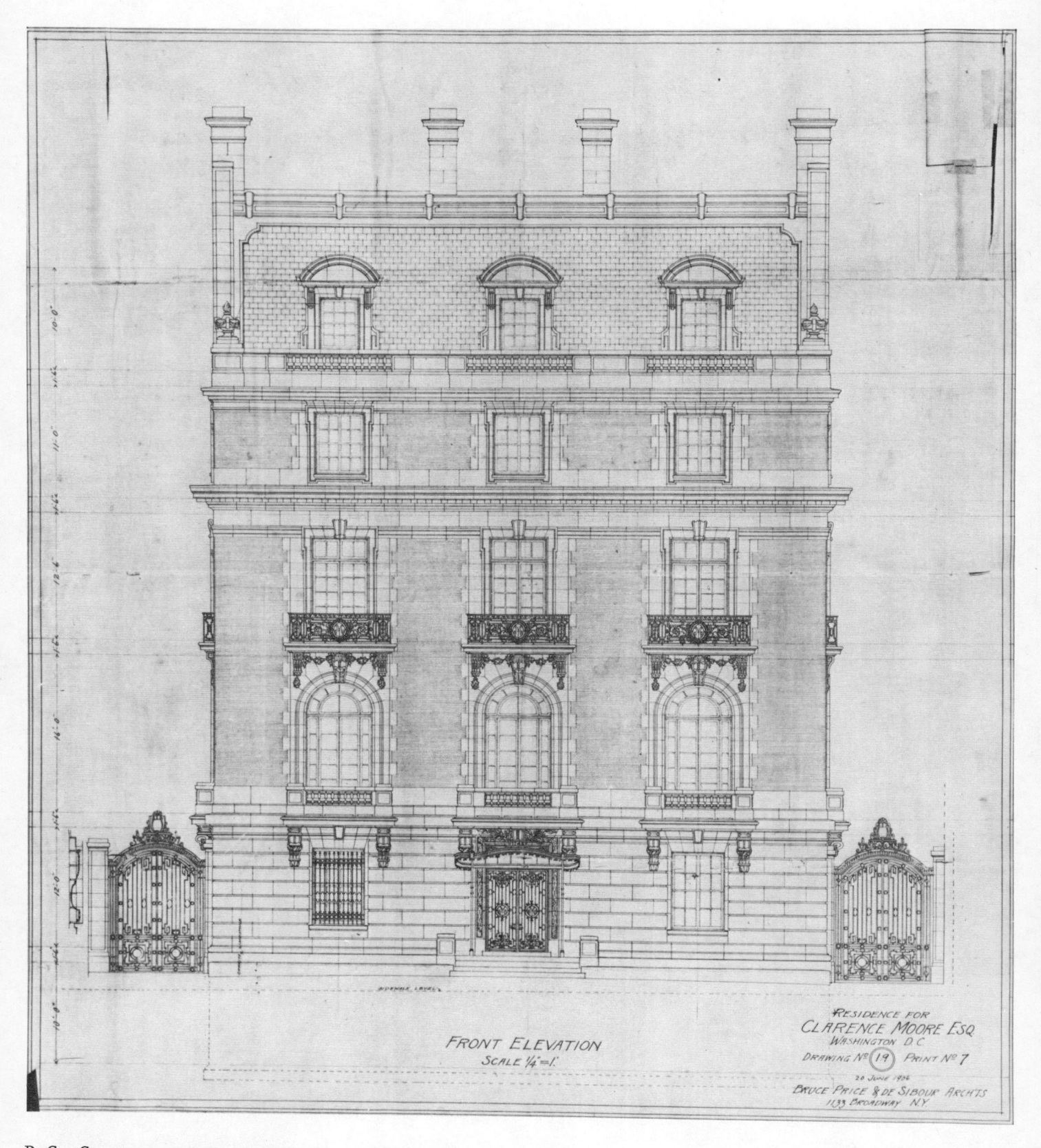

D.C. Government, Bureau of Licenses and Permits

40

CFA photo
Boucher 1970

Cornice Detail
Entrance Hall
HABS photo
Boucher 1972

Ground Floor Entrance Hall
HABS photo
Boucher 1972

Stair Hall Detail
Ground Floor
HABS photo
Boucher 1972

Ground Floor Stair Hall
HABS photo
Boucher 1972

Hall Sconce
Ground Floor
HABS photo
Boucher 1972

Dining Room
First Floor
HABS photo
Boucher 1972

Reception and Stair Hall
First Floor
HABS photo
Boucher 1972

Panelling Detail
First Floor Hall
HABS photo
Boucher 1972

1746 Massachusetts Avenue, N.W.

PART II. ARCHITECTURAL INFORMATION

    A. General Statement:

        1. Architectural character: This detached residence has a Louis XV exterior with 16th, 17th and 18th century French and English interior details.

        2. Condition: well-maintained despite minor partitioning and service alterations.

    B. Exterior Description:

        1. Overall dimensions: The four and one half story plus basement structure is 79'-6" from sidewalk to roof ridge. The elevations measure 59'-0" along the three bay north elevation (Massachusetts Avenue), 101'-0" along the composite four bay east elevation (the last two bays broken back 4"), 58'-8" along the three bay south elevation, and 101'-0" along the composite four bay west elevation, which has an 18'-6" south bay followed by a 31'-5" service bay broken forward 11'-0" from the building wall.

        2. Foundations: concrete footings and slab.

        3. Wall construction: Above a granite base is a limestone torus water table, a rusticated ground floor, and a frieze and block string course below a pedestal which supports the upper walls of Roman brick separated between the second and third floors by a limestone Tuscan entablature with a bracket cornice and a block cap flush with the building wall. The first, second and third floor window and door architraves are set in a limestone ground broken slightly forward.

        4. Structure: brick bearing walls, concrete floors, steel roofing members.

        5. Mechanical: The building is heated by an oil-burning, hot air furnace. The Otis passenger elevator is wood-panelled. The "Standard Electric Power Cellar (freight) Elevator" is 5'-0" by 4'-0". The dumbwaiter and lighting are electric.

        6. Porches, stoops, bulkheads, etc.: The north entrance has a 6'-6" wide stoop approached by four, 12'-0" wide, granite risers flanked by panelled limestone balustrades.

        Flanking the head of the entrance and ground floor windows are limestone consoles with swag and guttae. The string course breaks forward at each pair of consoles to support limestone first floor balconies with vase balusters and panelled end stops.

1746 Massachusetts Avenue, N.W.

The first floor window keystones are connected by limestone floral swags to flanking console brackets with pendants. The brackets support limestone second floor balconies with decorative cast iron railings each centered by a monogram bordered by rinceau and sprays. The basement is approached by a flight of concrete risers which descend into an areaway at the southeast corner of the building.

7. Chimneys: Visible from ground level are six limestone chimneys with Tuscan entablature caps (one each at the east and west walls, two at the front (north) mansard roof ridge and two at the south).

8. Openings:

    a. Doorways and doors: The original double door and transom of plate glass and decorative cast iron with centered monograms has been replaced. The limestone, pulvinated oak leaf architrave has a scroll keystone with foliate sprays.

    b. Windows: The ground, second and third floor windows and French doors are four lights wide. All are casement except for the ground and third floor bays where double-hung windows simulate casements. The first floor French doors have round-arched transoms and side lights; the second floor French doors have flat transoms. The ground floor has wrought iron, decorative bar grilles. The second floor has louvered shutters which fold into the architrave jamb.

    The ground floor windows have recessed limestone architraves, fillet and block sills, and panelled keystones which interrupt the string course.

    The first floor French doors have limestone, fascia and ogee architraves with acanthus leaf and scroll keystones and shell caps.

    The second floor French doors have crossette limestone architraves of fascia and backband with scrolled keystones which interrupt the second floor entablature architrave.

    The third floor windows have crossette limestone architraves of fascia and backband which interrupt the roof entablature architrave and frieze.

9. Roof:

    a. Shape, covering: The slate mansard roof has limestone fractables, and metal, pulvinated ridge caps and flashing with built-up roofing behind.

1746 Massachusetts Avenue, N.W.

  b. Cornice eaves: The limestone Tuscan entablature is capped at the north elevation by a raised panel balustrade with vase balusters centered over each bay, the end stops surmounted by a draped, limestone lamp.

  c. Dormers, cupolas, towers: Centered above each north bay is a double-hung, limestone dormer with side panels flanked by angular scrolls and capped by brackets which support a segmentally-arched pediment.

C. Interior Description:

1. Floor plans: On axis with the north central entrance is a ground floor vestibule, a five bay entrance hall and a stair hall. The entrance hall is flanked by an east library and two west reception rooms divided by a lavatory. The stair hall gives access to south service rooms, and a west elevator and service stair; the main stair ascends at the east, having a lavatory and east elevation entrance beneath its first landing.

   South of the first floor stair hall is the south dining room (Ambassador's office) and a southwest breakfast room. To the west are the elevator and service rooms and stair. North of the stair hall the reception corridor is flanked by east and west parlors, all three opening into the drawing room running the width of the Massachusetts Avenue elevation. (See plan.)

   South of the second floor living hall are three bedrooms and two baths. The service area is to the west and the major bedroom suites to the north flanking the hall. Ascending north within the master suite corridor is a secondary straight-run stair to the upper floors.

   Arranged around the north to south central hall, the third floor has bedroom suites and a southeast play room. The fourth floor has additional bedrooms and servants' quarters.

2. Spaces:

   Entrance vestibule:

   a. Flooring: black and white marble squares, laid diagonally, with black marble border.

   b. Baseboard: 9", tan and white-veined black marble with fascia cap.

   c. Walls: plaster to simulate limestone. Raised panels have rosette corner indentations.

   d. Cornice: cyma, dentil, cavetto, talon and ogee.

1746 Massachusetts Avenue, N.W.

e. Ceiling: There is a single raised panel with rosette corner indentations and cyma surround.

f. Doorways and doors: The side-lighted, double door to the entrance hall has decorative cast iron grilles of rosettes and leaf bars over plate glass with a centered lion mask in pattera.

g. Hardware: brass door handles.

h. Lighting: There are single, black-enamelled coach lights with concave glass panes at the east and west walls.

Entrance hall: (see photographs)

a. Flooring: white and black marble squares, laid diagonally, with black marble border.

b. Baseboard: 9", tan and white-veined black marble with fascia cap.

c. Walls: plaster to simulate limestone. The east and west walls are divided into three bays of raised panels with fascia and cyma mouldings flanked by opposed double door bays, each bay separated by fluted pilasters on plinths having limestone composite capitals.

d. Cornice: The full entablature has a fascia and cyma (plaster) architrave, a (limestone) frieze of anthemion and palmette separated by cornucopia and rosettes, with a (plaster) talon cap, and an enriched corona (wood) cornice. (See detail photograph.)

e. Ceiling: 11'-9" high. Wood beams frame cavetto and talon coffers centered with dropped pattera.

f. Doorways and doors: Each leaf of the opposed double door has three panels with a linen fold panel at the bottom, a central panel of urn with rinceau, and an upper panel of dolphins, male figures, masks, griffins and horse head masks in rinceau.

g. Hardware: silver, male head, connecting-bar terminals with leaf and tail handles.

h. Lighting: There are four, two-light, alabaster sconces each with a satyr holding bronze, paired cornucopia with opague glass light bowl terminals. The single, plaster, hanging bowl lamp has allegorical scenes in relief, a gilded metal rim and handles, and an alabaster pineapple pendant. (See detail photograph.)

1746 Massachusetts Avenue, N.W.

Library: (wood. Tudor manner.)

a. Flooring: basket weave parquetry.

b. Baseboard: 8", with bead cap.

c. Walls: There are seven rows of flat panels with cyma mouldings. Flanking the north window, the south mantle and between either west wall door are 2'-10" high cabinets below built-in bookshelves with a bound, oak leaf roll architrave.

d. Cornice: gouge frieze and talon.

e. Ceiling: 11'-9" high, plaster painted white. Geometric panels within floral ribs.

f. Doorways and doors: At either end of the west wall are double doors to the entrance hall (8'-6" high) with five flat panels and a double fascia with cyma architrave.

g. Hardware: Each door leaf has an 8 1/2" wide by 4" high by 1 1/2" deep brass rim lock having a lion mask escutcheon and fleur-de-lis panel with an acanthus "barbell" door knob.

h. Lighting: There are six, two-light, mirror-backed brass sconces, and two, five-light, brass chandeliers.

i. Heating: The south wall chimney mantle (8'-1" wide by 6'-6" high) has a limestone firebox surround with a cyma, bead and cavetto architrave on plinths, and six quatrefoil frieze panels with decorative carvings. A wood bolection moulding surrounds the whole and is capped by a cavetto shelf. The overmantle has two rows of linen fold panels.

Reception room: (painted white. Late Georgian manner.)

a. Flooring: carpeted.

b. Baseboard: 7", wood with bead cap.

c. Dado: raised panels with cyma moulding.

d. Chairrail: 2'-11" high, wood with bead, fascia and roll.

e. Walls: plaster. The southeast door interrupts one of the large flush panels which have pulvinated leaf mouldings. The windows and entrance hall door, in addition, are flanked by narrow, raised panels.

f. Cornice: There is a metope and triglyph frieze with decorative guttae, and volute modillions above the triglyph and between a talon moulding, and an astragal and talon cornice.

g. Ceiling: 11'-9" high, plaster with decorative center oval of swags, fan spandrels.

h. Doorways and doors: The natural wood double door to the entrance hall and the single south wall door both have three rows of paired panels and a double fascia, talon, and strapwork and leaf architrave.

i. Hardware: The brass rim locks, 6 1/2" wide by 3 1/2" high by 1 1/2" deep, each have a panel with a bead moulding and oval fan knob.

j. Heating: The south wall chimney has a grey-veined white marble hearth and a grey and white-veined black marble firebox surround. The mantle (6'-9" wide by 5'-1" high) has a cavetto and bead architrave surround, reed and flute pilasters, a reed and flute frieze broken forward as a lion mask over either pilaster, and a cyma and cavetto shelf. There is a raised overmantle panel within a leaf fascia and pulvinated guilloche frame.

Stair hall: (see photographs)

a. Flooring: black and white marble squares, laid diagonally, with black marble border.

b. Baseboard: 9", tan and white-veined black marble with fascia cap.

c. Walls: The plaster walls simulate limestone and have raised panels with fascia and cyma mouldings. Flat-panelled composite pilasters flank the stairwell openings.

d. Cornice: The full entablature has a fascia and cyma (plaster) architrave, a (limestone) frieze of anthemion and palmette separated by cornucopia and rosettes, with a (plaster) talon cap, and an enriched corona (wood) cornice.

e. Ceiling: 11'-9" high. Wood beams frame cavetto and talon coffers centered with dropped pattera.

f. Doorways and doors: Flanking the west wall chimney are single, three-panelled doors with a linen fold panel at the bottom, a central panel of urn with rinceau, and an upper panel of dolphins, male figures, masks, griffins and horse head masks in rinceau.

Under the stair landing at the east wall is a single door of plate glass and decorative cast iron.

g. Hardware: silver, male head, connecting-bar terminals with leaf and tail handles.

1746 Massachusetts Avenue, N.W.

    h. Lighting: There is a single, plaster hanging bowl lamp with allegorical scenes in relief, gilded metal rim and handles and alabaster pineapple pendant. Satyr sconces light the stair landings.

    i. Heating: The west wall chimney has a tan marble hearth and firebox surround. The plaster, limestone-simulated mantle (7'-9" wide by 6'-5" high) has three-quarter-engaged round plinths with decorative urn dados below beaded, spiral composite columns supporting 18" high rinceau brackets with scroll soffits. There is a bundled reed, mask and floriated fascia architrave, a frieze of palmette and anthemion separated by cornucopia and rosettes, and a dentil, egg and dart, corona, astragal and cyma shelf. The flush-panelled overmantle hood has raised cyma mouldings.

    j. Stair: The first four risers of this dog-leg stair are on a graduated convex curve; the whole ascends sixteen risers east to the first landing, and eleven additional risers west to the first floor. The closed stringer simulates limestone and supports 6" high by 6'-0" wide tan marble risers and treads. The banister has cast and wrought iron monogram escutcheons, leaf and tendril panels and a moulded oak handrail. (See photograph.)

The second flight ascends twelve risers east to the first landing, eight risers north to the second and twelve risers west to the second floor. Wood beams frame a cavetto and talon coffered ceiling.

First floor stair hall: (see photographs)

a. Flooring: herringbone parquetry, carpeted.

b. Baseboard: 5 1/2", wood with scotia cap.

c. Wainscot: (described by section; wood. See photograph.)

    (1.) linen fold panels and pedestal stiles.

    (2.) rinceau-panelled chairrail, 3'-9" high, between mask blocks at stiles.

    (3.) urn, mask, griffin and floral rinceau panels in cavetto and guilloche mouldings between alternating male and female term stiles ending at 6'-0" height. (See detail photograph.)

    (4.) rinceau mask rail panels between mask blocks at stiles.

    (5.) at 8'-0" height, cavetto and cyma cornice.

1746 Massachusetts Avenue, N.W.

d. Walls: The simulated limestone plaster walls continue behind the wainscot. The west chimney wall breaks forward 1'-3".

e. Cornice: floral rinceau panels between escutcheon blocks; cyma cornice.

f. Ceiling: 15'-0" high, plaster painted white. The coffers have rounded corners and rib bosses.

g. Doorways and doors: There are 9'-5" high double doors to the south dining room (Ambassador's office), the north drawing room, and the east and west parlors. Each leaf has four rows of panels with paired linen fold panels at the bottom followed by a griffin lock rail panel, paired medallion and trophy rinceau panels, and paired medallion rinceau panels at the top. The architrave is similar to the wainscot stiles except for the substitution of composite, fern leaf pilasters above the term stiles. The rinceau frieze over the door has mask block terminals, a bead and cyma cornice, and a broken segmental pediment with scroll terminals and rinceau tympanum.

    Flanking the west wall chimney mantle are single doors, each leaf similar to the wainscot and capped by a broken scroll pediment with rinceau mask tympanums.

h. Heating: The west wall chimney has a green marble hearth and firebox surround, and a cast iron, cartouche-panelled firebox. The wood mantle (7'-4" wide by 6'-3" high by 3'-1" deep) has plinths which support single, decoratively carved, composite columns, banded at the mid-shaft and supporting griffin rinceau beams projecting from the wall and terminated by masks. The entablature has a fascia architrave, allegorical frieze, and layered shelf.

    The 3'-7" high overmantle is one panel in depth. Three rinceau facing panels in gouge and guilloche mouldings are separated by male and female term stiles and terminated by decorative, three-quarter-engaged, composite columns. A rinceau frieze is broken by mask block stiles and capped by a layered cornice.

Dining room: (Ambassador's office. In the manner of Belton House dining room in Grantham, England, designed by William Stanton in 1685, with carvings attributed to Grinling Gibbons. See photograph.)

a. Flooring: herringbone parquetry.

b. Baseboard: 9 1/2", wood with cyma and bead cap.

c. Dado: raised panels of burled walnut veneer in a cyma moulding.

1746 Massachusetts Avenue, N.W.

d. Chairrail: 3'-2" high, wood with fascia and bead.

e. Walls: raised panels of burled walnut in a cyma moulding. At the room corners, over the west doors and flanking the door to the hall are high relief wood carvings.

f. Cornice: The cornice of corona and cyma courses between coves is terminated by talon.

g. Ceiling: 15'-0" high, plaster painted white. The central panel has tobacco leaf pulvination, a cove, and a ribbon roll moulding. Each corner is indented by flower and fruit, pulvinated roundels, connected by floriate border panels.

h. Doorways and doors: The three panel double door to the hall, 9'-5" high, has a bolection architrave, pulvinated frieze over the door and segmental pediment. Flanking the west wall chimney are single doors, 7'-5" high, with a fascia, bead and cyma architrave, pulvinated frieze over the door and segmental pediment.

i. Hardware: Each door leaf has an 8 1/2" wide by 4" high by 1 1/2" deep brass rim lock with a cherub panel, capped by a dolphin bolt lock, and a decorative oval knob.

j. Lighting: There are eight, three-light, escutcheon-backed, silver-plated sconces and a ten-light, baroque urn, arm and tassel, silver-plated chandelier.

k. Heating: The west wall wood chimney mantle (9'-0" wide by 6'-0" high) has a white and grey marble bolection firebox surround. The panelled pilasters support consoles which flank a swag and trophy frieze, and an acanthus, talon and cyma shelf. The overmantle has a raised panel capped and draped with carved pheasant, flowers and oak leaves.

Breakfast room: (wood, painted. Secretary's office.)

a. Flooring: carpeted.

b. Baseboard: 6", with cyma and bead cap.

c. Dado: flat panels.

d. Chairrail: 3'-5" high, fascia.

e. Walls: three rows of flat panels.

f. Cornice: cavetto and stepped fascia.

g. Ceiling: 15'-0" high, plaster painted white. The shallow dome within its flower and fruit pulvinated frame

1746 Massachusetts Avenue, N.W.

has floral wreath and spray spandrels, and is centered by a round, flower and fruit fixture rosette.

h. Doorways and doors: There are two, two-panelled doors, one each to the dining room and the northwest antehall.

i. Hardware: brass, star-patterned, bulbous door knobs.

j. Heating: The east wall, white marble chimney mantle (6'-6" wide by 4'-10" high) has pilasters with inlaid yellow marble fluting. The pilasters support a rosette and swag frieze interrupted at the center and over either pilaster by urn panels.

East parlor: (wood painted cream)

a. Flooring: herringbone parquetry.

b. Baseboard: 8", green-veined black marble with wood bead cap.

c. Dado: raised panels with cyma moulding.

d. Chairrail: The 3'-2" high, talon, fascia and cyma rail returns to the wall 2" before the door and window architraves.

e. Walls: raised panels with cyma moulding. The south chimney wall breaks forward 3 1/2" with three-quarter-round astragal corners. Resting on the chairrail and flanking the mantle are semicircular-arched shell niches with crossette, astragal and talon architraves and raised panels over either arch.

f. Cornice: cyma, talon, corona, astragal and cyma.

g. Ceiling: 15'-0" high, plaster painted white.

h. Doorways and doors: The double doors to the hall and drawing room have raised panels and a crossette architrave of astragal, fascia, talon, astragal and cyma mouldings. There is an acanthus bolection frieze over either door and an acanthus cavetto, corona, astragal and cyma cornice.

i. Windows: The floor to cornice architraves, similar to the doorways, have recesses for draperies.

j. Hardware: brass strapwork escutcheons for mortise locks.

k. Heating: The south wall chimney mantle (5'-7" wide by 4'-9" high) has a green-veined marble bolection surround within a wood talon frame. The overmantle panel has a high relief, palm leaf cap draped over floral cornucopia,

1746 Massachusette Avenue, N.W.

and flanked by floral swags terminated by paired **phe**asants with floral pendants linked by ribbon and tassel.

West parlor: (wood, painted cream; low office partition. Late 18th century English manner.)

a. Flooring: herringbone parquetry (covered in black asphalt tiles.)

b. Baseboard: 7", with bead cap.

c. Dado: single raised panels in cyma moulding.

d. Chairrail: 3' 1/2" high, fascia and roll.

e. Walls: The walls are divided into three sections with narrow panels of rosette guilloche at the bottom, flat panels in astragal, fascia and cyma, rosette-indented frames at the center, and plain panels at the top. The south chimney wall is broken forward 14".

f. Cornice: The full entablature has a fascia and cyma architrave, a plain frieze, and a cavetto, bead, bolection, corona and cyma cornice.

g. Ceiling: 15'-0" high, plaster painted white. At the center is an oval sunburst with a laurel surround, bordered at the cornice by a decorative running dog frieze.

h. Doorways and doors: Pairs of double doors, one each to the drawing room and hall have two, rosette-cornered raised panels in a fascia and cyma moulding. Over each door is a crossette rinceau panel.

i. Windows: The fascia and cyma architraves have recesses for draperies.

j. Hardware: Each door leaf has a brass rocaille rim lock, 7" wide by 3" high by 1" deep, with a decorative oval knob.

k. Heating: The south wall chimney hearth is covered by carpeting and the firebox is closed. The wood mantle (7'-0" wide by 4'-9 1/2" high) has a plain architrave surround, flanked by reeded panels, which support a horizontally fluted frieze interrupted by a central urn panel and broken forward over either reeded panel. Roll mouldings form the shelf. An overmantle mirror, within an astragal moulding, is capped by a crossette rinceau panel and flanked by vertical rosette panels.

Drawing room: (oak. Jacobean manner.)

a. Flooring: black asphalt tiles (modern).

1746 Massachusetts Avenue, N.W.

    b. Baseboard: 6", with cyma cap.

    c. Dado: Flat square panels are set within "L"-shaped panels.

    d. Chairrail: 5'-0" high, ogee.

    e. Walls: Flat square panels are set within "L"-shaped panels. The west chimney wall is broken forward 2'-7".

    f. Cornice: talon, alternating acanthus modillions and pattera, cyma.

    g. Ceiling: 15'-0" high, plaster painted white. Variously shaped geometric panels are framed by decorative floral ribs.

    h. Doorways and doors: There are three sets of double doors, one each to the east and west parlors and central hall, with paired linen fold bottom panels, a plain lock rail panel and an upper rectangle within "L"-shaped panels. The acanthus bolection architrave is capped by a plain pulvinated frieze and an ovolo, corona and cyma cornice.

    i. Windows: The four bays, three on Massachusetts Avenue and one at the east, have 14'-0" high acanthus bolection architraves.

    j. Hardware: Each door leaf has a brass key excutcheon, 8" wide by 3 1/2" high, having a decorative central rosette within a cartouche, and an oval acanthus knob. Each window has a brass extension bolt lock with a brass lever and rosette knob.

    k. Heating: The west wall chimney hearth is covered by asphalt tile and the firebox is closed. The wood mantle (10'-2" wide by 5'-10" high) has paired, fluted Ionic columns on strapwork drums which support guilloche consoles flanking a panelled frieze. The frieze is divided into three sections by paired strapwork consoles. The shelf is an ovolo.

       The overmantle 4'-0" high, is divided vertically into three crossette panels by alternating male and female terms, the central section sculpted to form a round-arched niche with floral spandrels. The terms support consoles which flank a panelled frieze below a dentil, ovolo, corona and cyma cornice.

D. Site:

1. Setting and orientation: The building faces north on a lot measuring 82'-4" on Massachusetts Avenue, 194'-7" on the east, 62'-7" on the southeast (public alley), 63'-0" on the southwest,

1746 Massachusetts Avenue, N.W.

and 162'-0" on the west.

2. Enclosures: Terminated at the north by limestone consoles, the lot is surrounded at the east, south and west by a limestone-capped, brick garden wall. Flanking the building and supported by limestone pylons are 16'-0" high, decorative cast and wrought iron double gates with segmental arches and excutcheon caps.

3. Outbuildings: none.

4. Walks: The north entrance is approached by a semicircular concrete drive with granite curbing. The south garden area has been paved for parking and service.

5. Landscaping: There are hemlock, azalea, boxwood and elm plantings at the north. A rectangular planted area separates the parking from the south side of the building.

1785 MASSACHUSETTS AVENUE, N.W., WASHINGTON, D.C.

CFA photo
Boucher 1970

Location: 1785 Massachusetts Avenue, N.W., Washington, D.C.; on the northeast corner of Massachusetts Avenue and 18th Street.

Present Owner: The Brookings Institution

Present Occupant: Seventeen Eighty Five Office Building

Present Use: Offices

Statement of Significance: Built as one of the first Washington apartment buildings for luxury living, the structure was designed to complement a surrounding beaux-art neighborhood. The composition of three principal elevations acts as a major pivotal point for an important residential boulevard and accents two street intersections. Its six units, with quarters for more than forty servants, were once occupied by some of the Capital's most distinguished personalities.

PART I. HISTORICAL INFORMATION

A. Lot and Square:

The building is located in Square 157, lot 800 (formerly lots 57 through 60 in John F. Olmstead's Subdivision of lots 30 through 38 of McRae's Subdivision of lots in Square 157).

B. Original and Subsequent Owners:

The following chain of title to the property shows the owners of the present structure and of any known preceding structures on the site:

1880 Deed March 10, 1880, recorded March 24, 1880 in
Liber 933 folio 406

John F. Olmstead et ux,
Hannah S.
   To
Belden Noble

"This Indenture...between John F. Olmstead and Hannah S. Olmstead his wife, of the City of Washington, D.C. of the first part, and Belden Noble of the State of New York of the second part...for and in consideration of the sum of Sixteen thousand nine hundred and twelve dollars ($16,912)...Lots...(57),...(58),...(59), and...(60) of John F. Olmstead's subdivision of Lots...(30) to...(38) of McRae's subdivision of Lots in Square...(157) as recorded in the Office of the Surveyor of the District of Columbia in Liber No. 10, folio 106, January 28, 1880..."

1905 Deed January 30, 1905, recorded February 1, 1905 in Liber 2885 folio 491

Adeline M. Noble
  To
Maud Noble Harlan

"This Indenture made...between Adeline M. Noble of Washington in the District of Columbia, widow of the late Belden Noble, party of the first part, and Maud Noble Harlan, of Chicago, in the State of Illinois, daughter of the grantor, party of the second part...for and in consideration of natural love and affection, and in further consideration of the sum of one (1) dollar...and one third of the following described Real Estate..."

Lots 57 through 60 in Square 157.

1906 Deed September 12, 1906, recorded September 19, 1906 in Liber 3022 folio 441

Mary Maud Noble Harlan
Nannie Yulee Noble (widow)
  To
Stanley McCormick

"...Being the same property of which Belden Noble died seised and possessed and which by will he devised to his wife, Adeline M. Noble and to his children, William Belden Noble, and the said Mary Noble Harlan. The said William Belden Noble has since died, and by his will he devised his interest in said property to his wife, the said Nannie Yulee Noble..."

NOTE: The Will of Stanley McCormick left his entire estate, which did not exceed $25,000,000, to his wife Katherine Dexter McCormick. Filed at D.C. Registrar of Wills, 4-1-47.

1950 Deed March 31, 1950, recorded April 25, 1950 in Liber 9191 folio 141

Katherine Dexter McCormick
  To
American Council on Education

"...Katherine Dexter McCormick, widow and devisee under the Will of Stanley McCormick, deceased..."

1785 Massachusetts Avenue, N.W.

1970   Deed January 2, 1970, recorded January 6, 1970 in
Liber 13065 folio 502

American Council on Education
To
The Brookings Institution

Source: Recorder of Deeds, Washington, D.C.

C. Date of Erection:

The building was begun late in 1915 and completed by 1917.

D. Building Permits:

The applications for the following building permits were filed by the architect, contractor or owner's agent and provide significant data:

No. 1987, October 25, 1915
Permit to build "one five story, brick and stone apartment house"
    Owner: Stanley McCormick
    Architect: J. H. de Sibour
    Builder: William P. Lipscomb & Co.
    Estimated cost: $350,000.

Filed with No. 1987, October 25, 1915
Application for Projections Beyond Building Line

No. 4705, May 1, 1916
Permit to install one electric passenger elevator
    Owner: Mrs. Stanley McCormick
    Contractor: A. B. See Elevator Co.
    Estimated cost: $2700.
    Location: Center of building

No. 4706, May 1, 1916
Permit to install one electric passenger and service elevator
    Owner: Mrs. Stanley McCormick
    Contractor: A. B. See Elevator Co.
    Estimated cost: $2700.
    Location: Center of building

No. 618, August 4, 1916
Permit to install one hand power freight elevator
    Owner: Mrs. Stanley McCormick
    Contractor: A. B. See Elevator Co.
    Estimated cost: $250.
    Use: Freight, ashes, etc.
    Location: Rear, on alley

1785 Massachusetts Avenue, N.W.

No. 3284, January 22, 1917
Permit to erect marquise
    Owner: Stanley McCormick
    Architect: J. H. de Sibour
    Contractor: William P. Lipscomb & Co.
    Estimated cost: $2900.

Source: D.C. Government: Department of Economic Development,
    Bureau of Licenses and Permits, Central Files.

E. Alterations and Additions:

After 1941 the building was used for offices and eventually partitioned.

F. Architect: J. H. de Sibour, Washington, D.C.

See biography of J. H. de Sibour under 1700 Massachusetts Ave., N.W.

G. Known Plans, Drawings, Elevations, etc.:

Typical floor plan.
The Architectural Record, Vol. LI (April 1922), plates.
"Apartment House at 1785 Massachusetts Avenue, Washington, D.C.
J. H. de Sibour, Architect"
(see reproduction)

Projection plans. Scale 1/4" = 1'
Recorded on microfilm with Permit No. 1987, October 25, 1915.
D.C. Government: Bureau of Licenses and Permits, Central Files.

Elevation and plan of marquise. Scale 1/4" = 1'
Recorded on microfilm with Permit No. 3284, January 22, 1917.
D.C. Government: Bureau of Licenses and Permits, Central Files.

H. Important Old Views:

Exterior photograph: Massachusetts Avenue and 18th Street facades.
The Architectural Record, Vol. LI (April 1922), plates.

Exterior photograph: Belden Noble House, 1785 Massachusetts
Avenue, N.W. Records of the Columbia Historical Society,
Washington, D.C.
(see reproduction)

Illustrations: "Residence of J. B. Noble" (exterior); and
"Hall and Staircase of J. B. Noble's Residence"

1785 Massachusetts Avenue, N.W.

<u>Harper's New Monthly Magazine</u>, Vol. LXV, no. 386 (July 1882), pp. 522-523. Records of the Columbia Historical Society, Washington, D.C.

I. Residents:

1. City and telephone directories list the following tenants:

    *1917-1940 Apartments
    1941-1942 British Purchasing Commission
    1943-1948 British Air Commission
    1949   British Commonwealth Scientific Office
    1951-1970 American Council on Education
    1971-1972 American Association of Physics
               American College Public Relations Association
               American Institute of Architects, National Office
               The Asia Society
               Consortium Curricular Evaluation
               Institutional Development & Economic Affairs
                   Service, Inc.
               National Architectural Accrediting Board, Inc.
               Polit-Econ Services
               Urban Design & Development Corp.

    *Apartment residents:

Katherine Judge	1917-1930, 1933-1940
Edwin Snow	1917
W. H. Bliss	1917
Roy A. Rainey	1918-1919
Henry R. Rae	1918-1919
John S. Cravens	1918-1919
Everitt V. Macy	1918-1919
Thomas F. Ryan	1920-1922
Robert Bliss	1920-1923
Mrs. W. A. Slater	1920-1921
Edwin T. Meredith	1921
Mrs. Harry W. Brown	1922-1928
Andrew W. Mellon	1922-1937
Sumner Welles	1921-1927
Mrs. Edward C. Walker	1923-1924
Don Gelasio Caetani	1924-1925
Mrs. Alvin T. Hert	1928-1937
McCormick Goodhear	1929-1931
William Butterworth	1930-1931
Alanson B. Houghton	1930-1934
A. Pearl Mesta	1931-1932
Mrs. Frederick H. Bugher	1937-1940
Mrs. George Mayre	1937-1940
Mrs. E. C. Douglas	1937

1785 Massachusetts Avenue, N.W.

2. Selected biographies:

Stanley F. McCormick (1875-1947), who built the McCormick Apartments, was the son of Cyrus McCormick, inventor of the reaper and founder of what was later the International Harvestor Company. He served as controller of the company and managed real estate for himself and his family until he was declared incompetent. His $36,000,000 estate was then managed by the Cook County (Illinois) Probate Court. His property at 1785 Massachusetts Avenue was part of the estate left to his wife, Katherine Dexter McCormick, upon his death.

Source: The New York Times, 1-20-47, 25:4 (obituary).

Andrew W. Mellon (1885-1937), the industrialist, lived on the fifth floor of the McCormick Apartments while serving as Secretary of the Treasury under Presidents Harding, Coolidge, and Hoover (1921-1933). From 1933 until his death, he lived intermittently in his Washington apartment while completing his plans for the National Gallery of Art.

Source: Who Was Who in America 1897-1942: A Companion Volume to Who's Who in America, Vol. I, Chicago: The A. N. Marquise Company, 1942.

The New York Times, 8-27-37, 1:1 (obituary)

Lord Duveen (1869-1939) was head of the London and New York art dealing firm of Duveen Brothers. He was influential in forming some outstanding art collections in America, including those of Frick, Bache, Widener, Morgan, Altman, Kress and Mellon. In 1936 he leased an apartment at 1785 Massachusetts Avenue in order to display an art collection for Andrew Mellon's benefit. As he said to Mellon," I have gathered them specially for you, things you ought to have. ...I shall arrange matters so that you can see those things at your convenience and leisure." Mellon bought the forty-two item collection for $21,000,000. (Duveen, pp. 270-273).

Sources: S. N. Behrman, Duveen, New York: Random House, 1951.

The New York Times, 5-26-39, 23:1 (obituary).

Robert Wood Bliss (1875-1962) was Chief of Western European Affairs in the State Department from 1920 to 1923 when he was appointed Minister of Sweden. From 1927 to 1933 he served as U. S. Ambassador to Argentina. Bliss and his wife, Mildred Barnes Bliss, had collected pre-Columbian and Byzantine art for many years. In 1940 Bliss donated his estate,

1785 Massachusetts Avenue, N.W.

Dumbarton Oaks, (Washington, D.C.) his art collection and a research library to Harvard University.

Source: The New York Times, 4-20-62, 27:2 (obituary).

William Butterworth (1864-1936) was president of the Illinois firm of Deere and Company from 1907 to 1930 when he became chairman of the board. Deere and Company was one of the world's largest farming machine manufacturers at that time. From 1916 to 1920 Butterworth was director of the U. S. Chamber of Commerce. He then served as its vice-president until 1926. From 1928 to 1931 he was president.

Source: Who Was Who in America 1897-1942: A Companion Volume to Who's Who in America, Vol. I, Chicago: The A. N. Marquis Company, 1942.

The New York Times, 6-1-36, 19:5 (obituary).

Alanson Bigelow Houghton (1863-1941) was president of the Corning Glass Works from 1910 to 1918 before becoming chairman of the board. He served as the American Ambassador to Germany from 1922 to 1925 and to Great Britain from 1925 to 1928. In 1928 he ran for U. S. Senator from New York and lost. From 1935 until his death, he was a trustee of Brookings Institution.

Source: Who Was Who in America, 1897-1942: A Companion Volume to Who's Who in America, Vol. I, Chicago: The A. N. Marquis Company, 1942.

Edwin Thomas Meredith (1876-1928) was the Secretary of Agriculture in the Cabinet of President Wilson (January 1920-March 1921).

Source: Who Was Who in America 1897-1942: A Companion Volume to Who's Who in America, Vol. I, Chicago: The A. N. Marquis Company, 1942.

Thomas Fortune Ryan (1851-1928) was a great financier in the fields of banking, insurance, railroads, and municipal transit. Other interests included oil, gas, coke, electricity, tobacco, lead, coal, rubber, and lumber. He was also one of the largest individual owners of diamond fields in the Belgian Congo.

Source: Who Was Who in America 1897-1942: A Companion Volume to Who's Who in America, Vol. I, Chicago: The A. N. Marquis Company, 1942.

1785 Massachusetts Avenue, N.W.

J. Previous Structure on the Site:

The Belden Noble house at 1785 Massachusetts Avenue, N.W. was torn down in 1915 or 1916 to provide a site for the present building. (see photograph)

In 1880 Belden Noble bought the corner site and built a three story and basement brick residence. Permit number 1586, issued June 14, 1880 provides the following information about the house:

>   Architect: Gray and Page
>   Builder: Davidson & Co.
>   Dimension: 45' (front) X 62' (depth) X 45' (rear)
>   Estimated cost: $50,000.

"The residence of Mr. J. B. Noble, designed by Messrs. Gray and Page, on the corner of Eighteenth Street and Massachusetts Avenue, is perhaps the best illustration in the city of what may be accomplished in massiveness and the ornamental in brick, without superficial adornment. It is thirteenth-century Gothic in its general effect..."
(Harper's New Monthly Magazine, July 1882)

In 1906 Stanley McCormick bought the property. The following repairs made to the house and stable in 1913 indicate that there seemed to be no plans to demolish at that time:

>   Permit No. 325, July 22, 1913
>   Owner: Cyrus McCormick Estate
>   Location: Lot 59, Square 157
>   Estimated cost: $4,000
>   "To change parlor story main stairs [and] pantry stairs -
>   remove non-bearing stud partition, enlarge pantry. To
>   put new window in pantry..., two new windows in parlor,
>   ...remove pier in drawing room. Put in two 10" I beams
>   to support brick logia above - fire proof beams - repairs
>   to floors, doors, windows throughout - change vestibule
>   stud partition - repair interior and exterior wood steps -
>   set new materials - repair side wood fence."

>   Permit No. 1169, September 12, 1913
>   Owner: Cyrus McCormick Estate
>   Contractor: William H. Furton
>   Estimated cost: $175.
>   "To convert existing brick stable into a private garage -
>   put in garage trap, water closet, basin, new treads to
>   existing steps and make minor repairs."

City directories give the following tenant information:

>   1883-1887   Belden Noble
>   1897   Adeline M. Noble, widow of Belden
>   1898   Enrique Dupuy de Lome, E.E. and M.P., Spain

1785 Massachusetts Avenue, N.W.

1900-1902	Duke de Arcos, E.E. and M.P., Spain
1903	Emilio De Ojeda, E.E. and M.P., Spain
1907	William Henry Moody, Associate Justice, Supreme Court
1914-1915	Stephen L. H. Slocum U.S. Army
1916	Vacant

Belden Noble Residence
Previously on Site
(Demolished 1915-1916)
Courtesy of the Columbia Historical Society
Proctor Collection

CFA photo
Boucher 1970

Opposite
Entrance Lobby
CFA photo
Boucher 1970

Typical floor plan
The Architectural Record
April 1922, pp. 344-5

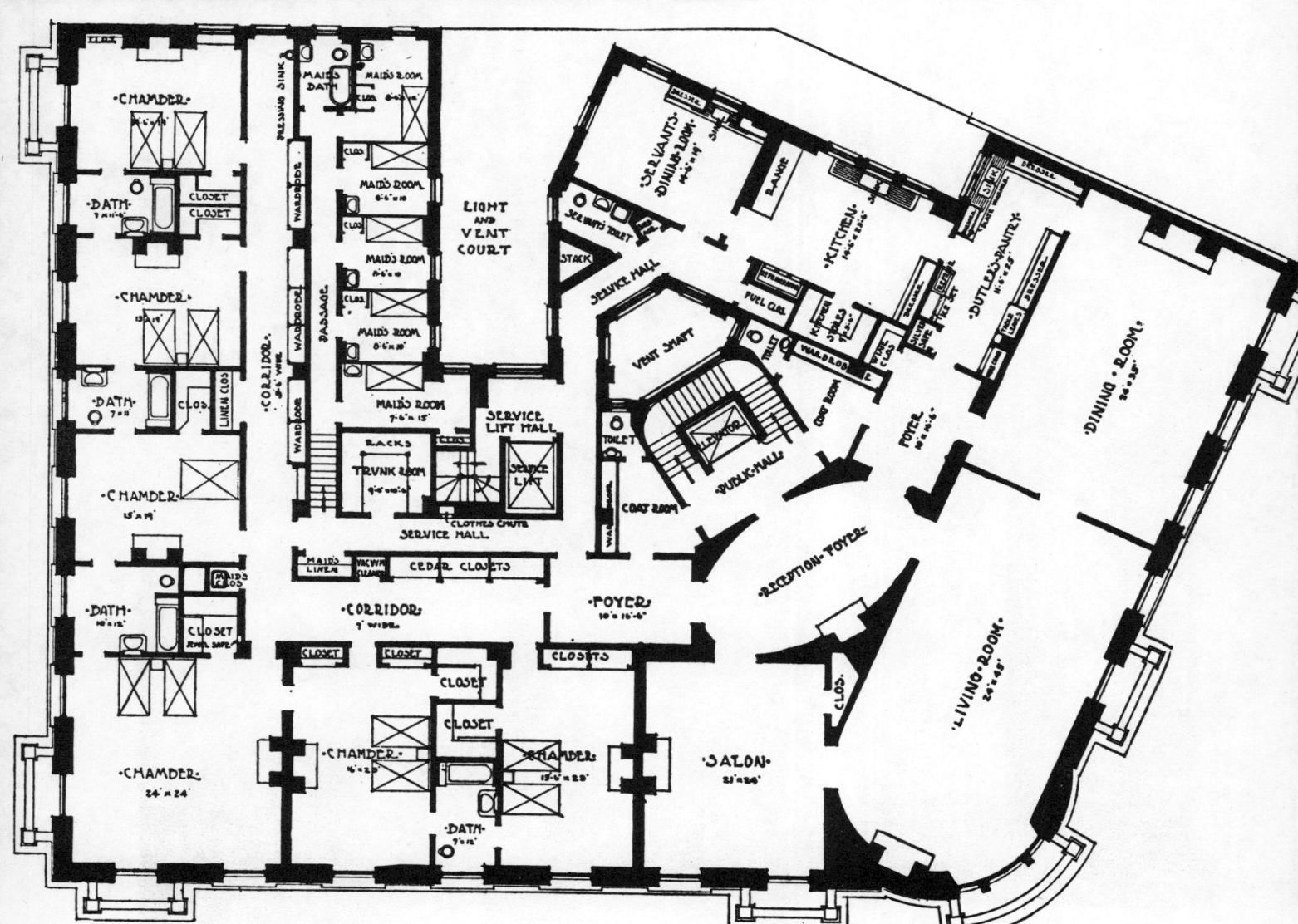

FIG. 131.—TYPICAL FLOOR PLAN—APARTMENT HOUSE AT 1785 MASSACHUSETTS AVENUE, WASHINGTON, D. C.
J. H. De Sibour, Architect.

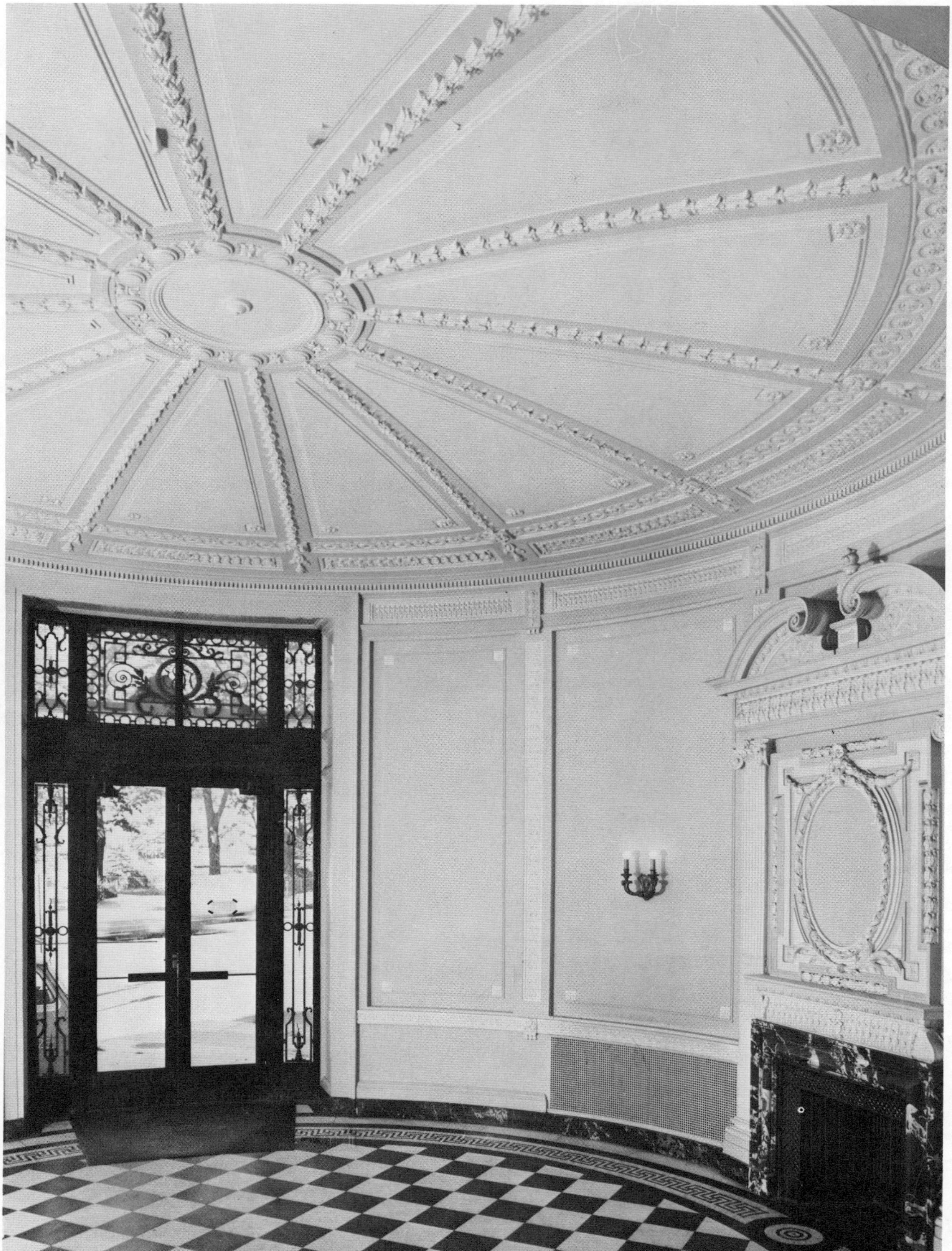

Typical Living Room
CFA photo
Boucher 1970

Detail Entrance Lobby
CFA photo
Boucher 1970

1785 Massachusetts Avenue, N.W.

PART II. ARCHITECTURAL INFORMATION

    A. General Statement:

        1. Architectural character: This semidetached, luxury apartment building has Louis XVI exterior details.

        2. Condition: Though the exterior is preserved, the interior has been altered for offices.

    B. Exterior Description:

        1. Overall dimensions: Including the one bay entrance bow, the four and one half story plus basement structure measures 79'-10" across the five bay Massachusetts Avenue elevation; 110'-10" across the seven bay 18th Street elevation; 100'-0" across the eight bay P Street elevation; 82'-5" on the northeast (including a light and vent court); and 66'-7" along the east party wall and light court.

        2. Foundations: concrete footings and slab.

        3. Wall construction: The base of this limestone-faced structure has a torus and cavetto water table which supports the rusticated first floor. The first floor is capped by a fret string course, which serves as window lintel punctuated by rosettes centered over each opening. A panelled false balustrade supports the smoothly surfaced second, third and fourth floors. Between the head and sill of the central windows on the third and fourth floors are decorative panels. This motif is repeated on the bow, at the same height.

        4. Structure: steel and brick.

        5. Mechanical: The building has a steam and stoker heating system. The original elevators, including the wood-panelled electric passenger elevator, the 5'-0" by 8'-1" electric freight elevator and the handpowered service elevator, were installed by the A.B. See Elevator Company. In 1961 an air conditioning system and replacement passenger elevator were incorporated.

        6. Porches, stoops, bulkheads, etc.: A basement areaway on 18th Street and Massachusetts Avenue runs beneath the limestone entrance stoop of four risers with scroll-terminated block balustrades. The balustrades support decorative iron panels capped by an iron and glass, radial marquise with a centered swag and wreath escutcheon.

        At the bow and end bays, limestone, urn-baluster balconies on concave consoles with swags break forward from the second floor false balustrade. The central bays have flush, urn-baluster balustrades.

All third floor bays have flush, oval guilloche balustrades supported by the second floor window cornices. The entablature of each third floor end bay acts as a limestone fourth floor balcony with decorative cast iron railings.

7. Chimneys: Nine chimneys serve 45 fireplaces. Those flanking the corner bow are limestone, approximately twenty feet high from dormer balcony to cap, with escutcheon and lion mask panels, a rosette frieze and a cornice cap.

8. Openings:

   a. Doorways and doors: The glazed, double door entrance, with decorative cast iron side lights and transom, has a limestone oak leaf and fret architrave.

   b. Windows: All bays are casements with transoms.

   The basement and first floor lack architraves. Each second floor end bay has a guilloche frieze broken forward over pendant consoles and supporting a shell and sprig pediment. The corresponding bay of the bow has a segmental pediment. Each inner bay crossette architrave has a guilloche frieze flanked by fluted brackets below a cyma cornice.

   The guilloche balconies of the end bays of each third floor elevation are interrupted by the second floor window pediments; their crossette architraves are capped by plain friezes flanked by concave brackets below a corona and cyma cornice which acts as base for the fourth floor balcony railings.

   The fourth floor bow and inner bays have block sills on brackets.

9. Roof:

   a. Shape, covering: The slate, convex mansard roof has a copper pulvinated ridge cap over a gouge frieze.

   b. Cornice, eaves: A limestone gouge frieze, punctuated by rosettes centered over each bay, acts as fourth floor window lintel. The cornice has dentils, modillions and cyma below a cast iron railing of ovals and running dog.

   c. Dormers, cupolas, towers: Each limestone dormer has pendant consoles below blocks which support the inner bay triangular pediments and outer bay shell and spray, segmental pediments. In addition, the dormer of the bow has a guilloche frieze.

C. Interior Description:

1. Floor plans: On axis with the first floor entrance is the circular lobby, the rectangular vestibule (approached by four risers), and the elevator and stair area. Single apartments flank the vestibule.

    The upper floors have identical plans. The stair and elevator landing gives access to an oval reception foyer. From the foyer a side foyer connects to the east service, kitchen and pantry area and the dining room (on Massachusetts Avenue). At the south is the living room and the salon. The west foyer (from the reception foyer) gives access to the west corridor (connecting service and the north corridor, lined by bedroom suites and baths). (See plan.)

    Ventilated by a light court at the east, the building core is subdivided into ten service levels.

2. Spaces:

    Entrance lobby: (see photographs)

    a. Flooring: black and white marble 12" squares, laid diagonally, bordered by fret mosaic.

    b. Baseboard: 6", tan-veined black marble with 6", wood fascia and cyma cap.

    c. Chairrail: 2'-8" high, applied wave moulding punctuated by rosettes and guttae.

    d. Walls: plaster. Between vertical guilloche panels centered over each chairrail rosette, are rosette-indented raised panels.

    e. Cornice: The plaster, gouge and tulip frieze, punctuated by floral blocks with guttae centered over each guilloche panel, is capped by a denticulated cornice with cyma.

    f. Ceiling: The 14'-0" high segmental dome of plaster is subdivided by radial bellflower ribs terminating at the center in pattera and at the ends in rosettes and tassels. The ribs flank raised panels, the rosettes are linked by a guilloche frieze and the tassels by leaf panels.

    g. Doorways and doors: The entrance door has a panelled jamb within a fascia and cyma architrave. The three-panelled double door to the vestibule is mahogany.

    h. Hardware: brass door handles.

    i. Lighting: There are four, two-light, brass-finished plaster sconces.

1785 Massachusetts Avenue, N.W.

j. Heating: The west wall chimney has a cast iron linen fold firebox with a lattice surround. The mantle has a white-veined, black marble bolection architrave which supports a wood, gouge and tulip frieze and an egg and dart shelf. The decorative wood overmantle has a crossette panel centered by an oval of bound bay leaves with sprays at the bottom and a key with swags at the top. Both sections are flanked by decoratively fluted Ionic pilasters on pedestals supporting a fascia and cyma architrave, a pulvinated leaf frieze, an egg and dart and corona cornice and a broken scroll pediment with central pedestal and urn. (See detail photograph.)

Vestibule:

a. Flooring: black and white marble 12" squares, laid diagonally, bordered by fret mosiac.

b. Baseboard: 6", tan-veined black marble with 6", wood fascia and cyma cap.

c. Chairrail: 2'-8" high, applied wave moulding punctuated by rosettes and guttae.

d. Walls: plaster. Between vertical guilloche panels centered over each chairrail rosette are rosette-indented raised panels.

e. Cornice: denticulated.

f. Ceiling: 14'-0" high, plaster painted white.

g. Doorways and doors: (none original).

h. Lighting: brass-finished, funnel-shaped sconces of more modern date.

i. Stair: The well of the half-turn stair with landings encloses an elevator shaft. The stair ascends nine risers north (on the right of the elevator), ten risers west and six risers south to the second floor. The stringer soffit is plaster and the risers and treads marble. The landings are black and white marble 12" squares. The design is repeated on all levels.

(The second floor sets precedence for all succeeding floors.)

Reception foyer:

a. Flooring: black and white marble 12" squares, laid diagonally.

b. Baseboard; 6", tan-veined black marble with 6", wood fascia and cyma cap.

1785 Massachusetts Avnue, N.W.

    c. Walls: plaster with raised panels.

    d. Cornice: corona and cyma.

    e. Ceiling: 14'-6" high, plaster painted white.

    f. Doorways and doors: The mahogany double doors with blind transoms, one to the living room and the other to the salon, have four rows of two panels per leaf and 12'-0" high crossette architraves with panelled jambs.

    g. Hardware: brass door handles and shell mortise lock escutcheons.

    h. Heating: The southwest wall limestone chimney mantle, with a patent bush-hammered finish, has fluted consoles with swags and a swag-centered wave frieze broken forward over either console.

<u>Side foyers</u>:

    a. Flooring: black and white marble 12" squares, laid diagonally.

    b. Baseboard: 6", tan-veined black marble with 6", wood fascia and cyma cap.

    c. Walls: plaster with raised panels.

    d. Cornice: corona and cyma.

    e. Ceilings: 14'-6" high, plaster painted white with recessed center panel.

    f. Lighting: Each corridor has an alabaster hanging light bowl with an urn and swag frieze and brass mounts.

<u>Dining room</u>: (partitioned for offices)

    a. Flooring: herringbone parquetry.

    b. Baseboard: 6", wood.

    c. Dado: plaster, raised panels in ogee moulding.

    d. Chairrail: 2'-6" high, applied rosette frieze.

    e. Walls: plaster, raised panels in ogee moulding.

    f. Cornice: modillion, corona and cyma.

    g. Ceiling: 14'-6" high, plaster painted white with lighting fixture rosette.

1785 Massachusetts Avenue, N.W.

h. Doorways and doors: The single doors at the corners of the north wall have a crossette architrave, pulvinated frieze and segmental pediment. They flank a door with a plain crossette architrave (not indicated in original plan).

i. Hardware: brass door knobs and shell mortise lock escutcheons.

j. Heating: The east wall chimney has a cast iron firebox and a black-veined, white marble mantle (5'-10" square) with a crossette architrave.

Living room: (see photograph)

a. Flooring: herringbone parquetry, carpeted.

b. Baseboard: 6", wood.

c. Dado: plaster, raised panels in ogee moulding.

d. Chairrail: 2'-6" high, fascia and cyma.

e. Walls: plaster, raised panels in ogee moulding.

f. Cornice: acanthus modillions and leaf talon above a modern indirect lighting cove.

g. Ceiling: The 14'-6" high, plaster ceiling is covered by accoustic tile.

h. Doorways and doors: The double doors with blind transoms to the reception foyer, dining room and salon, have four rows of two panels per leaf within 12'-0" high crossette architraves. The curved double door to the salon is recessed within a panelled jamb.

i. Hardware: brass rinceau and rosette door handles and pulvinated mortise lock escutcheons.

j. Lighting: There are eight, three-light, brass rosette sconces with crystal pendants. There are two, twelve-light, single tier, crystal chandeliers. The brass arms have pendant prisms. The rim band, connected to the crown by prism strands, is hung with three layers of prisms.

k. Heating: The west wall chimney has a cast iron linen fold firebox and a brown-veined, white marble mantle (6'-0" wide by 5'-8" high) with a bolection surround, a plain frieze with scroll terminals and a cyma, corona and cyma shelf.

Salon:

a. Flooring: herringbone parquetry.

b. Baseboard: 6", wood.

c. Dado: plaster, alternating wide and narrow raised panels within ogee mouldings.

d. Chairrail: 2'-6" high, fascia and cyma.

e. Walls: The plaster walls have alternating wide (plain) and narrow (decorated) panels within ogee mouldings.

f. Cornice: The full entablature has an egg and dart and decorative talon architrave; an anthemion frieze; and a corona and talon cornice.

g. Ceiling: 14'-6" high, plaster painted white with ceiling fixture rosette.

h. Doorways and doors: The double doors to the drawing room and reception foyer have four rows of two panels per leaf, and crossette architraves.

i. Hardware: brass, rinceau and rosette door handles with pulvinated mortise lock escutcheons.

j. Heating: The north wall chimney has a cast iron gouge and bundled-reed firebox, and a white marble mantle (5'-10" wide by 4'-0" high) with Tuscan pilasters which support a central swag frieze broken forward over either pilaster.

D. Site:

1. Setting and orientation: The building faces southwest on a lot measuring 79'-10" on Massachusetts Avenue (south); 110'-10" on 18th Street (west); 100'-0" on P Street (north); 82'-5" on the northeast (light court) and 66'-7" on the east.

2. Enclosures: A tubular metal railing protects the areaway.

3. Outbuildings: none.

4. Walks: A diagonal walkway cuts the intersection corner to the sidewalk and entrance stoop.

5. Landscaping: A narrow lawn and low shrubs surround the areaway and north elevation. Trees line the public sidewalk.

1801 MASSACHUSETTS AVENUE, N.W., WASHINGTON, D.C.

From Dupont Circle
CFA photo
Boucher 1970

Address: 1801 Massachusetts Avenue, N.W., Washington, D.C.

Significance: This building, with conglomerate 18th century details,
                    occupies a full block. Its location necessitated an
                    architectural treatment dependent upon three problems:
                    an intersection (18th Street and Massachusetts Avenue),
                    a circle (Dupont Circle), and three street facades
                    (Massachusetts Avenue, 18th Street, and P Street).

Present Owner: Sulgrave Club
Present Use: Private Club
Lot and Square: All of Square north of Square 137

HISTORICAL AND ARCHITECTURAL INFORMATION

Original Owner: Herbert Wadsworth
Original Use: Residence
Date of Erection: ca. 1900*
Architect: unknown**
Builder: Charles A. Langley*
Estimated cost: unknown**

Subsequent Owners:

   Martha Elbert Blow Wadsworth, widow of Herbert (1927-1932)
   Sulgrave Club (1932-   )

City and Telephone Directories List:

   1903-1904   Herbert Wadsworth
   1907-1917   Herbert Wadsworth
   1918   American Red Cross
   1919-1920   Herbert Wadsworth
   1921-1932   Vacant
   1933-1972   Sulgrave Club

Known Plans, Drawings, Elevations, etc.:

   Series of interior detail drawings in possession of Sulgrave Club.
   Unsigned and undated.

Important Old Views:

   Two exterior photographs showing: porte-cochere and view from southwest.
   The American Architect and Building News, Vol. XC (September 29, 1906).
   (see reproduction)

---
*   C. A. Langley applied for a projection permit in January 1900.
** Original building permit is missing.

1801 Massachusetts Avenue, N.W.

Building Dimensions:

    Stories: 3 and 1/2 plus basement

    Height: 40'-0" to eaves

    Bays: 9 bays on Mass. Ave.
           3 bay bow on Dupont Circle
           5 composite bays on P Street
           3 composite bays on 18th Street
           3 bay bow on corner of 18th Street and Mass. Ave.

    Widths: 136'-0" to apex of each bow on Mass. Ave.
            125'-0" on P Street
             76'-0" on 18th Street

Lot Dimensions:

    174'-10" on south (Mass. Ave.)
    159'-10" on north (P Street)
     71'- 6" on east (18th Street)

Major Alterations:

1. Installed new baths and decorated interior (1932).
2. Carriage entrance blocked (1932).
3. Passenger elevator installed (1934).
4. Built new marquise and altered vestibule (1952).
5. Passenger elevator installed (1954).

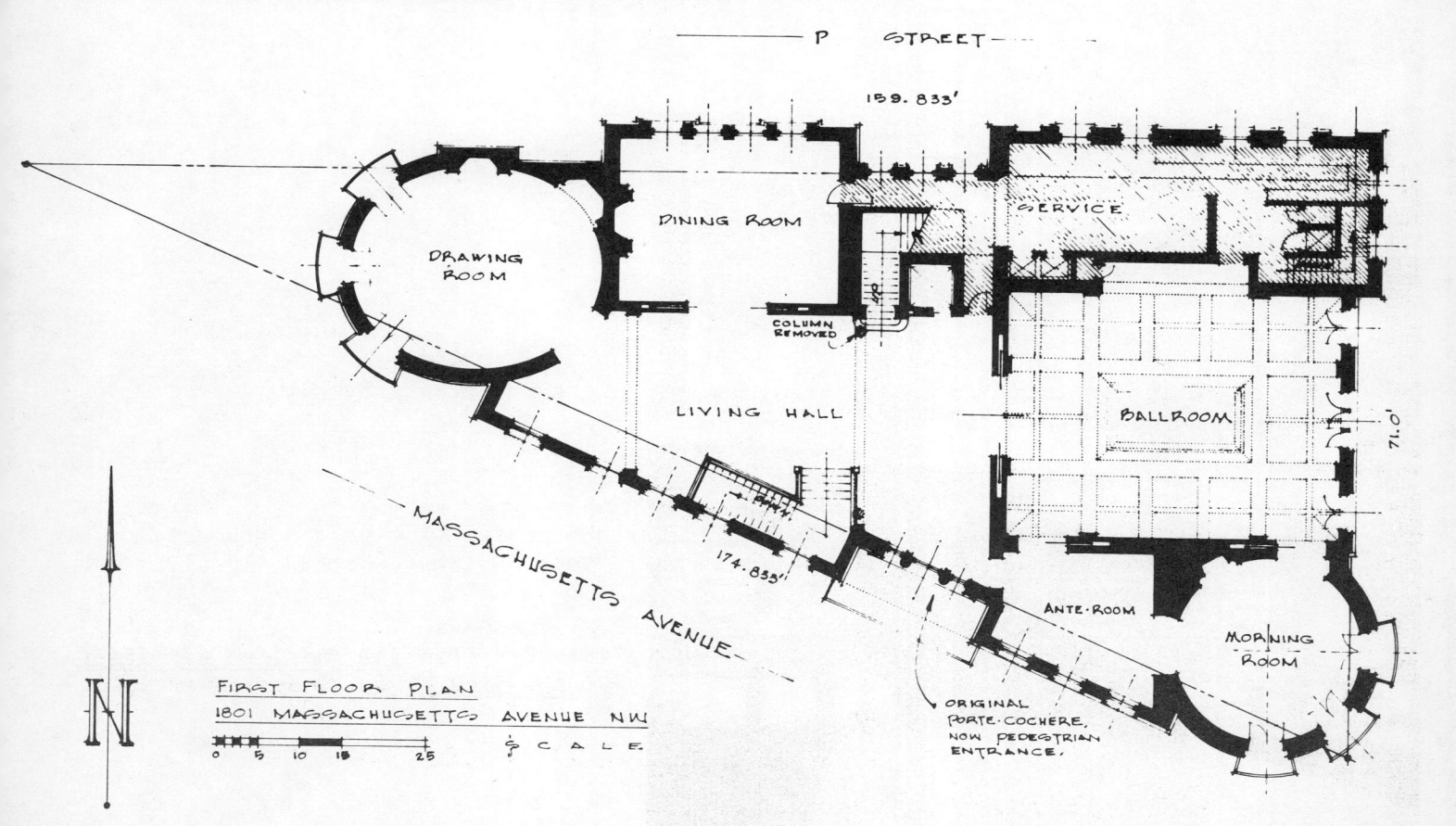

Massachusetts Avenue Elevation
CFA photo
Boucher 1970

Porte-cochere
Reprinted from The American Architect and Building News, 29 September 1906.

Ground Floor Stair Hall
CFA photo
Boucher 1970

First Floor
Drawing Room
CFA photo
Boucher 1970

Detail Drawing Room
CFA photo
Boucher 1970

Ballroom
CFA photo
Boucher 1970

Anteroom toward
Morning Room
CFA photo
Boucher 1970

Dining Room
CFA photo
Boucher 1970

15 DUPONT CIRCLE, N.W., WASHINGTON, D.C.

View from Dupont Circle
CFA photo
Alexander 1971

Location: 15 Dupont Circle, N.W., Washington, D.C.;
on the northeast corner of Dupont Circle
and P Street.

Present Owner: The Washington Club

Present Occupant: The Washington Club

Present Use: Private Club

Statement of Significance: This structure is a McKim, Mead and White example of neoclassicism in the decorative Italianate manner. The white marble and glazed terra-cotta building is heavily ornamented. The court, which breaks the south corner of the polygonal plan, gives added light to the interior and commands the approach of vehicular traffic around Dupont Circle.

PART I. HISTORICAL INFORMATION

　　A. Lot and Square:

　　The building is located in Square 136, original lot 2.

　　B. Original and Subsequent Owners:

　　The following chain of title to the property shows the owners of the present structure and of any known preceding structures on the site:

　　1900　Deed March 30, 1900, recorded April 4, 1900 in
　　　　　Liber 2490 folio 31

　　　　　Anna Howell Stewart
　　　　　　　To
　　　　　Elinor Medill Patterson

　　　　　"This Deed...Witnesseth that Anna Howell Stewart (widow), of the District of Columbia, party hereto of the first part, for and in consideration of Eighty-three thousand four hundred and six dollars...to her paid by Elinor Medill Patterson of said District of Columbia, party hereto of the second part...All of Original Lot...(2) in Square...(136)..."

　　1923　Deed March 17, 1923, recorded March 31, 1924 in
　　　　　Liber 5192 folio 44

15 Dupont Circle, N.W.

Elinor Medill Patterson, widow
        To
Countess Eleanor Patterson Gizycka

"...in consideration of love and affection and the sum of Ten dollars...Together with all household furniture and effects of every character and description contained therein, with the exception of silver and goldplate..."

NOTE: Will of Eleanor Patterson was recorded February 9, 1949 in Will Book No. 385 folio 398, Registrar of Wills, District of Columbia. The will stated:

"I give, devise and bequeath to the American Red Cross, of Washington, District of Columbia, my real estate improved by premises No. 15 Dupont Circle in said City of Washington, now occupied by me as my home, and all the furnishings in said premises except my family portraits and silver ware absolutely and in fee simple..."

1951 Deed March 1, 1951, recorded March 7, 1951 in Liber 9421 folio 562.

The American National Red Cross
        To
The Washington Club

"...Being the same property devised to grantor by Will of Eleanor Patterson, deceased (also known as Eleanor Medill Patterson and as Countess Eleanor Patterson Gizycka) by name and style of American Red Cross which is identical with the said The American National Red Cross. Said property being identical with 15 Dupont Circle, N.W...."

Source: Recorder of Deeds, Washington, D.C.

C. Date of Erection:

The building was begun in 1901 and completed in January 1903.

D. Building Permits:

The applications for the following building permits were filed by the architect, contractor or owner's agent and provide significant data:

No. 1905, June 10, 1901
Permit to build dwelling
   Owner: R. W. Patterson

15 Dupont Circle, N.W.

    Architect: McKim, Mead and White
    Builder: George A. Fuller Co.
    Estimated cost: $85,000.

No. 174, July 17, 1917
Permit to Repair or Reconstruct
    Owner: Mrs. Robert W. Patterson
    Architect: J. H. de Sibour
    Contractor: William P. Lipscomb & Co.
    "It is proposed to extend the present Wine Room out under the driveway a distance of 10'-0" by 12'-0" wide brick walls and reinforced concrete roof slab."

No. 177903, March 4, 1935
Permit to install elevator repair - changing D.C. to A.C. current

No. A 20984, June 13, 1951
Permit to Repair or Reconstruct
    "Make alterations to have building conform to required egress regulations for use as club building. Provide new toilet room."

No. A 21711, July 3, 1951
Permit to install concrete stair to second floor

    Source: D.C. Government: Department of Economic Development,
            Bureau of Licenses and Permits, Central Files.

E. Alterations and Additions:

To satisfy fire code regulations, a partition was constructed between the first floor foyer and the stairway to the bedroom floor.

A two story addition (with a dining room and foyer on the ground floor and a meeting room and a reception room on the second floor) was completed in 1956. The east wall windows of the original structure were closed and interior access doorways built for the addition.

F. Architect: McKim, Mead and White, New York City
           Stanford White, partner in charge

Stanford White, the son of Richard Grant White, noted Shakespearean scholar, and of the former Alexina Mease, was born in New York City November 9, 1853. White was educated in private schools and graduated from the University of New York. He had shown considerable talent in drawing and water color, but he was persuaded by his friend, John La Farge, to study architecture instead.

From 1872 until 1878, White worked as a draftsman in the office of Gambrill & Richardson in Boston. While there he became friends with

Charles F. McKim, another apprentice in the office; and with Augustus St. Gaudens, who was working under La Farge on mural decorations for H. H. Richardson's Trinity Church, Boston.

White left the firm in 1878 to travel in Europe. He spent some time sketching buildings in the towns surrounding Paris. St. Gaudens and McKim joined him later for a trip through southern France.

After his return to New York in 1880, White entered into a partnership with McKim and William Rutherford Mead - forming the firm of McKim, Mead and White. Mead was considered the more businesslike of the partners; and "although he gave less of his time to actual designing...he often not only conceived the scheme which was the basis of the whole design, but gave timely criticism which had vital bearing upon the finished work." McKim was "a calm, deliberate scholar - shy, cautious...He built decidedly in the grand manner, even to the point of austerity." White on the other hand was "exuberant, restless, a skyrocket of vitality. He worked at terrific pressure and produced a great many buildings, which are graceful and charming rather than imposing, and often profusely ornamented." (Sketches and Designs by Stanford White, pp. 15-17.)

The above noted book contains a "List of Works of McKim, Mead & White, in Which Stanford White Took a Leading Part." Two Washington, D.C. residences are included: the Residence of Thomas Nelson Page, 1759 R Street, N.W. (1897); and the Residence of Mrs. E. M. Patterson, 15 Dupont Circle, N.W. (1903). Also on the list:

> Residence of Robert Goelet, Newport, R.I. (1883)
> Residence of Charles L. Tiffany, N.Y.C. (1884)
> Residence of Joseph H. Choate, Stockbridge, Mass. (1887)
> Century Club, N.Y.C. (1891)
> Madison Square Garden, N.Y.C. (1891)
> Metropolitan Club, N.Y.C. (1894)
> New York University (1894)
> Residence of John Jacob Astor, Rhinebeck, N.Y. (1898)
> Residence of W.C. Whitney (interior), N.Y.C. (1900)
> Cullum Memorial Hall, West Point, N.Y. (1898)
> Knickerbocker Trust Co. (1904)
> Lambs Club, N.Y.C. (1905)
> Brook Club, N.Y.C. (1905)
> Gorham Building, N.Y.C. (1906)
> Tiffany & Co., N.Y.C. (1906)
> Residence of James L. Breese, Southampton, L.I. (1906)
> Residence of Payne Whitney, N.Y.C. (1906)

Stanford White was not interested in architectural design only. Besides planning "luxurious city and country homes in New York, Newport and the Berkshires, [he] designed furniture, and ransacked Europe for rugs, pictures, sculptures and hangings. He fashioned a railroad parlor-car and furnished James Gordon Bennett's yacht.

15 Dupont Circle, N.W.

He designed pedestals for Saint-Gaudens, and MacMonies, picture frames for Dewing, magazine covers for The Century and Scribner's, gravestones, book and program covers, and exquisite jewelry." (Dictionary of American Biography, Vol XX.)

On June 25, 1906, while attending the summer opening of the Madison Square Gardens Roof, Stanford White was shot and killed by Harry Thaw, a jealous husband.

Sources: Charles Moore, The Life and Times of Charles Follen McKim, New York: Houghton Mifflin Company, 1929.

L.G. White, Sketches and Designs by Stanford White, New York: The Architectural Book Publishing Company, 1920.

Henry F. Withey and Elsie R. Withey, Biographical Dictionary of American Architects (Deceased), Los Angeles: New Age Publishing Co., 1956.

Dumas Malone (ed.), Dictionary of American Biography, Vol. XX, New York: Charles Scribner's Sons, 1936.

The New York Times, "Thaw Murders Stanford White," 6-26-06, 1:5.

G. Known Plans, Drawings, Elevations, etc.:

Set of architectural drawings. Blueline prints. Scale 1/4" = 1'
McKim, Mead and White, Architects
New York Historical Society, NHi Roll #874
(see reproductions of ground and first floor plans)

H. Important Old Views:

Exterior photograph: view from southwest.
"Residence of R. G. Patterson, Dupont Circle, Washington, D.C., McKim, Mead & White, Architects."
The Architectural Record, Vol. XIII, no. 6 (June 1903), p. 493.

I. Residents:

1. City and telephone directories list the following tenants:

    1904-1905   R. W. Patterson
    1906   No listing
    1907-1909   Robert W. Patterson
    1910-1912   No listing
    1913   Mrs. Robert W. Patterson
    1914-1922   Mrs. Eleanor Patterson (widow of Robert)

15 Dupont Circle, N.W.

    1923   Mrs. Eleanor M. Patterson
    1924   Mrs. Robert Patterson
    1925   Countess Gizycka
    1926   Mrs. Eleanor Schlesinger
    1927-1930   Elmer Schlesinger
    1931-1932   Emily Patterson (probably Eleanor)
    1933-1935   Mrs. Eleanor Patterson, Publisher, The Washington Herald
    1936-1949   Mrs. Eleanor M. Patterson
    1950   Vacant
    1951-1972   The Washington Club

2. Biographies of the residents:

Robert Wilson Patterson (November 30, 1850 - April 1, 1910), the son of Rev. Robert Wilson and Julie A. (Quigley) Patterson, was born in Chicago. He was graduated from Williams College in 1871. After attending law school for a while, Patterson left to join the editorial staff of the Presbyterian "Interior." In 1873 he accepted the position of telegraph editor for The Chicago Tribune. Patterson married Eleanor Medill, daughter of Joseph Medill, who was the editor of the Tribune. When Medill died in 1899, his son-in-law received the vacated position. The Pattersons had two children: Joseph Medill and Eleanor (Cissy) Medill.

Sources: The National Cyclopedia of American Biography, Vol. XX, New York: James T. White & Company, 1929, p. 53.

            The New York Times, 4-2-10, 11:3 (obituary).

Mrs. Robert Patterson (died October 1935), formerly Eleanor Medill, was the daughter of Joseph Medill, editor of The Chicago Tribune.

> Mrs. Patterson moved operations to Washington for the same reason that Mrs. Marshall Field, Mrs. Edward Walsh and Mrs. Levi Leiter were erecting pleasure places there...Washington was the one city in the East where any woman with money and talent could set up housekeeping and become an important hostess. (Cissy Patterson, p. 16-17)

In 1893 she paid $83,000 for a site on Dupont Circle, and by 1903 she had reputedly spent $200,000 for what her daughter refered to as "the movie palace." (Cissy Patterson, p. 17)

Sources: Felicia Gizycka, "15 Dupont Circle - The Most Beautiful Palace of Them All", The Washingtonian Magazine, Vol. V, No. 11 (August 1970), pp. 46-49, 77-81.

           Alice Albright Hoge, Cissy Patterson, New York: Random House, 1966.

15 Dupont Circle, N.W.

Eleanor (Cissy) Medill Patterson (November 7, 1884 - July 24, 1948), the daughter of Robert W. and Eleanor M. Patterson, was christened Eleanor Josephine. The nickname "Cissy" was given by her older brother, Captain Joseph Medill Patterson, playwright, author, and publisher of The New York Daily News. For most of her life, Cissy was a well-known member of Washington society.

In 1902, her aunt, Mrs. Robert R. McCormick (formerly Katherine Medill), invited Cissy to Vienna where she was presented to the Austro-Hungarian court. During this trip, she met Count Josef Gizycka (of Blansko in the Moravian province of Austro-Hungary) in Paris. The Count followed her to St. Petersburg in 1903 and proposed. They were married April 14, 1904 at 15 Dupont Circle and left for Russia where their daughter, Felicia, was born in 1905. Matrimonial trouble in 1907 induced the Countess to flee to England. In 1908, Count Gizycka went to England, kidnapped the three year old Felicia, and took her back to Russia. Soon after, President Taft and prominent Russian citizens appealed to the Czar for Felicia's return. In August 1909, Felicia and her mother returned to the Unites States; and two years later the Countess filed for divorce, asking only for custody of the child. (The New York Times, 1-29-11)

Cissy married a New York corporate lawyer, Elmer Schlesinger, in 1925. During their marriage, the couple lived at 1010 5th Avenue, New York City and Port Washington, Long Island. (The New York Times, 2-21-29) After his death in 1929, Cissy had her name legally changed to Mrs. Eleanor Medill Patterson.

William Randolph Hearst, a friend, encouraged Cissy to take up journalism. Her first assignments included a series of hunting articles in 1920 from the Sawtooth Mountains in Idaho. In 1930, Hearst appointed her editor of The Washington Herald at $10,000 per annum, at which time the introduction of her column, "Interesting but not True," extended the popularity of the newspaper. (Post Biographies of Famous Journalists)

Through inheritances and purchases, Cissy Patterson eventually accumulated stock in The Chicago Tribune and The New York Daily News. By 1942 she had acquired both The Washington Times and The Washington Herald from William R. Hearst. The two papers were combined to form the Times-Herald, which Constance McLaughlin Green in Washington Capital City (page 418) called "pro-Americanism, pro-Hearst, pro-Marian Davies, and anti-everything else."

Using Eleanor Gizycka as a pen name for articles and publications, Cissy wrote two novels: Glass Houses (1926), a revealing story based on real Washington personalities; and Fall Flight (1928), a story of a wealthy American girl in pre-World War I Russia.

After Elmer Schlesinger's death, Cissy often used 15 Dupont Circle for entertaining, but by 1944 she was spending less time with the

15 Dupont Circle, N.W.

Times-Herald and her Washington residence. Her other homes, included: "Dower House" in Prince Georges County, Maryland, which was the original estate of Lord Baltimore and the hunting lodge of Lord Calvert; a summer house at Sands Point, Long Island; a winter home in Sarasota, Florida; a ranch near Jackson Hole, Wyoming; and an apartment at Carlton House, New York City. (The New York Times, 7-25-48)

Perhaps Cissy Patterson's well-known criticism of Washington society, her unusual dinner parties, and her numerous acquisitions of properties encouraged Robert S. Allen and Drew Pearson (her daughter's first husband) to write in Washington Merry-Go-Round:

> Eleanor Medill Patterson, formerly Mrs. Eleanor Schlesinger, formerly Countess Gizycka, formerly Eleanor Medill Patterson, one of the most gifted women in Washington...has dissipated her gifts, for the most part, on trivialities.

With Eleanor Patterson's death, the estate, estimated at $17 million, went to her family - except for the residence and its contents at 15 Dupont Circle, which were left to the American National Red Cross. (The Evening Star, 10-18-48)

Sources: John E. Drewery (ed.), Post Biographies of Famous Personalities, "Cissy is a Newspaper Lady" by Stanley Walker, New York: Random House, 1942, pp. 346-364.

Constance McLaughlin Green, Washington Capital City, 1879-1950, Princeton, New Jersey: Princeton University Press, 1963.

Alice Albright Hoge, Cissy Patterson, New York: Random House, 1966.

Robert S. Allen and Drew Pearson, Washington Merry-Go-Round, New York: Horace Liveright, Inc., 1931, pp. 10-15

Who's Who in The Nation's Capital 1938-1939, Washington, D.C.: Ransdell Incorporated, 1939.

The Evening Star, 10-18-48, B1:4.
The New York Times, 1-29-11, 3:5.
The New York Times, 2-21-29, 27:3 (Mr. Schlesinger's obituary).
The New York Times, 7-25-48, 49:1 (Mrs. Patterson's obituary).

15 Dupont Circle, N.W.

Elmer Schlesinger (November 20, 1880 - February 20, 1929) was raised in Chicago. He graduated in 1901 from Harvard University where he received his law degree in 1903. He began practice with the Chicago law firm of May, Meyer, Austrian and Platt. Eventually, his organization ability led to the directorship of The Chicago Tribune, The New York News, Liberty Magazine and the Libby-Owens Glass Company. From June 1921 until September 1922, Schlesinger was the vice-president and general counsel of the U.S. Shipping Board in Washington, D.C. He later joined the New York law firm of Chadbourne, Stenchfield and Levy.

His marriage to Halle Schaffner in 1911 ended in divorce in 1922. They had two children, Halle and Elmer. On April 11, 1925 Schlesinger married Eleanor Patterson Gizycka.

Sources: Who Was Who in American 1897-1942: A Companion Volume to Who's Who in America, Vol. I, Chicago: The A. N. Marquis Publishing Company, 1942.

The New York Times, 2-21-29, 27:3 (obituary).

The Washington Club is a women's organization. Under the Articles of Incorporation, the club was established for:

> ...literary purposes and mutual improvement;... That the particular business and objects of our said society are the establishment, maintenance and promotion of social intercourse; and to continue the work and organization heretofore inaugurated and carried on by the society incorporated by a certificate of incorporation recorded in the office of the Recorder of Deeds for the District of Columbia on the 8th day of May 1893, in Liber No. 6 folio 248 et seq. of the incorporation records of the District of Columbia.

Source: Incorporation Records of the District of Columbia. Recorded in Liber 28 folio 186 on March 25, 1911.

J. Events Connected with the Structure:

Soon after its completion in 1903, 15 Dupont Circle was the scene of many gala events:

> During Mrs. [Robert] Patterson's years in the house, she maintained a staff of 10 to 15 servants. Until the war they wore full livery and the house was always the scene of parties.
> (The Sunday Star, 1-2-55)

These lavish parties seem to have been prepared for the amusement of the "Three Graces of Washington:" Alice Lee Roosevelt, Countess Marguerite Cassini and Cissy Patterson.

The wedding between Cissy and Count Josef Gizycka in 1904 was considered a major event - with the Ambassadors, their wives, and staff of both Russia and Austria in attendance. Rev. Thomas S. Lee, Rector of St. Matthew's Church, performed the ceremony. (The Evening Star, 4-14-04; Cissy Patterson, p. 26)

The Patterson house was used by President and Mrs. Coolidge in 1927 while the White House was refurbished. "Although [Grace Coolidge] found the slantwise rooms 'a little cramped after the big square rooms at the White House' she liked them... 'Like most of the Washington houses this one was built with more thought given to the entertainment side of it than to the living side.' "(Grace Coolidge and Her Era, p. 218)

In June of 1927, Col. Charles A. Lindbergh was given a hero's welcome upon his return to the United States. He and his mother, Mrs. Evangeline Lodge Lindbergh, were guests of the Presidential family at 15 Dupont Circle. The house was besieged by cheering crowds for three days, demanding glimpses of the man who had flown the Atlantic. (The Evening Star, 6-10-27 and 6-12-27)

Alice Albright Hoge wrote in Cissy Patterson that the family rarely used the house after Mrs. Robert Patterson moved back to Chicago in 1923. However, Cissy, after her second husband's death in 1929, again opened the house to entertainment.

> According to her friends, the thing she liked most was a good argument and she frequently had guests who were sure of getting into one. At one memorable party she had six or seven presidential candidates together. (The Sunday Star, 1-2-55)

With her death in 1948, Cissy's will made public her desire that 15 Dupont Circle and all its contents go to the American National Red Cross. In April of 1949, The Red Cross opened the house to the public auction of the personal belongings and effects of Cissy Patterson. (The Washington Daily News, 4-29-49) Soon after, the Red Cross offered the building and all its furnishings (not previously auctioned) for sale at $700,000 (Times-Herald, 11-29-50); and in January of the following year the building was purchased by the Washington Club for approximately $450,000. The sale included a "number of Gobelin, Flemish and French tapestries, authentic period chairs, sofas and tables." (The Evening Star, 1-12-51)

Sources: Alice Albright Hoge, Cissy Patterson, New York: Random House, 1966.

15 Dupont Circle, N.W.

Ishbel Ross, Grace Coolidge and Her Era, New York: Dodd, Mead & Company, 1962

The Evening Star, 4-14-04, 5:5.
The Evening Star, 6-10-27, 1:1.
The Sunday Star, 6-12-27, 1:2.
The Evening Star, 1-12-51, 5:2.
The Sunday Star, 1-2-55, D4:1.
The Washington Daily News, 4-29-49, 21:1.
Times-Herald, 11-2-48, 1:2.
Times-Herald, 11-29-50, 23:4.

West Elevation
CFA photo
Boucher 1970

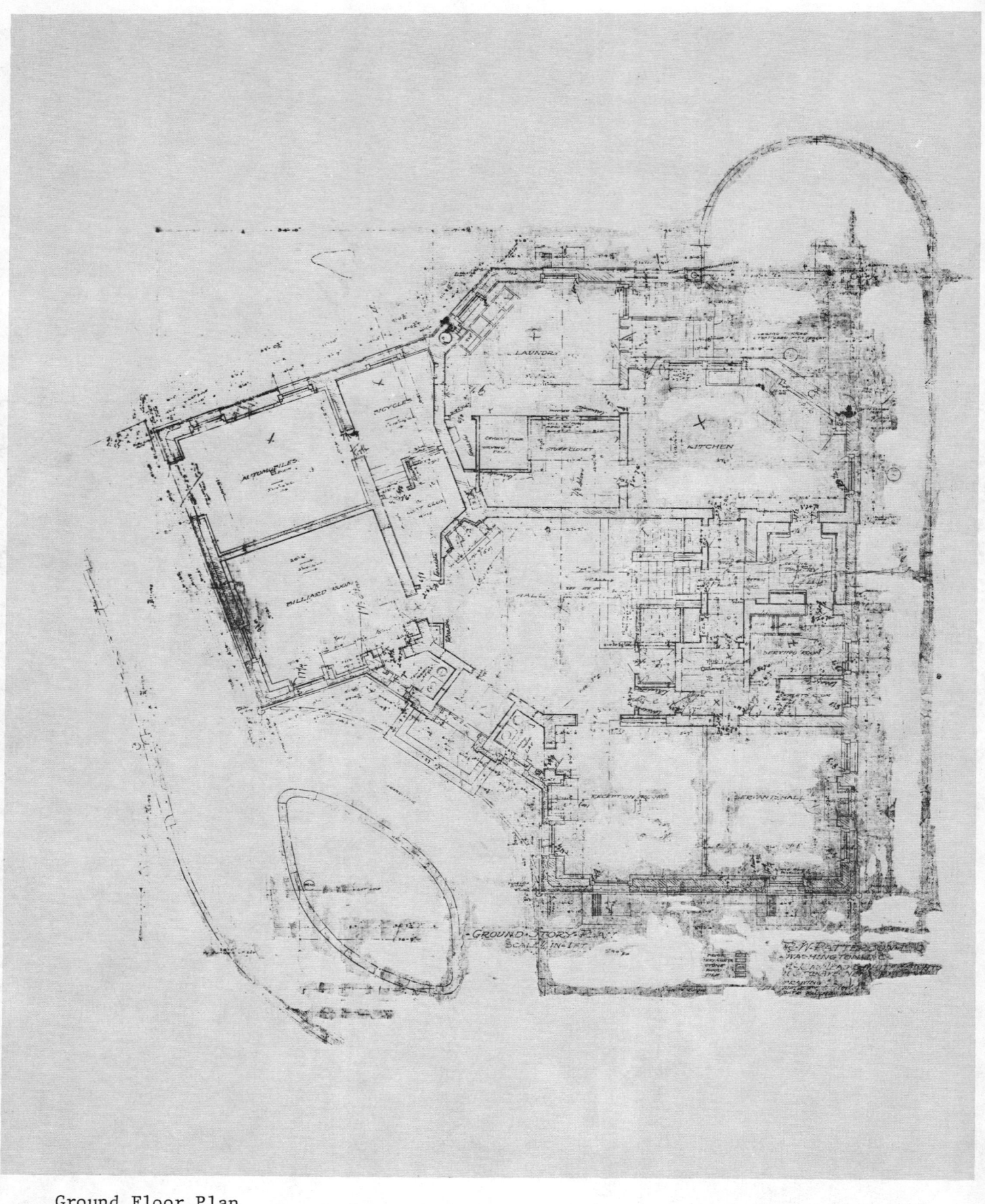

Ground Floor Plan
McKim, Mead and White, Architects
March 20, 1901
New York Historical Society

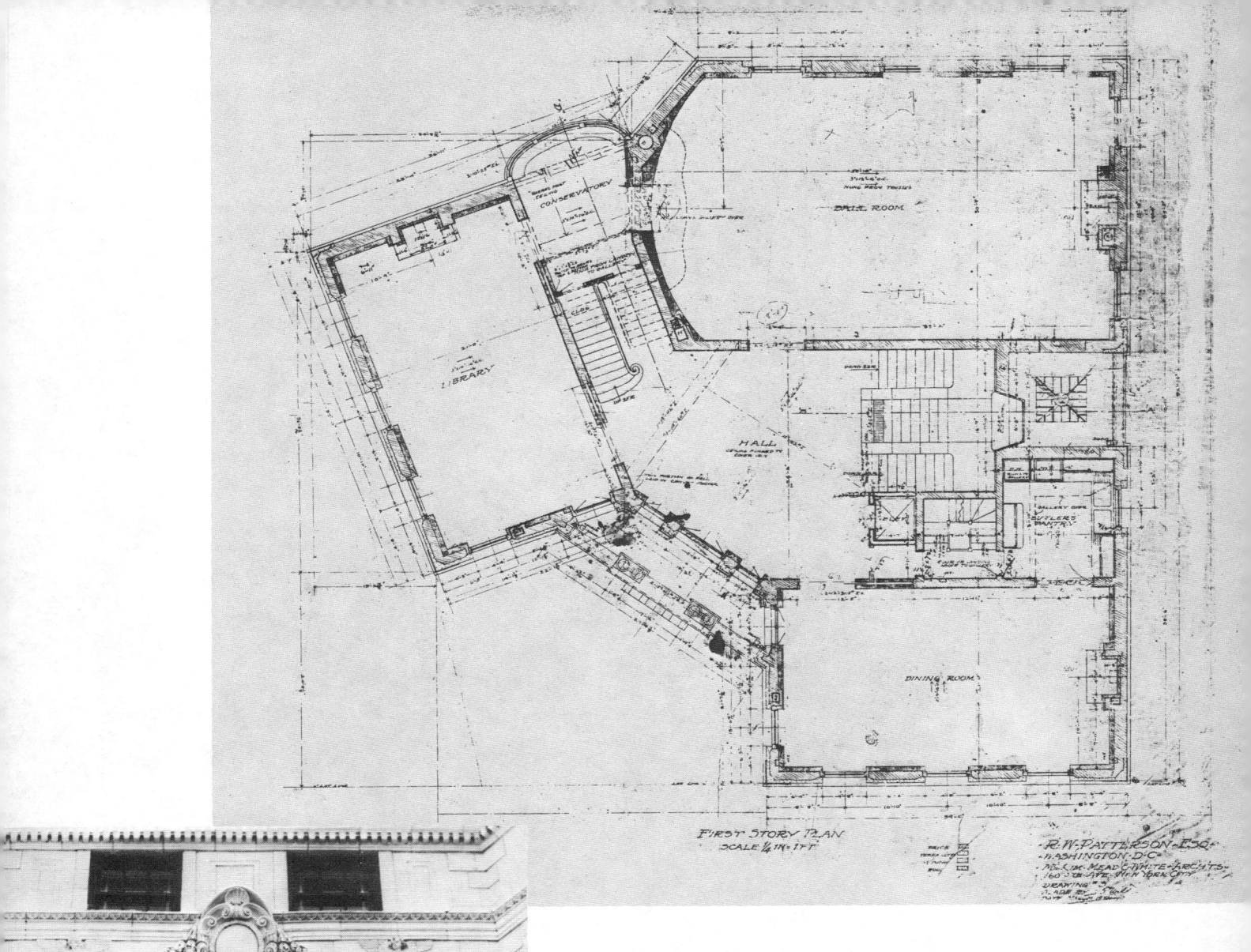

First Floor Plan
McKim, Mead, and White, Architects
March 19, 1901
New York Historical Society

Left
Detail Entrance Loggia
CFA photo 1973

Next page
Ballroom
CFA photo
Alexander   1971

Next page
Library
CFA photo
Alexander 1971

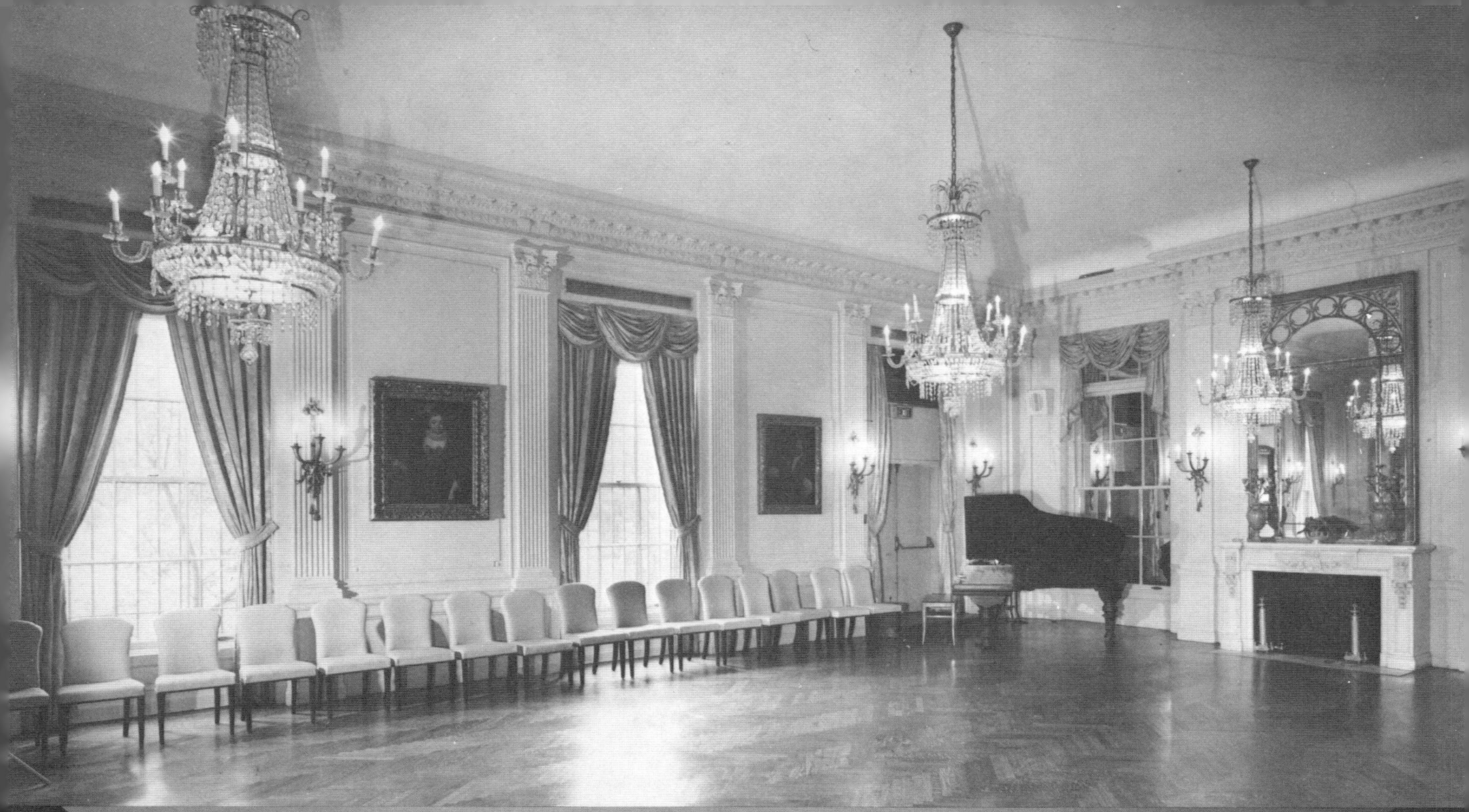

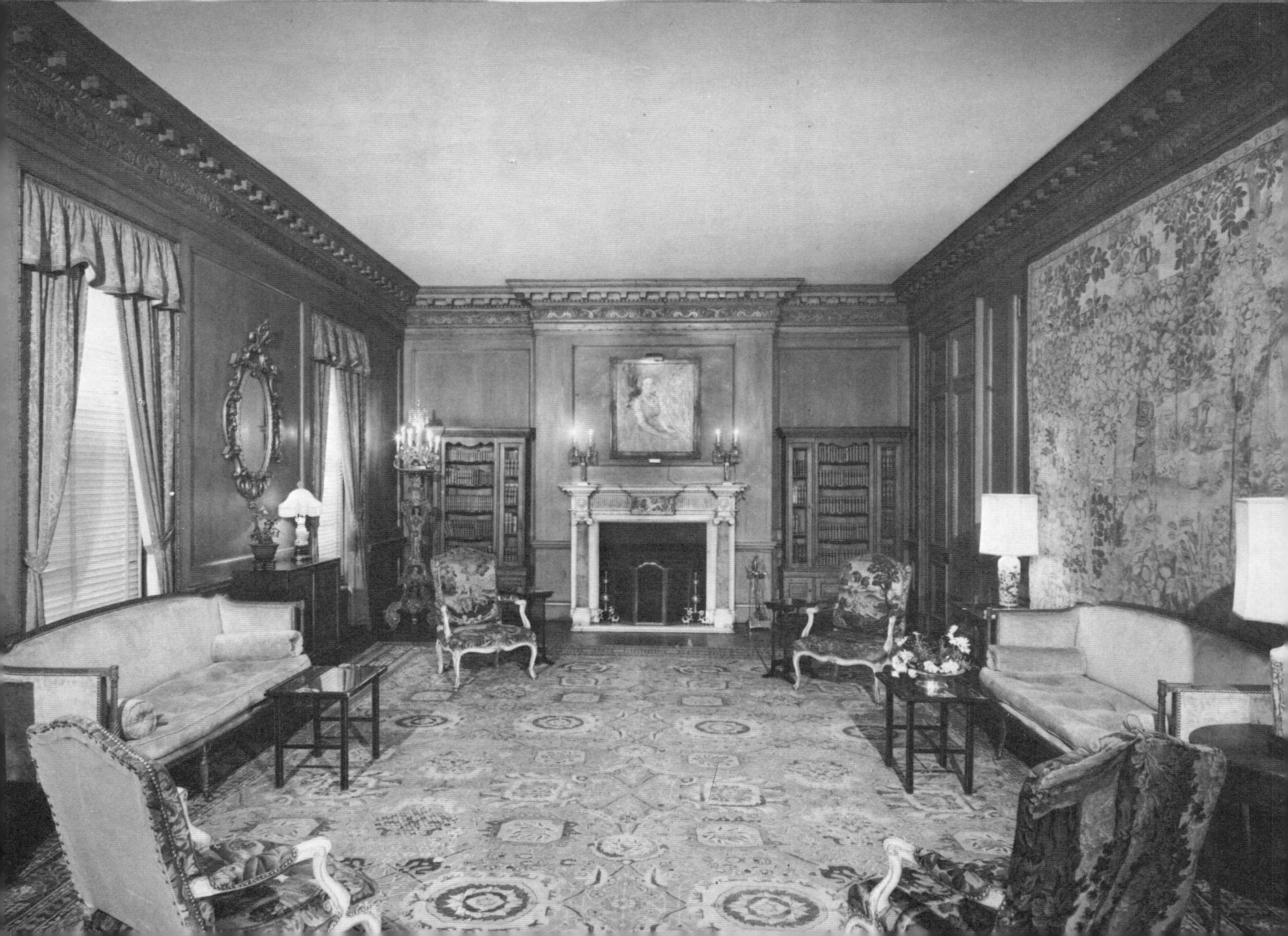

15 Dupont Circle, N.W.

PART II. ARCHITECTURAL INFORMATION

    A. General Statement:

        1. Architectural character: This detached structure is an example of the decorative neoclassic Italianate style.

        2. Condition: very good aside from minor regulation firecode changes and remodeling.

    B. Exterior Description:

        1. Overall dimensions: The four story plus basement structure measures 60'-0" from sidewalk to roof ridge. The 27'-5" wide entrance wall is set back from the street in an entrance court with obtuse angled, one bay, east and west elevations, respectively, 13'-7" and 14'-2" deep. The entrance wall supports a loggia, one bay (8'-0") in depth, with an 18'-6" wide back wall. The P Street and Dupont Circle, three bay elevations are both 39'-0". The northwest elevation is an obtuse angle whose sides measure 37'-8" from Dupont Circle and 11'-8". The east section of the 46'-0" north elevation is opened at ground level for service. The east wall is 83'-0", having a two story addition on P Street.

        2. Foundations: concrete footings and slab.

        3. Wall construction: The marble-faced structure has glazed terra cotta ornament. A low stone base supports the quoines and range-coursed walls of the ground floor. A Greek key string course acts as loggia balustrade and first floor window sill. The first and second floors have quoines with tooled edges. The first floor windows are separated by variegated marble panels in egg and dart mouldings with scroll bases and urn and festoon caps. Over each panel are additional panels each with a bib drape linked to fruit swags which flank escutcheons mounted over the first floor window pediments. Fruit and ribbon pendants hang from the corner swags on the street elevations. The lowest of these fruit clusters is supported by a cherub. Each second floor window has a scroll support and a scroll and flambeau mount, and is separated by variegated marble panels in egg and dart mouldings with mask and scroll bases. Over each of these panels is a winged figure which holds fruit swags attached with ribbon to the flambeau crowns over each window. The end figures on the street elevations stand on round panels with pendants. The third floor (attic) is the building entablature. The architrave is interrupted by a fruit and swag escutcheon which caps the central French door to the balcony over the loggia. The escutcheon swags are linked to winged figures over the side windows flanking the door. Above the fascia and talon architrave, the frieze has alternating windows and flat panels.

4. Structure: brick bearing walls.

5. Mechanical: The passenger elevator is by Otis, the lighting is electric and the heating is a gravity rise system.

6. Porches, stoops, bulkheads, etc.: The front entrance stoop is approached by three limestone risers. The Greek key string course, which acts as a cap for the loggia balustrade, supports two pairs of volute and swag, variegated marble columns on plinths with candelabra pilasters at each end. Candelabra pilasters flank the loggia doors. The loggia is capped by an Ionic entablature and an urn baluster balcony interrupted by panelled pedestals.

7. Chimneys: Visible from the street are seven, brick, panelled chimneys with limestone entablature caps (two over either street elevation, two at the north and one over the west end of the central facade).

8. Openings:

    a. Doorways and doors: The black enameled double entrance door has four, pattera-centered panels per leaf and a marble crossette architrave with a cyma cornice capped by a scroll and fruit swag escutcheon. The escutcheon interrupts the Greek key string course. The garage entrance on Dupont Circle has metal double doors. Glazed doors, capped by escutcheon friezes, give access to the loggia.

    b. Windows: All windows are double-hung. The ground floor windows have block sills and decorative wrought iron console grilles. The first floor windows rest on the Greek key string course. Each window has an astragal, fascia and talon architrave, anthemion and palmette frieze and raked cyma pediment. The second floor windows have fillet and block sills and astragal, fascia and talon, crossette architraves. The balcony door is flanked by narrow windows having a frieze within the talon architrave. The attic windows lack architraves.

9. Roof:

    a. Shape, covering: The truncated-hip roof, originally red tile, is presently covered by asbestos shingle with copper flashing.

    b. Cornice, eaves: dentils, acanthus modillions, corona and cyma.

    c. Dormers, cupolas, towers: skylights over corridors below flat section of roof.

C. Interior Description:

1. Floor plans: On axis with the southwest entrance is the ground floor vestibule and the polygonal entrance hall. To the northeast of the entrance hall, the main stair alcove is approached by two marble risers and a platform. The vestibule is flanked by lavatories with access from the southeast reception room and the northwest library (billiard room). Behind and to the south of the main stair is a servants' stair, pantries and an entrance hall elevator. East of the reception room, and north of the entrance hall and library are service areas, with the kitchen at the northeast. (See plan.)

   At the head of the main stair is the first floor polygonal foyer. Arranged around the foyer are: the elevator, servants' stair and pantry at the east; the southeast dining room on P Street; and the loggia on the south. The loggia connects the dining room to the southwest drawing room (library) on Dupont Circle. To the north of the drawing room is the family stair, behind which is a conservatory. The conservatory connects the drawing room to the northeast ballroom. (See plan.)

   The second floor contains bedroom suites arranged along a west-to-east corridor which terminates in a northeast foyer. The third floor has servants' quarters and storage rooms.

2. Spaces:

   Entrance hall:

   a. Flooring: polished terrazzo with a white marble border.

   b. Walls: plaster.

   c. Ceiling: plaster painted white.

   d. Heating: The north wall corner chimney has a limestone mantle in the 15th century Italianate manner, 5'-0" wide by 7'-0" high with a firebox 4'-0" wide by 5'-6" high. Narrow candelabra pilasters flank the firebox and support large acanthus scrolls decorated with Pan and flambeau side panels. The scrolls support a cantilevered entablature shelf having a bead and talon architrave, a rinceau frieze of winged mermen interrupted by a central cartouche, and an egg and dart, and cyma cap.

   Reception room:

   a. Flooring: carpeted.

   b. Baseboard: 6", wood.

   c. Walls: plaster.

d. Cornice: acanthus leaf cove.

e. Ceiling: plaster painted white.

f. Doorways and doors: The decorative crossette architraves are capped by plaster, swag and festoon panels.

g. Hardware: brass door handles.

h. Heating: The west wall chimney has a white marble mantle (3'-6" high) in the Georgian manner, with consoles and a spray frieze.

Billiard room:

a. Flooring: carpeted.

b. Baseboard: 6", wood.

c. Chairrail: 2'-6" high, wood fascia.

d. Walls: wood, built-in north and east wall bookshelves (modern).

e. Cornice: egg and dart with cyma.

f. Ceiling: plaster painted white.

g. Doorways and doors: crossette architraves.

h. Hardware: brass door knobs.

i. Heating: The south wall chimney has a plain, sand-cast mantle in the Georgian manner.

Main stair:

a. Stairway: The stair alcove and entrance hall are separated by marble Ionic columns in antis. The main stair ascends east ten risers to a landing with a recessed wall fountain. The landing is flanked by two additional landings approached by single risers from which the stair ascends west nine risers on two flights to the first floor foyer. The stair risers, treads and closed stringer are marble. The cast iron banister has rinceau and cartouche panels; and the handrail is bound in red velvet.

b. Fountain: Built into the east wall of the central landing is a grey and tan-veined, white marble fountain. On a large plinth is perched an eagle with spread wings supporting a shallow half-round bowl. The spigot projects from the mouth of a satyr's mask which is capped by a swan. Flanking candelabra pilasters with naive Ionic capitals and rosette bases support a fascia architrave, plain frieze and an egg and dart cornice. Over the cornice is a recessed fan within an egg and dart moulding capped by acroterion.

Foyer:

a. Flooring: herringbone parquetry.

b. Baseboard: 6", wood with cyma cap.

c. Walls: Between panelled wood pedestals and fluted composite pilasters are raised, corner-indented, plaster panels within beaded mouldings.

d. Cornice: fascia, talon, egg and dart, acanthus brackets, astragal and talon.

e. Ceiling: 12'-4" high, plaster painted white.

Dining room:

a. Flooring: 6", curly maple, common.

b. Baseboard: 5 1/2", wood with cyma cap.

c. Dado: raised panels.

d. Chairrail: 3'-0" high, wood, fascia and bead.

e. Walls: raised plaster panels.

f. Cornice: The full entablature has a fascia architrave, a plain frieze, and a dentil, egg and dart, and grooved bracket cornice.

g. Ceiling: 12'-4" high, plaster painted white.

h. Doorways and doors: crossette architraves.

i. Windows: crossette architraves with recesses for drapes.

j. Hardware: brass door handles.

k. Lighting: There are six, three-light, mirror-backed, crystal sconces (the arms tied in the manner of a fleur-de-lis). There is one, twelve-light, crystal chandelier, having two brass tiers with crystal beads. Brass leaves spring from its inverted, heavy brass canopy which has a rosette block band and a crystal pendant at the base. Over the canopy, the arms of the crystal mid-section have lotus candle holders.

15 Dupont Circle, N.W.

1. Heating: The east wall chimney has a cast iron firebox and a white marble mantle in the Georgian manner (7'-6" wide by 5'-6" high). Flanking stop-fluted Ionic columns support the central swag and ribbon frieze, broken forward over either column, and a denticulated shelf.

Library: (present drawing room: natural pine panelling. See photograph.)

a. Flooring: herringbone parquetry.

b. Baseboard: 7 1/2", cyma cap.

c. Dado: flat panels within cyma mouldings.

d. Chairrail: 3'-0" high, bead, cyma and fascia.

e. Walls: flat panels within cyma mouldings.

f. Cornice: The full entablature has an astragal, fascia and talon architrave; a strapwork, leaf and rosette, pulvinated frieze ; and an egg and dart, plain modillion, talon and cyma cornice.

g. Ceiling: 12'-4" high, plaster, **painted** white.

h. Doorways and doors: Each leaf of the wood, double doors to the foyer and conservatory has three raised panels in egg and dart mouldings. The architrave has a bound oak leaf roll, with fascia, astragal and talon mouldings.

i. Windows: The stiles and rails of the wall panelling form an architrave edged by astragal and recessed for drapes.

j. Hardware: brass door handles.

k. Heating: The north wall chimney has a marble hearth within an ogee moulding and a mantle in the Georgian manner (6'-6" wide by 5'-4" high). The white marble, egg and dart firebox surround is flanked by plinths with Ionic columns of yellow and pink marble. The full entablature shelf has an astragal architrave; an inlaid yellow and pink marble gouge frieze centered by a pink marble, rabbit and hound panel and broken forward over either column; and an egg and dart, and talon cap.

Ballroom: (see photograph)

a. Flooring: oak, herringbone parquetry.

b. Baseboard: 6", wood with cyma cap.

c. Dado: raised, corner-indented panels within cyma and bead mouldings.

15 Dupont Circle, N.W.

d. Chairrail: 3'-0" high, wood, cyma and bead.

e. Walls: raised, rosette-indented, plaster panels within cyma and bead mouldings. Flanking the chimney, doors and windows, and at the room corners, are fluted composite pilasters on raised panelled pedestals. The west wall is semielliptical, and the east chimney wall breaks forward 9".

f. Balcony: Over the central west wall door is a serpentine orchestra balcony supported by acanthus and festoon consoles with guttae. The stringer has a bead and binding moulding, and the painted and gilded, cast iron banister has a center medallion flanked by rinceau and gouge panels and united by a wave pattern. The background wall has panelled pilasters.

g. Cornice: The full entablature has a fascia and talon architrave; a running dog frieze with paired brackets above each pilaster and an egg and dart, acanthus bracket, astragal and talon cornice.

h. Ceiling: 14'-6" high, plaster painted white within a slight border cove.

i. Doorways and doors: The glazed double door to the foyer has a fascia architrave.

j. Windows: The beaded architraves have recesses for drapes. The windows flanking the chimney wall have been closed by the east addition; the glazing is replaced with mirror panes.

k. Hardware: brass door handles except at modern northeast fire escape door.

l. Lighting: There are ten, three-light, brass-finished plaster sconces with flambeau arms knotted together and joined by ribbon and tassels. There are three, twelve-light crystal chandeliers, their tasseled bowls and crowns connected by prism drapes. The brass arms and frames are encrusted with crystal beads. Each chandelier has three concealed light tiers.

m. Heating: The east wall chimney has a cast iron firebox with a musical cartouche, simulated lattice side panels and floral rinceau surround. The white marble mantle (6'-6" wide by 4'-0" high by 1'-0" deep) sits on baseboard plinths The plinths support flanking panelled pilasters with floral festoon caps; a gouge frieze, interrupted by a central musical panel and broken forward over either pilaster and a cyma shelf. The gilded overmantle mirror, in the late 18th century English manner, has columnettes which support a decorative muntin and a semicircular arch with flambeau spandrels.

15 Dupont Circle, N.W.

D. Site:

1. Setting and orientation: The building faces southwest across the east end of Dupont Circle and is set on an irregularly shaped lot measuring 128'-10" on the south (P Street); 64'-6" on the southwest (Dupont Circle); 164'-9" on the northwest; and 132'9" on the east.

2. Enclosures: none.

3. Outbuildings: none. A two story wing of two composite bays was added by the Washington Club to the east building wall.

4. Walks: There is a semielliptical concrete entrance drive linking P Street and Dupont Circle. Both the drive and public sidewalk are edged by limestone curbing.

5. Landscaping: The public sidewalk is bordered by clipped hedges. At the west, the property has ivy, with spruce, magnolia grandiflora and oak.

2020 MASSACHUSETTS AVENUE, N.W., WASHINGTON, D.C.

CFA photo
Boucher 1970

Location:	2020 Massachusetts Avenue, N.W., Washington, D.C.; on the southeast corner of Massachusetts Avenue and 21st Street.
Present Owner:	Republic of Indonesia
Present Occupant:	Republic of Indonesia
Present Use:	Chancery
Statement of Significance:	Originally a private residence, this detached structure with Louis XVI details is most conspicuous for its art-nouveau undulating walls and roof; its galleried and sky-lit, three story, "steamship" stairhall; its pastiche of applied ornament; and its colorful early occupants.

PART I. HISTORICAL INFORMATION

A. Lot and Square:

The building is located in Square 95, original lots 4 and 6. The original owner also built a stable in Square 67, lot 41 (formerly parts of original lots 8 and 9).

B. Original and Subsequent Owners:

The following chain of title to the property shows the owners of the present structure and of any known preceding structures on the site:

1901 Deed April 30, 1901, recorded April 30, 1901 in
Liber 2543 folio 403

Esther E. Hopkins
Bertha Hammond et vir
    To
Thomas F. Walsh

"...Esther E. Hopkins, widow of John S. Hopkins, Bertha Hammond (formerly Hopkins, sole heir at law of said John S. Hopkins, deceased) and Thomas V. Hammond, her husband, all of the District of Columbia...for and in consideration of Seventy four thousand two hundred and thirty dollars... to them paid by Thomas F. Walsh, of said District of Columbia...All of Original Lot...(6)... in Square...(95)..."

1902   Deed January 3, 1902, recorded January 4, 1902 in
Liber 2625 folio 288

Esther E. Hopkins et al
    To
Thomas F. Walsh

"...All of Original Lot...(4) in Square...(95). Subject however to an indebtedness of Fifteen thousand Dollars ($15,000) secured by Deed of Trust bearing date of January 6, 1896 and duly recorded in Liber No. 2079 folio 278..."

1927   Deed July 14, 1927, recorded July 19, 1927 in
Liber 5915 folio 135

American Security and Trust Company, Trustee
Carrie B. Walsh
    To
American Security and Trust Company, Trustee
Evalyn McLean

"This Deed...by and between the American Security and Trust Company, as Trustee under that certain deed in trust from Carrie B. Walsh, dated March 25, 1919 and recorded March 27, 1919 in Liber 4169 folio 123...said Trustee acting herein in exercise of the powers conferred by said deed in trust, and also by and with the consent of said Carrie B. Walsh, such consent being evidenced by her becoming a party to and executing these presents, and said Carrie B. Walsh, of the District of Columbia, parties hereto of the first part, and the American Security and Trust Company and Evalyn McLean, as Trustees under that certain deed in trust from said Evalyn McLean, dated June 21, 1920 and recorded June 28, 1920 in Liber 4393 folio 227..., said Trustees acting herein in exercise of the powers conferred by said last mentioned deed in trust, parties hereto of the second part.

"Witnesseth, that the said parties of the first part, for and in consideration of the grant and conveyance hereinafter made to said American Security and Trust Company as Trustee under the aforesaid deed in trust recorded in Liber 4169 folio 123...and in further consideration of...($56,500)...do... sell unto the said parties hereto of the second part in fee simple...All of lots, parts of lots and parcels of land in Squares...(222) and...(405), of which Thomas F. Walsh died seized and possessed...

"And this deed further witnesseth, that the said parties hereto of the second part, in consideration of the grant and conveyance hereinabove made to them as Trustees under the said deed in trust recorded in Liber 4393 folio 227...do hereby grant and convey unto said American Security and Trust Company as Trustee under deed in trust recorded in Liber 4169 folio 123...the following described land and premises, with improvements, easements and appurtenances thereunto belonging,...Lot...(41) in Thomas F. Walsh's Subdivision of lots in Square...(67), as **per plat** recorded in Liber 26 folio 109 of the Records of the Office of the Surveyor of the District of Columbia; also Lots...(4) and ...(6) in Square...(95)..."

Also lot 60, Square 252; lots 30, 31, 32, 33 in Square 252; and part of 38 in Square 95.

"To have and to hold the land and premises described above, ...unto and to the use of the said American Security and Trust Company, as Trustee under said deed in trust recorded in Liber 4169 folio 123...in fee simple, in severalty, but in trust nevertheless..."

NOTE: The Will of Carrie B. Walsh, was recorded July 11, 1932 in Will Book No. 183, page No. 190, Registrar of Wills, District of Columbia.

1951 Deed December 19, 1951, recorded January 2, 1952 in Liber 9623 folio 312

American Security and Trust Company, Trustee
 To
Republic of Indonesia

"This Deed...by and between American Security and Trust Company, Trustee under Deed in Trust from Carrie B. Walsh dated March 25, 1919 and recorded March 27, 1919 in Liber 4169 folio 123...and as Trustee under Deed in Trust from American Security and Trust Company, as Trustee and Evalyn McLean, dated July 14, 1927 and recorded in Liber 5915 folio 135... acting herein in exercise of the powers conferred by said Deeds in Trust, party hereto of the first part; and Republic of Indonesia, party hereto of the second part...for and in consideration of Three Hundred Thirty-five Thousand ($335,000) Dollars...Original Lots...(4) and...(6) in Square...(95)..."

Stable:

1901 Deed December 30, 1901, recorded December 31, 1901 in Liber 2595 folio 285

2020 Massachusetts Avenue, N.W.

Swope and Hamilton, Trustees
    To
Thomas F. Walsh

"...part of original lot...(8) in Square...(67); beginning for the same at the Northeast corner of said lot and running thence South along the rear line thereof...42 feet to the Southeast corner thereof; thence West along the South line thereof...47 feet; thence North...42 feet and thence East...47 feet to the point of beginning; together with a right of way for alley purposes over a part of said lot; beginning at a point in the North line thereof distant...47 feet from the Northeast corner thereof and running West along the North line of said lot...5 feet; thence South...62 feet to the South line thereof; thence East...5 feet and thence North...62 feet to the point of beginning..."

1901 Deed December 19, 1901, recorded December 31, 1901 in Liber 2595 folio 289

Edward J. Stellwagen et ux, Charlotte M.
    To
Thomas F. Walsh

"...Witnesseth that the parties of the first part for and in consideration of - $3260.62 - lawful money of the United States of America to them in hand paid by the party of the second part...have...conveyed...the following described land and premises...distinguished as part of original lot...(9) in Square...(67); beginning for the same at the Northeast corner of said lot and running thence South along the rear line thereof...55 feet...6 inches to the Southeast corner thereof; thence West along the South line thereof...47 feet, thence North...55 feet...6 inches and thence East...47 feet to the point of beginning...together with a right of way for alley purposes over a part of said lot beginning at a point in the North line thereof distant ...47 feet from the Northeast corner thereof and running thence West along the North line of said lot...5 feet thence South...55 feet...6 inches to the South line thereof; thence East...5 feet and thence North...55 feet...6 inches to the beginning..."

NOTE: April 7, 1902 Thomas F. Walsh subdivided the East 47 feet by 97.5 feet of original lots 8 and 9, Square 67, into lot 41. Recorded in Subdivisions Book 26 folio 109, Office of the Surveyor, District of Columbia.

Source: Recorder of Deeds, Washington, D.C.

2020 Massachusetts Avenue, N.W.

C. Date of Erection:

The building permit was issued in October 1901. In 1902, Thomas F. Walsh was first listed in the city directory at 2020 Massachusetts Avenue, N.W.. Walsh's daughter, Mrs. Evalyn Walsh McLean, wrote in Father Struck It Rich that the family moved into the house in the fall of 1903.

D. Building Permits:

The applications for the following building permits were filed by the architect, contractor or owner's agent and provide significant data:

No. 690, October 16, 1901
Permit to build dwelling
    Owner: Thomas F. Walsh
    Architect: Henry Anderson [Andersen], 1183 Broadway, N.Y.C.
    Builder: Newman & Smith, 367 Pleasant Avenue, N.Y.C.
    Estimated cost: $300,000.

No. 1531, April 9, 1902
Permit to build two-story private brick stable
    Owner: Thomas F. Walsh
    Architect: L. Morris
    Builder: Charles A. Langley
    Location: Lot 41, Square 67 (rear 2118 Mass. Ave.)
    Estimated cost: $15,000.

No. 962, November 18, 1902
Permit for Repairs, Alterations, etc.
    Owner: Thomas F. Walsh
    Mechanic: Otis Elevator Co.
    Estimated cost: $5705.
    "To install an electric dumbwaiter...and an electric elevator"

No. 131, July 20, 1903
Permit to erect a pergola with brick wall
    Owner: Thomas F. Walsh
    Architect: F. W. Carlyle
    Mechanic: George Hughes
    Estimated cost: $1500.
    "The above application is for a Pergola for the ornamental treatment of running vines and flowers. The brick wall in rear to be 9'-0" high and the front of large columns. The roof will be of wooden strips...on rear of lot on private property."

No. 262006, July 6, 1943
Permit to repair carriage house at rear of 2118 Mass. Ave.
    Owner: Mrs. Edward B. McLean

2020 Massachusetts Avenue, N.W.

        Occupant: War Workers Club
        Location: Lot 41, Square 67
        Value of improvement: $8550.
        "Renovate, remodel and install additional facilities - namely plumbing, electrical and construction of two sets of exit stairs."

Source: D.C. Government: Department of Economic Development, Bureau of Licenses and Permits, Central Files.

E. Alterations and Additions:

The Indonesian government has constructed an addition on the south side at basement level and partitioned the fourth floor ballroom into offices. A 1911 photograph (listed under "Important Old Views") shows that the carriage porch was once glazed.

F. Architect: Henry Andersen, New York City

Henry Andersen was born in Flensborg, Denmark June 20, 1852. At the age of 16 he was graduated from a private college in Copenhagen. After serving a few years with a mason contractor, he attended the Technical and Polytechnical Institute in Copenhagen. Andersen completed his studies in architecture at the Royal Academy of Art in Copenhagen and then emigrated to the United States where he was engaged in the offices of several architects before starting his own practice in New York in 1892.

Andersen designed several churches and many residences, apartment houses, stores and warehouses. Among his works were the Don Carlos Apartments, 76th Street and Madison Avenue; Acadia Apartments, 115th Street at 7th and St. Nicholas; Sans Souci Apartments, 30-32 West 124th Street; and the Lutheran Church of the Covenant - all in New York City. (Leslie's History of Greater New York)

It is fairly certain that the same Henry Andersen designed Thomas F. Walsh's residence in Washington, D.C.. Walsh's daughter, Evalyn Walsh McLean, wrote that "The architect was Henry Anderson, well known in 1902, and he was told by Father just what was wanted..." (Father Struck It Rich, p. 91) Anderson was spelled with an "o" instead of an "e" in this passage. However, a rendering of the mansion illustrated in the same book was signed "Henry Andersen, Architect, 1183 Broadway, N.Y." The Trow Business Directory of the Boroughs of Manhattan and Bronx, City of New York listed "Henry Andersen, architect, 1183 Broadway" in 1902. From 1898 through 1904 only one Henry Andersen was listed in the New York City directories under architects; and his address was indicated as 1180, 1181 or 1183 Broadway.

Sources: Evalyn Walsh McLean, with Boyden Sparkes, Father Struck It Rich, Boston: Little, Brown, and Company, 1936.

Leslie's History of Greater New York, Vol. III, of the
Encyclopedia of New York Biography and Geneology, New
York: Arkell Publishing Co., 1898.

G. Known Plans, Drawings, Elevations, etc.:

Plan of excavation. Ink on linen.
Filed with Permit No. 690, October 16, 1901

Rendering of 2020 Massachusetts Avenue, N.W.
"Henry Andersen, Architect, 1183 Broadway, N.Y."
Father Struck It Rich, by Evalyn Walsh McLean, p. 98.

H. Important Old Views:

Photograph of exterior showing glazed carriage porch.
Massachusetts Avenue Heights, Washington, D.C., Its Whereabouts, Its Purpose, Its Plan, and Its Attractiveness to Investor and Homeseeker, New York: Ballard and Alvord, 1911. (Washingtoniana Room, Martin Luther King Library, Washington, D.C.)

I. Residents:

1. City and telephone directories list the following tenants:

1902-1910	Thomas F. Walsh
1911	Mrs. Carrie B. Walsh
1912-1916	Edward Beale McLean
1917	Mrs. Carrie B. Walsh
1918	Vacant
1919	Charles P. Stone
1920-1930	Mrs. Carrie B. Walsh
1931-1935	Vacant
1936	U.S. Suburban Resettlement Administration
1937	U.S. Rural Electrification Commission
1938-1941	Vacant
1942-1951	American Red Cross, D.C. Chapter
1952-1972	Indonesian Embassy, Chancery

2. The following residents were included in volumes of *The Elite List: A Compilation of Selected Names of Residents of Washington City, D.C. and Ladies Shopping Guide*:

   1905   Mr. and Mrs. Thomas F. Walsh
               Mr. Vinson F. Walsh, Jr.

   1906-1908   Mr. and Mrs. Thomas F. Walsh
               Miss Evalyn L. Walsh

2020 Massachusetts Avenue, N.W.'

    1909-1911 Mr. and Mrs. Thomas F. Walsh
                   Mr. and Mrs. Edward Beale McLean

3. Biographies of the residents:

Thomas F. Walsh (1851-1910) was born in County Tipperary, Ireland. At the age of 19, he emigrated to the United States and two years later moved from Massachusetts to Colorado where he worked for a mining concern. As he saved money he would "grubstake" prospectors, and then become part owner of their mines when they struck gold. His own discovery and development of the Camp Bird Mine at Ouray, Colorado established him as the sole owner of one of the richest gold mines in the world. Mr. Walsh met and married the former Miss Carrie Bell Reed when he was a prospector.

In 1899 Thomas Walsh was appointed by President McKinley as one of the Commissioners from the United States to the Paris Exposition. While there, the Walshes entertained and traveled in lavish style. A Seine River steamer was converted into a "floating palace" on which a $40,000 dinner party was given for a group of "distinguished" men. Then Mr. Walsh "chartered a train of five palace cars, fitted it with silk and decorations which he had used upon his steamer and commenced a tour of France and Belgium. The late King Leopold of Belgium met Mr. Walsh at Ostend." (The New York Times, 4-9-10) King Leopold was interested in having Mr. Walsh invest in mining ventures in the Congo.

The Walshes moved from Leadville, Colorado to Washington near the turn of the century. In 1897-1898 they lived in a suite of rooms at the Cochran Hotel on 14th Street near K Street, N.W.. They purchased a furnished home from Conrad and Anna Jenness Miller at 1825 Phelps Place, N.W., in December 1898.

On April 30, 1901 land was purchased for their new home on Massachusetts Avenue, N.W. The Evening Star, May 16, 1901 reported that grading of the ground at the southeast corner of Massachusetts Avenue had begun:

> At present the lot is at a considerable height above the grade of the street...Owing to the extent of the space, which is about 150 feet square, this is an undertaking of some magnitude...It is probable...that the house, which will be of a size to correspond with the ample building space, will be constructed of stone, and will represent a high type of domestic architecture.

The Walsh residence is as large as the Star predicted it would be. It contains more than 50 rooms and includes a three story central stairhall with galleries.

> One grand dame recalls that at the time the mansion was built she thought it 'very good, very rich, and very ugly.' She continued: 'The story was that Mr. Walsh admired the architect of a German steamer, so he had that stairway built like those on an ocean liner.' (The New York Times, 1-28-68)

According to Mrs. Evalyn Walsh McLean, daughter of Thomas F. Walsh, the house cost $835,000 to build - exclusive of furnishings. Mrs. McLean wrote of the interior decorations:

> My father had hired Mrs. Anna Jenness Miller to scout around and help my mother buy just what was needed for that house; it was a job that lasted several years...She even went abroad to get some choicer paintings and the bric-a-brac we needed. Rugs from Persia, and aquarelles from dealers in the Boulevard Poissonniere in Paris, and from the Avenue Louise in Brussels; sometimes her shipments came from Montreux, Switzerland. How the money went! (Father Struck It Rich, page 92)

On May 1, 1902 Thomas Walsh sold the Camp Bird mine for $3,100,000 plus one fourth of the proceeds from the ore for $2,000,000 more, as well as $100,000 in stock.

On August 19, 1905 the Walsh's daughter Evalyn was injured and their son Vinson killed in an automobile accident at Newport, Rhode Island. Mr. Walsh died in April 1910.

Sources: American Biographical Directories, District of Columbia, 1908-1909, Washington, D.C.: The Potomac Press, 1908.

Evalyn Walsh McLean, with Boyden Sparkes, Father Struck It Rich, Boston: Little, Brown, and Company, 1936.

The Evening Star, 5-16-01, 16:5.
The Evening Star, 11-12-51, B3:1.
The New York Times, 4-09-10, 11:1 (obituary).
The New York Times, 1-28-68, 68:1.
The Sunday Star, 1-16-55, D4.
Times-Herald, 1-7-40, D8:1.

Edward Beale McLean, the son of John Roll and Emily Beale McLean, was born in Washington, D.C. in 1883. His father owned The Washington Post, The Cincinnati Enquirer, and for a while, the New York Morning Journal.

McLean eloped with Evalyn Walsh in 1908. Their first child,

2020 Massachusetts Avenue, N.W.

Vinson Walsh McLean was born at 2020 Massachusetts Avenue in 1909 and was soon known as the million dollar baby because of the two fortunes to which he was heir. The McLeans received so many kidnapping threats that Vinson was never left alone. In 1919, while staying at "Friendship", the McLean family estate on Wisconsin Avenue, N.W., Vinson ran away from the servants and was killed by a car. The McLeans eventually had three other children - John R., Edward B., Jr., and Emily Beale McLean.

Edward McLean's father died in 1916 leaving his fortune of $25,000,000 in trust until twenty years after the death of his son's children. Edward was barred from administering his father's estate until he brought suit and won editorial control of the two papers and management of the estate, though he was restricted to its income. (The New York Times, 7-28-41)

Through his newspapers, Mr. McLean became an influential man in the Republican party. He and his wife were often hosts to Senator and Mrs. Harding before the Presidential election; and when Harding was inaugurated in 1921, McLean served as head of the inaugural committee. While President, Harding was a guest of the McLeans at Palm Beach.

In 1924 McLean became involved in the Teapot Dome scandal concerning the leasing of naval oil reserves by the Department of Interior. As a favor for his friend, Albert B. Fall, Secretary of the Interior, McLean claimed that he had lent Fall $100,000. Actually, Fall had received the money from Edward L. Doheny, an oil magnate. After an investigation, McLean admitted to a Senate committee that he had not made the loan, but he denied knowing anything about the scandal in which Fall and Doheny were involved. (The New York Times, 3-13-24)

In 1930 Edward McLean's wife sued him for separate maintenance - charging desertion and non-support. She was awarded 40 percent of his monthly income so long as her share did not exceed $7,500. On October 4, 1933 she petitioned that a committee be appointed to manage her husband's finances. October 30, 1933 Edward McLean was declared insane and incapable of managing his affairs. He was confined to Shepard and Enoch Pratt Hospital at Towson, Maryland until his death in July 1941. (The New York Times, 7-28-41)

Sources: The Evening Star, 4-27-47, 1:2.
        The New York Times, 3-13-24, pp. 1-2 (Teapot Dome Scandal).
        The New York Times, 7-28-41, 13:1 (obituary).

Evalyn Walsh McLean (1887-1947), the daughter of Thomas F. Walsh and the wife of Edward B. McLean, was a well-known society figure in Washington, D.C.. She was also noted as the last private owner of the 44 1/2 carat Hope Diamond.

The New York Times, January 29, 1911, reported the purchase of the diamond:

> The sale was negotiated at Mr. McLean's residence 2020 Massachusetts Avenue by Pierre Cartier, of 712 Fifth Avenue, New York, the American representative of the jewelry firm of Cartier Frères, Paris...
>
> The diamond will...be worn by Mrs. McLean as a head ornament arranged in a bandeau, the large stone being placed immediately in front with other diamonds of lesser size studding the setting bands...
>
> The stone will be kept at the McLean mansion during the day and each night will be deposited in a safe deposit vault. When Mrs. McLean wears the gem at balls and receptions arrangements have been made to keep the safe deposit building open until after the function so that the stone may be safely stored away. A special automobile has been purchased to convey the guards to and from the trust company's building...

The Hope Diamond, now in the Smithsonian's Museum of Natural History, has a long history - from the Far East, to the courts of 17th century France, to England and the United States. Of its owners, some were either murdered, drowned, assassinated by revolutionaries or deserted by their wife - all of which led to the supersition that the diamond brought bad luck. Mrs. McLean never believed in this and wrote, "As a matter of fact, the luckiest thing about it is that, if I ever had to, I could hock it," which she did several times. (Father Struck It Rich, p. 179)

In 1932, Mrs. McLean was defrauded of $104,000 by Gaston B. Means, once termed by J. Edgar Hoover as the "worst crook" he had ever known. (The Evening Star, 5-3-72) Means had convinced Mrs. McLean that he would be able to use the money to achieve the release of the kidnapped son of Charles A. Lindbergh. He was convicted of the swindle in 1932 and sentenced to 15 years in prison, but the money was never recovered.

Sources: Evalyn Walsh McLean, with Boyden Sparkes, Father Struck It Rich, Boston: Little, Brown, and Company, 1936.

> The Evening Star, 4-27-47, 1:2 (obituary).
> The Evening Star, 4-28-47, 1:5 (obituary).
> The Evening Star, 5-03-72, 7:1.
> The Sunday Star, Magazine, 5-17-59, p.2.
> The Washington Daily News, 4-28-47, 3:5 (obituary).
> The Washington Post, 4-30-47, 6:6 (obituary).
> The Washington Post, Parade, 11-12-50, "Curse of the 'Hope'" by Frank DeBlois, p. 21.

J. Historical Events Connected with the Structure:

During the Theodore Roosevelt administration, the Walsh residence was the scene of some of the most lavish entertainment in Washington. The Evening Star, December 8, 1903 described one party.

> Mr. and Mrs. Thomas F. Walsh entertained at a dinner last night in their new home on Massachusetts Avenue which in every detail was one of the most sumptuous affairs ever given in the Capital...The dinner table was adorned with yellow orchids of a very beautiful variety, their coloring being the keynote to the superb decoration of the board, where a service of gold made from glittering nuggets taken fron the Camp Bird Mine, was used for the first time. A recital on the organ in the music room was an accompaniment to dinner.

The guest list included Admiral Dewey; Senator and Mrs. Wetmore; Senator and Mrs. Hanna; Senator and Mrs. Depew, the Belgian Minister and Baroness Moncheur; Mr. and Mrs. Wayne MacVeagh; Mr. and Mrs. John B. Henderson (of Boundary Castle); Mr. and Mrs. C. C. Glover; Mr. and Mrs. W. J. Boardman; Mr. and Mrs. Thomas Nelson Page; and others.

On December 29, 1903 a small ball and cotillion was given in honor of Miss Alice Roosevelt, the daughter of the President. Evalyn Walsh, who was too young to attend, wrote about the affair:

> The dancing began at eleven in the top floor ballroom, with its walls all yellow with brocade, with yellow hangings and yellow fabrics covering all the benches and chairs around the room. (Father Struck It Rich, p. 99)

Thomas Walsh often entertained on a grand scale. "At one New Year's Eve party 325 guests consumed 480 quarts of champagne, 288 fifths of Scotch, 48 quarts of cocktails, 40 gallons of beer and 35 bottles of miscellaneous liquors." (The New York Times, 1-28-68)

It was rumored that the Belgian King Leopold had accepted the Walshes' invitation to visit when he came to the United States in 1903 for the St. Louis Exposition. Mr. Walsh, in anticipation of the visit, supposedly rushed to complete the house. King Leopold never came to the United States, but his nephew, King Albert, and Queen Elizabeth came October 28, 1919 for three days. President Wilson was ill, so Vice President and Mrs. Marshall gave a state dinner at the Walsh mansion. Other guests at the dinner were the Duke of Brabant, later King Leopold III of the Belgians; the French Ambassador Jusserand and his wife; Chief Justice Edward Douglas White; Cabinet members, Senators and Representatives. After dinner, Queen Elizabeth presented Mrs. Walsh the "Order of Elizabeth, Queen of the Belgians" for her Belgian relief work during World War I. The Walsh house had been used by Washington volunteers to make garments for refugees. (The Evening Star, 10-29-19, 8:3)

Mrs. Walsh lived in the house until her death in 1932. Although her daughter Evalyn Walsh McLean inherited the house, she left it vacant since she was living at "Friendship". In August 1935 "2020" was rented to the Resettlement Administration. The newspapers reported that the government's New Deal agency paid $1600 per month rent. (The Evening Star, 7-19-35)

When the government moved out in 1937, the house remained vacant until 1941 when Mrs. McLean gave it rent free to the Washington Chapter of the American Red Cross. Red Cross women manufactured over 100,000 surgical dressings per month there. Other Red Cross activities located in the house included classes for nurses aides, the War Fund drive, and the headquarters for emergency first aid and the mobile canteen. (The Evening Star, 1-17-42)

In 1942 Mrs. McLean, at her own expense, renovated and furnished her carriage house at the rear of 2118 Massachusetts Avenue, N.W. so that it could be used as a club for women government workers.

On December 19, 1951 the Indonesian government purchased 2020 Massachusetts Avenue for $335,000. Although the building was to be used as a chancery, the Indonesians spent $75,000 for renovations and tried to preserve the character of the interior decoration. (The Sunday Star, 1-16-55)

Sources: The Evening Star, 12-08-03, 5:6.
          The Evening Star, 12-30-03, 5:5.
          The Evening Star, 10-29-19, 8:3.
          The Evening Star, 7-19-35, 2:5.
          The Evening Star, 7-30-35, B1:5.
          The Evening Star, 1-17-42, 16:2.
          The Evening Star, 12-31-42, 2:2.
          The Evening Star, 11-10-51, 3:2.
          The Evening Star, 11-12-51, B3:1.
          The Sunday Star, 1-16-55, D4:5.

2020 Massachusetts Avenue, N.W.

The New York Times, 1-28-68, 68:1.
The Washington Daily News, 6-28-37, 9:2.
The Washington Herald, 8-8-35, 29:3.
The Washington Post, 10-28-19, pp. 1-2.
The Washington Post, 10-29-19, 1:1, p. 3.
Times-Herald, 1-7-40, D8:1.
Times-Herald, 6-12-40, 1:2.
Times-Herald, 7-17-45, 9:5.

Opposite
CFA photo
Commercial Photo Co.
ca. 1945

CFA photo
Boucher 1970

MASSACHUSETTS AVENUE

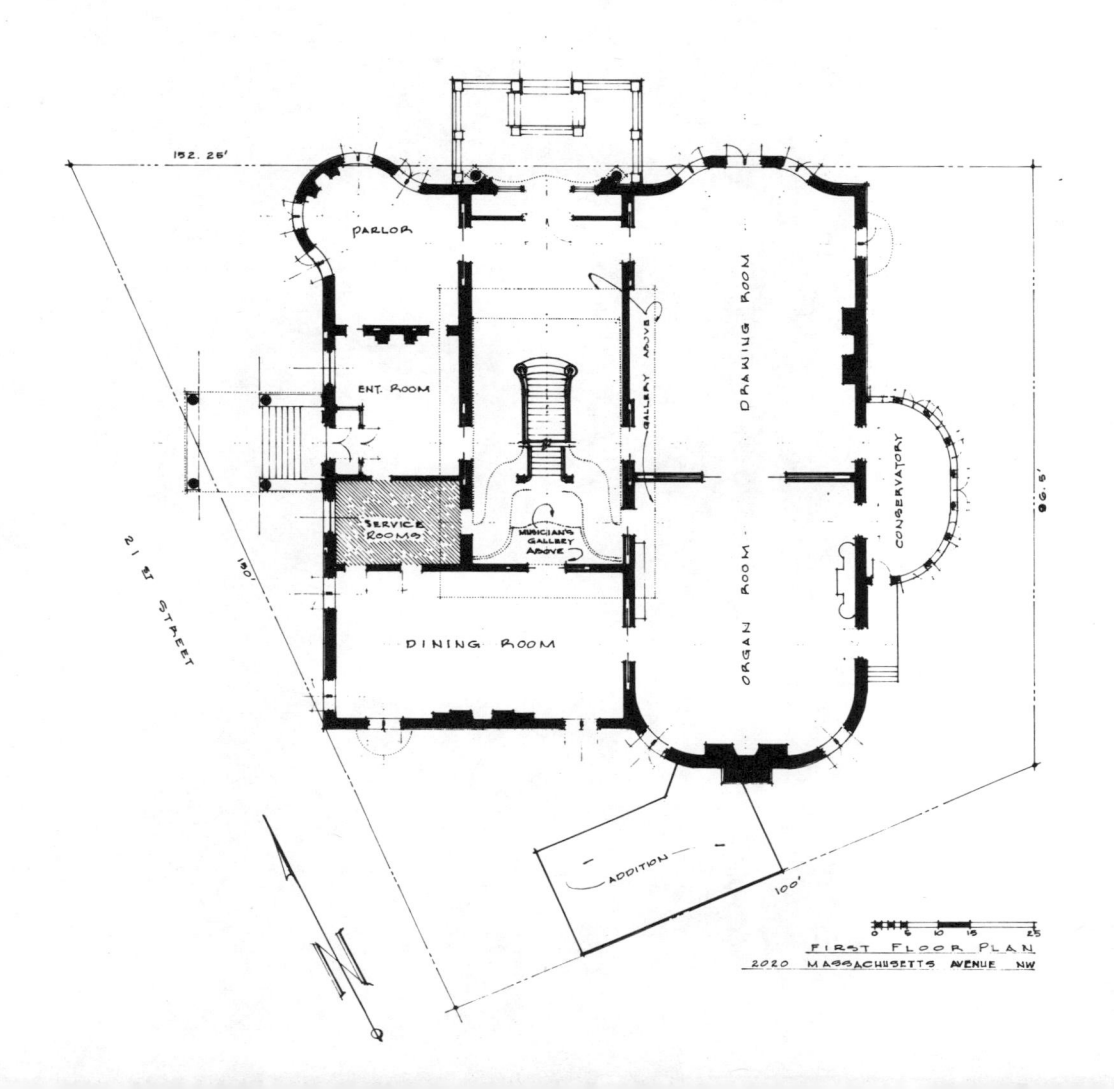

FIRST FLOOR PLAN
2020 MASSACHUSETTS AVENUE NW

Light Fixture
Entrance Vestibule
CFA photo
Boucher 1970

Central Hall
CFA photo
Boucher 1970

Skylight
Central Hall
CFA photo
Boucher 1970

Entrance Room Mantle
CFA photo
Boucher 1970

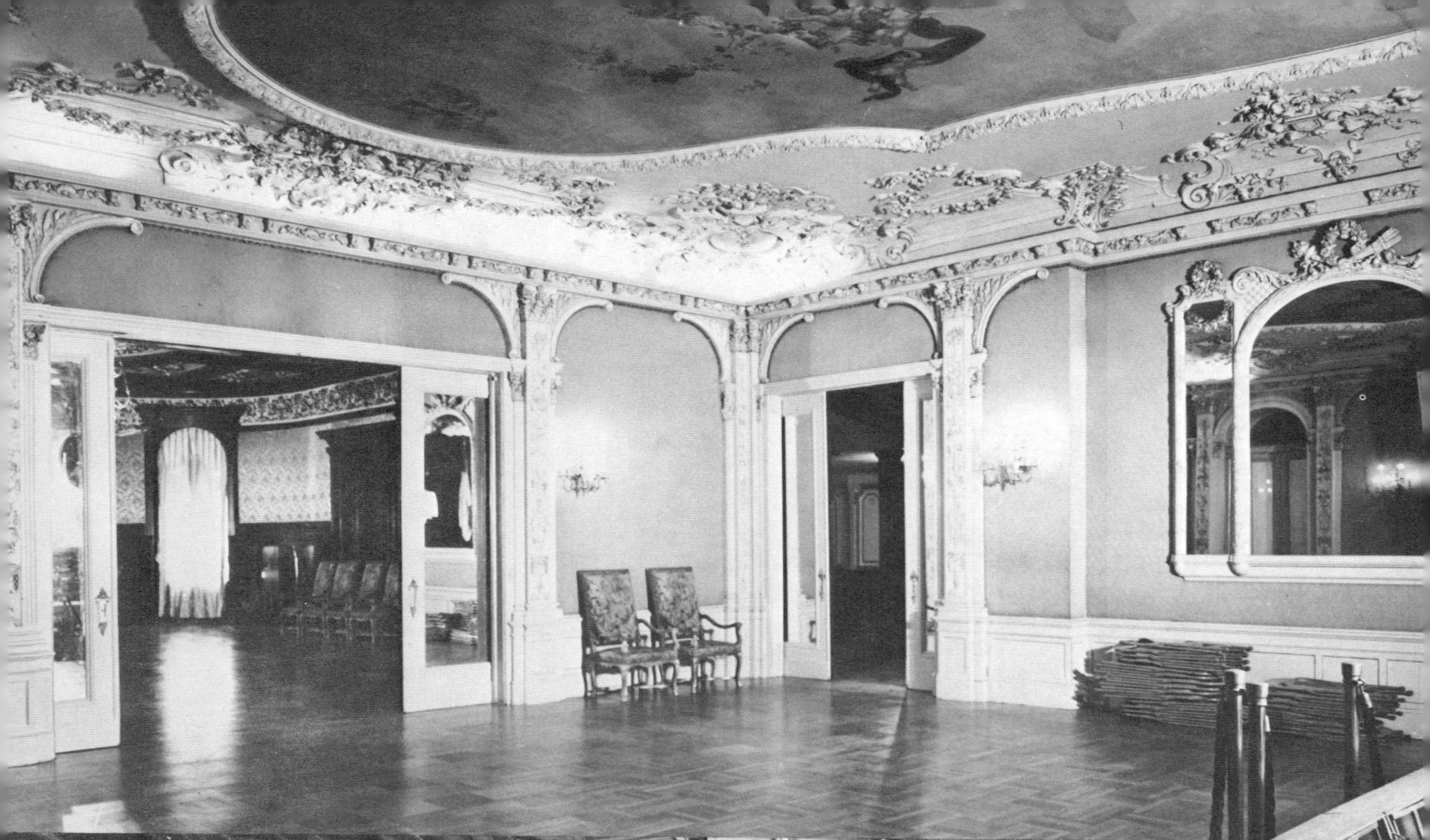

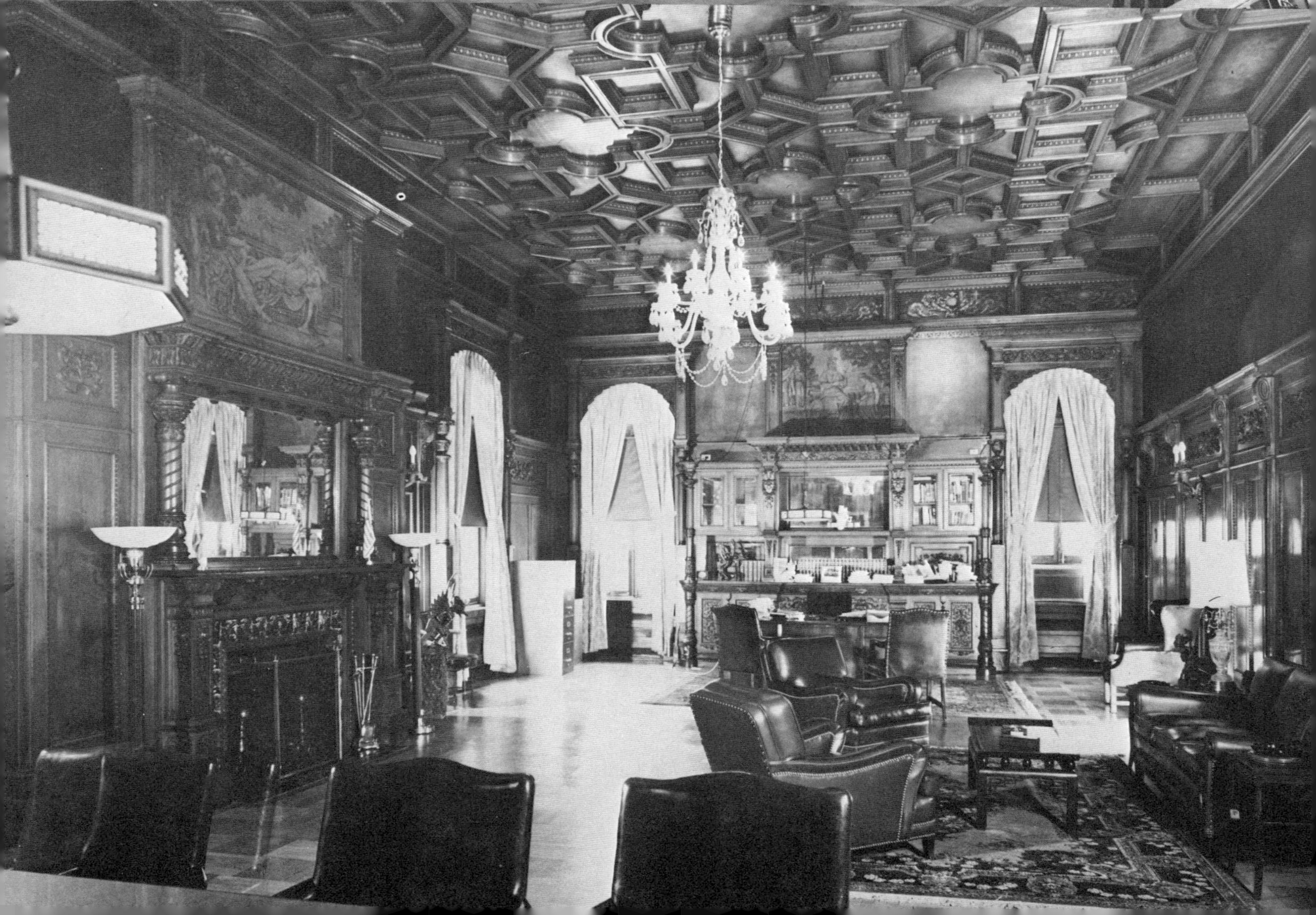

Detail Organ
CFA photo
Boucher 1970

Opposite Top
Drawing Room
CFA photo
Boucher 1970

Opposite Bottom
Dining Room
CFA photo
Boucher 1970

Organ Room
CFA photo
Boucher 1970

2020 Massachusetts Avenue, N.W.

PART II. ARCHITECTURAL INFORMATION

    A. General Statement:

        1. Architectural character: This detached structure combines renaissance, baroque and rococo details within an art-nouveau parti.

        2. Condition: well maintained, minor alterations not having effected the general scheme.

    B. Exterior Description:

        1. Overall dimensions: The three and one half story plus basement structure measures 64'-6" at its highest point. The 75'-0" north elevation (Massachusetts Avenue) begins at the east end with a three bay swell, followed by a composite entrance bay and a four bay bow rounding the northwest corner onto 21st Street. The 90'-0" west facade contains five additional bays, a carriage porch second from the north. At the western end of the south elevation are two bays with a second floor oriole, and at the eastern end a two bay swell. The east elevation has a projecting, single story, metal and glass conservatory below five upper bays, to the north of which is a second floor oriole.

        2. Foundation: concrete footings and slab.

        3. Wall construction: The building has a rock-faced granite base capped by a blind limestone balustrade which serves as first floor window sill. The upper walls are tan Roman brick divided by two limestone string courses: one at the impost of the first floor windows; the second, of cyma and corona, serving as second floor sill.

        4. Structure: brick bearing walls.

        5. Mechanical: The building is heated by a gravity rise hot air system. The lighting is electric. The dumbwaiter and passenger elevator are by Otis. The bank of kitchen ice boxes are by the Fritts Refrigeration Construction Company.

        6. Porches, stoops, bulkheads, etc.: A rock-faced limestone base supports the marble columns for the 21st Street metal carriage porch which has a rosette frieze, ogee pediments and glazed vault. (The glazed panels between the columns have been removed.)

        The rectangular terrace of the pedestrian entrance on Massachusetts Avenue is approached by two flights of stone risers. The terrace balustrade of urn balusters breaks out from the blind balustrade of the building wall. A second story loggia, centered over the pedestrian entrance, has an urn-balustered balcony, marble Ionic columns which support semicircular arches with cartouche keystones, and a bracketed cornice.

The north and west first floor windows rest on shallow, bracketed and urn-balustered, limestone balconies. The north, south and east second floor windows have decorative cast iron balcony panels.

7. Chimney: Visible from the ground are eight, Roman brick chimneys (two on the east, two on the west, one each above the bow and both swells, and one above the two flush bays on the south) each with limestone quoines, a plain entablature frieze, a segmental pediment centered by an escutcheon, and a block cap.

8. Openings:

   a. Doorways and doors: The Massachusetts Avenue, Louis XVI, double door entrance, with a semicircular headed fan and side lights, has decorative rinceau cast iron grilles over plate glass. The limestone architrave is moulded, recessed and interrupted by a scrolled escutcheon keystone. The architrave sits in a limestone frame which swells at the center and flairs outward at the ends. Both ends are terminated by volute and swag columns. The full entablature architrave and frieze are interrupted by the semicircular-arched doorway architrave. The cornice breaks forward from the second story string course and acts as the loggia balcony.

   From underneath the carriage porch nine stone risers ascend to the glazed double door with semicircular fan. The door is flanked by paired pilasters which share the first floor string course as capital.

   b. Windows: Both the first and second floor casements have Louis XVI, ogee and shell sashes. The first floor windows have engaged Ionic columnettes which support semicircular arches with beaded jambs and decorative escutcheon keystones. The second story windows have beaded, limestone architraves each with a console-supported corona cornice. The double-hung, segmentally-arched, third story windows have crossette architraves and scroll keystones. The arches interrupt the architrave and frieze of the building entablature.

   Exceptions to the above include:

   (1.) over the north entrance: the semicircular arches of the loggia.

   (2.) flanking the west entrance: single double-hung windows capped by blind panels, flanked by engaged columnettes and divided by the first floor string course from elliptical lunettes over swags.

(3.) above the west entrance: single broken scroll and urn pedimented bay flanked by limestone scrolls with obelisk terminals.

(4.) on the south elevation over the west bay: single second floor oriole with a limestone base and metal, segmental dome.

(5.) on the east elevation: the elliptical conservatory with a granite base and blind, limestone balustrade, capped by a row of paired windows which share stained-glass transoms. The paired windows are separated by cast iron, Corinthian columnettes which support an iron cornice capped by anthemion filigree and a segmental, copper dome.

(6.) on the east elevation over the north bay: single, second floor, five bay oriole, treated as the conservatory though having an ogee roof and lacking cornice filigree. The base is formed by the second story string course.

9. Roof:

   a. Shape, covering: The red tile mansard roof, consistent with the wall curvature, is capped by copper flashing with an embossed circle motif, behind which the roofing is built-up.

   b. Cornice, eaves: The entablature has an architrave, a striated frieze, and a dentil and bracket cornice capped by a continuous limestone balcony of urn balusters with swag panels at the chimneys and corners.

   c. Dormers, cupolas, towers: The built-up roof is pierced by a skylight, approximately 20'-0" wide by 40'-0" long, and carries the former roof garden. The fourth floor dormers are double-hung and fanlighted. Between each dormer is an oculus. The dormers and oculi are capped by limestone hoods with scroll and shell keystones and volute label stops.

C. Interior Description:

1. Floor plans: All first, second and third floor rooms radiate from the three story, galleried and skylit central hall. On axis with the first floor north entrance is the central hall and stair, and the south dining room. On the northeast is the drawing room, connected to the southeast organ room, both with access to the east conservatory. On the northwest is the parlor, connected to the carriage porch entrance room (a service area and central hall elevator between the west entrance and dining room). (See plan.)

Screened by the south walls of the second and third floors in the central hall are straight-run stairs. The bedrooms are connected by baths and family rooms. The northeast and northwest second floor bedrooms and connecting baths share a gallery giving access to the loggia over the north entrance.

The fourth floor has servants' quarters, a billiard room and a ballroom, one wall of which looks over the top of the Tiffany-style skylight illuminating the central hall. Over the first is a second skylight in the fourth floor roof.

2. Spaces:

North entrance:

a. Walls: pink marble with marble settees in east and west walls.

b. Ceiling: 15'-0" high, gilded plaster, rosettes within squares within octagonal coffers.

c. Doorways and doors: The oak, double door to the hall has a fanlight and flanking, fluted Ionic pilasters.

d. Lighting: Over either settee is a convex, fish scale, art-nouveau sconce of milk glass within a bronze, fruit swag, dolphin and flambeau surround. (See detail photograph.)

Central hall: (described in four sections: stair, first floor, first gallery and second gallery. See photographs.)

Stair:

The freestanding, "Y" shaped, art-nouveau central stair ascends south 17 risers from a flaired base to an orchestra landing where a canvas sounding screen allows music to be heard in the dining room to the south. The screen forms the wall between the stair and dining room. From the landing the stair divides and ascends east and west 15 risers to the south bays of the second floor gallery. Mahogany, escutcheon and spray balustrade panels are separated by panelled pilasters. The handrails terminate in low acanthus leaf statuary bases.

Ground floor:

a. Flooring: basket weave with triangular parquetry border.

b. Baseboard: 6", with cyma cap.

c. Dado: wood with flat panels in bolection moulding.

d. Chairrail: 2'-6" high, wood, beaded fascia.

e. Walls: Plaster panels are set within (gilded) egg and dart, fascia, and (gilded) anthemion applied mouldings with decorative corner treatments. The doorways are flanked by wood, fluted composite pilasters on pedestals.

f. Cornice: The 15'-0" high, plaster ceiling, formed by the second floor gallery at the north, has gilded floral pattern in octagonal coffers within guilloche bands.

g. Doorways and doors: The east and west walls have two sets of opposed double doors (two with access to the drawing room, one to the parlor and one to the west entrance room). The south wall has a double door to the dining room. Each has a panel over the door with a fleur-de-lis arabesque cap. There is a single door to the organ room and one to the elevator.

h. Hardware: gold-plated, inset door pulls.

i. Lighting: There are six, 2'-0" high, five-branched, gilded-bronze, flambeau sconces, each branch holding a pair of lights in glass rose petals. The light switches are concealed in the millwork.

First gallery:

a. Baseboard: 6", wood with cyma cap.

b. Dado: wood with flat panels in bead moulding.

c. Chairrail: wood, double fascia.

d. Walls: Plaster panels are set within (gilded) egg and dart, fascia and (gilded) anthemion applied mouldings with decorative corner treatments.

e. Wall cornice: plaster; gilded, fruit and winged figure frieze, and fascia.

f. Gallery: supported by the ground floor cornice is an escutcheon and spray panel balustrade interrupted by wood pedestals and fluted composite columns.

g. Gallery ceiling: plaster, geometric coffers in gilded and applied, bead and bay leaf, pulvinated mouldings.

h. Gallery cornice: The full entablature of wood has a fascia architrave, panel frieze and modillion cornice.

i. Doorways and doors: The wood doors each have corner rosette panels, a fascia architrave, a wreath and spray panel over the door, and an egg and dart cornice.

j. Hardware: gold-plated oval door knobs.

k. Lighting: five-light brass sconces.

Second gallery:

a. Baseboard: 6", wood with cyma cap.

b. Dado: wood with flat panels in bead moulding.

c. Walls: Plaster panels are set within (gilded) egg and dart, fascia and (gilded) anthemion applied mouldings with decorative corner treatments.

d. Ceiling cornice: plaster; gilded, fruit and winged figure frieze, fascia.

e. Gallery: Supported by the first gallery cornice is an escutcheon and spray panel balustrade interrupted by panelled stops.

f. Ceiling: plaster, geometric coffers in gilded and applied, bead and bay leaf, pulvinated mouldings. The hall is covered by a coved, stained-glass, three-panelled skylight having an oval, floral centerpiece on an ochre field.

g. Doorways and doors: The single panel doors have crossette architraves, wreath and spray panels over the doors and cyma cornices.

h. Lighting: incandescent fixtures above the skylight.

Dining room: (see photograph)

a. Flooring: basket weave parquetry.

b. Baseboard: 8", wood with cyma cap.

c. Wainscot: The 9'-0" high wainscot has flat panels in egg and dart mouldings, topped by a row of applied rinceau panels separated by scroll consoles, and capped by a bead, corona and cyma cornice.

d. Buffet: The west wall 9'-0" high, wood buffet, has a beaded baseboard, candelabra dado panels, separated by columnettes and terminated at the ends by spiral Ionic columns on bulbous bases, and a decorative ovolo counter. The counter back wall is divided into three sections: the center a mirror flanked by terms; the ends panels terminated by decorative columnettes supporting a gouge frieze. Over the frieze is a central mirror flanked by glazed cabinets. The three sections are separated by volute and swag terms. The cabinets are terminated by decorative, Ionic columnettes which support an egg and dart architrave and a central frieze capped by a modillion, corona, and egg and dart cornice. Over the central cornice is a tapestry flanked by panelled Ionic pilasters which support a corona and cyma cornice.

- e. Walls: plaster painted green, except stair landing screen and tapestries.

- f. Cornice: dentil architrave and painted rinceau, urn and flambeau, panel frieze.

- g. Ceiling: 15'-0" high, wood with quatrefoil, square and diamond coffers in the 17th century English manner.

- h. Doorways and doors: Wood double doors are set in the lower section of the wainscot.

- i. Windows: The windows, with semicircular arches and rinceau spandrels, are flanked by 5'-0" high pedestals with short, urn and volute columns which support plain panels capped by a rinceau frieze, and a corona and cyma cornice.

- j. Lighting: There are four, two-light, bronze escutcheon sconces with reeded cornucopia arms. There is a two-tier, twelve-light crystal arm, pendant and drape chandelier. The light switches are concealed in the millwork.

- k. Heating: The south wall oak chimney mantle has a blue and green floral tile firebox surround with a brass rinceau tile guard. Flanking rinceau pedestals support cartouche-panelled pilasters and acanthus modillions between cavetto and cushion pilasters. The overmantle mirror is flanked by bulbous bases for cushion and volute columns which support a rinceau frieze, a modillion, egg and dart, corona and cyma cornice, and a tapestry flanked by panelled, composite pilasters, capped by an egg and dart, corona and cyma cornice.

Entrance room:

- a. Flooring: basket weave parquetry.

- b. Baseboard: 6", wood with cyma cap.

- c. Dado: wood with flat panels in cyma moulding.

- d. Chairrail: 2'-6" high, wood, fascia and cyma.

- e. Walls: plaster painted white. The doors and windows are flanked by wood, fluted composite pilasters on pedestals. At the west wall is a 12'-0" high, gilded rocaille mirror with a flower basket cap.

- f. Cornice: pulvinated architrave and baroque escutcheon corners.

g. Ceiling: 15'-0" high, plaster painted white.

h. Doorways: Each wood double door has a panelled frieze and fleur-de-lis arabesque cap.

i. Hardware: gold-plated door pulls and handles.

j. Lighting: There are 2'-0" high, five-branched, gilded bronze, flambeau sconces. Each branch holds a pair of lights in glass rose petals. The light switches are concealed in the millwork.

k. Heating: The west wall chimney has a marble hearth with rectangular insets. The green marble mantle has a torus firebox surround of bundled-leaf ormolu framed by a marble bolection in a crossette architrave with floral ormolu pendants at the corners. The architrave is capped by a ribbon and leaf ormolu torus, a shallow marble hood with ormolu acanthus mounts, and an enriched ormolu lip terminated by a marble block cap. (See detail photograph.)

Northwest parlor:

a. Flooring: basket weave parquetry.

b. Baseboard: 6", with cyma cap.

c. Walls: plaster. Mirrors in applied mouldings alternate with tapestries in rocaille panels.

d. Ceiling: plaster, coved, cherub frescos.

e. Windows: The windows have broken-scrolled pediments capped by panels of shepherds and shepherdesses.

f. Hardware: gold-plated door pulls.

g. Lighting: recent crystal chandelier. The light switches are concealed in the millwork.

h. Heating: The northwest corner chimney has a bronze-finished, wood, rocaille mantle.

Drawing room: (see photograph)

a. Flooring: basket weave with diamond parquetry border.

b. Baseboard: 8", with bead cap.

c. Dado: flat panels.

d. Chairrail: 2'-6" high, bead, fascia and cyma.

e. Walls: pink damask. Flanking the openings and at the room corners are Corinthian candelabra pilasters on pedestals which in turn are flanked by secondary pilasters supporting concave, tobacco leaf scrolls. At the west wall is a rocaille triptych mirror with pulvination, and lattice and wreath ornaments.

f. Cornice: alternating flambeau, shell, spray and swag panels interrupted by gilded brackets.

g. Ceiling: 15'-0" high, plaster painted pink, green and gold. The ceiling border has rocaille cartouches, escutcheons, swags, shells and sprays; the center has a curvilinear canvas in the late 18th century manner with a pulvinated leaf surround.

h. Doorways and doors: The sliding double doors are mirror panelled. The glazed conservatory door has a semicircular arch with tobacco leaf spandrels and panelled jamb.

i. Hardware: gold-plated rocaille door pulls.

j. Lighting: five-light brass sconces.

k. Heating: The east wall chimney has a cream onyx mantle in rocaille with flanking consoles and overmantle triptych mirror similar to that on the west wall.

Organ room: (see photographs)

a. Flooring: basket weave parquetry.

b. Baseboard: 8", wood with cyma cap.

c. Display cases: There are 6'-0" high, built in cabinets of wood with glass doors and rinceau splash boards.

d. Walls: green damask.

e. Organ: At the east wall is a 14'-6" high, baroque-style wood organ with flanking rinceau panels, curved at the ends. Over the keyboard and panels, the pipe sections have wreath, musical instrument and floral carvings.

f. Cornice: 2'-6" high, gilded, plaster rinceau frieze.

g. Ceiling: 15'-0" high, plaster painted pink, green and blue. The ceiling border is divided by beams into gilded rocaille cartouche and escutcheon panels. The central quatrefoil of rinceau and rosette bands is outlined in wood and broken by plaster ceiling fixture escutcheons at either end.

h. Doorways and doors: The semicircular-arched windows and conservatory door have floral spandrels. Flanking each arch are panelled composite pilasters which support staggered entablatures that interrupt the room frieze. The remaining doors with flat lintels terminate below the room frieze.

i. Hardware: gold-plated door handles.

j. Lighting: There are two, five-petal, mother-of-pearl chandeliers, with bronze and gilded rocaille filigree and pendant. The lights are hung by five chains with connecting swags. The light switches are concealed in the millwork.

k. Heating: The south wall chimney mantle has a swan and rinceau, copper firebox surround and flanking pairs of composite columns which support a bead architrave, a triglyph and escutcheon metope frieze and a bead shelf. The overmantle has a round panel with rocaille spandrels. The panel is flanked by rocaille mirrors between composite columnettes on pedestals.

D. Site:

1. Setting and orientation: The building faces north on a lot measuring 152'-3" on the north (Massachusetts Avenue); 96'-6" on the east; 100'-0" on the south; and 150'-0" on the west (21st Street).

2. Enclosures: The grounds and sidewalks are separated by a 6" curb.

3. Outbuildings: At the south is a one story, flat-roofed wing at basement level, connected to the main block by a passageway.

4. Walks: A north walk leads from the sidewalk between two stone posts to the entrance steps and terrace. The west drive passes in an arc under the carriage porch. A service drive and entrance are located in the rear, at the kitchen-basement area.

5. Landscaping: Adjacent to the conservatory and exposed to the street is an east garden. The surrounding lawns contain young trees, and shrubs line the north walk and west driveway.

2118 MASSACHUSETTS AVENUE, N.W., WASHINGTON, D.C.

James R. Dunlop, Inc.

Location: 2118 Massachusetts Avenue, N.W., Washington, D.C.; on the south side of Massachusetts Avenue between 21st and 22nd Streets.

Present Owner: The Society of the Cincinnati

Present Occupant: The Society of the Cincinnati

Present Use: National Headquarters and Museum

Statement of Significance: Originally a private residence commissioned for lavish entertaining, this limestone, detached structure is one of the largest and costliest homes in the city. The dissimilar facades of the north entrance with its court and the south garden elevation are attributable to the English manner during the first half of the 18th century. In addition, each major interior space is designed as a stylistic entity.

PART I. HISTORICAL INFORMATION

A. Lot and Square:

The building is located in Square 67, lot 42 (formerly original lots 14 and 15). Other lots included in the property are: lot 43 (formerly part of original lot 4); lot 49 (formerly part of original lot 5 and part of original lot 6); lot 803 (formerly part of original lot 5); and lot 805 (formerly part of original lot 6).

B. Original and Subsequent Owners:

The following chain of title to the property shows the owners of the present structure and of any known preceding structures on the site:

1901 Deed May 23, 1901, recorded May 25, 1901 in Liber 2583 folio 155

Mary E. Patten, et al.
　　To
Isabel Anderson

"...Mary E. Patten, Josephine A. Patten, Edith A. Patten and Helen Patten (all unmarried), of the District of Columbia ...Isabel Anderson of Boston, Massachusetts...Original Lots ...(14) and...(15) in Square...(67)..."

NOTE: Internal Revenue Stamp affixed: $93.00. At this time the tax was imposed at the rate of $.50 per $500. The value of the conveyance was therefore approximately $93,000.

November 26, 1902 lots 14 and 15, Square 67, were combined into lot 42 by Isabel Anderson. Recorded in Subdivisions, Liber 27, folio 135, Office of the Surveyor, District of Columbia.

1901 Deed May 25, 1901, recorded May 28, 1901 in Liber 2578 folio 116

Edward J. Stellwagen, Trustee
    To
Isabel Anderson

"...Edward J. Stellwagen, Trustee under a certain Deed-in-Trust from Francis G. Newlands and others dated January 16, 1901 and duly recorded in Liber 2569 folio 18...All that part of Original Lot...(4) in Square...(67) contained within the following metes and bounds namely: Beginning for the same at the Northeast corner of said lot and running thence West on an alley...30 feet wide; ...62 feet...2 inches to the Northwest corner of said lot; thence South on an alley...15 feet wide...64 feet; thence East...62 feet...2 inches to the East line of said lot; and thence North...64 feet to the place of beginning...in consideration of $4973.33..."

1903 Deed January 6, 1903, recorded January 23, 1903 in Liber 2680 folio 408

Edward J. Stellwagen, Trustee
    To
Isabel Anderson

"...for and in consideration of Seven hundred seventy-seven ...Dollars...All that part of original lot...(4) in Square ...(67) contained within the following metes and bounds, viz:- Beginning for the same on the East line of said lot at a point distant...64 feet South of the Northeast corner of said lot and running thence South on said East line,...10 feet, thence West parallel with the North line of P Street, ...62 feet...2 inches to the West line of said lot, thence North on said West line...10 feet, and thence East...62 feet ...2 inches, to the place of beginning..."

NOTE: April 3, 1903 the North 74 feet by full width of original lot 4, Square 67, was subdivided into lot 43 by Isabel Anderson. Recorded in Subdivisions, Liber 28, folio 25, Office of the Surveyor, District of Columbia.

1907 Deed March 5, 1907, recorded May 15, 1907 in Liber 3073 folio 258

Katherine Medill McCormick
    To
Isabel Anderson

"...Part of Original lot...(5) in Square...(67) contained within the following metes and bounds, viz: - Beginning for the same at the Northeast corner of said lot and running thence West along the South line of a public alley, 30 feet wide, 47.17 feet to the East line of another public alley, 30 feet wide; thence South along the East line of said alley, 74 feet; thence East 47.17 feet to the West line of a public alley 15 feet wide; thence North along the West line of said alley, 74 feet to the place of beginning..."

1912 Deed June 6, 1912, recorded June 7, 1912 in Liber 3519 folio 388

Oscar W. White et ux,
Agnes L.
    To
Larz Anderson

Lot 49 in Oscar W. White's subdivision of lots in Square 67.

NOTE: May 27, 1910 Oscar W. White combined parts of original lots 5 and 6, Square 67, into lot 49. Recorded in Subdivisions, Liber 40, folio 15, Office of the Surveyor, District of Columbia.

1937 Deed July 28, 1937, recorded May 15, 1939 in Liber 7347 folio 73

Isabel Anderson
    To
The Society of the Cincinnati

"This Deed...by and between Isabel Anderson, of the State of New Hampshire, devisee under the Will of Larz Anderson, deceased, party of the first part; and the Society of the Cincinnati...party of the second part..."

2118 Massachusetts Avenue, N.W.

Lots 43, 49, and part of Original lot 5 in Square 67.

1938   Deed May 16, 1938, recorded May 15, 1939 in
Liber 7347 folio 71

Isabel Anderson
    To
The Society of the Cincinnati

"...Lot...(42) in Isabel Anderson's combination of lots in Square...(67)...subject to the restrictions that said property shall not be used for commercial or residential purposes, or for any purpose other than as the National Headquarters of the Society of the Cincinnati, or a public museum, or by corporations or associations organized and operated for educational or charitable purposes of a nonsectarian nature, which restrictions are to be in effect during the life of Isabel Anderson of Webster, New Hampshire..."

1972   Deed February 23, 1972, recorded February 29, 1972 in
Liber 13318 folio 534

Virginia Josie Calvagno
    To
The Society of the Cincinnati

"...Part of Original Lot 6 in Square 67 described as follows: Beginning for the same on the North line of "P" Street, at the Southwest corner of said lot and running thence North 100 feet; thence West 20 feet; and thence South 100 feet to the place of beginning..."

Source: Recorder of Deeds, Washington, D.C.

C. Date of Erection:

The building was begun in 1902 and completed in 1905.

D. Building Permits:

The applications for the following building permits were filed by the architect, contractor or owner's agent and provide significant data:

No. 660, October 9, 1902
Permit to build dwelling
    Owner: Larz Anderson
    Architect: Little & Browne

2118 Massachusetts Avenue, N.W.

    Builder: Connery and Wentworth
    Estimated cost: $200,000.

Filed with No. 660, October 9, 1902
Application for projections beyond building line, No. 40671
    "Four areas on Massachusetts Avenue front to be covered with iron gratings."

Filed with No. 660, October 9, 1902
Application for fence
    "To erect fence more than 10' high on dividing line and the balance of proposed fence will be erected on alleys at least 15' wide...fence...will be 13" thick."

Filed with No. 660, October 9, 1902
Application for permit for repairs, alterations, etc.
    "Four areas...covered with stone capping and iron grating. Also two coal hole chutes with solid cover of iron." All on east side of building.

No. 1699, April 30, 1903
Permit to build stable
    Owner: Capt. Larz Anderson
    Architect: Little & Browne
    Builder: Connery and Wentworth
    Estimated cost: $25,000.
    Location: Lot 43, Square 67
    Completed: 99% complete, April 11, 1904

No. 754, October 23, 1903
Permit to install handpowered carriage elevator in stable
    Owner: Isabel Anderson
    Mechanic: Fauret LeRoy & Co.
    Estimated cost: $340.

No. 660A, February 10, 1904
Permit to install elevator
    Occupant: L. Anderson
    Mechanic: Whittier Machine Co.
    Estimated cost: $3200.

No. 660B, August 5, 1904
Permit to install elevator
    Occupant: L. Anderson
    Mechanic: Whittier Machine Co.
    Estimated cost: $3000.

No. 2776, December 20, 1915
Permit to Repair or Reconstruct Building
    "Fireproof basement story of elevator shaft and stairway. Install fireproof doors on dumbwaiter openings in basement and first floor."

No. 229319, January 7, 1940
Permit to repair Rear 2118 Massachusetts Ave., N.W. (stable)
    Owner: Society of the Cincinnati
    Cost of improvements: $1000.
    Location: Lot 43, Square 67
    "Remove portion of second floor construction to provide additional headroom for badminton court. Install new steel."

No. 291304, December 24, 1946
Permit to repair Rear 2118 Massachusetts Avenue, N.W. (stable)
    Owner: Society of the Cincinnati
    Lessee: August King-Smith
    "Make such exits and entrances to first floor of building in order to satisfy code regulations."

Source: D.C. Government: Department of Economic Development, Bureau of Licenses and Permits, Central Files.

E. Alterations and Additions:

There have been no significant changes made to the building. The Society of the Cincinnati has made only minor changes for security purposes.

F. Architects: Little & Browne, Boston, Massachusetts

<u>Arthur Little</u> (1852-1925) was the senior partner in the firm of Little & Browne, Boston, Massachusetts. He was graduated in architecture from the Massachusetts Institute of Technology in 1875 and continued his studies in France. After extensive travelling in Europe, he returned to Boston. In 1877 he started his own practice and in 1889 formed a partnership with Herbert W. C. Browne.

> Mr. Little's best known works were in the field of domestic architecture. He designed urban and country homes as well as large suburban estates ...During the early part of this century his firm designed the residence, stables and gardens at Prides Crossing, Mass., for William S. Spaulding; also at Prides Crossing, estates of Henry Clay Frick, Edwin C. Swift and Robert S. Bradley; and the home of the Hon. George von L. Meyer (former ambassador to Italy) at Hamilton...The firm's outstanding architectural achievement, however, was at 2118 Massachustts Avenue between 1902 and 1905. (<u>Biographical Dictionary of American Architects (Deceased)</u>)

<u>Herbert W. C. Browne</u> (1860-1946) was a partner in the firm of

2118 Massachusetts Avenue, N.W.

Little & Browne for over fifty years. He attended the Boston Museum School of Fine Arts, and then toured Europe and studied architecture in Paris and Florence. Before the partnership was formed, Browne worked in the office of Jacques & Ranteul, Boston.

Source: Henry F. Withey and Elsie R. Withey, Biographical Dictionary of American Architects (Deceased), Los Angeles: New Age Publishing Co., 1956.

G. Known Plans, Drawings, Elevations, etc.:

Plan of projections on Massachusetts Avenue. Ink on linen.
Plan of projections on east side. Ink on linen.
Partial plan for basement, showing east side. Blueprint.
Filed with Permit No. 660, October 9, 1902.

Sectional elevation and floor plan of service elevator. Blueprint.
Filed with Permit No. 660A, February 10, 1904.

Sectional elevation and floor plan of passenger elevator. Blueprint.
Filed with Permit No. 660B, August 5, 1904.

Floor and site plans. Published in The Larz Anderson House in Washington, New York: Society of the Cincinnati, August 15, 1938.
(see reproductions)

H. Important Old Views:

Exterior photograph of carriage house. Dated January 1965.
Photograph by Harry L. Cleveland.
Archives of The Society of the Cincinnati

Photographs: Great Hall and stables, south elevation and north gate.
Photographs by Dunlop and Davis.
Archives of The Society of the Cincinnati
(see reproductions)

Photographs: Great Hall, grand staircase, exterior from Massachusetts Avenue.
The Washington Times, 2-19-38, p. 19.

Photographs: Great Hall, gallery, dining room, first floor library, and French salon (first drawing room).
The Washington Post, "Potomac," 2-18-62, p. 10-12.

Photographs: Great Hall, winter garden (conservatory), entrance courtyard.
The Washington Star, "Sunday Magazine," 7-24-66, p. 10-12.

I. Residents:

1. City and telephone directories list the following tenants:

2118 Massachusetts Avenue, N.W.

    1906-1937   Larz Anderson
    1938   Mrs. Isabel Anderson
    1939-1942   Society of the Cincinnati
    1943   U.S. Joint Radio Board
    1944-1972   Society of the Cincinnati

2. Biographies of the residents:

<u>Larz Anderson</u> (1866-1937) was the son of General Nicholas Longworth Anderson and Elizabeth Coles (Kilgour) Anderson of Cincinnati, Ohio. Larz's great grandfather, Colonel Richard Clough Anderson (1750-1826) was a founder of the Society of the Cincinnati. In 1891, after one year at Harvard Law School, Mr. Anderson was appointed Second Secretary of the U.S. Embassy at London by President Benjamin Harrison. In 1893 President Grover Cleveland appointed him First Secretary of the Embassy at Rome. While in Rome he met Isabel Weld Perkins, whom he married in Boston on June 10th, 1897.

From 1898 to 1899 Mr. and Mrs. Anderson stayed with his parents at 1530 K Street, N.W. General Anderson's home had been designed about 1882 by his college friend, Henry Hobson Richardson. The house was destroyed around 1925, and the Carlton Hotel built in its place.

During the Spanish American War, Larz Anderson served as a Captain and then as Assistant Adjutant General of the Second Army Corps. After the war "until 1911 he devoted himself to outside interests, passing most of the time with his wife in Washington and Boston, where they were prominent in society." (<u>The New York Times</u>, 4-14-37)

They also made at least one trip abroad during this period. While in England, March 1906, Mr. Anderson wrote:

> We have been seeing about the furniture for the English drawing room [in Anderson House] and have been in the hands of Cowtan, who does all Mr. [Pierpont] Morgan's work, and of whom Miss Anne Morgan spoke when she visited our house. (<u>Larz Anderson: Letters and Journals of a Diplomat</u>, p. 189)

In 1911 President Taft appointed Larz Anderson Minister to Belgium. One year later, he was appointed Ambassador to Japan. In addition to their tours with the diplomatic service, the Andersons went on several cruises throughout the world - including: South America (1927); Africa (1928); the Mediterranean (1929); the East, including Indian, British Malaya, the Dutch East Indies, Siam, Indochina, and Borneo (1931); the South Seas (1934); and Central America (1935).

2118 Massachusetts Avenue, N.W.

Also, the Anderson's were "eventually to travel into every state of the Union, as well as into Canada and Mexico." (<u>Larz Anderson: Letters and Journals of a Diplomat</u>, p. 172.)

Sources: Isabel Anderson (ed), <u>Larz Anderson: Letters and Journals of a Diplomat,</u> New York: Fleming H. Revell Co., 1940.

<u>Richard Orr Denby, The Society of Cincinnati and Its Museum</u>, published by The Society of the Cincinnati, 1967.

<u>American Biographical Directories, District of Columbia</u>, 1908-1909, Washington, D.C.: The Potomac Press, 1908.

<u>Who's Who in the Nation's Capital</u>, 1938-1939, Washington, D.C.: Ransdell Inc., 1939.

<u>The New York Times,</u> 4-14-37, 25:1 (obituary).

<u>Isabel Weld Perkins Anderson</u> (1876-1948) was heir to the $17 million fortune accumulated by her grandfather, Stephen Weld, in his East Indian tradings.

> As the wife of a distinguished diplomat, Mrs. Anderson gained wide-spread social success. But she earned for herself even greater fame as an author and philanthropist, and through her First World War service. (<u>The New York Times</u>, 11-4-48)

Mrs. Anderson was the author of plays, poetry, fiction and accounts of her travels. She also edited her husband's journals and the letters and journals of Larz's father, General Nicholas Longworth Anderson. Her poetry included: "The Welds", "William Gordon Weld", and "William Fletcher Weld" ("The Weld Trilogy"); "Angkor Thom"; and "Cambodian Lullaby" - all published in 1937. Two of her plays were: "Freedom", which deals with a few episodes in the life of her father, George Hamilton Perkins; and " A City Built in a Night" - published in 1933 and 1937 respectively.

She was most prolific in writing children's stories and plays. Some of the titles which have been found are:

> Sir Frog Goes a Travelling (play)
> Topsy Turvy and the Gold Star
> Little Madcap's Journey (play)
> The Witch in the Woods (play)
> Justice Whisker's Trial (play)
> Merry Jerry (play)
> Dick Whittington

2118 Massachusetts Avenue, N.W.

>   The Gee Whiz (play)
>   King Foxy of Muir Glacier (play)
>   The Red Flame
>   Captain Ginger Goes Travelling
>   Captain Ginger, Eater of Dreams
>   Captain Ginger's Fairy
>   Captain Ginger's Sunboy
>   Captain Ginger Aboard the Gee Whiz

The travel writings describe most of Isabel and Larz Anderson's diplomatic assignments and around-the-world cruises. Some of these books are:

>   The Spell of Japan (1914)
>   The Spell of Belgium (1915)
>   The Spell of the Hawaiian Islands and the Phillippines (1916)
>   Zigzagging (1918)
>   Circling South America (1927)
>   Circling Africa (1928)
>   A Yacht in the Mediterranean (1929)
>   In Eastern Seas (1931)
>   Zigzagging the South Seas (1934)

During World War I, Isabel participated in Red Cross work in Washington. Then in September 1917, she left for Europe for eight months of service in the Red Cross canteen at Epernay and in hospitals on the Belgium and French fronts. For her service Mrs. Anderson was awarded the French Croix de Guerre, the Royal Belgian Medal of Elizabeth with Red Cross, and the American Red Cross Canteen Medal.

Sources: Isabel Anderson (ed), Larz Anderson: <u>Letters and Journals of a Diplomat</u>, New York: Fleming H. Revell Co., 1940.

<u>Who's Who in the Nation's Capital, 1938-1939</u>, Washington, D.C.: Ransdell Inc., 1939.

<u>The New York Times</u>, 11-4-48, 29:3 (obituary).

<u>The Society of the Cincinnati</u>

After Mr. Anderson's death in 1937, Mrs. Anderson gave the house and its surrounding land to the Society of Cincinnati to be used as a museum and national headquarters. A resolution made at the annual meeting of the Virginia Society of the Cincinnati on October 30, 1937 stated:

> Mrs. Larz Anderson, Litt. D., LL.D. nee
> Isabel Weld Perkins, daughter of gallant
> Commodore George Hamilton Perkins...in
> carrying out the wishes of her late husband, has offered the Society of Cincinnati their beautiful home in Washington
> ...at 2118 Massachusetts Avenue...

An act of Congress passed February 24, 1938 granted the house exemptions from local taxation provided it was maintained as a "national museum for the custody and preservation of documents, relics and archives, especially those pertaining to the American Revolution, accessible to the public...at reasonable hours."

The deed, recorded May 15, 1939 in Liber 7347 folio 71 at the Recorder of Deeds, Washington, D.C., states the conditions under which Isabel Anderson donated the residence. (See chain of title.)

The Society of the Cincinnati is a non-political body organized in 1783 by the officers of the American Army who had served in the Revolutionary War. General Washington was the first President General of the Society. Membership is hereditary. One male descendent of each qualified officer in the Continental Army or Navy is eligible for membership in one of the thirteen state Societies or the French Society.

Sources: Richard Orr Denby, <u>The Society of the Cincinnati and Its Museum</u>, published by the Society of the Cincinnati, 1967.

J. Historical Events Connected with the Structure:

Anderson House was used during World War I for Belgium Relief work, for Red Cross work for the blind, and as housing for French officers. At the time, Larz Anderson was a member of the first Central Belgian Relief Committee, and also a member of the original Red Cross Council of the District of Columbia.

June 18, 1917 the Belgian mission arrived in Washington and stayed in the Anderson's home for three weeks. The Andersons had turned the building over to the mission while they were out of town.

Larz wrote that "Anderson House has had a good deal of experience in entertaining foreign guests, and it has proved a fine setting for the purpose. It was arranged for stately functions of a limited size, and its approaches and successions of rooms make a suitable background." (<u>Larz Anderson: Letters and Journals of a Diplomat</u>, p. 606.) In the spring of 1929, the Andersons gave several dinners before leaving the city for the summer. The French and Japanese Ambassadors were the guests for one and the

2118 Massachusetts Avenue, N.W.

Italian and Belgian Ambassadors for another. Larz wrote:

> Our dinners proved successful. The house was full of flowers, - azaleas, orchids, lillies and tulips. We remained, I believe, the only house in Washington, except the Embassies, which turned out the servants in full-dress livery, shorts and stockings, buckled shoes, and braided coats. These dinners were swan songs to the old order.
> (Larz Anderson: Letters and Journals of a Diplomat, p. 558)

The Andersons again gave up their house for visiting dignitaries. In 1931, while on a cruise through the Far East, they received a telegram from Secretary of State Stimson requesting the use of Anderson House for the King and Queen of Siam during their visit to Washington. The King and Queen arrived April 28 and left May 2. During their stay at Anderson House, a succession of royal functions took place. President and Mrs. Hoover were received in the English drawing room. "Vice President Curtis, Chief Justice Hughes, and big wigs were placed according to precedence in the long gallery and then introduced in order by State Department officials into the drawing room." (Larz Anderson: Letters and Journals of a Diplomat, p. 610)

The Society of the Cincinnati continued the Anderson tradition of offering the house for charitable uses and official government functions. In 1941 the Washington Committee for Refugees in England worked there to prepare warm clothes for a half million needy English. (Times-Herald, 7-31-41) Then in January 1942, the Navy Department took over the house for the duration of the war. (The Washington Post, 1-17-42 and 1-19-42)

Members of the Society use the house for private parties, dances and teas; and the President, Vice President and members of the Cabinet and Supreme Court may give official functions there. Otherwise, Anderson House is now a museum of portraits, sculpture, flags, swords, and other relics of the American Revolution and the Anderson family.

Sources: Isabel Anderson (ed), Larz Anderson: Letters and Journals of a Diplomat, New York: Fleming H. Revell Co., 1940.

The Sunday Star, 1-18-42, B 7:2.
The Washington Post, 1-17-42, 3:1.
The Washington Post, 1-19-42, 10:1.
The Washington Post, "Potomac", 2-18-62, pp. 10-12.
The Washington Times, 2-19-38, 19:4.
The Washington Star Sunday Magazine, 7-24-66, pp. 10-12.
Times - Herald, 7-31-41, 20:5.

Front Elevation
CFA photo
Alexander 1971

Plan, Building Projections
D.C. Government, Bureau of
Licenses and Permits

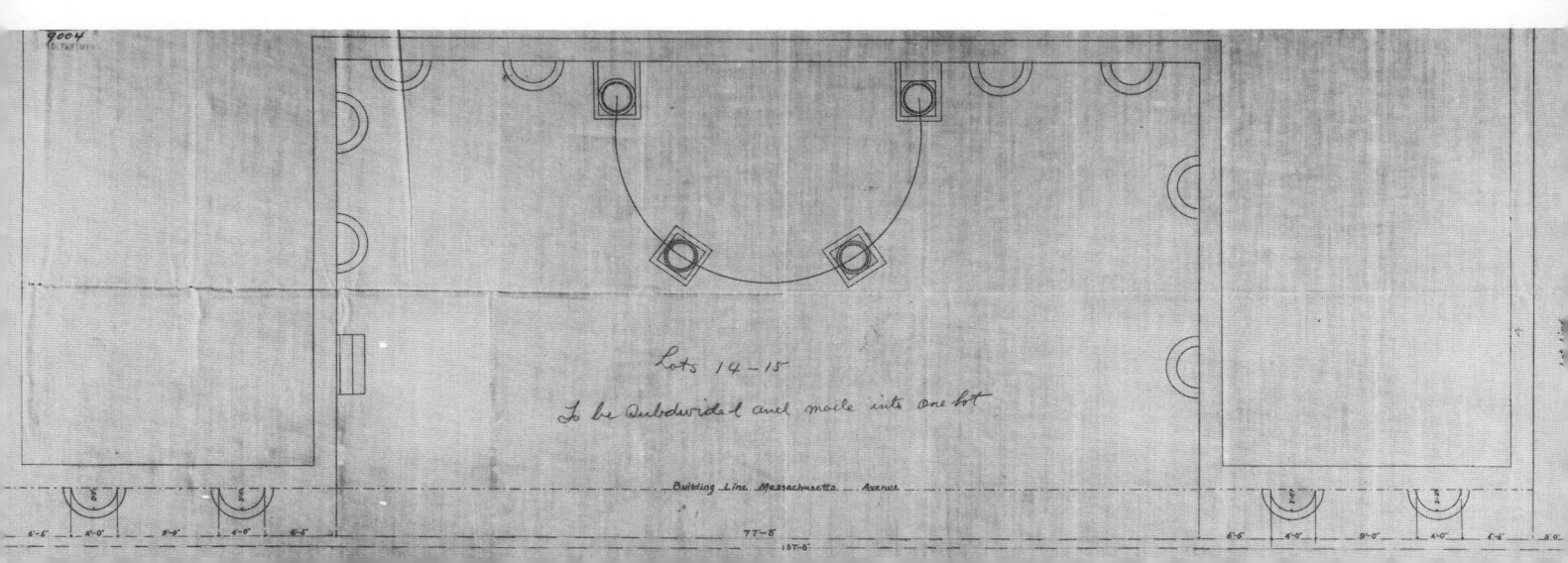

Rear Elevation
James R. Dunlop, Inc.

Opposite
Floor Plans
Courtesy Society of the Cincinnati

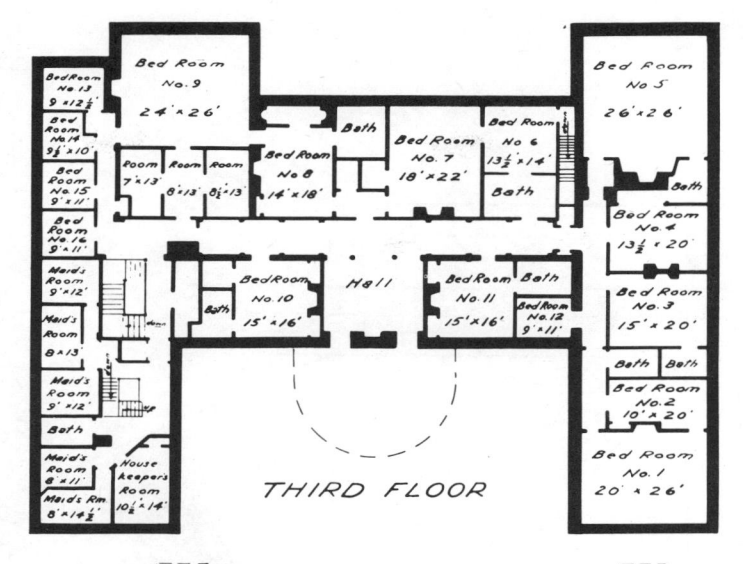

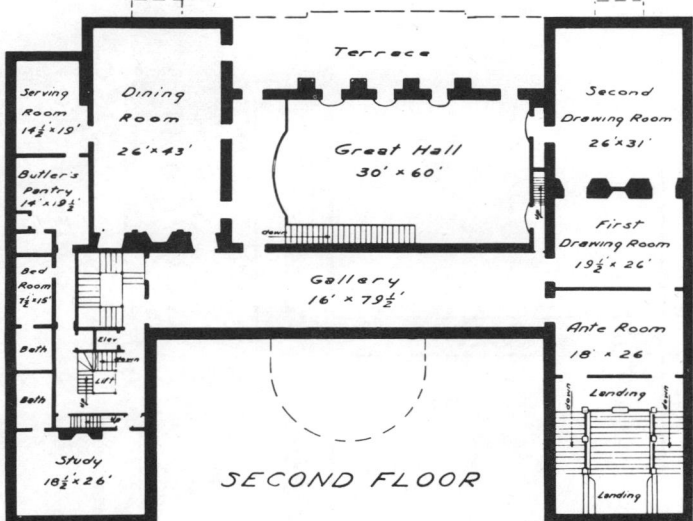

FLOOR PLANS

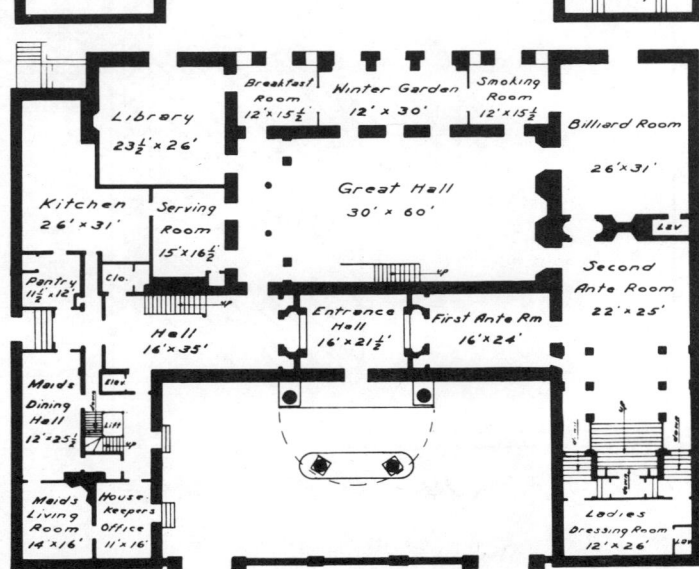

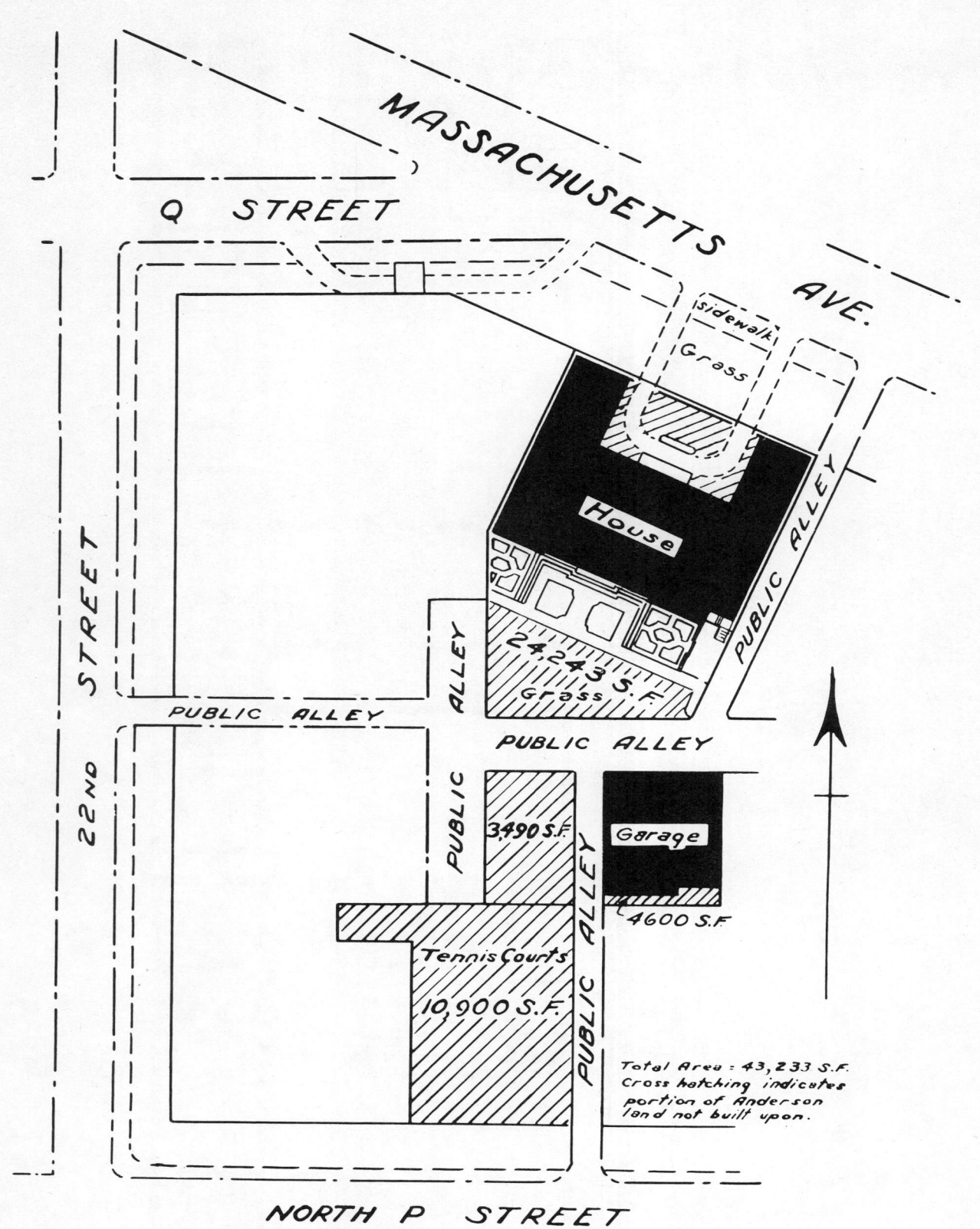

PLOT PLAN
Scale 1" 80'

Stables
(Demolished)
James R. Dunlop, Inc.

Opposite
Site Plan
Courtesy Society of the Cincinnati

165

Detail Cornice and Ceiling
Great Hall
CFA photo 1973

Great Hall
CFA photo 1973

Great Hall
James R. Dunlop, Inc.

Detail Great Hall Stair
CFA photo 1973

Detail Overmantle
Great Hall
CFA photo 1973

Detail Great Hall
CFA photo 1973

Detail Mantle
Great Hall
CFA photo 1973

Second Floor Gallery
City News Bureau, Inc.

Detail Woodwork
Gallery
CFA photo 1973

Second Drawing Room
City News Bureau, Inc.

Winter Garden from Breakfast Room
CFA photo 1973

Dining Room
City News Bureau, Inc.

Detail Winter Garden
CFA photo 1973

2118 Massachusetts Avenue, N.W.

PART II. ARCHITECTURAL INFORMATION

    A. General Statement:

        1. Architectural character: This detached structure is first half 18th century English in manner with similar details found in the works of Tallman, Gibbs, Campbell, Sampson and Kent. The interior spaces are eclectic.

        2. Condition: excellent.

    B. Exterior Description:

        1. Overall dimensions: The three story plus basement structure measures 66'-6" from sidewalk to roof ridge. The "H"-shaped plan is 137'-8" wide by 106'-0" deep. The symmetrical, eleven bay north elevation (Massachusetts Avenue) has a recessed seven bay carriage court which is 79'-8" wide by 38'-7" (two bays) deep. The court has a centered, three bay, two story portico and an entrance screen with gates.

        The eight bay south elevation has an off-center ground floor conservatory below a first floor terrace measuring five bays (63'-0") wide by one bay (12'-0") deep. Flanking the conservatory are composite bays, both 30'-3" wide. At the east, a single bay (15'-4" wide) breaks back 9'-0". The east elevation has a mezzanine fourth floor.

        2. Foundation: concrete footings and slab.

        3. Wall construction: The north and south elevations are faced with grey limestone. The base has a torus water table. The rusticated ground floor supports a panelled false balustrade, its cap acting as first floor window sill. The first and second floors are smooth limestone. The three central bays of the carriage court break forward six inches for the portico.

        Over the south elevation terrace, the three central bays of both floors are separated by single, half-engaged, two story Ionic columns on pedestals. Above the ground floor, the south elevations of both flanking bays are framed by two story Ionic pilasters on pedestals.

        4. Structure: concrete, brick and steel.

        5. Mechanical: The building has a hot water heating system. Air conditioning was added after 1940. Both passenger elevators were installed by the Whittier Machine Company of New York. The lighting is electric.

6. Porches, stoops, bulkheads, etc.: The two story, three bay, semicircular portico has fluted composite columns and pilasters on pedestals. The composite entablature has an oak leaf soffit and an urn-baluster balustrade.

   The south terrace (ground floor garden) is divided into three sections corresponding to the division made by the conservatory and flanking bays. From the conservatory and side sections, four marble risers descend to the central terrace.

   The three central bays of the conservatory break forward slightly with the balustrade of the first floor terrace. The terrace continues the line of the false balustrade, while similarly treated balconies supported on acanthus consoles break forward from the flanking Venetian bays.

7. Chimneys: Visible from ground level are seven chimneys faced with smooth limestone, each with block cap.

8. Openings:

   a. Doorways and doors: The north entrance double door is flanked by rustication and capped by a semicircular fan, the voussoir arch of which has a decorative keystone. There is a single service door at the east and west walls of the carriage court.

   Leading onto the portico balcony are two, semicircular-arched and recessed French doors with crossette architraves and decorative keystones. The doors flank a circular statuary niche within a bay leaf architrave.

   The bays flanking the south conservatory have a glazed double door with side lights separated by rustication. The doors and side lights have decorative keystones. Separated by rustication and capped by decorative keystones, each of the three central bays of the conservatory has a glazed double door with a semicircular fan. Flanking these bays are additional glazed double doors with semicircular fans, glazed spandrels and side lights with transoms. The doors and side lights are separated by single Tuscan columns.

   The first floor terrace has French doors with transoms and crossette architraves. The three central bays have semicircular pediments; the flanking bays have triangular pediments supported on leafy consoles.

   b. Windows: The single bays flanking the north entrance are treated in the same manner as the door with the exception of a flat voussoir lintel which replaces the fan. The remaining ground floor carriage court windows have panelled

2118 Massachusetts Avenue, N.W.

keystones and lack architraves. The street bays have crossette architraves and acanthus keystones. Except for the Gibbs surround of the three central portico windows, the first floor bays rest on the projecting panels of the false balustrade. Their architraves support tablets which are flanked by consoles and capped by a cyma cornice. The second floor crossette window architraves have acanthus keystones.

The south elevation first floor terrace is flanked by Venetian windows. The recessed east bay has a crossette and tablet window architrave. The second floor windows have square sashes and fascia architraves. The bay over either Venetian window is flanked by narrow side windows. Over the first floor terrace is an east loggia. The window of the east bay has a crossette and keystone architrave.

9. Roof:

   a. Shape, covering: Over the entrance portico, the slate, truncated-hip roof is interrupted by a pediment with a carved tympanum.

   b. Cornice, eaves: The north elevation has an egg and dart, modillion and cyma cornice capped by a panelled balustrade with acorn and finial stops and a central tablet over both wings. The south elevation has a fascia architrave; a pulvinated frieze terminating with the bays flanking the conservatory; and an egg and dart, modillion and cyma cornice capped by tablets (as at the north elevation). The projecting entablature above each half-engaged column is topped by a bulbous urn.

   c. Dormers, cupolas, towers: A skylight illuminates the east stair well.

C. Interior Description:

1. Floor plans: The ground floor centered entrance hall of the "H"-shaped plan is entered from the south side of the carriage court. Flanking the hall are the west "chapel" (an anteroom for the west reception hall) and the east stair hall. A serving room with access to a ballroom (the "Great Hall") south of the entrance hall lies between the east hall and a southeast library. The northeast wing and the area east of the pantry and library are devoted to kitchens and servants. South of the ballroom is the conservatory, which is divided into three sections: the central winter garden, the east breakfast room and the west smoking room. The smoking room has access to the southwest billiard room which is opposite the library. The billiard room is on axis with the west reception hall (connected to both the ballroom and "chapel"), and the northwest stair aisle and hall. (See plan.)

2118 Massachusetts Avenue, N.W.

The northwest first floor stair landing is on a north to south axis with an anteroom and two drawing rooms. Overlooking Massachusetts Avenue to the north, the gallery runs east from the anteroom and first drawing room. The gallery gives access to a secret passage at the southwest; the ballroom balcony (beyond which is the first floor terrace) and its stair; and the southeast dining room. Further to the east are the hall stair, servants' quarters, pantries and a northeast study. (See plan.)

The third floor, which contains various bedroom suites, will not be included in this study.

2. Spaces:

Entrance hall:

a. Flooring: The pink on grey marble floor is linearly divided into three square sections; an oval in the central section flanked by hexagons. The squares are bordered by diamond forms at the north and south. Two stone risers ascend to the east and west doorway alcoves.

b. Baseboard: 8", grey stone.

c. Walls: 9'-2" high, stone. The east and west doorway alcoves are flanked by tan marble, fluted, Roman Doric columns which support a semicircular arch. The arch has a false perspective jamb (pierced by niches) and soffit.

d. Ceiling: 13'-9" high, frescoed barrel vault linearly divided into three square coffers flanked by similar rectangular coffers. The flanking coffers are intersected by the barrel vaults over the entrance wall windows and door.

e. Doorways and doors: The 8'-0" high, east and west, wood double doors have stone fascia architraves. The wood entrance door is separated from its semicircular fanlight by a plain panel.

f. Lighting: polygonal, brass and opaque glass, ceiling lantern.

"Chapel": (anteroom to west reception hall)

a. Flooring: The white marble floor is centered by a purple rectangle having chamfered corners. Within the rectangle the purple stone is cut in sections which form an oval. The whole is framed within a purple border.

b. Baseboard: 6" wood. The baseboard projects from the wall to form a platform for 9'-2" high choir seats and back panels, reported to have come from 17th century Naples.

c. Wainscot: 3'-6" high wood seats with scroll and paw legs; alternating human and griffin arms; and a continuous back band of guilloche. The arms support figure consoles buttressed against pedestals and half-engaged, composite columns with decorative stop-fluting. Rinceau friezes break forward over the consoles. The whole is capped by a talon, dentil, egg and dart, corona and cyma cornice.

d. Walls: frescoed with polychromatic emblems of various societies.

e. Ceiling: 13'-9" high, fresco similar to walls.

f. Doorways and doors: 8'-0" high cased openings in stone architraves, at both east and west.

g. Lighting: There is a brass, Arabic censor chandelier with bronze female figure handles and mounts.

East stair hall:

a. Flooring: The marble floor has white squares with chamfered corners of yellow insets.

b. Baseboard: 6 1/2", pink, grey and white marble.

c. Chairrail: 3'-0" high, wood.

d. Walls: raised wood panels painted cream.

e. Cornice: cavetto, corona and cyma.

f. Ceiling: 14'-2" high, plaster painted white.

g. Doorways and doors: The 8'-0" high wood double doors have pink stone architraves. All doors are capped by decorative talon, except for the northeast semicircular archway which has a keystone and pulvinated architrave.

h. Stair: The stair ascends twenty-one risers east to a landing, two risers north to a second landing, two risers north to a third and five risers west from the third landing to the first floor. The treads, stringer brackets, and handrail are natural wood. The banister is decorative cast iron.

Library: (natural wood)

a. Flooring: 2", common hardwood.

b. Baseboard: 5", with additional 2" ogee cap.

c. Dado: raised panels in talon moulding.

d. Chairrail: 2'-8" high, fret.

e. Walls: two rows of panels similar to dado. Above the north wall chairrail are four bays of bookshelves. The bays are separated by narrow panels with statuary console bases beginning 7'-0" from the floor.

f. Cornice: wood with dentils, egg and dart, acanthus modilions and cyma.

g. Ceiling: 13'-9" high, plaster with centered quatrefoil.

h. Doorways and doors: At either end of the west wall are 7'-11" high wood double doors which swing into the jamb.

   The fascia architraves support bay leaf pulvination which is interrupted by a centered tablet and capped by a pediment.

i. Hardware: garland and leaf, brass door knobs.

j. Lighting: There are four, bust and wreath, bronze sconces each with three, leaf and mask arms.

k. Heating: The east wall red, grey and black marble chimney mantle (6'-10" wide by 4'-6" high) has a plain firebox surround flanked by Corinthian columns. Each column has a white marble base and capital, and a pink fluted shaft, which supports a plain, denticulated entablature.

Ballroom: (The two story "Great Hall" is described by floor. See photographs.)

Ground floor:

a. Flooring: Squares of herringbone parquetry are surrounded by herringbone within a geometric border of pink, orange and grey marble insets.

b. Baseboard: 8 1/2", pink stone.

c. Chairrail: 3'-5" high, pulvinated.

d. Walls: The plaster walls with recessed panels in talon mouldings are 13'-9" to the east balcony soffit. The treatment of the plaster simulates limestone. The south wall is divided into five bays by composite pilasters of pink stone on pedestals. Both end bays are separated from the central arches by projecting panels. Four composite columns with pink stone spiral shafts on grey pedestals support the east balcony.

e. Cornice: Dividing the ground floor from the first is a 2'-0" entablature having a fascia architrave, pink stone ogee frieze and a decorative cyma cornice.

f. Doorways and doors: The mirror-panelled double doors in false perspective jambs (flanking the west wall chimney) and the three glazed double doors (of the south wall central bays) are 8'-0" high, with fanlights and talon architraves with keystones. The wood double doors of the south wall end bays and those to the library, serving room and east hall (the door at the west end of the north wall is false) each has a pulvinated architrave and a statuary base keystone within an oval niche ornamented by sprays.

g. Lighting: There are six, nine-light, two-tier, crystal and gilded metal sconces.

h. Heating: The east wall alabaster chimney mantle (7'-4" wide by 7'-2" high) has candelabra pilasters and ogee hood blocks which support a decorative architrave broken forward over either block. Above the architrave is an arabesque frieze and a talon, egg and dart, gouge and talon shelf. The overmantle, which is broken forward slightly, has a talon panel flanked by pendants and consoles which support the ground floor entablature. The entablature is capped by a broken pediment with centered escutcheon.

i. Stair: The north wall stair ascends twenty-six cantilevered stone risers east to the first floor balcony. The decorative bronze banister, with paired scroll supports, has a wood handrail.

First floor:

a. Flooring: The marble floor of the concave east balcony has six-point stairs composed of tan hexagons and pink triangles bordered in black and tan.

b. Baseboard: The 8 1/2" cyma-capped baseboard extends around the balcony and across the top of the ground floor entablature.

c. Chairrail: 2'-9" high, punctuated by statuary console bases above each south wall ground floor pilaster.

d. Walls: plaster treated as on ground floor. Decorative plaster panels between each south wall bay are interrupted over both projecting ground floor panels by single statuary niches.

e. Cornice: wood, partly gilded. The cornice has cyma, astragal, egg and dart, acanthus modillions (which alternate with rosette coffers), corona and ogee.

f. Ceiling: 33'-8" from ground floor to first floor ceiling. Wood beams outline gilded rinceau and escutcheon panels in roundel and square coffers.

g. Doorways and doors: Each of the five south wall bays, the two east wall and two west wall bays has 14'-0" high, glazed French doors with transoms and fascia architraves. Those doors not on the balcony, open onto semielliptical bronze balconies. The exception is the 8'-1" high, wood double door from the balcony to the gallery. It has centered roundel panels within a fascia architrave which supports an acanthus bolection frieze interrupted by a centered tablet and capped by a semicircular pediment.

h. Hardware: decorative brass handles.

i. Lighting: There are two, bell-shaped, four-tier, crystal and gilded metal, modern chandeliers.

Conservatory: (three linear chambers: east breakfast room, central winter garden and west smoking room.)

a. Flooring: The marble floor of each chamber has a four-part geometric pattern in tan, gray, white, blue and black. The design is repeated three times in the central chamber.

b. Baseboard: 6", stone.

c. Chairrail: 2'-9" high, stone.

d. Walls: The north walls of the east and west chambers are frescoed. The central chamber has gilded wood trellis work terminated at lintel height by a fret frieze. The trellis work is interrupted by alternating doors and mirror-panelled pilasters. Two glass partitions with doors separate the three chambers.

e. Ceiling: 12'-11" high, plain plaster. The central chamber has trellis work.

f. Doorways and doors: Aside from the outside doors listed under "Exterior Description", the double doors from the side chambers to the ballroom, library and billiard room have crossette stone architraves with cavetto caps. Each of the three fanlighted bays from the central chamber to the ballroom has a stone, fascia and roll architrave with panelled keystone.

2118 Massachusetts Avenue, N.E.

g. Lighting: Each chamber has a three-light, mask and swag, lamp chandelier with opaque glass globes. Flanking the ballroom doors of the side chambers are single-light, mask and cornucopia, bronze sconces. Each has an opaque glass globe.

Billiard room: (presently a museum. Natural wood.)

a. Flooring: herringbone parquetry.

b. Baseboard: 5 1/2" with cyma cap.

c. Chairrail: 2'-9" high.

d. Walls: Above the doors and between each opening are single raised panels in talon mouldings. The doors and windows are flanked by pedestals at chairrail height below panelled composite pilasters.

e. Cornice: The bracket, corona and cyma cornice breaks forward over each pilaster.

f. Ceiling: 13'-9" high, plaster painted white. Decorative ribs frame hexagons and squares in the 17th century English manner.

g. Doorways and doors: The wood double doors have pink stone architraves.

h. Hardware: brass swag door pulls.

i. Lighting: There are eight, single-light, acanthus baroque sconces. Flanking the north wall chimney are single, triple-light, one-armed, gilded torch sconces girdled by a mask band.

j. Heating: The north wall chimney has a cast iron firebox with a "Trophy-of-War" back panel. The pink stone mantle (6'-7" wide by 4'-11" high) has a grey stone frieze surround with semicircular corners. The overmantle panel has a pulvinated acanthus moulding.

Northwest stair: (separated from the billiard room by a frescoed passage with east and west niches and tray ceiling. Described in three sections: reception hall, stair aisle and stair hall.)

Reception hall:

a. Flooring: The white marble floor is centered by a grey rectangle (with chamfered corners) surrounded by a second rectangle with corners tangent to squares.

b. Baseboard: 10", black stone.

c. Chairrail: 3'-0" high.

d. Walls: The frescoed walls simulate sculptured "Trophy" panels and statuary niches.

e. Cornice: An alternating triglyph and decorative metope frieze is capped by an acanthus and palmette cove.

f. Ceiling: The geometry of the mouldings for the 13'-9" high plaster ceiling is similar to the floor. It has a rectangular central panel, outlined by a foliate frieze, with corner squares and flanking rinceau panels centered by pattera. The whole is framed by an egg moulding.

g. Doorways and doors: The wood double doors have scagliola fascia architraves, each with tablet and pediment cap.

h. Windows: The west wall windows have scagliola bolection architraves.

i. Lighting: recently added crystal and brass chandeliers.

j. Heating: The south wall chimney has a cast iron firebox with floral panels. The pink stone mantle (7'-4" wide by 5'-2" high) has a pulvinated spiral surround and a bolection frieze with rope border. The overmantle fresco depicts the Society's medals.

Stair aisle:

a. Flooring: The white marble floor is divided into three sections: the center aisle has a grey square enclosing two concentric octagons; and the side aisles, each separated into three bays, have triangles within squares.

b. Baseboard: 10", grey stone.

c. Walls: The three aisles are separated by single rows of Tuscan columns on 3'-0" high pedestals. Pilasters of similar design flank raised panels capped by decorative tablets.

d. Cornice: The center aisle is framed by a triglyph and plain metope frieze.

e. Ceiling: The 13'-9" high center aisle ceiling is centered by a crossette panel of plaster with bundled leaves set between each corner spray. The pilasters and columns support side aisle beams and tray vaults.

Stair hall:

a. Stair: The grey stone stair ascends from the center aisle seventeen risers north to a landing laid in marble with an orange rectangle within a red octagon. The stair divides with two sets of three risers ascending east and west to additional landings, each of which has a white and grey marble oval within an orange surround. Single flights of twelve risers accend south from both landings to the first floor. This last double ascent has bronze rinceau balustrade panels and grey stone handrails with block and scroll newels.

b. Baseboard: 6 1/2".

c. Chairrail: 3'-8" high.

d. Walls: plaster treated to simulate limestone.

e. Cornice: acanthus scotia and recessed cove.

f. Ceiling: The pulvinated bay leaf border surrounds a guilloche frieze which frames a central roundel with spandrels and a pulvinated fruit moulding.

g. Doorways and doors: On line with the last stair ascents are two, south wall, wood double doors with roundel-centered panels and white, grey and purple marble, fascia and cyma architraves. Each architrave supports a bolection frieze(interrupted by a decorative tablet)and an egg and dart pediment.

h. Lighting: There are six, four-light, brass, "Trophy-of-War" sconces, and one bronze, Arabic censor chandelier with a "topnot" light crown.

Anteroom:

a. Flooring: white and yellow marble tiles in a fret motif with black and yellow border.

b. Baseboard: 8", purple marble.

c. Wainscot: 4'-6" high fresco simulates a dado and chairrail.

d. Walls: frescoes depict commemorative events.

e. Cornice: guilloche, cavetto (painted grey and partly gilded) and decorative cove.

f. Ceiling: The 16'-4" high plaster ceiling has a colorful center of paired roundel frescoes framed by a corner-indented rectangle.

g. Doorways and doors: The 8'-2" high wood double doors have roundel-centered panels and white and grey marble bolection architraves which support a white marble frieze with blue insets and a broken pediment with floral basket.

h. Windows: The windows have wood bolection architraves.

i. Lighting: There is a one-tier, sixteen-arm, gilded chandelier. The arms project from a ribbed tray above a bowl-like body and pendant formed by griffins.

First drawing room: (French manner.)

a. Flooring: herringbone parquetry.

b. Baseboard: 5" purple marble base with 1 1/2" gilded cap.

c. Dado: Both the dado with recessed panels in gilded cyma mouldings and the chairrail project 2" into the room.

d. Chairrail: 3'-0" high, gilded bead on cream fascia.

e. Walls: painted cream with gilded ornamentation. Above a band of horizontal guilloche and rosette friezes are silk damask panels in gilded mouldings. Flanking the south wall chimney and rounding the room corners are gilded, palmette and escutcheon, rocaille panels.

f. Cornice: cream architrave with gilded astragal below cove with panel mouldings.

g. Ceiling: 16'-4" high, plaster with central polyfoil moulding in rocaille.

h. Doorways and doors: The east and north wall wood double doors have roundel-centered panels; the double doors at the south are recessed into alcoves. All doors have white and purple marble bolection architraves, each supporting a cavetto base for a floral and fruit canvas in the 17th century manner.

i. Windows: The talon window architraves surround false perspective friezes which simulate panelled jambs.

j. Hardware: brass swag door pulls.

k. Lighting: Flanking the south chimney are two, three-light, gilded lily sconces. There is also a two-tier, sixteen-light, rocaille chandelier with crystal fruit.

l. Heating: The south wall white marble chimney mantle in the 18th century French manner (6'-7" wide by 3'-10" high), has splayed scroll terms and a central escutcheon. The gilded overmantle mirror is in the late baroque manner.

Second drawing room: (English manner. See photograph.)

a. Flooring: herringbone parquetry.

b. Baseboard: 5" tan and pink marble base with 1", gilded, bundled leaf torus and 2" cyma reversa cap.

c. Chairrail: 3'-1" high, interrupted by full length central east and west wall panels and by pedestals with gilded caps.

d. Walls: Over each pedestal is a narrow flat panel. Flat panels with gilded fret corners and talon mouldings flank the single, east and west wall, full length panels. The larger panels are capped by gilded rocaille tablets.

e. Cornice: painted cream with gilding. The cornice has dentils, egg and dart, corona (with rocaille soffit), cavetto and talon.

f. Ceiling: 16'-4" high, gilded rocaille.

g. Doorways and doors: The north wall double doors, painted cream with gilded rocaille panels, are set in recessed semicircular archways with gilded jambs and grey and white marble pulvinated architraves. Both doors are capped by talon panels centered by an oval niche with gilded jardinaire scroll base, sprays and swags.

h. Hardware: gold-plated, swag door pulls.

i. Lighting: There are eight, three-light, gilded rocaille sconces, and one, single-tier, sixteen-light, brass baroque chandelier.

j. Heating: The north wall chimney has empire andirons having porcelain urns each with brass base, drapes, hooves, swags and finial mount. The white marble mantle (7'-9" wide by 4'-7" high) has a yellow marble firebox surround. The flanking foliate-panelled console terms support a foliate swag and central basket frieze (which is broken forward over either term), and an egg and dart, corona and talon shelf. The overmantle has a gilded rocaille mirror.

Gallery: (see photographs)

a. Flooring: The marble floor is set in five linear sequences of concentric octagons within squares.

b. Baseboard: 7 1/2", maroon marble with gilded, bundled roll cap.

c. Chairrail: 3'-0" high, talon.

d. Walls: The raised wood panels in egg and dart mouldings are covered by tapestries. The west wall doorways are recessed within a roundel-panelled alcove.

e. Cornice: concave acanthus moulding.

f. Ceiling: The 16'-4" high plaster ceiling has a cove border divided into alternating rectangular and roundel panels. A pulvinated leaf moulding separates these panels from nine, alternating, octagonal and roundel panels.

g. Doorways and doors: At the east and west walls are two sets of wood double doors each having a semicircular arch with sculpted fan, scrolled keystone, and maroon bolection architrave. The east wall doors have roundel-centered panels of pierced carving.

h. Windows: wood bolection architraves.

i. Lighting: There are three, six-light, crystal arm, bead and pendant, chandeliers (recently added).

Dining room: (natural wood. See photographs.)

a. Flooring: The marble floor has an orange border surrounding a geometric pattern of black and white circles and triangles on a green ground.

b. Baseboard: 4" black and green marble base with a 2" torus cap.

c. Dado: flat panels.

d. Chairrail: 3'-0" high.

e. Walls: hung with tapestries.

f. Cornice: astragal and egg and dart.

g. Ceiling: 16'-4" high, plaster, pulvinated fruit and foliate roundel within rectangular border frieze.

h. Doorways and doors: The wood double doors flanking the north wall chimney have centered roundel panels and black and green marble bolection architraves. Each architrave supports a wood frieze with a spray keystone and a geometric statuary niche flanked by cornucopia and capped by an escutcheon with drapes and swags. The east wall wood double door to the serving room has raised panels and a marble bolection architrave flanked at the head by consoles which support a wood frieze and cornice.

i. Windows (French doors): wood bolection architraves and valances capped by urn finials.

j. Hardware: brass swag door pulls.

k. Lighting: There are four, seven-light, bronze flambeau sconces with female figures composing the bowl and cherubs, putti and ramsheads the shaft. There is a more recent, single-tier, ten-light, crystal body, pendant and drape chandelier.

l. Heating: The north wall torquoise marble chimney mantle (7'-1" wide by 4'-11" high) has a pulvinated firebox surround and a bolection architrave. The overmantle tapestry panel is framed by wood, floral and fruit, sprays and pendants. The chimney wall is flanked by half-engaged, fluted Corinthian columns. The room cornice breaks forward over either column.

D. Site:

1. Setting and orientation: The building faces north on a lot measuring 140'-10" on Massachusetts Avenue; 158'-6" on an east alley; 107'-11" on a south alley; 105'-9" on the southwest; and 105'-4" on the west.

2. Enclosures: The carriage court limestone screen is terminated at the ends by iron-panelled gates within Tuscan semicircular archways flanked by three-quarter-engaged Tuscan columns. The columns support full entablatures each having a guttae architrave, plain frieze, dentil cornice and a segmental pediment.

   The south garden is bordered by limestone and brick walls. The side terraces are bordered at the east and west by limestone screens with statuary niches.

3. Outbuildings: The brick stable and garage on the adjoining property to the south has been destroyed. (See interior photograph.)

4. Walks: The carriage court is paved in exposed aggragate, as are the south garden terraces.

5. Landscaping: The avenue is lined by elms. Between the public sidewalk and the house the grass is bordered by ivy and various flowering shrubs. The south garden was formally planted with ivy, clipped evergreens and flowering shrubs, the south wall shaded by various trees.

2121 MASSACHUSETTS AVENUE, N.W., WASHINGTON, D.C.

CFA photo
Alexander 1971

Location :   2121 Massachusetts Avenue, N.W., Washington, D.C.;
                        on the northeast corner of Massachusetts and
                        Florida Avenues.

Present Owner: Cosmos Club

Present Occupant: Cosmos Club

Present Use: Private Club

Statement of   This detached residence is a good example of Louis XVI
Significance: exterior detailing, in this case applied to a structure
                        reminiscent of J. A. Gabriel's Petit Trianon (1762-1768)
                        at Versailles. As reputedly stipulated by the Townsends,
                        the present building incorporates parts of an earlier
                        home. The lot, nearly an acre in extent, occupies a
                        dominant corner site defined by the intersection of Que
                        Street, Massachusetts and Florida Avenues. Olmsted
                        Associates may have designed the landscaping for the
                        site.

PART I.   HISTORICAL INFORMATION

   A.   Lot and Square:

   The building is located in Square 66, lot 71 (formerly lots 14 and
   15). Lots 41 and 42 in Square 66 are also included in the property.

   B.   Original and Subsequent Owners:

   The following chain of title to the property shows the owners of
   the present structure and of any known preceding structures on the
   site:

   1871   Deed June 14, 1871, recorded June 15, 1871 in
          Liber 649 folio 415

          August Miller et ux
                  To
          Curtis J. Hillyer

          "...for and in consideration of the sum of Twenty-five thou-
          sand dollars ($25,000)...to them in hand paid by the said
          party of the second part...All of Square...(66) as laid out
          and recorded on the original plan of said city..."

2121 Massachusetts Avenue, N.W.

1892   Deed March 4, 1892, recorded March 7, 1892 in
Liber 1660 folio 367

Curtis J. Hillyer et ux, Angeline
             To
Edward J. Stellwagen

"Lot...(14) and part of lot...(15) of Curtis J. Hillyer's recorded subdivision of Square...(66) said part of lot...(15) being contained within the following metes and bounds viz.: Beginning for the same at the south east corner of said lot, running thence North westerly on and with the North line of Massachusetts Avenue...178.25 feet; thence North easterly at right angles to said North line of Massachusetts Avenue...137.07 feet to the south line of a public alley; thence south easterly on and with the south line of said public alley,...69.28 feet; thence East 61.9 feet to the West line of a public alley; thence south 53.4 feet to the line of lot...(14); thence West 10.95 feet; thence south westerly 14.65 feet; and thence south on and with the dividing line between lots...(14) and...(15) to the line of Massachusetts Avenue the place of beginning..."

(This is a description of lot 14 and the eastern part of lot 15.)

1892   Deed July 8, 1892, recorded July 14, 1892 in
Liber 1715 folio 93

Edward J. Stellwagen, Trustee
        To
Angeline Hillyer

"This Indenture...by and between Edward J. Stellwagen Trustee under certain deed in trust recorded in Liber 1660 folio 367...party of the first part and Angeline Hillyer of the District of Columbia party of the second part...conveyed...Lot...(14) and [eastern] part of Lot...(15) of Curtis J. Hillyer's subdivision of Square...(66) said part of Lot...(15) being described by metes and bounds as follows..." (Refer to liber 1660 folio 367 as recorded above.)

1898   Deed December 5, 1898, recorded December 22, 1898 in
Liber 2342 folio 445

Curtis J. Hillyer et ux, Angeline
             To
Mary Scott Townsend

2121 Massachusetts Avenue, N.W.

"This Deed...Witnesseth, that Curtis J. Hillyer and Angeline Hillyer, his wife, the said Angeline Hillyer acting herein also in her own right, of the District of Columbia, parties hereto of the first part, for and in consideration of Ten dollars in current money...to them paid by Mary Scott Townsend of the said District of Columbia, party hereto of the second part...do hereby...convey .. .. the following described land and premises, with the improvements thereon and the easements and appurtenances thereunto belonging, situate and lying in the City of Washington...All of lot... (14) in said Curtis J. Hillyer's subdivision of Square... (66), as said subdivision and the plat thereof are recorded in Liber No. 12 folio 55 of the Records of the Office of the Surveyor of said District. Also all that part of Lot...(15) in said subdivision of said square contained within the following metes and bounds, namely: Beginning for the same on the North line of Massachusetts Avenue, at the South eastern corner of said Lot...(15), and running thence North westerly along with said North line of said Avenue,...278.25 feet, more or less, to the South eastern corner of that part of said lot...(15) [which was] conveyed by said parties hereto of the first part by Deed bearing date June 7, 1894 and recorded in Liber No. 1931 folio 81 to Laura F. McCartney and by her husband, conveyed to John G. Moore, by Deed bearing date June 7, 1897 and recorded in Liber No. 2240 folio 6 of said Land Records; thence North easterly along and with the East line of said part of said lot...137.07 feet, more or less, to a public alley; thence south easterly along and with the South line of said alley...170.0 feet...to a point ...61.9 feet West of the West line of a ...24 feet wide alley; thence East 61.9 feet more or less to the Western line of said last named alley; thence south easterly following said ...alley...23.4 feet; thence South...30.01 feet; thence West 10.95 feet; thence south westerly...14.65 feet intersecting a straight line drawn due North of the point beginning, at a distance of...104.8 feet from said point of beginning; and thence South...104.8 feet, to the point of beginning...being all of said Lot...(15) excepting the part thereof conveyed as aforesaid to McCartney, and by said McCartney conveyed to said Moore. Subject nevertheless, to five Deeds of Trust on parts of said subdivided Lot...(15), recorded respectively in Liber No. 2273, folio 331 et seq.; Liber No. 1778, folio 156 et seq.; Liber No. 2188, folio 256 et seq.; Liber No. 2188, folio 264 et seq.; and Liber No. 2188, folio 269 et seq. of the aforesaid Land Records, securing payment of incumbrances aggregating Sixty-five thousand, five hundred dollars ($65,500) which the said Mary Scott Townsend assumes to pay as part of the consideration for this conveyance..."

2121 Massachusetts Avenue, N.W.

(This is a description of lot 14 and the eastern and middle parts of lot 15.)

1894 Deed June 7, 1894, recorded June 11, 1894 in
Liber 1931 folio 81

Curtis J. Hillyer et ux, Angeline
      To
Laura F. McCartney,
wife of John W.

"...for and in consideration of Thirteen Thousand six hundred and eleven and 50/100 dollars ($13,611.50)...to them in hand paid...have...conveyed...the following described land and premises...distinguished as part of lot...(15) in C. J. Hillyer's subdivision of Square...(66) beginning for the same at the south west corner of said lot and square being also the intersection of the north line of Massachusetts Avenue with the east line of Boundary Street now Florida Avenue; thence south easterly at right angles to the north line of Massachusetts Avenue...55.33 feet; thence north easterly at right angles to the north line of Massachusetts Avenue...137.07 feet to the south line of a public alley; thence north westerly with said south line of said public alley to the east line of Boundary Street...and thence with the east line of said street to the north line of Massachusetts Avenue the place of beginning, containing 3889 square feet of land, more or less. Subject however, to a certain Deed of Trust dated January 10, 1893 recorded in Liber No. 1778, folio 139 securing a note of...Six thousand dollars ($6,000), which said note is included in and forms part of the consideration hereinbefore named in this Deed..."

(This is a description of the western part of lot 15.)

1897 Deed June 7, 1897, recorded June 28, 1897 in
Liber 2240 folio 6

Laura F. McCartney et vir
      To
John G. Moore

"...John G. Moore, of the City and State of New York, party of the second part...Part of lot...(15) in C. J. Hillyer's subdivision of Square...(66)..." (See Liber 1931, folio 81 as recorded above.)

1898 Deed November 24, 1898, recorded December 12, 1898 in
Liber 2354 folio 295

John G. Moore et ux, Louisa
        To
Elverton R. Chapman

Western part of lot 15 in Square 66.

1898 Deed December 10, 1898, recorded December 12, 1898 in Liber 2354 folio 300

Elverton R. Chapman (unmarried)
        To
Mary Scott Townsend

"This Deed...witnesseth that Elverton R. Chapman (unmarried) of New York City, State of New York party hereto of the first part, for and in consideration of Fifteen thousand, five hundred fifty-six dollars ($15,556)...to him paid by Mary Scott Townsend of the District of Columbia party hereto of the second part...conveyed...Part of Lot...(15) in C. J. Hillyer's subdivision of Square...(66) as per plat recorded in Liber 12, folio 55 of the Records of the Office of the Surveyor of the District of Columbia contained within the following metes and bounds..." (Refer to Liber No. 1931, folio 81 as recorded above.)

NOTE: The Will of Mary Scott Townsend was recorded in Will Book No. 169, folio 534 and admitted to probate April 14, 1931.

Mary Scott Townsend leaves all property to her daughter, Mathilde Townsend Welles.

The Will of Mathilde Townsend Welles was recorded in Will Book No. 396, folio 138 and admitted to probate November 2, 1949.

1950 Deed January 12, 1950, recorded March 8, 1950 in Liber 9157, folio 552

Sumner Welles,
Bruce Baird and
National Savings and Trust Co.
Trustees
    To
Cosmos Club

"This Deed...by and between Sumner Welles, Bruce Baird and National Savings and Trust Company, Trustees under the last Will and Testament of Mathilde Townsend Welles, acting herein in exercise of the power confered by said Will, parties hereto of the first part; and Cosmos Club, a body corporate, duly incorporated under the laws of the District of Columbia, party of the second part...for and in consideration of the sum of Three hundred and sixty-four thousand, six hundred and thirty-five dollars ($364,635)...Lots...(14) and...(15), and...(41) and...(42) in C. J. Hillyer's subdivision of Square ...(66) as per plat recorded in Liber 12, folio 55 of the Records of the Office of the Surveyor of the District of Columbia..."

Lot 41 and lot 42 adjoin lot 15 at the northeast.

Source: Recorder of Deeds, Washington, D.C.

C. Date of Erection:

The house was begun early in 1899 and completed by 1901.

D. Building Permits:

The applications for the following building permits were filed by the architect, contractor or owner's agent and provide significant data:

Permits missing from the files of the D.C. Government:

No. 920, December 22, 1898
No. 1582, May 9, 1899
No. 105, July 15, 1904
No. 364, July 20, 1909
No. 662, August 8, 1912
No. 799, August 16, 1912

Permits found:

No. A 23589, August 31, 1951
Permit to Excavate

No. A 23784, September 7, 1951
Permit to raze stable at rear

No. A 27522, January 31, 1952
Permit to build addition
    Owner: Cosmos Club
    Architect: Horace W. Peaslee
    Estimated cost: $225,000.
"Build one brick and concrete addition to private club as per plans ($100,000). Also relocations of partitions for bedrooms, and baths, new kitchens. Facilities, general

2121 Massachusetts Avenue, N.W.

miscellaneous repairs. Remove upper story of stable ($125,000)."

No. A 28448, March 7, 1952
Permit to Install Passenger Elevator
    Owner: Cosmos Club
    Mechanic: Haughton Elevator
    Estimated cost: $16,000.
    Location: center of building

No. A 28457, March 7, 1952
Permit to Install Freight Elevator
    Owner: Cosmos Club
    Estimated cost: $16,000.
    Location: rear of building

No. A 46398, August 12, 1953
Permits for Repairs, Alterations, etc.
    Owner: Cosmos Club
    Architect: Julian E. Berla
    Estimated cost: $500.
    "Rearrange exterior stairway from east parking lot to basement and provide an entrance to coat room through the barber shop."

Source: D.C. Government: Department of Economic Development, Bureau of Licenses and Permits, Central Files.

E. Alterations and Additions:

A 19'-0" by 24'-0", second story, tin-roofed north addition was made to the house in 1904 by the architects, Carrère and Hastings. Some modifications occured in the building after 1915 as revealed in a comparison of the present interiors with photographs taken in that year. (See Francis Benjamin Johnston photographs.) These changes include: the replacement of the first floor brocatelle wall coverings, the replacement or removal of the detailing in the first floor reception and anterooms, and the replacement of the library mantle.

In 1942 the stable was converted into a Service Canteen by the installation of kitchens for the American Women's Volunteer Service. When the property was leased to the Canadian Women's Army Corps in 1943, the house had to be modified in order to provide for the 150 women stationed there. (Refer to plans in the Director's office of the Cosmos Club.) Dormitory rooms were located on the first, third and fourth floors. The dining room became the combined mess and recreation hall, while the library was turned into the officers' dining room.

Extensive modifications were made after the purchase of the property by the Cosmos Club in 1950. Seventeen architect members of the

Cosmos Club formed a group called "The Associated Club Architects." A contract dated May 10, 1950 provided for a design competition to be held in two stages with a winner to be selected within 60 days. (Cosmos Club Bulletin, Vol. 3, No. 8, June 1950, pages 2-3) Horace Peaslee was awarded the contract to convert the building for club use.

Peaslee's changes included a new roof, plumbing, wiring, heating, rearrangements of the interior, a modernized kitchen, an enlarged dining room and an auditorium - all for an estimated $390,000. Because of building code requirements, the doorways between the reception room and the ballroom were closed; and the open central stair was closed off from surrounding rooms. In addition, the building was subdivided into fire blocks. (Cosmos Club Bulletin, Vol. II, No. 7, July - August 1958, page 6)

In 1952, a five story north addition (with three third floor dining rooms and an enlarged Members' Dining Room) was opened. (Cosmos Club Bulletin, Vol. 15, Nos. 6-7, June - July 1952, page 8) At the time, a west entrance was provided for access to the Ladies Dining Room in the new wing. Eight columns in the Byzantine manner (which had earlier supported arches in a garden pavilion) and an Italianate fountain (which had earlier been set in the garden wall of the coach house) formed the major architectural framework of the new facitity. Many parts of the original building were offered for sale after the remodeling was completed. These included marble mouldings, electric fixtures, oak-panelled doors, and ironwork, a list of which is found in the Cosmos Club Bulletin of May 1953.

In 1958 funds were voted to restore murals on the first floor. Henri Courtais of New York was the restoration artist. (The Washington Post, 4-2-58, with a photograph showing the artist and mural)

The 1960 remodeling for an estimated $408,000 included the following changes:
- Basement: modernization of the kitchen areas, including an expanded dining room and lounge for the staff.
- Grd. fl.: changing the board room and offices into a taproom.
- 1st fl.: enlargement of original dining room by addition of space for three private rooms convertible into one room.
- 2nd fl.: six convertible dining rooms and a new board room.

The Cosmos Club purchased land at 2168 Florida Avenue and at No. 5 Hillyer Court to provide room for the east extension designed by the architect, Frank W. Cole, and completed in May 1962 by the contractor, George Lipscomb and Co.. Further remodeling in 1971 included alterations to the ground floor service area.

F. Architects: Carrère and Hastings, New York City.

John Merven Carrère (November 9, 1858 - March 1, 1911), the son of John M. Carrère a coffee plantation owner and resident of Baltimore, was born in Rio de Janeiro. His mother, Anna Louisa Maxwell, was also of Baltimore. As a youth, Carrère studied at the Institute Breitenstein at Grenchen, Switzerland. While attending the École des Beaux Arts, he studied under Leon Ginain and graduated with the Diplome d' Architecte in 1882. In 1883 Carrère joined the firm of McKim, Mead and White. Shortly thereafter, he formed a partnership with Thomas Hastings. His marriage in 1886 was to the former Marian Sidonia Dell of Houston and San Francisco.

Carrère was the chief architect and chairman of the architectural board for the gardens, decorations and grounds of the 1901 Pan American Exposition in Buffalo. He helped found the Fine Arts Federation, the Municipal Art Commission of New York City, and the Society of Beaux Arts Architecture, of which he was twice president. He was also twice president of the American Institute of Architects and a trustee of the American Academy at Rome. Carrère worked on the city commissions of: Grand Rapids, Michigan (1909), Hartford Connecticut (1911), and Cleveland, Ohio.

His book City Improvement from the Artistic Standpoint (1908) was highly influential. The architect's death in 1911 was the result of a collision between his taxi cab and a street car.

A few of the more important buildings designed by the firm include:

    Ponce de Leon Hotel, St. Augustine, Florida (1887)
    Alcazar Hotel, St. Augustine, Florida (1888)
    Grace Methodist Church, St. Augustine, Florida (1887)
    Presbyterian Church, St. Augustine, Florida (1890)
    Central Congregational Church, Providence, Rhode Island (1891)
    Hotel Laurel-in-the-Pines, Lakewood, New Jersey (1891)
    Benedict estate, Greenwich, Connecticut (1891)
    Jefferson Hotel, Richmond, Virginia (1893)
    "Bellafontaine" (Giraud Foster residence;), Lenox, Mass. (1897)
    Ganbrill estate, Newport, Rhode Island (1898)
    "Blairsden" (Blair estate), Peapack, New Jersey (1898)
    Richmond Borough Hall, New York City (1903-07)
    McKinley Monument, Buffalo, New York (1903)
    Approaches and architectural work of Manhattan Bridge, New
        York City (1905)
    Royal Bank of Canada, Montreal (1906)
    "Whitehall" (Flagler residence), Palm Beach, Florida (1901)
    Guggenheim residence, Elberton, New Jersey (1903)
    First Church of Christ Scientist, New York City (1898)
    Carnegie Institute, Washington, D.C. (1906)
    Goldwin Smith Hall at Cornell University (1903)
    Woolsey Hall and Memorial Hall at Yale (1906)
    Senate and House Office Buildings, Washington, D.C. (1905-06)

2121 Massachusetts Avenue, N.W.

New (Century) Theatre, New York City (1906-09)
New York Public Library, (1897, completed 1911)
Portland City Hall, Maine (1911)

Sources: Dumas Malone (ed.), <u>Dictionary of American Biography</u>, Vol. III, New York: Charles Scribner's Sons, 1932.

<u>A. I. A. Quarterly Bulletin</u>, April - June, 1911.

<u>The New York Times</u>, 3-2-11, 9:3 (obituary).

<u>Thomas Hastings</u> (March 11, 1860 - October 22, 1929), the son of Thomas Samuel Hastings, pastor of the West Presbyterian Church, and of Fanny de Groot, was born in New York City. Hastings left Columbia University to study under Jules André at the École des Beaux Arts where he received his Dipolme d' Architecte in 1884. While in Paris he met Carrère. Later he returned to New York and joined the firm of McKim, Mead and White. In 1900 Hastings married the former Helen R. Benedict, daughter of Commodore E. C. Benedict of Greenwich, Connecticut.

Hastings, as a partner in the firm of Carrère and Hastings, helped formulate the Hartford city plan; worked on Mt. Vernon Square in Baltimore; and designed the industrial town of Duluth, Minnesota for United States Steel. The Pulitzer fountain and Plaza Hotel in New York City were equally noted works. His projects in England (including Devonshire House apartments in London) resulted in the award of the Royal Gold Medal of the Royal Institute of British Architects in 1922 and the distinction of chevalier of the Legion of Honor.

From 1910 to 1917 Hastings was a member of the Commission of Fine Arts in Washington, D.C. - during which time he was co-author of <u>Six Lectures of Architecture,</u> published in 1917. The architect's death in 1929 resulted from an appendicitis attack.

Some of the more important projects produced after the death of John Carrère include:

Tower of Jewels, Panama Pacific Exposition, San Francisco (1914)
Richmond County Court House, Staten Island, New York
Frick residence, Fifth Avenue, New York City
Knoedler Galleries, Fifth Avenue, New York City
Alexander Building, Fifth Avenue, New York City
St. Ambrose Chapel, Cathedral of St. John the Divine, New York City
Memorial Amphitheatre, Arlington Cemetary, Virginia
Princeton Battle Monument, Princeton, New Jersey
Lafayette monument base, court of the Louvre, Paris
Altar of Liberty and Victory Arch, Madison Square, New York City (temporary, 1919)
Standard Oil Company, Broadway, New York City

2121 Massachusetts Avenue, N.W.

   Sources: Dumas Malone (ed.), <u>Dictionary of American Biography</u>,
        Vol. VIII, New York: Charles Scribner's Sons, 1932.

        <u>The Architectural Forum</u>, Vol. LI, No. 6 (December 1929),
        page 35.

        <u>The New York Times</u>, 10-23-29, 29:1 (obituary).

G. Known Plans, Drawings, Elevations, etc.:

   Plans of building as it was in 1950 and a large selection of subsequent plans showing additions and alterations. Also a set of plans stamped "Preliminary", which are unsigned and undated (see reproductions). Files of the Cosmos Club.

   Ground and main floor plans.
   <u>The Architectural Record</u>, Vol. X, No. 4 (April 1901).
   (see reproductions)

H. Important Old Views:

   1. Cosmos Club's photograph album

      Exterior views:

      a. South facade
      b. Entrance drive and building from the east (see reproduction)
      c. Entrance drive and building from the west
      d. Entrance driveway
      e. Along south wall from the west
      f. View from across Massachusetts Avenue
      g. Same (exterior views indicate photographs taken before 1905)
      h. Detail of entrance door from sidewalk
      i. Garden, corner of Florida and Massachusetts Avenues
      j. Florida Avenue carriage house

   2. Francis Benjamin Johnston photographs, ca. 1915; Library of Congress, Prints and Photographs Division, Lot 2427

      Exterior views:

      a. Nearly direct view of entrance facade
      b. View from southwest of entrance facade
      c. Detail of entrance including marquise

      Interior views:

      a. Entrance hall, northeast corner (see reproduction)
      b. Entrance hall, northwest corner (see reproduction)
      c. Reception hall, fireplace wall

d. Dining room, west bay (see reproduction)
e. Ballroom, north musicians' alcove
f. Ballroom, looking north (see reproduction)
g. Library, southwest corner
h. Library, northwest corner (see reproduction)
i. Library, fireplace and wall (see reproduction)
j. Reception room, northwest corner
k. Reception room, fireplace and wall (see reproduction)
l. Anteroom, fireplace and wall (see reproduction)
m. Dining room, fireplace and wall (see reproduction)
n. East reception room, ground floor (see reproduction)

3. Percy C. Stuart, "Recent Domestic Architecture in Washington, D.C., Residence of Mrs. R. H. Townsend," The Architectural Record, Vol. X, No. 4 (April 1901), pages 425-437.

   a. Exterior looking north
   b. Entrance hall looking northeast
   c. Main stair, entrance hall from west
   d. Entrance hall, looking west from main stair
   e. Dining room looking south
   f. Reception hall looking southeast
   g. Ballroom looking northeast
   h. First floor reception room looking northeast
   i. Library looking northeast

4. Newspaper photographs

   Exterior views:

   a. View of stables, The Washington Daily News, 1-16-42.
   b. Facade, The Washington Star Pictorial Magazine, 11-23-52.
   c. Facade, The Washington Post, 1-23-56.

   Interior views:

   a. Interior of stables, The Washington Daily News, 1-16-42.
   b. Library mantle, The Washington Post, 1-12-50.
   c. Ballroom, The Washington Post, 1-12-50.
   d. Ballroom (refurbished), The Evening Star, 8-19-52.
   e. Dolly Madison Room, reception hall, anteroom, library, auditorium, and ladies dining room, The Washington Star Pictorial Magazine, 11-23-52.
   f. Lounge, The Washington Post, 1-23-56.

I. Residents:

1. City and telephone directories list the following tenants:

   1876-1899 Curtis J. Hillyer

2121 Massachusetts Avenue, N.W.

```
1900         Vacant
1901-1902    Richard H. Townsend
1903-1913    Mathilde and Mary S. Townsend
1914-1931    Mary S. Townsend
1932         Vacant
1933-1939    Sumner B. Welles
1940-1942    Vacant
1943         Sumner Welles
1944-1949    No listing found
1950-1972    Cosmos Club
```

2. The Cosmos Club lists among its most prominent members:

Presidents of the United States

    William Howard Taft
    Herbert Hoover
    Woodrow Wilson

Nobel Prize Winners

A. A. Michelson	Physics	1907
Woodrow Wilson	Peace	1919
Robert A. Millikan	Physics	1923
Arthur H. Compton	Physics	1927
Sinclair Lewis	Literature	1930
Harold Urey	Chemistry	1934
I. I. Rabi	Physics	1944
Lord John Boyd Orr	Physics	1949
Edwin M. McMillan	Chemistry	1951
Glenn T. Seaborg	Chemistry	1951
Vincent DuVigneaud	Chemistry	1955
Juan Ramon Jimenez	Literature	1956
George W. Beadle	Medicine & Physiology	1958
Willard F. Libby	Chemistry	1960
R. S. Mulliken	Chemistry	1956
Robert Hofstadter	Physics	1961
Melvin Calvin	Chemistry	1961
Charles H. Townes	Physics	1964
Eugene P. Wigner	Physics	1963
William Shockley	Physics	1956
Edward M. Purcell	Physics	1952

Pulitzer Prize Winners

Henry Adams	Biography	1919
Charles Warren	History	1923
James Truslow Adams	History	1923
William Allen White	Editorial Writing & Biography	1923
Jay N. Darling	Cartoon	1924, 1943

201

2121 Massachusetts Avenue, N.W.

Michael I. Pupin	Biography	1924
Edward Channing	History	1911
Sinclair Lewis	Letters	1926 (refused)
Samuel F. Bemis	History & Biography	1927 1950
Bernadotte E. Schmitt	History	1931
Archibald MacLeish	Poetry & Drama	1933, 1953 1959
Tyler Dennett	Biography	1934
Felix Morley	Editorial Writing	1936
Ralph Barton Perry	Biography	1936
Thomas L. Stokes	Local Reporting	1959
Ray Slannard Baker	Biography	1940
Carlos Bomulo	Foreign Correspondent	1942
Stephen Bonsal	History	1945
Leo Sowerby	Music	1946
Herbert Elliston	Editorial Writing	1949
Roy Franklin Nichols	History	1949
Herbert L. Block	Cartoon	1942, 1954
Bruce Catton	History	1954
Walter Lippman	Special Citation	1958
Allen Drury	Letters	1960
Arthur Walworth	Biography	1958
Merlo J. Pussey	Biography	1952
J. A. Livingston	Journalism	1965
Herman Wouk	Fiction	1951
William J. White	Biography	1955

3. Biographies of the residents:

Richard H. Townsend (1850-1902) was born in Philadelphia. Around 1892, after his retirement as President of the Erie and Pittsburgh Railroad, he moved to Washington. As stated in The Washington Post, January 11, 1950, Townsend and his wife, the former Mary Scott, commissioned the firm of Carrère and Hastings to rebuild the Hillyer mansion "in the style of the Petit Trianon." Shortly after the house was completed, Townsend fell from a horse, fracturing his skull, and died November 27, 1902. (The Evening Star, 11-28-02)

Mary Scott Townsend (died March 1931), wife of Richard H., was the daughter of Colonel William L. Scott and the former Mary Matilda Tracy, who lived at 22 Jackson Place, N.W., on Lafayette Square, Washington, D.C.. Colonel Scott was a member of Congress (1884-1888) and a railroad and coal executive.

Because of the belief in a story told in childhood that she would encounter evil if she were to live in a totally new house, Mrs. Townsend stipulated that the Hillyer residence (see

202

2121 Massachusetts Avenue, N.W.

photograph) be incorporated into a new structure.("In Haunted Washington" by Rene Bache) It was at her father's home that Mrs. Townsend began corresponding with Frederick Law Olmsted, Jr., about the design of the gardens around her new residence on Massachusetts Avenue. (Olmsted Associates Papers, Job # 296, Manuscripts Division, Library of Congress: letter dated 6-18-00)

After her husband's death in 1902, Mrs. Townsend remained at 2121 Massachusetts Avenue, where she is said to have spent as much as $240,000 a year for lavish entertainment, including food, payroll for 34 servants and their uniforms, and heat and electricity. (Times-Herald, 8-30-49)

Sources: Dumas Malone (ed.), "William L. Scott", Dictionary of American Biography, Vol. III, New York: Charles Scribner's Sons, 1932.

Olmsted Associates - Papers, Job # 296, Manuscript Division, Library of Congress, letter dated 6-18-00.

"In Haunted Washington", Rene Bache. Clipping in binder: "Historic Houses - General Articles", Washingtoniana Room, Martin Luther King Library.

Times-Herald, 8-30-49, 12:1.

Mathilde Townsend (died 1949), daughter of Richard and Mary Townsend, was said to be the richest girl in Washington. Her marriage in 1910 to Senator Peter Goelet Gerry of Rhode Island ended in divorce in 1925. That same year she married Sumner B. Welles, who later was to become the Under Secretary of State for Franklin D. Roosevelt. Mrs. Welles died while vacationing in Switzerland, and shortly thereafter her husband offered the Massachusetts Avenue house for sale.

Source: Times-Herald, 8-30-49, 12:1.

Sumner Benjamin Welles (October 14, 1892 - September 24, 1961) was born in New York City. After he was graduated from Harvard in 1914, he entered the State Department where in 1920 he became Assistant Chief of the Division of Latin American Affairs. In 1933 he served as Ambassador to Cuba, returning that December to his new appointment as Assistant Secretary of State under Cordell Hull. The following May he became Under Secretary of State. Welles kept the Government well-informed during the 1938 Munich crisis and during his fact finding tour of Rome, the Vatican, Berlin, Paris, and London in 1940. In 1941, he "accompanied President Roosevelt to the historic meeting with

2121 Massachusetts Avenue, N.W.

Sir Winston Churchill aboard the battleship Prince of Wales off Newfoundland, that resulted in the Atlantic Charter" (The New York Times, 9-25-61). Due to friction with Cordell Hull, Welles resigned his position in 1943.

Welles is remembered as an architect of the Roosevelt Administration's Good Neighbor Policy with Latin America - also, "as chairman of a State Department committee formed during World War II to outline post war international cooperation plans. Mr. Welles drafted proposals later used in modified form as the basis of the United Nations."(The New York Times, 9-25-61)

His marriage in 1915 to Esther Slater produced two sons and ended in divorce in 1923. In 1925, Welles married Mathilde Scott Townsend, the former Mrs. Gerry; and after her death in 1949, he married Mrs. Harriette Post in 1953. During his retirement, Welles divided his time between Oxon Manor in Oxon Hill, Maryland; 1840 24th Street, N.W. Washington; and his summer residence in Bar Harbor, Maine. Harvard University Press has published several of his books, including:

> Naboth's Vineyard (1928)
> Four Freedoms (1942)
> The Time For Decision (1944)
> Where Are We Headed (1946)
> Seven Decisions that Shaped History (1950)

Sources: Who's Who in The Nation's Capital, 1934-1935, Washington, D.C.: Ransdell Incorporated, 1935.

The New York Times, 9-25-61, 1:6 (obituary).

The New York Times, 9-26-61, 5:3.

The Cosmos Club was founded by John Wesley Powell, a reknowned explorer and scientist, after a meeting on November 16, 1878 with a number of gentlemen sharing similar interests. The auditorium of the present club was dedicated and named in his honor. The Club membership includes distinguished men in the fields of science, literature, and the fine arts.

The club was first located in rented rooms of the Old Corcoran building on 15th Street and Pennsylvania Avenue, N.W. (now demolished). The Club leased the house at 23 Madison Place in December 1882; purchased the Dolley Madison House (number 27) on June 1, 1886 for $40,000; and then bought number 25 Madison Place in 1907. Number 25 and the adjacent house (number 23) were demolished and in 1909-1910; the new building was added in their place. In 1917 further expansion resulted from the purchase of the Benjamin Ogle Tayloe house (now 25 Madison Place). An act of Congress approved March 31, 1930 gave authority to the

Secretary of the Treasury to acquire all private property on Madison Place. In 1940 the Federal Government finally made the purchase after an offer of $1,000,000 was accepted by a full meeting of the Club on March 27, 1940. The buildings were then rented by the Cosmos Club for twelve years, during which time it sought to buy suitable quarters. Property on H Street between 17th and 18th Street, N.W. was subsequently acquired, but problems in obtaining materials in the immediate post war period resulted in inaction.

Finally, in September 1950, the Club bought the Townsend House, which appropriately had been designed by John M. Carrère, a member of the Club from 1905 until his death in 1911. The initial remodeling and subsequent alterations were also carried on by some members of the Club. Horace W. Peaslee, a member from 1926 until his death in 1959, was the architect and Charles H. Tomkins, a member from 1926 until his death in 1956, was the contractor for the 1951 work on the building. The 1961 and 1962 enlargements were handled by architect Frank E. Cole, who joined the Club in 1958, and builder George W. Lipscomb, who joined in 1942.

Source: Paul H. Oehser, "The Cosmos Club of Washington: A Brief History", Records of the Columbia Historical Society of Washington, D.C., 1960-1962, pp. 250-265.

J. Historical Events Connected with the Structure:

As with similar large homes along Massachusetts Avenue, the Townsend residence has known various functions. During the first few weeks of 1933, Mr. and Mrs. Welles acted as hosts to Franklin D. Roosevelt before he entered the White House. In 1941, after the Welles family moved to Oxon Manor, the mansion was considered for use by the British Mission. (Times-Herald, 2-27-41) This apparently never occured, but in January 1942 the American Women's Volunteer Service was allowed to use the stables as a canteen. In 1943 the house was occupied by the Canadian Women's Army Corps Headquarters detachment, and the stables were vacated by the A.W.V.S., who were replaced by "British auxiliary territorials."

In late 1949 Sumner Welles indicated that he would be willing to sell the property. His wife, Mathilde, had died in Switzerland, and he no longer wished to retain the house. The Cosmos Club membership authorized the purchase of the building for $364,635 on January 10, 1950.

Sources: The Cosmos Club Bulletin, Vol. 3, No. 4, February 1950, page 2.

The Evening Star, 1-20-33, 4:2.

2121 Massachusetts Avenue, N.W.

The Washington Daily News, 1-18-33, 21:3.
The Washington Daily News, 1-16-42, 31:1.
Times-Herald, 2-27-41, E 1:3.
Times-Herald, 8-08-43, 3:3.

Hillyer Residence prior to 1898
On Site of Present Club
Courtesy of Columbia Historical Society

CFA photo
Boucher 1970

Entrance Drive
ca. 1950
Courtesy of the Cosmos Club

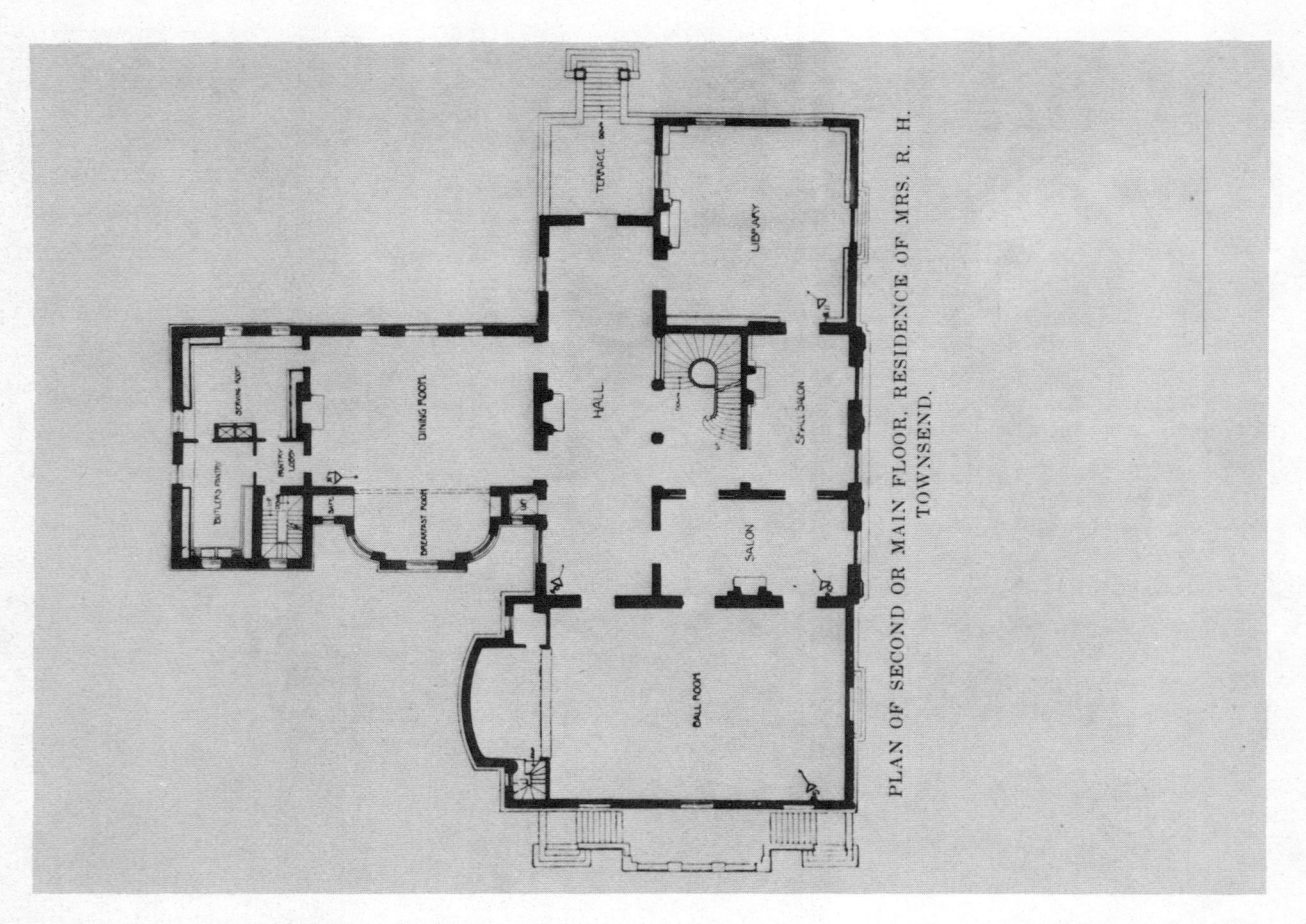

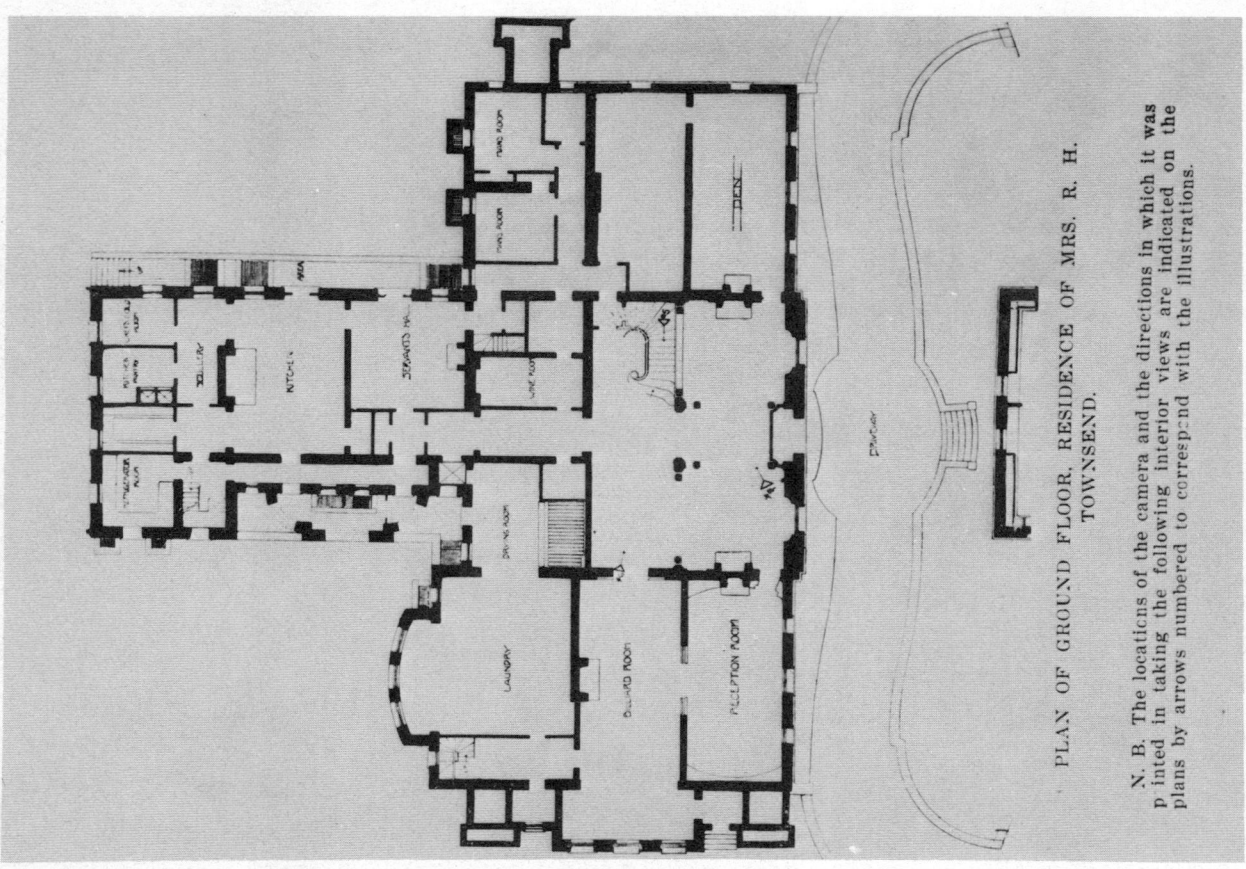

Floor Plans as published in Architectural Record, April 1901, Volume 10

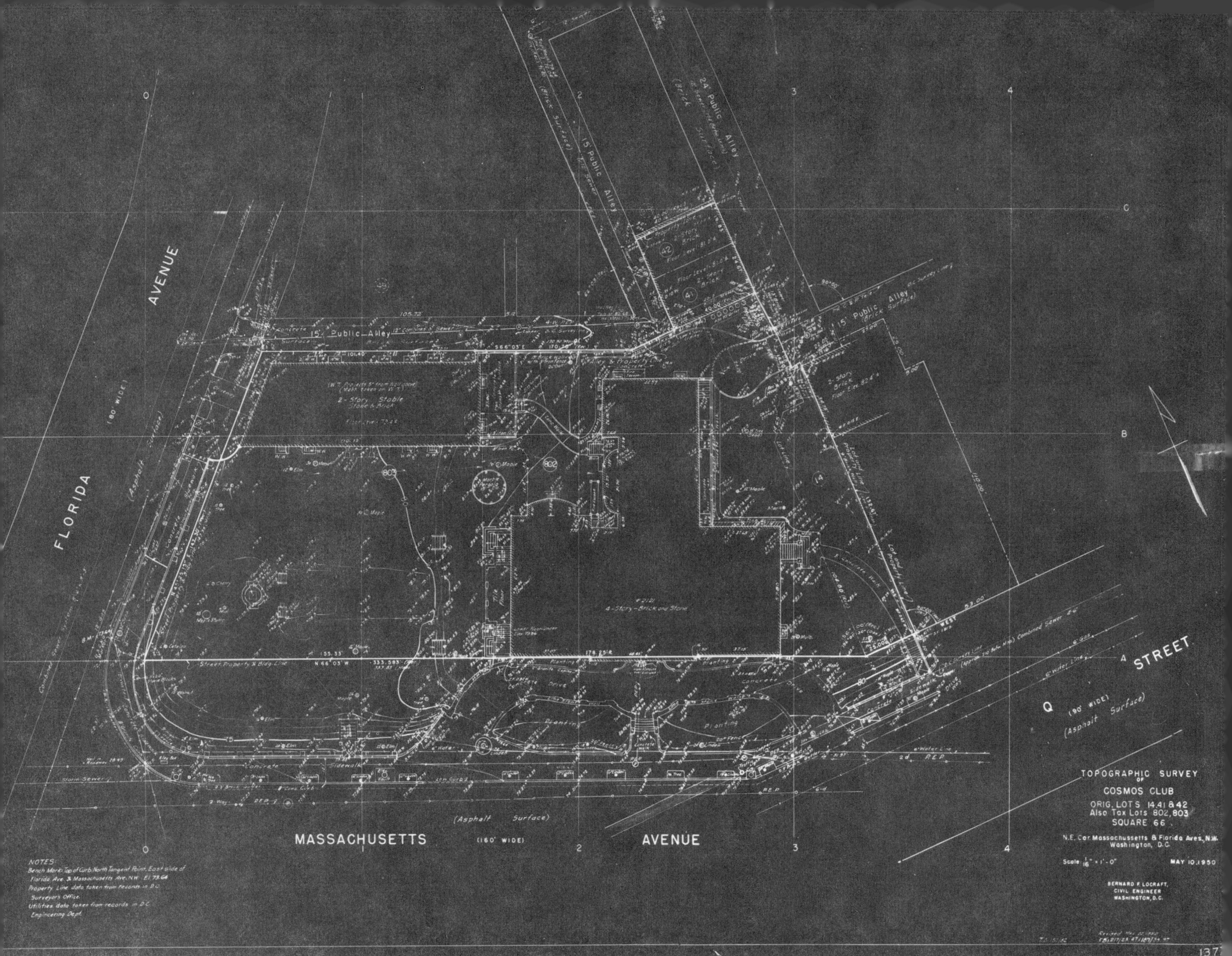
TOPOGRAPHIC SURVEY
OF
COSMOS CLUB
ORIG. LOTS 14, 41 & 42
Also Tax Lots 802, 803
SQUARE 66
N.E. Cor. Massachussetts & Florida Aves. N.W.
Washington, D.C.
Scale 1/16" = 1'-0"
MAY 10, 1950
BERNARD F. LOCRAFT,
CIVIL ENGINEER
WASHINGTON, D.C.
NOTES:
Bench Mark: Top of Curb, North Tangent Point, East side of Florida Ave. & Massachusetts Ave. N.W. El. 73.64
Property Line data taken from records in D.C. Surveyor's Office.
Utilities data taken from records in D.C. Engineering Dept.
MASSACHUSETTS
(160' WIDE)
AVENUE
(Asphalt Surface)
FLORIDA
AVENUE
(80' WIDE)
(Asphalt Surface)
Q
STREET
(90' WIDE)
(Asphalt Surface)
24 Public Alley
(Brick Surface)
15' Public Alley
15' Public Alley
(Brick Surface)
15' Public-Alley
2-Story Stable
Stone & Brick
2-Story Brick
#2121
4-Story-Brick and Stone
Street Property & Bldg. Line
N 66° 03' W
333.593'
155.33'
178.251'
101.40
105.75
110.00'
53.00'
Planting
Concrete
Drive
Sidewalk
Storm Sewer
802
803
14
41
42

SECOND FLOOR PLAN

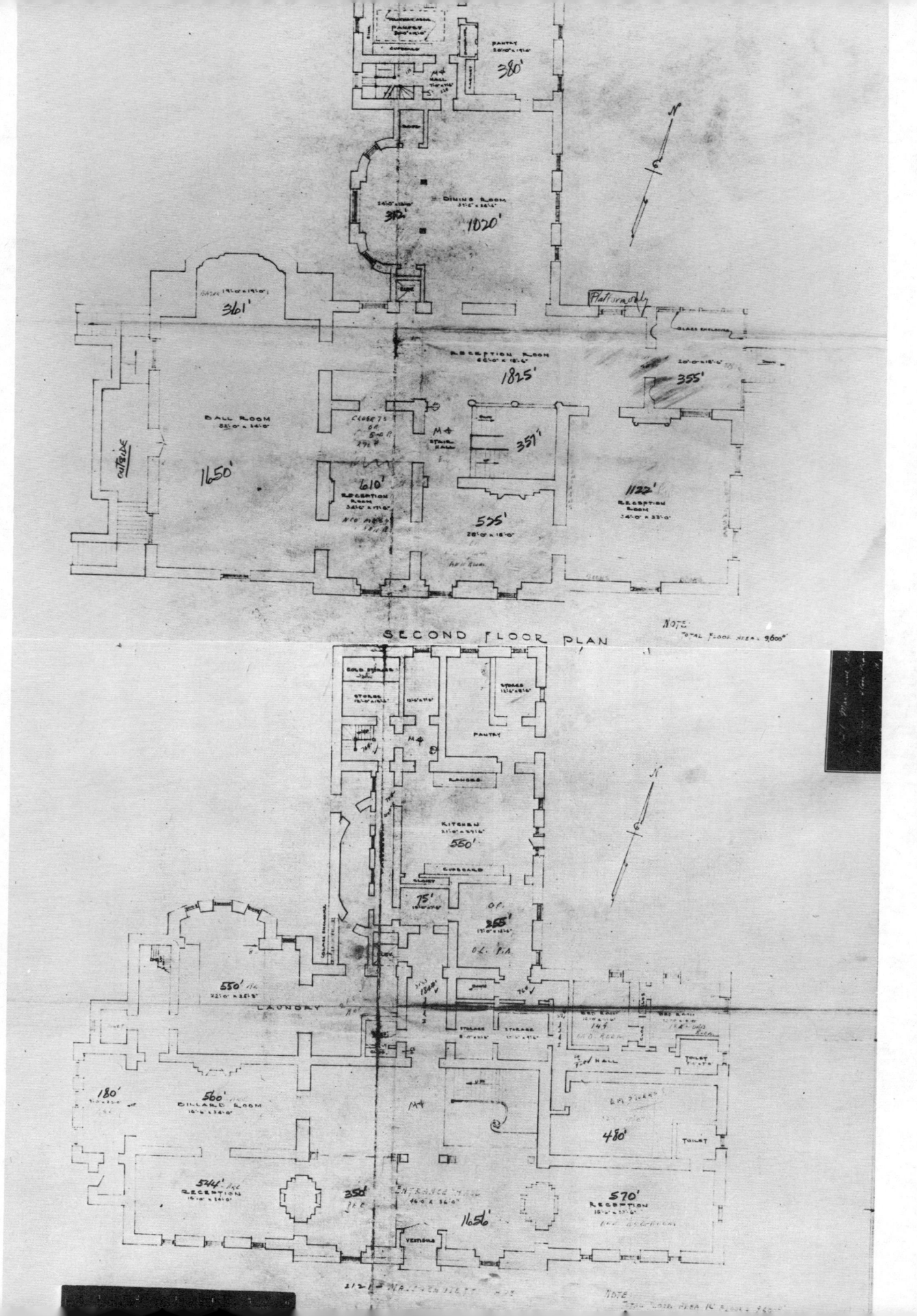

Copy photos of unsigned,
undated drawings
"Proposed Floor Plans
2121 Mass. Ave., N.W.
Bluprint #11"
Courtesy of the Cosmos Club

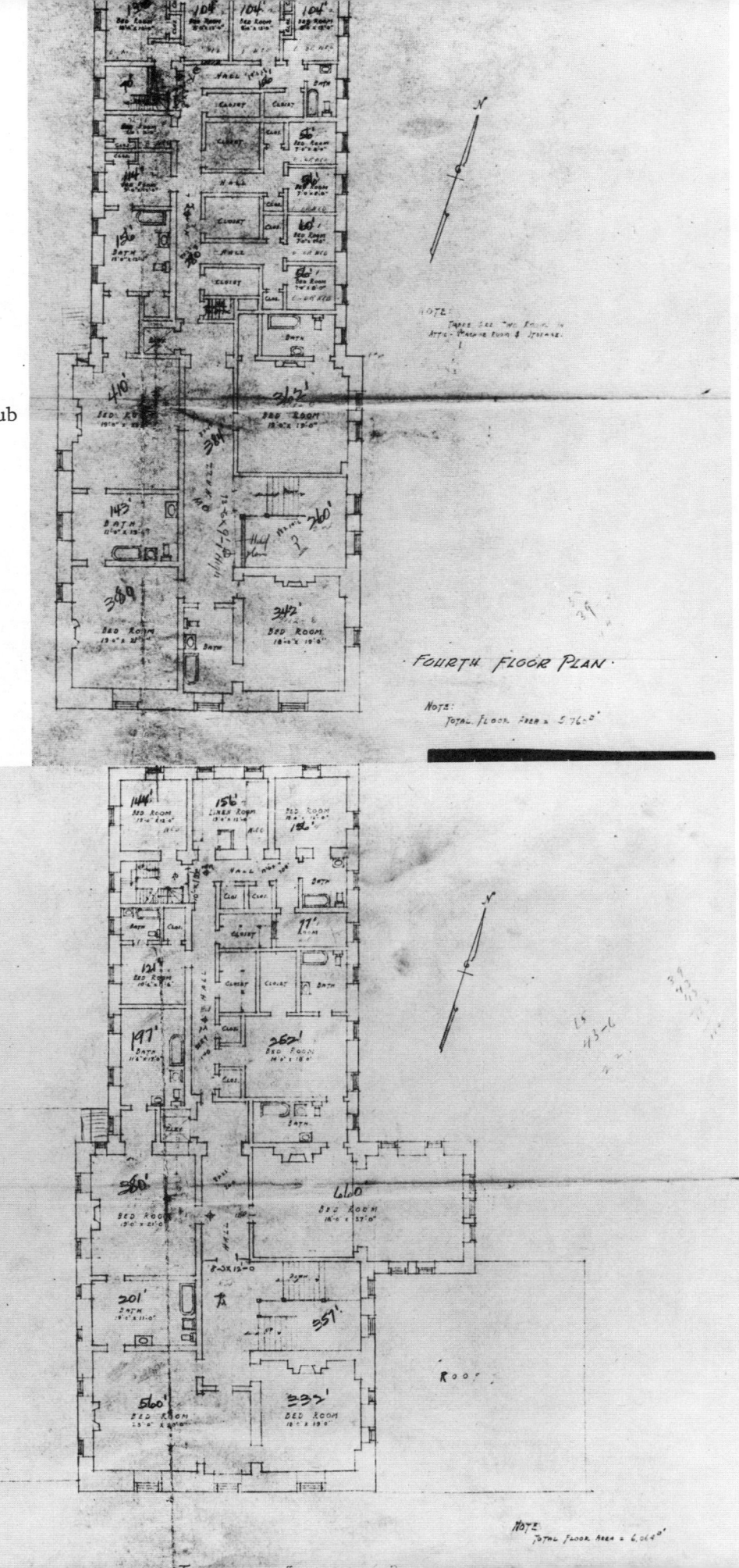

Entrance Hall looking west
ca. 1915
Francis B. Johnston Collection
Library of Congress

Entrance Hall looking east
ca. 1915
Francis B. Johnston Collection
Library of Congress

East Reception Room, ground floor
ca. 1915
Francis B. Johnston Collection, Library of Congress

Anteroom Library (Small Salon)
ca. 1915
Francis B. Johnston Collection, Library of Congress

Library
ca. 1915
Francis B. Johnston Collection
Library of Congress

Library
1971
Courtesy of the National Geographic Society

Detail Library
ca. 1915
Francis B. Johnston Collection, Library of Congress

Detail Library as published in
The Washington Post: 12 January 1950
Courtesy of the Cosmos Club

Dining Room
ca. 1915
Francis B. Johnston Collection
Library of Congress

Opposite
Detail Dining Room
ca. 1915
Francis B. Johnston Collection
Library of Congress

221

Ballroom
ca. 1915
Francis B. Johnston Collection
Library of Congress

222

Opposite
First Floor Reception Room
(Salon)
Francis B. Johnston Collection
Library of Congress

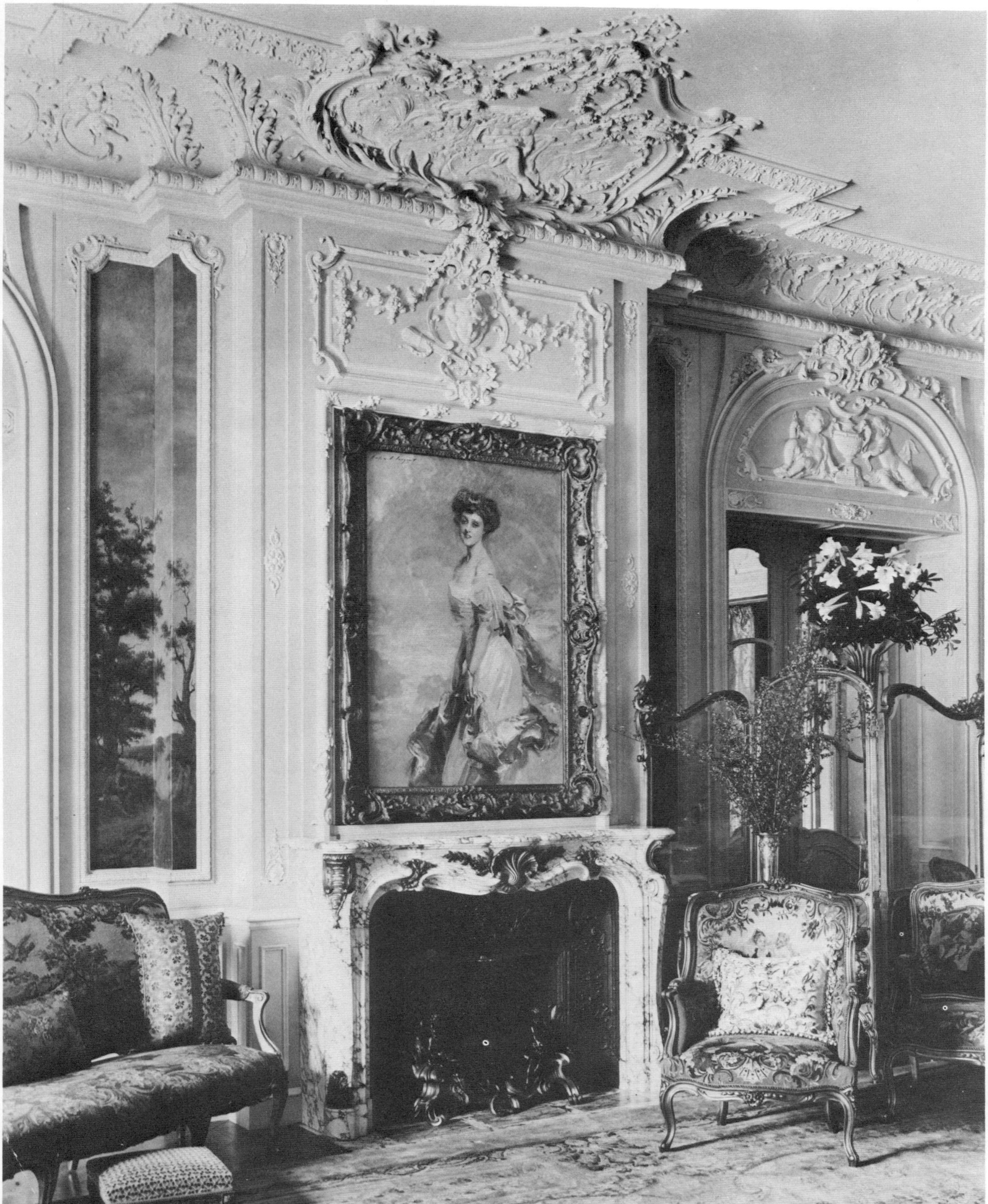

2121 Massachusetts Avenue, N.W.

PART II. ARCHITECTURAL INFORMATION

    A. General Statement:

        1. Architectural character: Incorporating part of the structure of an earlier residence, this detached building in the mid 18th century French manner has eclectic interior details.

        2. Condition: The original building is well maintained despite extensive additions and alterations for semipublic use.

    B. Exterior Description:

        1. Overall dimensions: The three and one half story plus basement structure has flanking two story wings. The three bay central pavilion measures 48'-6" on Massachusetts Avenue and 123'-9 1/2" through the dining room to the north wall of the original pantry. The composite bay wings measure 38'-3 1/2" wide, with the east wing 57'-9 1/2" deep and the west wing 62'-8 1/2".

        2. Foundations: concrete footings and slab.

        3. Wall construction: A granite base to window sill height supports the limestone walls. The rusticated ground floor is capped by a full entablature string course. The frieze is elaborated across the central pavilion while the corona cornice acts as base for a plinth course. The plinth course breaks forward for the two story, fluted, composite pilasters of the central pavilion. The wings have quoines and corner-indented raised panels which flank the central first floor windows and are capped by masks with swags, drapes and pendants.

        4. Structure: brick bearing walls and steel roofing members.

        5. Mechanical: The 1952 Haughton six passenger elevator has a capacity of 1000 pounds. The low pressure steam heating system is produced by paired, gas-fired, International Boiler furnaces installed in 1952. Approximately 60% of the building is centrally cooled by a Carrier Air Conditioning system. The lighting is electric.

        6. Porches, stoops, bulkhead, etc.: Flanking the limestone entrance step are decorative cast iron panels and consoles which support a glazed convex iron marquise with fleur-de-lis fringe and center escutcheons.

        The plinth course is interrupted at the central pavilion openings by decorative cast iron railings, and at the wings by a limestone, urn baluster and block balcony on concave consoles with drape, pendant and rosette.

7. Chimneys: Visible from Massachusetts Avenue are four limestone chimneys, two each at the east and west elevations of the central pavilion.

8. Openings:

    a. Doorways and doors: The glazed double entrance door has cast iron grilles and a rectangular transom with escutcheon and spray grille. The limestone Gibbs surround has a pulvinated bay leaf architrave with a fish scale keystone and floral spray.

    b. Windows: The ground floor, double-hung, four-light windows have decorative cast iron grilles. The central pavilion has ovolo limestone sills. The central windows of the wings are capped by swag panels flanked by the first floor balcony consoles (which interrupt the string course frieze) and by narrower two-light openings.

    The first floor has casement and transom windows with Ionic architraves on a raised ground. The wing bays have plain keystones. The architraves of the central pavilion break upward to encase guilloche panels and are flanked by acanthus consoles, capped by a corona and cyma cornice. The cornice drip moulds curve back toward the wall as the ground for the second floor windows which have crossette, Ionic architraves flanked at the base by scrolls and interrupted at the head by a scrolled keystone and floral swags.

9. Roof:

    a. Shape, covering: The central pavilion has a slate mansard roof, the east and west walls capped by limestone. A pulvinated copper ridge masks the built-up roofing. The wings each have a slate curb roof, the built-up roofing separated by a pulvinated copper ridge with copper escutcheons at each hip.

    b. Cornice, eaves: Interrupted by the second floor window heads, the entablature architrave and frieze break forward over each pilaster. The composite entablature supports an urn-balustered parapet with raised panel blocks centered over each pilaster. The wings have a cavetto and cyma cornice which supports a raised panel balustrade, pierced by oval guilloche bays.

    c. Cupolas, towers, dormers: The casement dormers over the central pavilion rise above a low attic wall behind the balustrade. Each have a blind fan, a torus architrave with keystone, and a segmental hood flanked by scrolls.

C. Interior Description:

1. Floor plans: The ground floor vestibule breaks forward into the entrance hall which is the width of the central pavilion. The entrance hall, containing the main stair, is flanked by the southeast reception room (now partitioned for offices), a northeast storage chamber (now additional offices), the southwest reception room (now the ladies' lounge) and the northwest billiard room (now the ladies' entrance hall). At the north the laundry, storage, kitchen, pantry and servants' rooms have been greatly altered by additions and remodeling to accomodate present needs. (See original plan.)

   The first floor central stair hall was open (now closed) to the rectangular reception hall at the north. The stair and reception hall gave access to the ballroom in the west wing, the library and conservatory (now enclosed) in the east wing, the reception and anterooms at the south, and the dining room and pantries at the north. (See original plan.) Note that due to the location of the stair, reception hall and dining room, the axis has shifted slightly to the east of the facade center line.

   The principal bedrooms occupy the second and third floors, with the major suites to the south and the third floor servants' quarters to the north.

2. Spaces: (This section is illustrated through photographs taken by Francis Benjamin Johnston prior to 1920. Any comments which indicate changes in the spaces are based on the same collection.)

   Entrance hall: (painted white. Opposite the centered vestibule at the south are paired piers and grey-veined, white marble, Ionic columns. The columns and piers serve as a screen which helps to divide the entrance hall into six bays. See photographs.)

   a. Flooring: grey-veined, white marble squares laid diagonally within a green-veined, black marble border. (A seven inch high marble stairway platform has been removed.)

   b. Baseboard: 9", stone plinth course with torus cap.

   c. Walls: raised plaster panels in rosette-indented and plain, fascia and cavetto mouldings.

   d. Cornice: Carried across the piers on an east and west beam the cornice has a running dog frieze and an egg and dart moulding, both divided into sections by swag and guttae consoles, capped by continuous corona, astragal

2121 Massachusetts Avenue, N.W.

and acanthus talon courses. Dividing the space into six bays are two additional beams, not as deep as the cornice described above, having egg and dart, corona, astragal and acanthus courses.

e. Ceiling: 14'-0" high, plaster painted white.

f. Doorways and doors: The modern, glazed, double door from the vestibule has a transom and side lights with decorative cast iron grilles. The natural wood, single doors flanking the east and west chimney walls each have a single carved panel capped by a plaster frieze, a cyma cornice and a decorative urn tablet. All doorways have been closed except those to the vestibule and at the southeast. The doorway to the billiard room (present ladies' entrance hall) has been removed and filled in. The north wall casement opening on axis with the vestibule gives access to the service area and the modern, ground floor dining rooms.

g. Heating: The east and west wall chimneys, with identical mantles, each have a green-veined, black marble hearth and a cast iron firebox with a cherub and spray back panel, and flambeau and spray sides. The plaster mantles, in the Louis XIV manner (4'-11" wide by 5'-8" high), each have a pulvinated bay leaf surround and an ogee frieze interrupted by a pink marble, central roundel with hood and scrolls. The shelf is divided into three sections: the cavetto ends supported decorative urns, the elevated center a classical bust.

East reception room: (painted light grey. The west mantle and the original brocatelle have been removed. Low partitioning divides the room into offices. See photograph.)

a. Flooring: common 2" hardwood, parquetry border.

b. Baseboard: 6 1/2", wood with torus cap.

c. Dado: raised panels in cyma moulding.

d. Chairrail: wood, bead, fascia and block.

e. Walls: applied fascia and cyma mouldings. Ionic pilasters with plain plinths, torus and astragal bases and decorative stop fluting flank the west wall chimney and east window. The pilasters divide the north and south walls into single bays flanked by pairs of smaller bays.

f. Cornice: The full entablature has a narrow architrave of talon, a plain frieze, and an egg and dart, corona and talon cornice.

g. Ceiling: 14'-0" high, plaster painted light grey.

h. Doorways and doors: To the left of the west wall chimney is a door of raised panels in ovolo mouldings set within a raised panel jamb. The west bay of the north wall has a door of raised panels in ovolo mouldings within an ovolo architrave flanked by pilasters. Both doors are capped by an urn and rinceau plaster panel.

i. Hardware: brass door handles with mortise lock escutcheons.

j. Lighting: three-light sconces removed.

k. Heating: The west wall, white marble chimney mantle has been removed. The semicircular-arched overmantle mirror within a bound bay leaf moulding is capped by a floral wreath with floral swags attached to acanthus spandrels. Flanking the mirror are floral panels.

West reception room: (present ladies' lounge: no longer accessible from entrance hall.)

a. Flooring: carpeted.

b. Baseboard: 3 1/2", wood.

c. Dado: The rosette-indented, raised panels are natural wood with gilded mouldings and additional painted graining.

d. Chairrail: 2'-11" high, wood with beading.

e. Walls: gold silk over padding. The east chimney wall breaks forward.

f. Cornice: The full entablature has a talon architrave, a gilded rinceau frieze on a grey ground, and an egg and dart cornice.

g. Ceiling: The plaster ceiling is divided into three linear bays by shallow beams with bead and talon mouldings. Each panel is centered by a decorative plaster moulding in the late 18th century manner.

h. Doorways and doors: The permanently closed, wood, single door (southeast) to the entrance hall has a gilded guilloche lock rail. This door and the casement opening to the former billiard room each have a fascia and gilded cyma architrave capped by a panel of gilded wreath, flambeau and sprays with scroll terminals, and a cyma, corona and talon cornice.

i. Hardware: brass, rocaille door handle (southeast) and panelled mortise lock escutcheon.

2121 Massachusetts Avenue, N.W.

j. Lighting: There are six, two-light, ribbon and tassel, brass sconces with scrolled flambeau arms.

k. Heating: The east wall chimney has a green-veined, black marble hearth with white rectangular insets and a cast iron lattice firebox with classical frieze surround. The green-veined, black marble mantle (4'-5" wide by 3'-7" high) has flanking consoles with brass leaf caps, a frieze centered by an oval brass panel and broken back over either console, and a cavetto shelf. The crossette frame of the beveled overmantle mirror has brass swags and a wood tablet cap with brass keystone and sprays.

<u>Billiard room</u>: (painted white. Now the ladies' entrance hall. Remodeled to accomodate present function. Doorway to main entrance hall is closed and new passage opened at northeast.)

a. Flooring: basket weave parquetry.

b. Baseboard: 7", wood with cyma cap.

c. Chairrail: 2'-7 1/2" high, leafy pulvination.

d. Walls: plaster with applied mouldings of bound "bachelor-buttons."

e. Cornice: egg and dart, fascia, tassel, astragal, talon, corona and talon.

f. Ceiling: The plaster ceiling is divided into three bays of north to south beams edged by a palmette talon moulding.

g. Doorways and doors: The 8'-0" high doorway openings at the northeast, northwest and south are flanked by panelled Tuscan pilasters capped by an entablature broken forward over either pilaster. The west entrance, post and lintel archway has paired Tuscan pilasters capped by acanthus consoles which support paired beams.

h. Lighting: Flanking the south doorway are two-light, brass cornucopia sconces.

i. Heating: The north wall chimney has a white marble hearth, and a cast iron firebox with an escutcheon back panel and fleur-de-lis surround. The white marble mantle (5'-11" wide by 5'-11" high) has panelled pedestals with fluted acanthus consoles capped by acanthus scrolls which support a guilloche moulding, a griffin, cherub and wreath frieze, and an egg and dart, dentil and cyma shelf.

2121 Massachusetts Avenue, N.W.

Stairway:

Within the main entrance hall, the stair ascends eight risers (7" high) north to the first landing and seventeen risers west to the first floor. The stringer soffit panel of plaster is rosette-indented. The risers and treads are limestone. The cast iron railing of wreath, flambeau and spray terminates at the base in a scroll and at the first floor in a panelled marble newel, tapered at the base and supporting a bronze of the "Four Muses" in turn capped by a single, six-light, brass candelabrum. The stair continues to the second and third floors.

First floor reception room: (painted pale blue with grey trim. Mid 18th century Germanic manner. The decorative panels over the doors and the east mirror, the allegorical scenes in the ceiling cove and the run-plaster work (except over the mantle, the mirror, the south window and at the ceiling corners) have been removed. See photograph.)

a. Flooring: herringbone parquetry.

b. Baseboard: 6 1/2", wood with ovolo cap.

c. Dado: wood panels formed by applied cyma moulding.

d. Chairrail: 3'-0" high, wood ovolo.

e. Walls: painted panels of bucolic scenes in rocaille ovolo mouldings. The east wall breaks forward slightly for a chairrail to cornice mirror.

f. Cornice: plaster, with a fascia and enriched lip architrave and a decorative rocaille cove terminated by a pulvinated moulding.

g. Ceiling: 14'-9" high, plaster painted white.

h. Doorways and doors: The rocaille mirror-paned, double doors flanking the west chimney wall to the ballroom are permanently closed. The doors have been brought forward flush with the wall. Each doorway, capped by a three-point-arched panel, has a bolection architrave and floral escutcheon key with rocaille sprays.

i. Windows: Interrupting the baseboard, the floor length window has a three-point-arched, ovolo architrave, recessed for drapes.

j. Lighting: There are six, five-light, brass, rocaille sconces.

k. Heating: The west wall chimney has a white, grey and tan-veined marble hearth with grey rectangular insets, and a cast iron firebox with a cherub and flambeau back panel, lattice sides and a concave, rinceau surround. The rocaille, cream marble mantle (5'-7" wide by 4'-0" high) has a curvilinear architrave, centered by a gilded shell and flanked by splayed consoles with gilded caps. The bundled ogee overmantle moulding originally contained a Sargent portrait capped by a mask-centered rocaille panel with floral swags and pendants.

<u>Anteroom to library</u>: (The original brocatelle has been replaced by pale blue rosette-indented panels in gilded talon mouldings on a raised ground. The pulvinated guilloche frieze has been replaced by a flat rinceau frieze. The swags joining the semicircular arch spandrels and the keystone of the overmantle mirror have been removed. The bound acanthus leaf doorway architraves have been replaced by a egg and dart crossette moulding. The overdoor crescent-shaped rocaille canvasses and frames have been replaced by tablets with end scrolls and rectangular canvasses in plain frames. See photograph.)

a. Flooring: herringbone parquetry.

b. Baseboard: 6 1/2", wood with ovolo cap.

c. Dado: flat wood panels in ovolo moulding.

d. Chairrail: 2'-7" high, wood ovolo.

e. Walls: plaster with applied panel mouldings, painted. The north wall chimney breaks forward.

f. Cornice: The full entablature has a fascia architrave with astragal and gadroon, a rinceau frieze and an egg and dart, corona and talon cornice.

g. Ceiling: 14'-9" high, plaster painted white with bundled reed border.

h. Doorways and doors: The east and west wall single casement openings (8'-9" high) each have an egg and dart, crossette architrave capped by a spray frieze with scroll terminals and a bucolic panel canvas. (A northwest doorway with a similar architrave has been closed to the stair hall.)

i. Windows: Interrupting the baseboard, the floor length windows each have a three-point arch with leaf and spray spandrels and a pulvinated bay leaf architrave, recessed for drapes.

j. Lighting: There are six, five-light, brass sconces, each with flambeau base and reeded, volute arms.

k. Heating: The north wall chimney has a white marble hearth with grey rectangular insets, and a cast iron firebox with an allegorical rocaille back panel, lattice sides and a concave rocaille surround. The white marble mantle (5'-9" wide by 4'-1" high) has flanking columns tapered toward the base, with decorative stop fluting and arrow shaft brass capitals which support a rocaille frieze of ribbon, bow and vine, brass applique, broken forward as rosettes over either column. The overmantle mirror is capped by a gilded, semicircular-arched putti panel and framed within decorative pulvination broken by a gilded, scrolled keystone. The chimney mantle and mirror are flanked by gilded ribbon, spray and floral pendant panels.

Library: (The plain ground of the chairrail and the original acanthus leaf bookcase caps have been replaced by gadrooning. The decorative platform over the central sections have been removed. The original brocatelle has been replaced by wood panels. The carved library table is now in the ballroom. The window at the right of the chimney has been replaced by a door. The north wall wood mantle of male terms, marquetry frieze, segmental back panel and flanking composite pilasters has been replaced. See photographs.)

a. Flooring: basket weave parquetry.

b. Baseboard: 6", ovolo cap.

c. Bookcase: built-in and broken forward from the walls. The central section of the east, west and south wall bookcases are separated by panelled, composite pilasters from the lower (5'-9" high), flanking bays which are capped by a gadrooned moulding.

d. Walls: panels formed by applied cyma mouldings.

2121 Massachusetts Avenue, N.W.

    e. Cornice: The fascia cornice has dentil, astragal and egg and dart mouldings of plaster painted to simulate wood.

    f. Ceiling: 14'-9" high, plaster. The ceiling has geometric rinceau panels, painted white and separated by wood beams with plaster crossing bosses and talon edging, painted to simulate wood.

    g. Doorways and doors: The 8'-9" high doorway openings to the anteroom and the conservatory, and the door at the west of the north wall mantle (the doors replaced by bookshelves), are capped by a decorative escutcheon panel and encased in a floor to cornice ovolo architrave.

    h. Windows: Interrupting the baseboard, the floor length windows each have an ovolo architrave, recessed for drapes, with a three-point arch and flambeau spandrels.

    i. Hardware: brass door handles with lattice escutcheon.

    j. Lighting: The four-light sconces have been removed.

    k. Heating: (original mantle replaced by following) The north wall chimney has a grey marble hearth and a cast iron firebox with an allegorical back panel, fleur-de-lis side panels and a concave strapwork surround. The plaster mantle in the 16th century manner is 10'-0" wide by 6'-5" high. It has flanking plinths and cluster columns with decorative shafts which support a fascia architrave, a wreath and rinceau frieze, and an egg and dart, corona and cyma shelf. The overmantle, an additional 5'-4" high, is terminated at the ends by candelabra pilasters with cherub capitals. Between the pilasters are two roundel panels centered by dragons, separated by decorative flambeau and capped by a shell and cherub frieze, and a talon, astragal, dentil and talon cornice. (Photographs in the possession of the Cosmos Club indicate this mantle to be a plaster copy of the original found at the Chateau of Blois.)

Reception hall: (natural oak. Divided into three linear bays by beams and pilasters broken forward from the south wall. The central south wall bay originally opened over the main stair. The space between the pilasters and balustrade has been filled in.)

    a. Flooring: basket weave parquetry.

    b. Baseboard: 7 1/2", quarter-round cap.

    c. Dado: panels formed by cyma moulding.

d. Chairrail: 3'-4" high, cyma.

e. Walls: The dado and similar wall panels are separated by floor to cornice, fluted Corinthian pilasters (the plaster capitals painted to simulate wood.)

f. Cornice: The full entablature has an egg and dart architrave, a plain frieze interrupted by paired brackets, and a corona and talon cornice. This extends across the ceiling beams. The mouldings are plaster, painted to simulate wood.

g. Ceiling: 14'-9" high, plaster painted white with pulvinated border moulding and a leafy fixture rosette centered in each bay.

h. Doorways and doors: The two doors in either end bay and those flanking the north wall chimney each have a bolection architrave with a cyma reversa, corona and cyma cornice, capped by a panel centered with a decorative roundel plaque and sprays.

i. Lighting: Each bay has a nine-light, single tier, gilded plaster, rocaille chandelier with grape pendant.

j. Heating: The north wall chimney has a white-veined, purple marble hearth with grey rectangular insets, and a cast iron firebox with a concave gouge surround. The white-veined, purple marble mantle in the manner of Louis XIV is 6'-11" wide by 5'-10" high. It has an ovolo architrave flanked by consoles each capped by a brass acanthus leaf and swags. The consoles support an inverted cyma frieze, centered by a brass rocaille mask with sprays, and terminated by brass acanthus leaves. The shelf is of cyma and corona.

Dining room: (original brocatelle panels replaced by wood. Plaster mouldings painted to simulate wood. See photographs.)

a. Flooring: basket weave parquetry.

b. Baseboard: 6", wood with quarter-round cap.

c. Dado: raised wood panels in cyma moulding.

d. Chairrail: 3'-4 1/2" high, wood ovolo.

e. Buffet: The south wall maroon and white marble buffet (8'-4" wide by 3'-6" high) has paired consoles with brass lion mask applique which support the serving counter. The marble splash board, an additional 3'-1" high, has scroll terminals and a centered brass mask and leaf cap.

f. Walls: flush panels in ovolo moulding with rocaille corners. The west alcove is separated from the main space by a screen of two pairs of composite columns and pilasters all with decorative stop fluting. The north chimney, the south buffet and the openings within the main space are flanked by similar composite pilasters.

g. Cornice: The full entablature has a talon, astragal and egg and leaf architrave, a plain frieze, and an ovolo, astragal, corona, shell talon and fascia cornice.

h. Ceiling: The west alcove columns have acanthus modillions which support panelled beams. The beams divide the main ceiling into three bays of frescoed plaster panels. The cornice is carried around each bay.

i. Doorways and doors: The 9'-0" high openings each have a decorative, three-point arch frieze and bolection architrave.

j. Hardware: The brass, baroque door handles have mortise lock lattice escutcheons, two inches wide by 1'-8" high.

k. Lighting: There are twelve, five-light, brass, baroque sconces each with a term, swag and mask base from which the arms spring.

l. Heating: Above the north wall door within the alcove, is a heating duct covered by a lattice grille centered with duck, leaf and ribbon, bronze applique (a wood panel above the opposing wall door is centered by a similar decorative motif).

The north wall chimney has a maroon marble hearth with black rectangular insets, and a cast iron firebox with an allegorical rocaille back panel, lattice sides, and a decorative concave surround. The white-veined, maroon marble mantle (7'-11" wide by 5'-0" high) has an ovolo architrave and flanking, panelled pilaster piers, capped by consoles which support a pulvinated frieze and an ovolo, corona and ovolo shelf. (The photograph shows the original brass applique which has been removed.)

Ballroom: (painted soft grey with gilding. The double doors to the reception room have been replaced by lighted cabinets. The chandeliers have been removed. See photographs.)

a. Flooring: basket weave parquetry.

b. Baseboard: 6 1/4", wood with quarter-round cap.

c. Dado: raised, corner-indented, wood panels in ovolo moulding.

d. Chairrail: 3'-3 1/2" high, wood ovolo.

e. Walls: Above the chairrail are rocaille panels which alternate between semicircular-arched openings and mirrors. At the arch impost block, the walls are divided by a fascia and ovolo course, interrupted above each panel by gilded rocaille urns, the floral sprays and clusters centered in an additional line of rocaille panels. Above the chairrail the semicircular-arched mirrors each have gilded applique and a floor to cornice fascia and bolection architrave with a gilded escutcheon and ribbon cap. Composite pilasters with decorative stop fluting, frame the central musicians' alcove which breaks back from the north wall.

f. Cornice: The egg and dart architrave and panel frieze is interrupted by elaborate, paired scrolls over the musicians' alcove pilasters. Above the frieze are astragal, cavetto and pulvinated mouldings capped by a decorative rocaille cove. Within the cove and centered above each wall, is a lunette flanked by dragons. At the ceiling corners similar devices are flanked by putti. The cove is terminated by bound leaf pulvination.

g. Ceiling: plaster. A border of applied mouldings surrounds three recessed ceiling bays. The north and south bays each have an elliptical rocaille panel edged by a roll moulding and bordered by lattice spandrels. The center bay of bundled-reed and pulvination supported by a bracketed cove centered with lunettes and masks, frames a round allegorical canvas which has a pulvinated surround and lattice spandrels.

h. Doorways and doors: The doors and either panel flanking the musicians' alcove, have semicircular arches with rose tinted paintings in rocaille lunettes. The doorways and windows have fascia and bolection architraves with gilded escutcheons and ribbon caps.

i. Hardware: brass rocaille window cranks and knobs.

j. Lighting: There are twelve, five-light, crystal pendant and bead, brass sconces with reeded rocaille arms.

D. Site:

1. Setting and orientation: The building faces south on Massachusetts Avenue within an angular lot measuring 358'-7" at the south; 147'-4" at the west (intersection of Massachusetts Avenue, Florida Avenue and 22nd Street); 232'-7" at the north (alley); and 170'-3" at the east.

2. Enclosures: Flanking either wing and broken forward so as to line the rear of the semielliptical driveway, are rusticated and stepped, limestone garden walls, each stepped segment centered by a raised panel. Mask and griffin vases terminate the walls at the driveway entrances. Lining the front of the drive is an oval guilloche, limestone balustrade terminated by scrolls. At the west, the property is enclosed by a retaining wall which supports an 8'-0" high decorative wrought iron fence.

3. Outbuildings: The rectangular, brick carriage house at the northwest (presently the auditorium at 2170 Florida Avenue) retains its 4'-0" high random ashlar granite base and ten inch limestone water table. The original slate mansard roof has been removed and replaced by a full height, second story.

4. Walks: Granite curbing lines the semielliptical entrance driveway and public sidewalk. Six granite risers flanked by oval guilloche and scroll, limestone balustrades on granite bases are on axis with the entrance door from Massachusetts Avenue. The original configuration of the west garden walks has been altered.

5. Landscaping: Though correspondence between Mrs. Townsend and the Olmsted Brothers of Brookline, Massachusetts, is extant, it is not known how much of the original landscaping (if anything) was designed by that firm. In 1952, the remodeling architect, Horace Peaslee, was forced to destroy part of the grounds for the club additions and parking facilities. The present plantings include azaelea, juniper, elm, wysteria, dogwood and magnolia.

2200 MASSACHUSETTS AVENUE, N.W., WASHINGTON, D.C.

CFA photo
Boucher 1970

Location: 2200 Massachusetts Avenue, N.W., Washington, D.C.; on the south side of Massachusetts Avenue, and bordered by 22nd Street (formerly Boundary Street) and Que Street.

Present Owner: Grand Duchy of Luxembourg

Present Occupant: Grand Duchy of Luxembourg

Present Use: Embassy residence

Statement of Significance: This limestone structure in the Louis XV manner is skillfully balanced with Louis XVI details. The building conforms to an irregular-shaped lot, which is defined by Massachusetts Avenue, Que Street, 22nd Street, and the west party line. Each street elevation is treated as a major facade. Those on the avenue and 22nd Street act together as a focal point for the convergence of the thoroughfares. Occupied as a residence throughout its history, the house and its original service facilities remain unchanged.

PART I. HISTORICAL INFORMATION

A. Lot and Square:

The building is located in Square 2511, lot 38 (formerly lot 38 in Block 5, "Kalorama Heights").

B. Original and Subsequent Owners:

The following chain of title to the property shows the owners of the present structure and of any known preceding structures on the site:

1907   Deed March 5, 1907, recorded May 15, 1907 in
Liber 3073 folio 259

Katherine Medill McCormick
         To
Isabel Anderson

"...Lot...(38) in James B. Nicholson's Subdivision of lots in Block...(5) 'Kalorama Heights', as per plat recorded in Liber County No. 9 folio 102 of the Records of the Office of the Surveyor of the District of Columbia..."

1908   Deed February 8, 1908, recorded February 10, 1908 in
        Liber 3137 folio 104

        Isabel Anderson et vir
              To
        Margaret Gray Stewart

        "This Deed made...by and between Isabel Anderson (acting and
        contracting in relation to her sole and separate estate) and
        Larz Anderson, her husband, of the District of Columbia,
        parties of the first part, and Margaret Gray Stewart of the
        District of Columbia, party of the second part, for and in
        consideration of the sum of Twenty Thousand (20,000) Dollars
        to them paid by the party of the second part, do hereby grant
        and convey...Lot...(38) in James B. Nicholson's subdivision
        of part of Block...(5) 'Kalorama Heights'..."

1931   Deed May 26, 1931, recorded June 8, 1931 in
        Liber 6564 folio 255

        Helen S. De Vore
              To
        Mary E. Stewart

        Lot 38 in James B. Nicholson's Subdivision of part of Block
        5, "Kalorama Heights":"...now known for purposes of taxation
        as Lot 38, Square 2511. Also parts of Lots...(19),...(20),
        and...(21), in Block...(3), 'Kalorama Heights'..now known
        for purposes of taxation as Lot 813, Square 2510...The
        interest hereby intended to be conveyed being the one-half
        undivided interest in said described properties which the
        said party of the first part inherited as one of the two
        heirs-at-law of Margaret G. Stewart..."

1941   Deed March 5, 1941, recorded March 8, 1941 in
        Liber 7578 folio 222

        Mary E. Stewart
              To
        H.R.H. The Grand Duchess of Luxembourg

        Lot 38, Square 2511."...for and in consideration of the sum
        of Forty thousand (40,000) Dollars..."

1962   Deed March 12, 1962, recorded March 15, 1962 in
        Liber 11767 folio 236

2200 Massachusetts Avenue, N.W.

      H.R.H. Charlotte, The Grand Duchess of Luxembourg
     and H.R.H. Prince Felix of Luxembourg, her husband
          To
     The Government of Luxembourg

     "Witnesseth, That in consideration of $160,000 Dollars the parties of the first part do grant unto the party of the second part...Lot 38, Block 5,'Kalorama Heights'..."

     Source: Recorder of Deeds, Washington, D.C.

C. Date of Erection:

The building was begun in 1908 and completed in 1909.

D. Building Permits:

The applications for the following building permits were filed by the architect, contractor or owner's agent and provide significant data:

No. 2811, March 24, 1908
Permit to build dwelling
    Owner: Alexander Stewart
    Architect: Bruce Price and de Sibour
    Builder: George A. Fuller Co.
    Estimated cost: $92,000.

Filed with No. 2811, March 24, 1908
Application for Building Projections, No. 69748, February 12, 1908
    1 area: 6' X 4' (on Mass. Ave.)
    2 areas: 7'-6" X 4' (on Mass. Ave.)
    1 area: 14'-6" X 4' (on Mass. Ave.)
    2 areas: 6' X 4' (on 22nd St.)
    1 area: 6' X 4' (on Que St.)
    1 area: 40' X 4' (on Que St.)
    1 porch: 16' X 4" (on Mass. Ave.)
    Steps to main entrance: 10' X 7' (on Mass. Ave.)

No. 3229, April 20, 1908
Permit for Hoisting Engine

No. 4156, June 25, 1908
Permit to erect one electric passenger elevator
    Owner: Alexander Stewart
    Mechanic: Otis Elevator Co.
    Dimensions: 4'-2" X 3'-6"
    Estimated cost: $2780.

2200 Massachusetts Avenue, N.W.

Source: D.C. Government, Department of Economic Development, Bureau of Licenses and Permits, Central Files.

E. Alterations and Additions:

No significant changes have been made.

F. Architect: J. H. de Sibour (Bruce Price & de Sibour, New York City)

See biography of J. H. de Sibour under 1700 Massachusetts Avenue.

G. Known Plans, Drawings and Elevations, etc.:

Elevation and plan of elevator. Blueprint.
Filed with Permit No. 4156, June 25, 1908
    Elevation: scale 1/2" = 1'
    Plan: scale 1" = 1'
    Otis Elevator Co.

"Plan showing Projection of Entrance areas, etc."
Ink on linen. Scale 1/8" = 1'
Filed with Permit No. 2811, March 24, 1908
    "Bruce Price & de Sibour, Architects
    1133 Broadway, New York"

H. Important Old Views: none found.

I. Residents:

1. City and telephone directories list the following tenants:

1910-1912	Alexander Stewart
1913-1916	Mrs. Margaret G. Stewart
1917-1918	Vacant
1919-1920	Mrs. Alexander Stewart, widow
1921-1932	Mrs. Margaret Stewart
1933-1937	Mrs. Mary E. Stewart
1938-1941	Vacant
1942-1955	Luxembourg Legation (residence and chancery)
1956-1972	Luxembourg Embassy (from 1962 residence only)

2. The following residents were included in volumes of <u>The Elite List: A Compilation of Selected Names of Residents of Washington City, D.C. and Ladies Shopping Guide</u>:

2200 Massachusetts Avenue, N.W.

    1909-1911   Mr. and Mrs. Alexander Stewart
                    Miss Mary Stewart
                    Miss Stewart

    1913   Mrs. Alexander Stewart

    1914-1918   Mrs. Alexander Stewart
                    Miss Mary Stewart
                    Miss Helen G. Stewart

    1924   Col. and Mrs. Daniel B. Devore

3.   Biographies of the residents:

<u>Alexander Stewart</u> was born in the Province of New Brunswick, Canada on September 12th, 1829. In 1849 he moved to Wausau, Wisconsin where he was employed by a small lumber company. He rose to manager and eventually, through investments, gained control of "a great deal of lumber land in Wisconsin and Michigan" and some of the western states. (<u>The Washington Post</u>, 5-25-12) Active in politics, Stewart was a delegate to the 1884 Republican National Convention; and from 1895 through 1901, he served three terms as a United States Congressman from Wisconsin.

In 1908 his wife, Margaret Gray Stewart, purchased a lot at 2200 Massachusetts Avenue for $20,000. Shortly afterwards, Alexander Stewart was issued a permit to build a $92,000 residence on this site.

May 24, 1912 Mr. Stewart died at his home - leaving his wife, Margaret, and three daughters: Mrs. Margaret Lindsay, Miss Mary Stewart, and Miss Helen G. Stewart (later Mrs. Daniel Devore).

Sources: <u>Who Was Who in America 1897-1941: A Companion Volume to Who's Who in America, Vol. I</u>, Chicago: The A. N. Marquis Co., 1942.

          <u>The New York Times</u>, 5-25-12, 13:6 (obituary).
          <u>The Washington Post</u>, 5-25-12, 2:3 (obituary).

<u>Mrs. Margaret G. Stewart</u> continued to live in the house until her death around 1931. According to the city directories, her daughter Mary lived there through 1937 and then left the house vacant until she sold it three years later.

<u>Luxembourg</u> established their Legation in Washington in 1940 at the Shoreham Hotel. April 4, 1940 **M.** Hughes Le Gallais presented his credentials as Chargé D'Affaires to Secretary of State Hull. In November of the same year, his status was raised

to that of Minister. The Legation received embassy status in 1955.

The Grand Duchess of Luxembourg, H.R.H. Charlotte, purchased 2200 Massachusetts Avenue from Mary E. Stewart in March 1941 "for and in consideration of Forty thousand (40,000) Dollars. (Deed recorded March 8, 1941 in Liber 7578, folio 222) Miss Stewart evidently settled for far less than the property was worth, since its total assessed value in 1941 was $104,118 (ground: $27,118; improvements: $77,000). (Lusk's D.C. Assessment Directory Service, 1941) The Grand Duchess did not live in the house, but spent her time in Montreal and London, where her ministers in exile were located during the German occupation of her country. The house was used instead by the Luxembourg Legation, which moved its residence and chancery there in 1941.

The Times-Herald reported on October 9, 1941 that "The Dowager Grand Duchess of Luxembourg, Maria Anna, is at her country's legation on Massachusetts Avenue for an indefinite stay." The Dowager Grand Duchess was 80 years old at the time and was to die in September 1942.

In January 1962, the government of Luxembourg bought another building, 2210 Massachusetts Avenue, to serve as the chancery. Three months later, the government acquired The Grand Duchess Charlotte's property for $160,000 and continued to use it as the Embassy residence.

Sources: Lusk's D.C. Assessment Directory Service, Washington, D.C.: Rufus S. Lusk, 1941 (Assessments as of June 30 1941)

The Evening Star, 4-7-40, D.2:1.
Times-Herald, 10-9-41, 16:6.

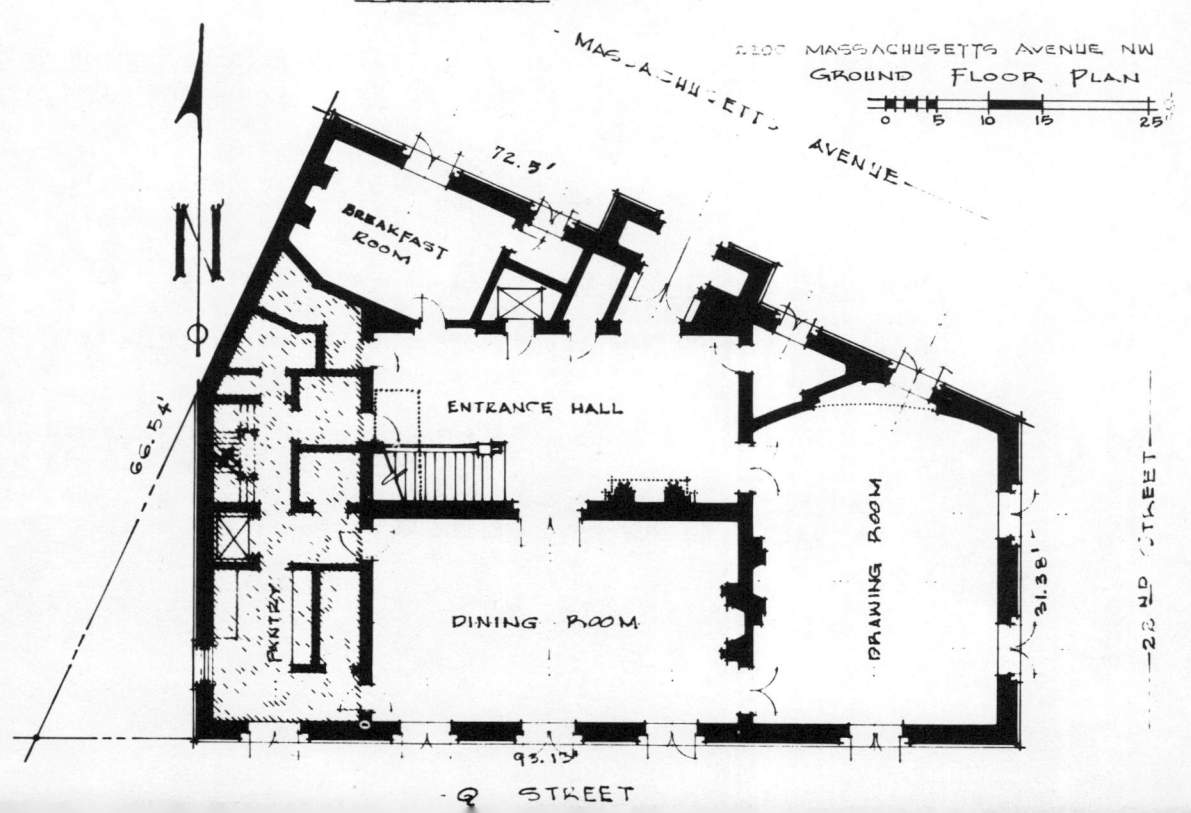

CFA photo
Boucher 1970

Entrance Hall
CFA photo
Boucher 1970

Breakfast Room
CFA photo
Boucher 1970

Drawing Room
CFA photo
Boucher 1970

248

Dining Room
CFA photo
Boucher 1970

Entrance Hall Mantle
CFA photo
Boucher 1970

PART II.   ARCHITECTURAL INFORMATION

    A.   General Statement:

        1.   Architectural character: This semidetached structure has a Louis XV exterior, Jacobean and Georgian interior details, and a polygonal plan.

        2.   Condition: very good.

    B.   Exterior Description:

        1.   Overall dimensions: The three and one half story plus basement structure measures 60'-0" from north sidewalk to roof ridge. The five bay south elevation (Q Street) is 93'-2"; the two bay east elevation (22nd Street), 31'-4"; the five bay north elevation (central entrance on Massachusetts Avenue), 72'-6"; the west party wall, 30'-0"; and the single bay southwest service entrance, 32'-6".

        2.   Foundations: concrete footings and slab.

        3.   Wall construction: The building has tan limestone facing. A smooth base serves as window sill for the rusticated first floor, which is capped by bead, fascia and block string courses. Two story flat panels on smooth plinths flank recessed second and third story window bays. Separating the second floor windows from those of the third floor are lamp, spray and swag panels.

        4.   Structure: brick bearing walls.

        5.   Mechanical: The structure retains its Bryant, hot air furnace, and Dryer Manufacturing Corporation clothes washer and drier (patented 1907). The lighting is electric. The elevator is by Otis.

        6.   Porches, stoops, bulkheads, etc.: The north entrance vestibule is formed by the building base and first floor rustication which together break forward as a simicircular-arched Tuscan entrance having a scrolled keystone and floral swag spandrels. The line of the first floor string courses is carried across as a full entablature with bead architrave, tulip in gouge frieze, and corona and cyma cornice. The cornice is capped by a balustrade of oval guilloche with raised end blocks. The guilloche balustrade, repeated under the second floor windows, continues the wall plinth line.

        7.   Chimneys: Visible from the street is a west wall brick chimney with a limestone block cap and metal hood.

8. Openings:

   a. Doorways and doors: The semicircular-arched, plate glass double door from the vestibule to the entrance hall has decorative, cast iron bar grilles surrounded by guilloche, with a rosette panel at bottom and lyre motif at top. The arched transom has a decorative wreath.

   b. Windows: All windows are four lights across, except for those of two lights which flank the central north bays.

   The first floor has casements and the upper two floors have double hung windows which simulate casements. All windows have transoms except for those on the third floor. The first floor has block architraves with scrolled keystones. The second floor has semicircular-arched Tuscan architraves with console keystones and floral spandrels, the narrower bays having Tuscan architraves with scrolled keystones. Resting on decorative wall panels, the third floor windows have crossette Tuscan architraves.

9. Roof:

   a. Shape, covering: slate, mansard roof with pulvinated, copper ridge cap and flashing.

   b. Cornice, eaves: The building has a tulip in gouge frieze, punctuated by rosettes centered over each bay and wall panel; and a modillion and cyma cornice. The cornice supports a panelled balustrade with balusters centered over each window bay.

   c. Dormers, cupolas, towers: Centered over each window bay are semicircular-arched windows having hood moulds with label stops, bracket supports, and scroll keystones.

C. Interior Description:

1. Floor plans: The entrance hall, with the main stair at the west, is entered via the north vestibule. The hall has access to all major first floor rooms. In the east wall of the hall is a door to a triangular closet, the angle of which is formed by the north building wall. A double door through the east wall of the hall leads to the drawing room, which in turn is connected to a dining room. The dining room, located south of the entrance hall, leads into the pantry. The pantry connects to the service stair, and cloak and storage rooms which are directly west of the main stair and connected by a door to the entrance hall. The breakfast room, set at an acute angle to the hall, is entered from the west end of the entrance hall north wall. A lavatory, entered from the breakfast room, and a hall elevator and closet, are set between the breakfast room and north vestibule. (See plan.)

The main stair ascends one story to the second floor, which is similar in arrangement to the first floor and contains an east library over the drawing room and the principal bedroom suites. The family stair (located above the first floor entrance), ascends in an ellipse from the second floor to the third and fourth.

2. Spaces:

Entrance hall: (see photographs)

a. Flooring: basket weave parquetry.

b. Baseboard: 4", wood with bead cap.

c. Wainscot: The 8'-0" high, wood wainscot has four rows of linen fold panels, recessed for the breakfast, drawing and dining room doors, and capped by a bracket and cavetto cornice.

d. Walls: The simulated limestone, plaster walls are recessed to form lancet arches over the breakfast, drawing and dining room doors. The south chimney wall breaks forward.

e. Cornice: scotia, bead, bracket, corona, bead, cyma and bead.

f. Ceiling: The 14'-0" high, plaster ceiling has square panels of ribs with bosses, and trefoil and fleur-de-lis fixture rosettes at the east and west.

g. Doorways and doors: The wood double doors to the breakfast, drawing and dining rooms have two linen fold panels below an acanthus diamond-within-square panel. The single doors to the west service stair and cloak room, the north closet and elevator, and the east closet, are concealed in the wainscot.

h. Hardware: brass door handles; single doors having brass pendant pulls set in stiles.

i. Lighting: There are two, six-light, gilded wood, acanthus leaf, baroque chandeliers.

j. Heating: Opposite the entrance door, the south wall limestone chimney mantle, in the Gothic manner (6'-0" wide by 8'-0" high) has a Tudor-arched firebox surround, single flanking plinths with cluster columns, a coved architrave four quatrefoil facing panels with linen fold side panels, an ivy frieze and a bracket cornice with hood overmantle. (See detail photograph.)

k. Stair: The oak stair ascends sixteen risers west to the first landing, seven risers north to the second landing and seven risers east to the second floor. The newel is buttressed by a decorative console, and the balustrade has carved rinceau panels of fruit, flora and fauna. At the wall is a velvet rope handrail looped through bundled reed, brass rings.

Drawing room: (late Georgian manner. See photographs.)

a. Flooring: herringbone parquetry.

b. Baseboard: 8", wood with torus, cavetto and bead cap.

c. Chairrail: 2'-8" high, wood with ogee, fascia and bead.

d. Walls: The pale yellow, plaster walls have applied fascia and bead mouldings. The north wall is a bow, and the west chimney wall breaks forward.

e. Cornice: The full entablature has an enriched architrave, a palmette and anthemion frieze, and a dentil, egg and dart, and astragal cornice.

f. Ceiling: 14'-0" high, plaster, painted.

g. Doorways and doors: At either end of the west wall is a double door to the entrance hall and the dining room. Both sets of three, raised, mahogany panels are capped by paired raised panels and framed by a double fascia and cyma architrave.

h. Windows: The alcove formed by the north wall bow has two windows; the west one is false, having mirrored panes.

i. Hardware: bundled reed, brass door handles set in stiles.

j. Lighting: Flanking the west wall chimney mantle are single, three-light, crystal arm and pendant sconces. Each sconce has a crystal body, and brass base, pendant and urn cap. There is one, tear-drop, paired-arm, fourteen-light chandelier with brass, grape and leaf girdle, flambeau bowl ribs, and pendant and fern leaf crown, all connected by crystal bead and prisms drapes and pendants.

k. Heating: The west wall chimney has a panelled cast iron firebox. The yellow marble, white trimmed mantle (6'-0" wide by 5'-0" high) has flanking Ionic pilasters with figure panels which support a talon architrave; a frieze broken forward at the center and over the pilasters; and a denticulated shelf. The overmantle gilded mirror has a semicircular arch and flanking columnette side lights. (See detail photograph.)

Dining room: (Jacobean manner, wood. See photograph.)

a. Flooring: basket weave parquetry.

b. Baseboard: 6", with bead cap.

c. Walls: There are four rows of diamond-within-square panels. The east chimney wall breaks forward.

d. Cornice: ogee, bracket, fascia, ogee and cyma.

e. Ceiling: 14'-0" high, plaster painted white; trefoils, quatrefoils and roundels bordered by rinceau ribs in grape and leaf.

f. Doorways and doors: There are two double doors, one to the drawing room and one to the entrance hall; and two, single doors to the pantry at the west. All doors have two diamond-within-rectangle panels. A bolection architrave with a bracket cornice surrounds the doors and their panel caps.

g. Hardware: brass, pendant door handles set in stiles.

h. Lighting: There are two, three-light, silver-plated sconces.

i. Heating: The east wall chimney mantle (6'-0" wide by 7'-0" high) has a white marble firebox surround flanked by mask-panelled, limestone plinths supporting serpentine human terms with naive Ionic capitals capped by iron escutcheon blocks. Above the wood architrave, the frieze is separated into three panels by diminuitive fishscale pedestals supporting female busts. The frieze is capped by a gadroon bedmould, and a corona and cyma shelf.

Breakfast room: (early Georgian manner; wood painted yellow.)

a. Flooring: herringbone parquetry.

b. Baseboard: 6", with quarter-round cap.

c. Walls: four rows of flat panels.

d. Cornice: fascia, corona and cavetto.

e. Ceiling: 14'-0" high, plaster painted white. Slight cove.

f. Doorways and doors: The east leaf of the raised panel double door from the hall is false. The fascia architrave is capped by an egg and dart cornice. The door to the lavatory is concealed in the panelling.

g. Hardware: bundled-reed, brass door handles set in stiles.

h. Lighting: Flanking the north window are single, two-light, Islamic intaglio and pendant, brass sconces.

i. Heating: The west wall, wood and plaster chimney mantle (6'-0" wide by 5'-0" high) has a white-veined, black marble firebox surround, a wood, egg and dart architrave flanked by scroll-capped pilasters with floral pendants; a central frieze mask with floral drapes and swags broken forward over the scrolls in a rosette motif; and a talon, corona and cyma shelf. The head of the overmantle panel has fruit and floral pendants suspended from swagged clusters. (See detail photograph.)

Second floor hall:

a. Flooring: basket weave parquetry.

b. Baseboard: 4", wood with bead cap.

c. Wainscot: 8'-0" high, wood linen fold panels.

d. Walls: plaster to simulate limestone.

e. Ceiling: 12'-0" high, plaster painted white.

f. Doorways and doors: The double doors have linen fold and acanthus leaf, diamond-within-square panels.

g. Hardware: oval, incised, brass door knobs.

h. Heating: The south wall tan limestone chimney mantle has a Tudor arch with a plain architrave and an overmantle of linen fold panels.

i. Stair: North of the south wall mantle, the elliptical spiral stair ascends twenty-three risers (generally east) to the third floor and twenty risers to the fourth. On the second floor treads flair out to one of two newels which has oriental fret panels; a diminuitive swag and rosette frieze; a square urn with Ionic capital; and a glyph frieze cap. The left banister is panelled and capped by a six inch wide, moulded handrail; the right handrail has fluted and tapered, flambeau-shaped balusters.

D. Site:

1. Setting and orientation: The building faces north on a lot measuring 72'-6" on the north (Massachusetts Avenue); 31'-4" on the east (22nd Street); 93'-2" on the south (Q Street); and 66'-6" on the west.

2. Enclosures: There is a concrete retaining wall on the east and a console-terminated limestone retaining wall on the west.

2200 Massachusetts Avenue, N.W.

3. Outbuildings: none.

4. Walks: The semicircular north entrance drive and southwest service entry are edged by limestone curbing.

5. Landscaping: An oval bed of roses is surrounded by the drive and the public sidewalk. Clipped hedges, holly, mountain laurel and azaleas elsewhere.

2201 MASSACHUSETTS AVENUE, N.W., WASHINGTON, D.C.

CFA photo
Boucher 1970

Location: 2201 Massachusetts Avenue, N.W., Washington, D.C.;
                   on the northwest corner of Massachusetts Avenue
                   and 22nd Street (formerly Boundary Street).

Present Owner: George Howard Bechtel

Present Occupant: Lodgers

Present Use: Argyle Terrace (Rooming House)

Statement of   This brick structure was designed by Paul J. Pelz,
Significance: associate architect of the Library of Congress. The
                   residence is a late example of the Queen Anne and
                   Romanesque revivals, modified by 16th century north
                   European renaissance details. The house occupies a
                   prominent site at the northwest corner of a major
                   intersection, which includes 22nd Street, Massachu-
                   setts Avenue, and Florida Avenue. The property has
                   one of the city's earliest "automobile" houses de-
                   signed as an integral part of the architectural
                   scheme.

PART I. HISTORICAL INFORMATION

   A. Lot and Square:

   The building is located in Square 2512, lot 800 (formerly part of
   lot 1 in Block 7 of "Kalorama Heights").

   B. Original and Subsequent Owners:

   The following chain of title to the property shows the owners of
   the present structure and of any known preceding structures on the
   site:

   1899 Deed November 27, 1899, recorded December 13, 1899 in
         Liber 2475 folio 57

         Anna E. L. Beaman et vir,
         George H.
                 To
         Alice Townsend Miller

         "This Indenture made...by and between Anne E. Lovett Beaman
         and George H. Beaman, her husband, both of the District of
         Columbia (residing at the time of the making...of these
         presents in the city of Paris, France) parties of the first
         part and Alice Townsend Miller of said District party of the

259

second part: Witnesseth that the parties of the first part for and in consideration of Twelve Thousand five hundred (12,500) Dollars...conveyed...unto the party of the second part...Lot...(1) in Block...(7) 'Kalorama Heights' as per plat recorded in Liber County No. 7 folio 34 of the Records of the Office of the Surveyor of the District of Columbia..."

1913 Deed January 27, 1913, recorded February 1, 1913 in Liber 3575 folio 476

Alice Townsend Miller
    To
William F. Dennis

"This Deed made...by and between Alice Townsend Miller of New York City, party hereto of the first part, and William F. Dennis of the District of Columbia, party hereto of the second part;...Part of Lot...(1) in Block...(7) 'Kalorama Heights', as per plat recorded in Liber County No. 7, folio 34 of the Records of the Office of the Surveyor of the District of Columbia, described as follows: - Beginning for the same at the Southeast corner of said lot, and running thence Northwesterly along the Northerly line of Massachusetts Avenue,...49.82 feet to the Southeast corner of the part of said lot conveyed to Emeline D. Lovett by Deed recorded in Liber 2558, folio 167 of the Land Records of said District; thence along the Easterly line of the land so conveyed to said Lovett, North...23 degrees ...57 minutes East,...41.67 feet to the Northeast corner of the land so conveyed; thence along the North line of the land conveyed as aforesaid, North...66 degrees...3 minutes West,...18/100 of a foot to the Westerly line of said Lot...(1); thence Northeasterly, along said Westerly line...58.33 feet to the Northwest corner of said lot; thence Southeasterly along the North line of said lot,...5.56 feet to the Northeast corner of said lot; and thence South along the East line of said lot and the West line of Twenty-second Street...109.42 feet to the point of beginning..."

1923 Deed August 9, 1923, recorded October 5, 1923 in Liber 5081 folio 473

William F. Dennis et ux,
Clara R.
    To
James D. Hobbs
Thomas P. Bones
(joint tenants)

2201 Massachusetts Avenue, N.W.

1925 Deed September 1, 1925, recorded September 23, 1925 in
Liber 5599 folio 185

James D. Hobbs
Thomas P. Bones
(joint tenants)
    To
Gustave Nassauer

"...Subject to an encumbrance of record, which the party of the second part assumes and agrees to pay..."

1926 Deed October 4, 1926, recorded November 17, 1926 in
Liber 5878 folio 266

Henry J. Robb
Howard A. Burns, trustees
    To
Harry Wardman
Thomas P. Bones
(joint tenants)

"Whereas, Gustave Nassauer (widower) heretofore made and executed a certain Deed of Trust bearing date on the tenth day of September, 1925 and thereby conveyed the...land and premises...unto James D. Hobbs and Howard A. Burns...And whereas default having been made in the payment of said debt, the parties of the first part...on the 14th day of September, 1926, ...did sell same at public auction unto Harry Wardman and Thomas P. Bones as Joint Tenants...for the sum of Twenty Thousand ($20,000) Dollars..."

1928 Deed September 20, 1928, recorded October 17, 1928 in
Liber 6236 folio 464

Harry Wardman
Thomas P. Bones
(joint tenants)
    To
Lincoln Properties Company, Inc.

"...Subject to a duly recorded Deed of Trust of Forty Thousand ($40,000) Dollars..."

1932 Deed October 18, 1932, recorded October 19, 1932 in
Liber 6694 folio 137

William K. Quinter
James D. Hobbs, Trustees
    To

2201 Massachusetts Avenue, N.W.

Edward R. True, Jr.

"Whereas, Harry Wardman and Thomas P. Bones, joint tenants heretofore made and executed a certain Deed of Trust,...on the 15th day of December 1927...duly recorded in Liber 6038 at folio 127 and whereas, default having been made in the payment of said debt, the parties of the first part...did sell the same at public auction unto Edward R. True, Jr.,... for the sum of Forty-five Thousand Dollars ($45,000)..."

1940   Deed February 7, 1940, recorded February 9, 1940 in Liber 7439 folio 577

Edward R. True, Jr., unmarried
      To
Evelyn C. Dodge
Rose B. Covington
(joint tenants)

1947   Deed May 12, 1947, recorded May 23, 1947 in Liber 8495 folio 343

Rose B. Covington
      To
Evelyn L. Dodge

"...All right, title and interest to...Part of Lot...(1) in Block...(7) of John F. Rodgers and Edward J. Stellwagen, Trustees' subdivision of part of a tract of land known as 'Kalorama Heights'..."

1960   Deed November 15, 1960, recorded November 22, 1960 in Liber 11518 folio 25

Evelyn C. Dodge
Evelyn D. Kirk (formerly Evelyn L. Dodge)
(joint tenants)
      To
Oscar Cox

1967   Deed July 5, 1967, recorded August 2, 1967 in Liber 12781 folio 238

Louise B. Cox
      To
Bernard Singer

2201 Massachusetts Avenue, N.W.

"...Louise B. Cox, widow and not remarried, also known on record as Louise Black Cox, in her own right and devisee under the last will of Oscar Cox, (also known as Oscar Sydney Cox)..."

1967 Deed August 3, 1967 recorded August 7, 1967 in Liber 12782 folio 562

Bernard Singer, widower
    To
Claire Shinderman

"...an undivided one-fourth (1/4) interest in and to...Part of Lot 1 in Block 7..."

1973 Deed February 5, 1973, recorded February 13, 1973 in Liber 13448 folio 452

Bernard Singer, widower
Claire Shinderman et vir,
Abraham
    To
George Howard Bechtel

Source: Recorder of Deeds, Washington, D.C.

C. Date of Erection:

The building was begun in March 1900 and completed in 1901.

D. Building Permits:

The applications for the following building permits were filed by the architect, contractor or owner's agent and provide significant data:

No. 1330, March 27, 1900
Permit to build dwelling and "automobile house"
    Owner: Capt. Frederick A. Miller, U.S.N.
    Architect: Paul J. Pelz
    Builder: F. H. Duehay
    Estimated cost: $35,000.

No. 3721, February 11, 1913
Permit to Repair or Reconstruct Building
    Owner: W. F. Dennis
    Architect: Reginald W. Geare
    Contractor: James J. Galvin

2201 Massachusetts Avenue, N.W.

>Estimated cost: $300.
>"The removal of a chimney breast now in place and the rebuilding of same in another position."

No. 4954, April 17, 1913
Permit to Repair or Reconstruct Building
>Owner: W. F. Dennis
>Architect: R. W. Geare
>Contractor: J. J. Galvin
>Estimated cost: $200.
>"to erect an enclosed porch on the north side of residence at 2201 Mass. Ave. N.W.. Back of building line."

No. 2381, October 14, 1920
Permit to Repair or Reconstruct Building
>Owner: W. F. Dennis
>Contractor: James J. Galvin
>"build one 2-story tile conservatory 13' X 15' - make repairs to bay window projection 5' X 16'."

No. 229925, February 23, 1940
Permit to Repair or Reconstruct Building
>Owner: Rose Covington
>Contractor: Jaffe-Dove, Inc.
>Estimated cost: $80.
>How occupied: dwelling
>"Cut opening through mansard roof, install window, patch roof, and plaster. One rafter will be cut and double header installed above and below window."

No. 275470, January 11, 1945
Permit to Repair or Reconstruct Building
>Owner: Evelyn Dodge
>Designer: P. S. Dove
>Contractor: Jaffe-Dove Const.
>Estimated cost: $900.
>How occupied: rooming house
>"Build 3 dormer windows in slate roof to replace old ones... Window area to be not less than 1/8 of floor area of room in which each is placed."

Source: D.C. Government, Department of Economic Development, Bureau of Licenses and Permits, Central Files.

E. Alterations and Additions:

According to building permits, the following alterations or additions were to be made: removal and rebuilding of chimney breast in 1913; erection of enclosed porch on north facade in 1913; and addition of a two-story tile conservatory in 1920. If they were built, the enclosed porch and tile conservatory were subsequently removed.

2201 Massachusetts Avenue, N.W.

F. Architect: Paul J. Pelz, Washington, D.C.

Paul Johann Pelz (1841-1918), the son of Eduard Ludwig and Henrietta (Helfensrieder) Pelz, was born in Germany. His father went to New York in 1851 while Paul remained in Germany with his mother until his education was completed. After joining his father in Hoboken, N.J. in 1858, Paul was apprenticed to a New York architect, Detlef Lienau. By 1864 Pelz had become the chief draftsman for the firm. Two years later, he left Lienau's office and went to Washington, D.C. where he eventually became chief draftsman of the U.S. Lighthouse Board.

In 1873 Pelz and John L. Smithmeyer, another Washington architect, won a competition for the design of the Library of Congress. Thirteen years later, Congress authorized construction of the library. Smithmeyer was appointed architect of the project, but was removed after a disagreement over the choice of construction materials. Pelz was then retained by Gen. Thomas L. Casey, Chief of Engineers, U.S. Army, to carry out the original design.

Other buildings designed by Smithmeyer and Pelz were: Academic Building, Georgetown University, Washington, D.C.; U.S. Army and Naval Hospital, Hot Springs, Ark.; Carnegie Library and Music Hall, Allegheny, Pa.; Administration Building at the Clinic Hospital, University of Virginia; and the Chamberlain Hotel, Fort Monroe, Va.. Independently, Mr. Pelz planned a number of residences and office buildings in Washington. (Withey, p. 466) One office building was the McGill Building located at 9th and G Streets, N.W. (destroyed in 1973).

Pelz was married twice. His first wife, Louise Dorothea Kipp of Hoboken, N.J., died in 1894 - leaving two children: Carl Eduard and Beatrice. February 23, 1895, Pelz married Mrs. Mary Eastbourne (Ritter) Meem.

Sources: The National Cyclopedia of American Biography, Vol. XXV, New York: James T. White & Company, 1936, pp. 424-425.

Who Was Who in America 1897-1942: A Companion Volume to Who's Who in America, Vol. I, Chicago: The A. N. Marquis Co., 1942.

Dumas Malone (ed.), Dictionary of American Biography, Vol. XIV, New York: Charles Scribner's Sons, 1932.

Henry F. Withey and Elsie R. Withey, Biographical Dictionary of American Architects (Deceased), Los Angeles: New Age Publishing Co., 1956.

The Sunday Star, 3-31-18, 3:4 (obituary).

2201 Massachusetts Avenue, N.W.

G. Known Plans, Drawings, Elevations, etc.: none found.

H. Important Old Views:

Photograph: exterior view from east.
<u>A History of the City of Washington, Its Men and Institutions</u>,
by the Washington Post Co., 1903, p. 429.
(see reproduction)

I. Residents:

1. City and telephone directories list the following tenants:

    1901-1907   Frederick A. Miller
    1908-1913   No listing found
    1914   William F. Dennis
    1915-1917   Charles N. Riker
    1918-1921   William F. Dennis
    1922   Vacant
    1923   Costa Rican Legation
                  Salvadorean Legation
    1924-1926   Costa Rican Legation
    1927-1933   Vacant
    1934   William P. Blair, Farm Credit Adm.
    1935   Mrs. Inez P. Poier, furn. rms.
    1936   Ernest J. (Inez P.) Poirior, salesman
    1937   Mrs. Inez P. Poirior
    1938   Ernest J. (Inez J.) Poirior, restr. 1240 22nd;
                  home 2201 Mass.
    1939   Mrs. Inez Poirior
    1940   Theodore (Hazel A.) Hoffman
    1941-1948   Mrs. Evelyn C. Dodge
    1949-1968   Argyle Terrace, rms.
    1969-1972   Singer's Argyle Guest House
    1973   Argyle Terrace

2. The following residents were included in volumes of <u>The Elite
   List: A Compilation of Selected Names of Residents of Washington City, D.C. and Ladies Shopping Guide</u>:

    1901-1902   Frederick A. Miller, Lieut. Commander and Mrs.

    1903-1904   Frederick A. Miller, Lieut. Commander and Mrs.;
                  Miss Edith Miller

    1905-1907   Frederick A. Miller, Lieut. Commander and Mrs.;
                  Miss Edith Miller; Miss Alice Miller

    1908-1910   F. A. Miller, Commander and Mrs. and drs.
                  2201 Mass. Ave. and Lakewood, N.J.

2201 Massachusetts Avenue, N.W.

    1911   F. A. Abercrombie-Miller, Commander and Mrs.;
                    The Misses Abercrombie-Miller

    1913   Mr. and Mrs. Walcott R. Tuckerman
                    Mrs. F. A. Abercrombie-Miller
                    Miss Miller

    1914-1918 Mr. and Mrs. W. F. Dennis
                    Mr. and Mrs. C. M. Riker

3. Biographies of the residents:

Frederick Augustus Miller, the son of Frederick A. M. and Martha Mason Abercrombie Miller, was born in Elkton, Maryland on June 12, 1842. After his education in local schools and Trinity College in Hartford, Connecticut, he joined the Navy on September 11, 1861 as a master's mate. During the Civil War, Miller participated in several battles, including Donaldsonville and Mobile, Ala. - as well as skirmishes along the Mississippi River. He achieved the rank of lieutenant-commander in 1882; retired from active service as a captain on November 30, 1885; and for his Civil War service was promoted to commander in 1906.

After his retirement, Commander Miller lived in Washington, D.C. where he was treasurer of St. John's Orphanage; director of the Workingman's Club; a director of the Eye, Ear, and Throat Hospital; a regent of the Blind Men's Home; and member of the board of directors of American Security and Trust Company. His social activities included membership in the Metropolitan, Cosmos, and Chevy Chase Clubs.

His home at 2201 Massachusetts Avenue was constructed between 1900 and 1901. Since few houses had been built this far west on the avenue at the time, Commander Miller was considered bold.

> Frederick Augustus Miller...is one of the staunchest believers in the future of Washington, which he predicts will in the course of a few years not only be the most beautiful city in the world, but is fast becoming the Mecca for the wealth, fashion and culture of the United States. With the courage of his convictions, within the past few years Captain Miller erected at the northwest corner of Massachusetts Avenue and Twenty-second street one of the most beautiful homes in the national capital. No expense was spared in this work, and the house stands boldly forth on the bluff it occupies, as one of the best examples of the architect's (Pelz) art and skill... The hand carving which adorns the newels,

> cornices and arches are works of art, while
> in design it is plainly discernible that
> Captain Miller's beloved profession fur-
> nished the theme for the many nautical fig-
> ures that there abound...(A History of Wash-
> ington, Its Men and Institutions, p. 429)

Miller died in 1909 leaving his wife Alice Townsend Miller and three children: Edith, Alice, and Townsend Miller. A letter filed with his will states that "Since the date of the execution of this will [1903] the testator's name was legally changed to Abercrombie-Miller, so that the will is filed as that of Commander Frederick Augustus Abercrombie-Miller, United States Navy."

Sources: American Biographical Directories, District of Columbia, 1908-1909, Washington, D.C.: The Potomac Press, 1908.

The Washington Post Co., A History of the City of Washington, Its Men and Institutions, ed. by Allan B. Slauson, Washington, D.C.: The Henry E. Wilkens Printing Co., pp. 429-430.

Countess Alice de Castellane, Commander Miller's daughter, died in 1965 at the age of 80. She had been graduated from the National Cathedral School in 1903 and married to Frederick A. de Peyster of New York in 1907. Having been divorced from her first husband, she remarried in 1930 to Count Bohdan de Castellane of Poland, a former Czarist cavalry officer. They lived in France until the Nazi invasion and then moved to Washington, D.C. The Countess was survived by five children: Frederick A. de Peyster, Jr., Woodbury, N.Y.; James A. de Peyster, Palm Beach, Fla.; Mrs. James Todd, Bedford Village, N.Y.; Mrs. Eric von Raits, Woodbury, N.Y.; and Mrs. J.S. Brittain Walker, Washington, D.C.

Source: The Washington Post, 5-28-65, B 7:5 (obituary).

William F. Dennis bought 2201 Massachusetts Avenue from Mrs. Miller in 1913 and owned it until 1923. The Evening Star, May 3, 1946 stated that Mr. Dennis, a resident of Washington for more than 35 years had been "prominent in the real estate business" in Washington since 1912. However, the city directories indicate that he and his family lived in the Massachusetts Avenue residence and apparently did not lease it as later owners were to do. Dennis also was a partner in the civil engineering firm of Rinehart & Dennis until his retirement in 1924. He died in May 1946 at the age of 85 - leaving his wife, Clara R.; two nephews, John and Albert Dennis; his son-in-law, Charles N. Riker; and his brothers, Albert and Percy Dennis.

Sources: The Evening Star, 5-3-46, 12:5 (obituary).
The Evening Star, 5-28-46, 7:5.
The Washington Post, 5-4-46, B 7:4 (obituary).

During the 1920's and 1930's the house changed hands several times: James D. Hobbs and Thomas P. Bones in 1923; Gustave Nassauer in 1925; Harry Wardman and Thomas P. Bones in 1926; and Edward R. True, Jr., in 1932.

James D. Hobbs, an associate of Harry Wardman, was at one point vice president of Wardman Real Estate Properties. (See biography of Harry Wardman under 2234 Massachusetts Avenue, N.W.) He left the organization in 1930. Two years later, he filed for bankruptcy - having more than 100 creditors and debts over $19 million. "The liability total includes liability on a suit brought against him and others in New York by Gustave Nassauer for $14,525,000." (The Evening Star, 6-4-32)

Sources: The Evening Star, 6-4-32, 16:2.
The Washington Herald, 5-25-32, 1:3.
The Washington Post, 6-4-32, 1:6.

Thomas P. Bones, born in South Dakota, came to Washington in 1900 at the age of 15 and worked as a carpenter with Harry Wardman. He eventually became Wardman's partner and vice president of his company until the late 1920's. "He directed construction for...Harry Wardman on the Carlton Hotel, the Hay-Adams Hotel, The Wardman Park Hotel and Cathedral Mansions. At the time of his death [in 1951] he was associated with the Henry J. Robb real estate firm here." (The Washington Post, 7-27-51)

Sources: The Evening Star, 7-26-51, 30:4 (obituary).
The Washington Post, 7-27-51, B 2:3 (obituary).

The residence was leased to the Costa Rican and Salvadorean Legations from 1923 through 1926 and then apparently left vacant until 1934. City directories show that "Mrs. Inez P. Poier" (or Mrs. Inez P. Poirior?) offered furnished rooms in 1935. Building Permit No. 275470, dated January 11, 1945, also shows that 2201 Massachusetts Avenue had become a rooming house - as it has remained to the present.

Oscar Sydney Cox, who bought the building in 1960, was the author of the Lend-Lease Act in 1940. "Mr. Cox, a native of Portland, Me., was one of the most popular personalities on the Washington scene during the war years. His unfailing good humor and ready wit made him a favorite of President Roosevelt and a frequent guest at informal White House dinners." (The New York Times, 10-6-66)

2201 Massachusetts Avenue, N.W.

After working for a New York law firm from 1929 to 1934 and with the city's corporation counsel until 1938, Mr. Cox came to Washington where he served in the government until 1945. His government positions were: assistant to the general counsel of the Treasury Department, 1938-1941; general counsel of the Lend-Lease Administration, 1941-1943; general counsel of the Office of Emergency Management, 1941-1943; Assistant Solicitor General of the U.S., 1942-1943; and general counsel of the Foreign Economic Administration, 1943-1945. For his role in providing economic assistance to foreign nations, Mr. Cox was decorated by the governments of France, Belgium, Italy, and the United States.

He then entered private law practice in Washington and was senior partner of Cox, Langford & Brown when he died in 1966. Mr. Cox was survived by his wife, the former Louise Black, of Washington, D.C.; two sons, Warren J. Cox of Washington, D.C. and Peter W. Cox of Bath, Me.; two brothers, Sydney of Silver Spring, Md. and Morris of Portland, Me.; and a sister, Mrs. Samuel Goldsmith of Portland, Me.

Sources: The New York Times, 10-6-66, 47:1 (obituary).
         The Washington Post, 10-7-66, B 4:1 (obituary).

A History of the City of Washington, Washington Post Co., 1903

CARRIAGE HOUSE

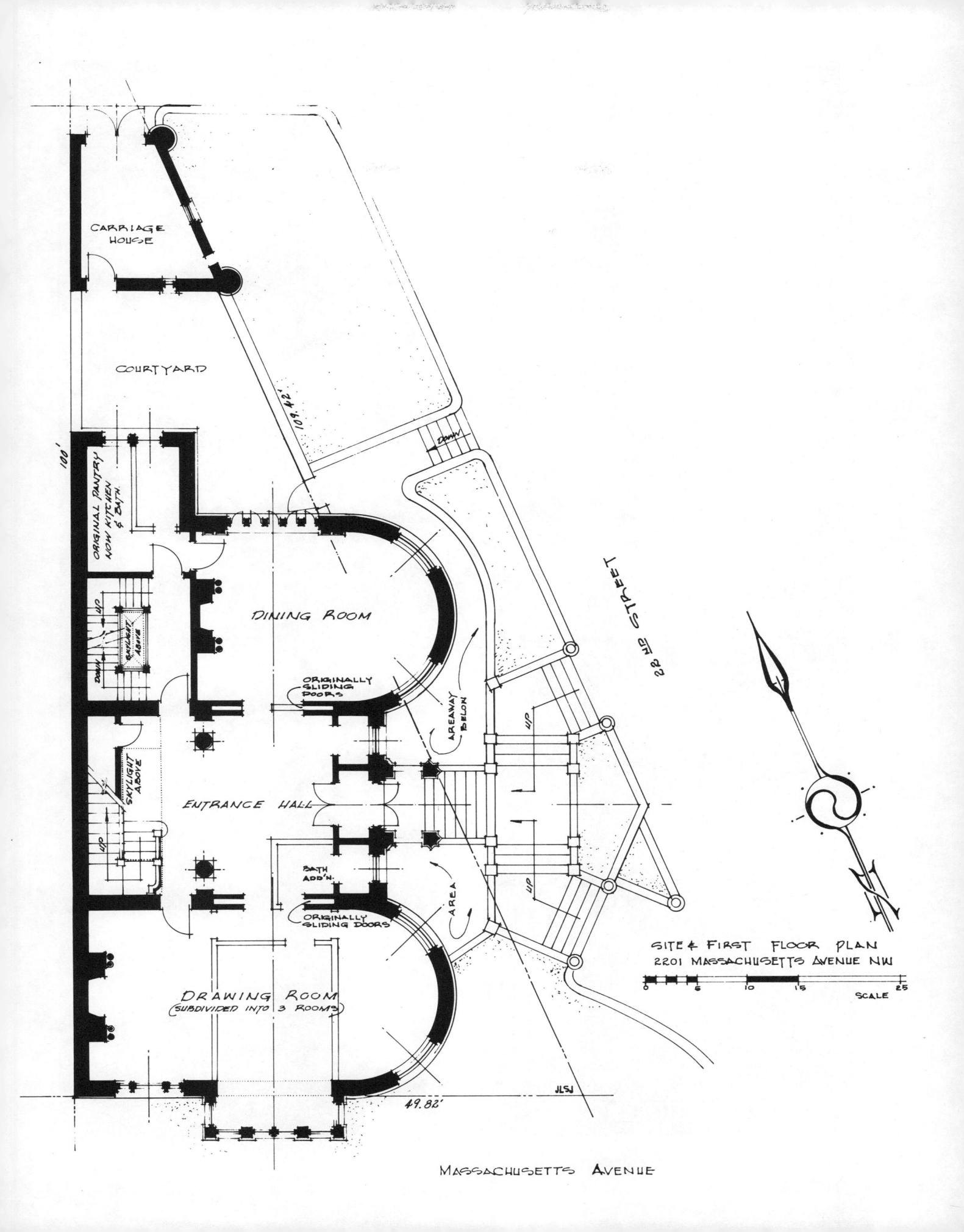

COURTYARD

100'

109.42'

ORIGINAL PANTRY NOW KITCHEN & BATH

SKYLIGHT ABOVE

DOWN

UP

DINING ROOM

ORIGINALLY SLIDING DOORS

AREAWAY BELOW

SKYLIGHT ABOVE

UP

ENTRANCE HALL

BATH ADD'N.

AREA

UP

ORIGINALLY SLIDING DOORS

DRAWING ROOM
(SUBDIVIDED INTO 3 ROOMS)

22 ND STREET

JLSJ

49.82'

MASSACHUSETTS AVENUE

SITE & FIRST FLOOR PLAN
2201 MASSACHUSETTS AVENUE NW

0 5 10 15 25
SCALE

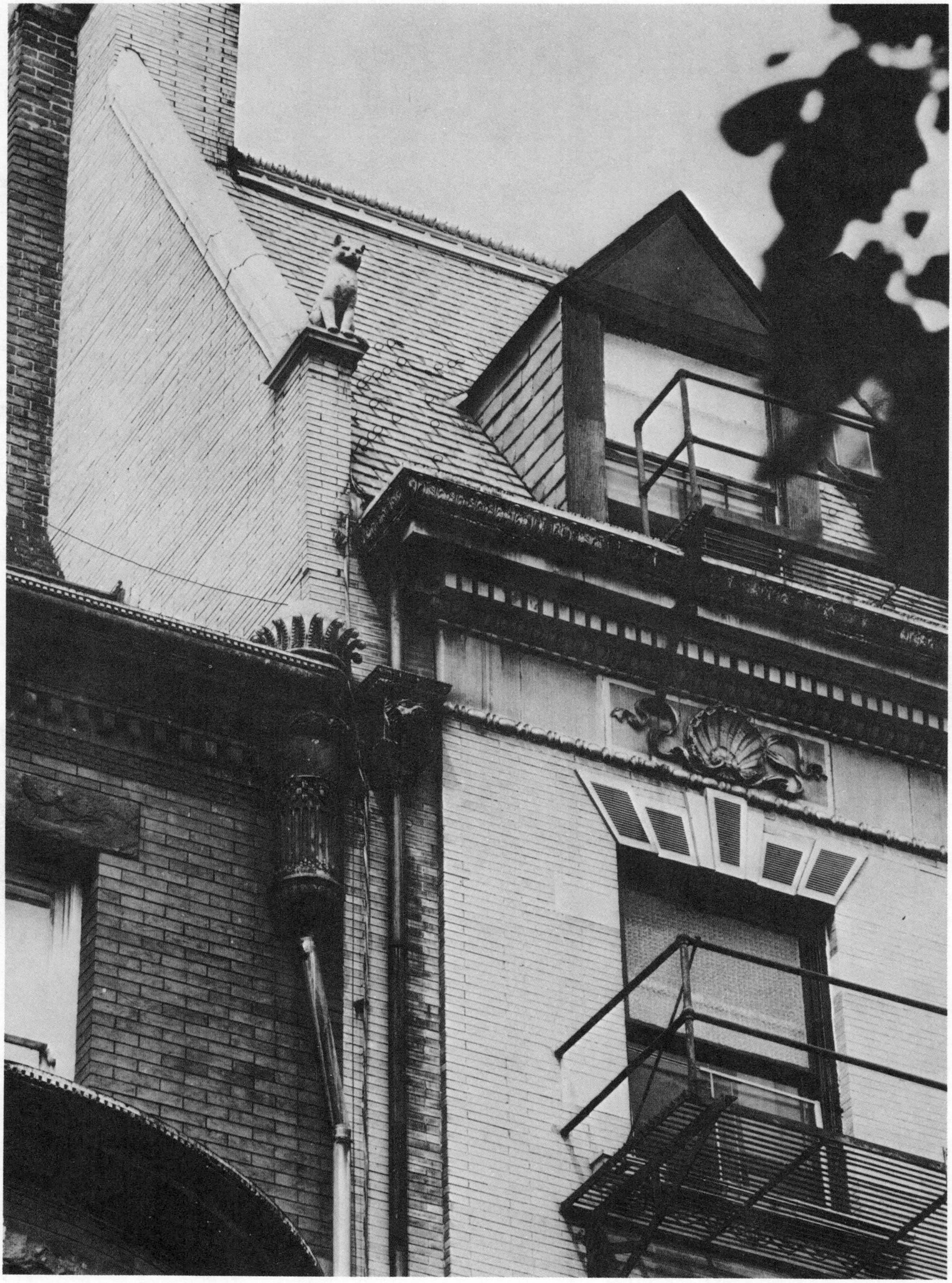

Entrance Detail
CFA photo 1973

Opposite
Detail Exterior
CFA photo
Boucher 1970

274

Above
Dining Room
CFA photo
Boucher 1970

Opposite
Dining Room
CFA photo
Boucher 1970

Mantle Detail
Dining Room
CFA photo
Boucher 1970

2201 Massachusetts Avenue, N.W.

PART II. ARCHITECTURAL INFORMATION

    A. General Statement:

        1. Architectural character: This semidetached structure has an exterior with 16th century North European Renaissance details.

        2. Condition: fair, with partitioning and plumbing installations.

    B. Exterior Description:

        1. Overall dimensions: The basement and attic, three and one half story structure measures 44'-0" from sidewalk to eaves. The three bay east entrance on 22nd Street has flanking two bay bows. The two bay (34'-0") south elevation on Massachusetts Avenue has an east end, first floor bay window. The west party wall is 66'-0" and the composite east bay of the north elevation (34'-0") breaks back 8'-6".

        2. Foundations: concrete footings and slab.

        3. Wall construction: The raised basement has two stone bands of random rustication terminated at the top of the voussoir window lintels by a plain stone frieze capped by a first floor window sill string course. A plain, stone frieze separates the yellow Roman brick walls of the first and second floors. The frieze, interrupted by a swag panel at either entrance elevation bow, rests on first floor window lintel tablets and acts as sill for the second floor windows. A string course over the entrance serves as sill for the central third floor bay. A crossette swag panel separates the two third floor bays of either bow.

        4. Structure: brick bearing walls with wood floor and roof systems.

        5. Mechanical: The building has a hot water, hand-fired, coal heating system. The lighting is electric.

        6. Porches, stoops, bulkheads, etc.: The stone entrance stoop and porch on 22nd Street is approached by two sets of risers, splayed out from center line and bordered by cheek walls and turned stops. They ascend separately six risers from the south and five risers from the north to separate midlandings from which five additional risers, with panelled balustrades and square posts, ascend to a common second landing which overlooks the street. From this second landing (with mosaic floor, rusticated retaining wall and decorative balustrade with posts), a final set of seven risers ascends over a basement areaway to the entrance porch, each side pierced by a single three-point arch flanked by composite piers on pedestals and capped

by a staggered entablature with fascia architrave, plain frieze, dentil cornice and balustrade with single decorative panels, pedestals and urns.

7. Chimneys: Visible from the street are two chimneys. The chimney set at right angles to the north wall retains its decorative terra cotta frieze capped by brick smoke vents.

8. Openings:

   a. Doorways and doors: Each leaf of the oak, double door entrance has a raised rectangular panel intersected by a centered oval with scrolls at bottom and top.

   b. Windows: Each basement window head has rounded corners and a voussoir lintel with panelled keystone. The first floor has double-hung windows with transoms, each having a console supported cornice and tablet cap. The second floor double-hung windows have stone voussoir lintels and scroll keystones. The third floor double-hung windows have stone sills (on brackets) and voussoir lintels.

   The exceptions include:

   (1.) the first floor, tripartite, southwest bay with its keystone and semicircular arch on panelled pilasters.

   (2.) the 13'-6" wide, 4'-2" deep, southeast bay window. The frieze capping the rusticated basement wall is punctuated by panels over which single, composite pilasters separate each section of the side and facade openings; the bay is capped by a plain entablature and balustrade (with centered decorative panel) which is an extension of the building frieze;

   (3.) the first floor northeast bay, called the Admiral Farragut window, with a keystone and semicircular arch on panelled pilasters;

   (4.) the casement window and transom over the entrance, in turn flanked by smaller casement windows without scroll keystones; and

   (5.) the two casement windows with decorative flat hoods which flank the third floor central bay over the entrance.

9. Roof:

   a. Shape, covering: The entrance elevation bows each have a conical slate roof which extends the depth of the building, both united by a central mansard pierced by a skylight and extended over the north elevation by a second mansard with a quatrefoil and finial, stone parapet. The conical peaks each have a metal finial, their extended roof ridges capped by decorative copper flashing.

b. Cornice, eaves: The entablature has an astragal architrave, a **striate**d frieze punctuated by shell and ribbon panels centered over each bay, and an astragal, egg and dart, dentil and corona cornice with an acanthus cyma, copper gutter. The cornice does not extend over the central bays of the entrance.

c. Dormers, cupolas, towers: Of the six dormers (two each over the south and north elevations and one centered over each bow) the three south dormers have been replaced. The original stone dormers each have flanking composite pilasters and a plain entablature capped by a swag tablet and a scroll pediment. The third story central bay and the entablature frieze over the entrance break slightly forward for a dormer with splayed composite piers. The piers flank the window area and support a stone entablature and brick parapet with pedestal stops, centered pediment and finial.

C. Interior Description:

1. Floor plans: The basement floor is arranged along a north to south corridor with access to the former northeast kitchen, the east servants' hall and the northwest service stair; the remaining area devoted to mechanical and storage.

   The east entrance vestibule and flanking window seat alcoves project into the central front hall which is separated from the west stair by a modillioned beam on fluted Ionic columns. The south drawing room has access to both the hall and stair, as do the northeast dining room and the northwest service stair and pantry. Bathroom partitioning occupies the southwest corner of the hall and the drawing room is partitioned into three rooms and a corridor. (See plan.)

   The second floor north to south corridor gives access to a southwest library and three bedroom suites on 22nd Street. The third floor is arranged similarly. The fourth floor contains servants' quarters.

2. Spaces:

Entrance vestiblue:

a. Flooring: centered mosaic medallion with Greek key border.

b. Wainscot: 5'-0" high, green and brown mosaic with Pompeiian swags on a grey ground.

c. Walls: plaster painted white.

d. Cornice: wood, cyma.

e. Ceiling: oak, plain coffers.

f. Doorways and doors: The wood double door to the hall has bevelled glass panels and a transom.

g. Hardware: The street door has decorative brass oval knobs.

h. Lighting: hanging glass globe in iron leaf and vine mesh.

Front hall:

a. Flooring: basket weave parquetry with cherry border.

b. Baseboard: 6", wood with cyma cap.

c. Wainscot: oak-panelled, 4'-6" high. The remaining window alcove (north) has a bench with back rest, console arm and decorative rosettes.

d. Walls: plaster painted white.

e. Cornice: wood, cyma.

f. Ceiling: 11'-8" high, plaster center. The corner coffers of the wood border have centered pattern.

g. Doorways and doors: The remaining window alcove (north) is framed by a semicircular arch on consoles. The wood, sliding double doors from the hall to the dining and drawing rooms each have a fascia architrave with flower basket frieze cap. There are single wood doors at the northwest and southwest. The single door under the stair is capped by a floral scroll pediment.

h. Lighting: hanging, opaque glass globe in stair hall.

Stair:

The main stair ascends five risers to a square landing, one riser west to a second landing, fourteen risers north to a third, and four risers east to the second floor. The oak risers, treads and stringer have an obelisk baluster railing which terminates at the panelled newel in an acanthus scroll. The three story stair has a skylight.

a. Cornice: third floor, alternating swag and flambeau frieze, with dentil cornice.

b. Ceiling: skylight in paired diamond pattern with plaster rosette border.

2201 Massachusetts Avenue, N.W.

Drawing room: (partitioned into three rooms and a corridor.)

a. Flooring: basket weave parquetry with cherry border.

b. Baseboard: 6", painted wood with cyma cap.

c. Walls: plaster, painted.

d. Cornice: dentils, egg and dart.

e. Ceiling: 11'-8" high, plaster painted white.

f. Doorways and doors: The wood, sliding double door to the hall has a fascia architrave with swag frieze flanked by modillions and capped by a cyma cornice.

g. Windows: The southeast bay window has a raised-panel, wood dado and an architrave opening of fascia and rinceau capped by an escutcheon-centered scroll pediment.

h. Lighting: There are two-light, tulip cup and leaf base, bronze sconces.

i. Heating: The west wall chimney mantle (6'-0" wide by 5'-0" high) has a green-veined white marble firebox surround, flanking paired and fluted Ionic columns, a ribbon and garland architrave, a shell and floral swag frieze, and an egg and dart shelf.

Dining room: (see photographs)

a. Flooring: basket weave parquetry with cherry border.

b. Baseboard: 6", wood with cyma cap.

c. Dado: two rows of raised wood panels, small over large.

d. Chairrail: 5'-0" high, bead and fascia.

e. Walls: plaster painted white.

f. Ceiling: The 11'-8" high, plaster ceiling is bordered by wood beams and coffers and centered by two circles, their intersection framing an escutcheon and acorn spray rosette.

g. Doorways and doors: The wood, sliding double door to the hall has a fascia architrave with fruit frieze flanked by rosettes and consoles which support a modillion cornice.

h. Windows: The Admiral Farragut Memorial window on the north wall has a raised-panel, wood dado, a serving counter and five, green crown glass, casement openings between alternating panelled pilasters. The pilasters support a semicircular, nautical transom of green and blue glass with a wood, console keystone, and shell and ribbon spandrels. The window is flanked by crossette-panelled pedestals each supporting paired Ionic pilasters below a plain architrave, a frieze and a staggered dentil and cyma cornice. The windows of the bow each have a fascia architrave with midpoint consoles.

    i. Lighting: There is a gilded leaf, crystal pendant, brass chandelier with four curvilinear arms and a light bulb crown.

    j. Heating: There are built-in, fret and quatrefoil, brass wall registers beneath each window sill.

The west wall chimney has a brown tile hearth and a cast iron shell and ribbon firebox. The wood mantle (7'-0" wide by 5'-6" high) has a brown tile firebox surround; paired flanking Ionic columns; a recessed dolphin, shell and floral frieze, broken forward in shell and ribbon over either set of paired columns; and a plain shelf with center swell. The bevelled overmantle mirror has a crossette architrave flanked by scrolls.

Library: (second floor)

    a. Flooring: 2", common hardwood.

    b. Baseboard: 6", wood with cyma cap.

    c. Walls: plaster. Flanking the west chimney wall are built-in cabinets which support bookcase bays (with doors of beveled glass painted over) bordered by paired composite columnettes.

    d. Cornice: denticulated.

    e. Ceiling: plaster painted white.

    f. Heating: The west wall chimney has a cast iron firebox. The wood (3'-6" high) mantle has a maroon tile firebox surround; flanking composite columns on pedestals; a plain architrave; paired consoles flanking a decorative frieze;and a cyma shelf. The overmantle mirror has flanking composite pilasters and cyma cornice capped by a roundel panel to ceiling height with flanking decorative consoles.

D. Site:

    1. Setting and orientation: The building faces east on a lot

measuring 109'-5" on 22nd Street, 49'-10" on Massachusetts Avenue, 100'-0" on the west and 5'-7" on the north alley.

2. Enclosures: An oval guilloche stone balustrade borders on the south. Ten foot high brick walls connect the building to its north garage. Enclosing a courtyard the wall is pierced by a decorative iron street gate within a stone, semicircular archway. The lot is enclosed by a cyclopean stone retaining wall and an iron fence at the northeast.

3. Outbuildings: The northeast brick garage, with access from the north alley, has round corner projections, a semicircular-arched street entrance for dogs, a stone architrave with brick frieze and stone cornice, and a slate mansard roof with stone ridges and finials.

4. Walks: courtyard, concrete.

5. Landscaping: The lawn on Massachusetts Avenue has English ivy, with beech, linden, maple and spruce trees.

2230 MASSACHUSETTS AVENUE, N.W., WASHINGTON, D.C.

CFA photo
Alexander 1971

Address: 2230 Massachusetts Avenue, N.W., Washington, D.C.

Significance: This row house, in the 16th century Belgian manner, is noteworthy for its limestone and terra-cotta exterior ornament.

Present Owner: Edward T. Hines
Present Use: Residence
Lot and Square: Square 2511, lot 5 (formerly in Block 11, "Kalorama Heights")

HISTORICAL AND ARCHITECTURAL INFORMATION

Original Owner: James C. Hooe (1907-1920*)
Original Use: Residence
Date of Erection: 1907
Architect: George Oakley Totten, Jr.
Builder: Charles A. Langley
Estimated cost: $25,000.

Subsequent Owners:

    May M. Govin (1920-1927)
    C. Augustus Simpson and his wife, Elizabeth Darlington (1927-1946)
    Bernard Singer and his wife Sadie (1946-1952)
    Mr. and Mrs. Edward T. Hines (1952-   )

City and Telephone Directories List:

1908-1911	James C. Hooe
1912-1917	George T. Oliver
1918-1919	Edward N. Hurley
1920	Vacant
1921	Ralph R. Govin
1922	Vacant
1923-1925	Ralph R. Govin
1926-1927	Vacant
1928-1935	Augustus C. Simpson
1936	Fred L. Payne
1937	Ervin R. Whitman
1938-1939	Rev. Wilson A. Beall
1940	Mansion Club
1941	John Hoffman
1942-1943	Mrs. Hattie Hoffman
1944-1946	Mansion Club

---

* The property was sold by the Union Trust Company of Washington, D.C., trustees under the will and testament of James C. Hooe.

1947   No listing found
1948   Mrs. Sadie Singer
1949-1951   Bernard Singer, rooms
1952-1954   No listing found
1955-1956   Eddie Hines
1957-1959   No listing found
1960-1962   Edward T. Hines
1963   No listing found
1964-1965   Edward T. Hines
1966-1968   No listing found
1969-1972   Edward T. Hines

Known Plans, Drawings, Elevations, etc.:

Front elevation. Blueprint. Scale 1/4" = 1'
Filed with Permit No. 3806, May 9, 1907
    "Res. for James C. Hooe, Esq.
    No. 2230 Massachusetts Ave.
    Washington, D.C.
    George Oakley Totten, Jr., Archt."
(see reproduction)

Important Old Views: none found.

Building Dimensions:

   Stories: 3 and 1/2 plus basement

   Height: approx. 57'-0" to roof ridge

   Bays: 3 composite bays on Mass. Ave.

   Widths: 28'-6" on Mass. Ave.
              83'-2" at west (with set backs)
              20'-0" at south
              83'-2" at east (party wall)

Lot Dimensions:

   28'-6" on north (Mass. Ave.)
   28'-6" on south
  100'-0" in depth

Major Alterations:

Relocated partition and installed door and window for new bathroom on first floor (5-21-52, Permit No. A 31563).

CFA photo
Boucher 1970

D.C. Government
Bureau of Licenses and Permits

―MASSACHUSETTS AVENUE―

DRAWING ROOM

100'

28.5'

FIRST FLOOR PLAN
2230 MASSACHUSETTS AVENUE N.W.
0 5 10 15 25 SCALE

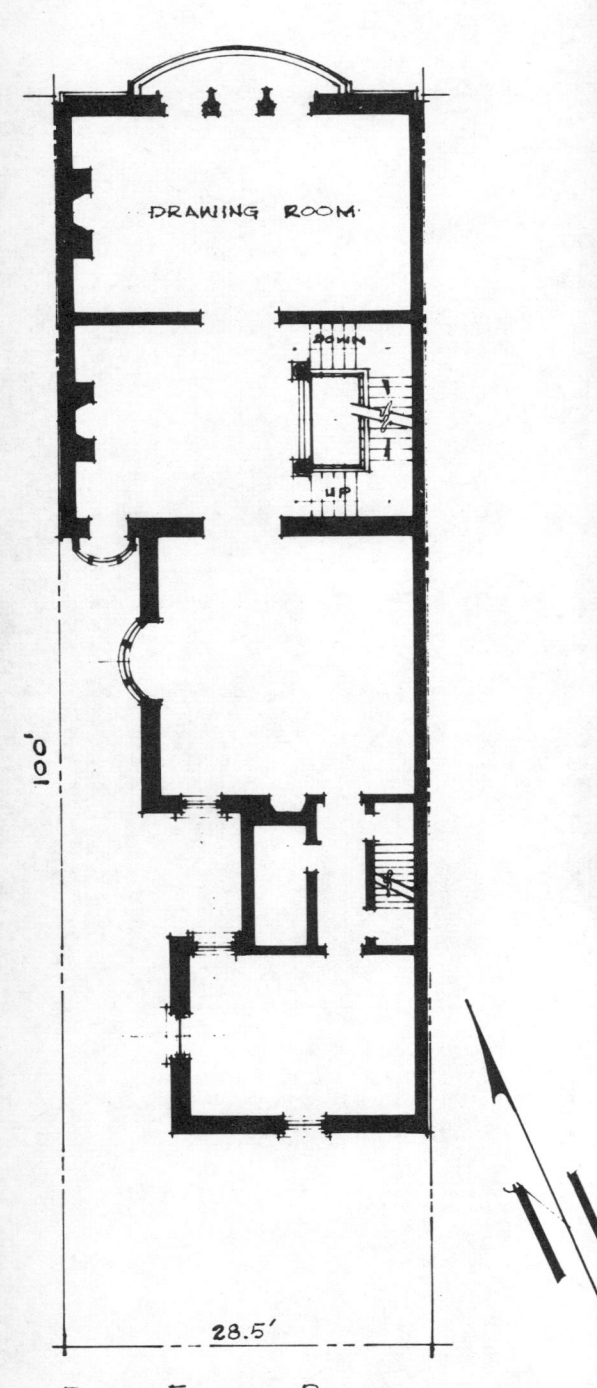

Balcony Detail
CFA photo
Alexander 1971

2234 MASSACHUSETTS AVENUE, N.W., WASHINGTON, D.C.

HABS photo
Boucher 1972

Location: 2234 Massachusetts Avenue, N.W., Washington, D.C.;
                     on the south side of Massachusetts Avenue and
                     Sheridan Circle.

Present Owner: The Government of Ireland

Present Occupant: The Government of Ireland

Present Use: Chancery

Statement of
Significance: This semidetached limestone residence in the Louis XVI
                     manner has two major facades (Massachusetts Avenue and
                     Sheridan Circle). The structure covers most of the
                     fan-shaped lot except for a small section which serves
                     as a light well. The interior circulation and rooms
                     which are designed about a central stair hall, as well
                     as the combination of reflective surfaces and natural
                     light, produce an illusion of greater space.

PART I. HISTORICAL INFORMATION

   A. Lot and Square:

       The building is located in Square 2511, lot 41 (formerly part of
       lot 3 in Block 5, "Kalorama Heights").

   B. Original and Subsequent Owners:

       The following chain of title to the property shows the owners of
       the present structure and of any known preceding structures on the
       site:

       1906 Deed May 16, 1906, recorded May 17, 1906 in
             Liber 2950 folio 398

             William Pitt Kellogg et ux,
             Mary E.
                     To
             Henrietta M. Halliday

             This Deed...Witnesseth, That William P. Kellogg and Mary E.
             Kellogg, his wife, both of the State of Louisiana, temporarily
             residing in the District of Columbia, parties hereto of the
             first part, in consideration of Twelve Thousand Six Hundred
             and Sixty-three ($12,663) Dollars, do hereby grant unto Hen-
             rietta M. Halliday, of the District of Columbia, party hereto
             of the second part, in fee simple, the following described

land and premises...situated in the County of Washington, District of Columbia, namely: Part of Lot...(3) in Block ...(5) 'Kalorama Heights', as per plat thereof recorded in Liber County # 7, folio 34, of the Records of the Office of the Surveyor of the District of Columbia, described by metes and bounds, as follows: Beginning for the same at the most northerly corner of said Lot...(3) and running thence southwesterly on Sheridan Circle...21.676 feet to land conveyed to Mary Eddy Driggs, by Deed recorded among the Land Records of the District of Columbia, in Liber # 2166, folio 351; thence southeasterly along the line of said Driggs land...83.91 feet to a point in the dividing line line between lots...(3) and...(4) distant...26.41 feet northeasterly from the most southerly corner of said Lot... (3); thence northeasterly with the dividing line between Lots...(3) and...(4)...73.59 feet to the southerly line of Massachusetts Avenue; and thence northwesterly on said southerly line...52.28 feet to the place of beginning..."

NOTE: June 26, 1908 Henrietta M. Halliday subdivided part of lot 3, Block 5, "Kalorama Heights", into lot 41. Recorded in County Book 23, folio 187, Office of the Surveyor District of Columbia.

1911 **Deed** January 31, 1911, recorded February 1, 1911 in Liber 3390 folio 481

Henrietta M. Halliday, widow of Edward C.
    To
Anna Jenness Miller

Lot 41 in Henrietta M. Halliday's Subdivision of parts of Block 5, "Kalorama Heights."

1916 Trust January 21, 1916, recorded January 21, 1916 in Liber 3861 folio 131

Anna Jenness Miller, widow
    To
Hobbs and Quinter, Trustees

"...Whereas, the said Anna Jenness Miller is justly indebted unto Harry Wardman in the full sum of Twenty-one Thousand seven hundred and fifty dollars...the party of the first part, in consideration of the premises and of one dollar lawful money...has granted unto the parties of the second part, in fee simple..."

Lot 41, Block 5, "Kalorama Heights."

2234 Massachusetts Avenue, N.W.

1916   Trustee's Deed August 10, 1916, recorded August 11, 1916 in
Liber 3914 folio 108

James D. Hobbs
Hubbert R. Quinter
    To
Howard A. Schladt

"...And Whereas, default having been made in the payment of the...debt, the parties of the first part, in execution of the trust declared in said Deed [Liber 3861, folio 131],... after previous public advertisement...for eleven days in the Evening Star Newspaper proceeded to make sale of said land and premises and appurtenances, and on the eighth day of August 1916...did sell the same at public auction unto Howard A. Schladt who as the highest and best bidder therefor, became the purchaser...for the sum of Twenty-one Thousand ($21,000) Dollars subject to a prior Deed of Trust for Fifty Thousand ($50,000) Dollars..."

1916   Fee Simple Deed August 22, 1916, recorded September 5, 1916 in
Liber 3918 folio 147

Howard A. Schladt, unmarried
    To
Bernhardt Meuser

1916   Deed October 31, 1916, recorded October 24, 1916 in
Liber 3929 folio 131

Bernhardt Meuser et ux,
Elizabeth
    To
Charlotte Jane Isabelle McDonald

"This Deed...by and between Bernhardt Meuser and Elizabeth Meuser, his wife, of the City of Chicago, State of Illinois, parties hereto of the first part, and Charlotte Jane McDonald, of the City of Washington, District of Columbia, party of the second part...the parties of the first part do hereby grant unto the party of the second part, in fee simple...[lot 41, Block 5, 'Kalorama Heights'] subject to an encumbrance of record in the amount of Fifty Thousand dollars ($50,000), which the party of the second part assumes and agrees to pay as part of the consideration for these presents..."

1926   Deed March 1, 1926, recorded March 2, 1926 in
Liber 5680 folio 481

2234 Massachusetts Avenue, N.W.

>
> Isabelle, Marchioness of Huntley
> (formerly Charlotte J. I. McDonald)
>   To
> Harry Wardman
> James D. Hobbs
> (joint tenants)

1929 Deed November 8, 1929, recorded February 2, 1930 in
Liber 6407 folio 459

>
> Harry Wardman
> James D. Hobbs
>   To
> Robert N. Taylor
> K. Parrish Wood, Jr.
> (joint tenants)

1929 Fee Simple Deed November 9, 1929, recorded January 3, 1930 in
Liber 6408 folio 216

>
> Robert N. Taylor
> K. Parrish Wood, Jr.
> (joint tenants)
>   To
> Lillian R. Wardman, Trustee

1930 Deed July 11, 1930, recorded July 12, 1930 in
Liber 6465 folio 469

>
> Lillian R. Wardman, Trustee
>   To
> Garnett Crossan Dick

1945 Deed January 12, 1945, recorded January 29, 1945 in
Liber 8063 folio 411

>
> Garnett Crossan Douglas
>   To
> Ronald Ferree Dick

"This Deed...by and between Garnett Crossan Douglas (formerly Garnett Crossan Dick) of the City of Newport...State of Rhode Island, party hereto of the first part; and Ronald Ferree Dick, of the said City of Newport, party hereto of the second part ..."

1945 Deed September 19, 1945, recorded September 29, 1945 in
Liber 8162 folio 515

2234 Massachusetts Avenue, N.W.

>Garnett Crossan Douglas
>(Ancilliary Guardian of the Estate of
>Ronald Ferree Dick, a minor)
>   To
>Margaret Good Van Clief (devisee under the Will of
>Ray Alan Van Clief, deceased)
>
>"...for and in consideration of the sum of One Hundred and five thousand ($105,000) Dollars..."
>
>NOTE: The Will of Margaret Good Van Clief was recorded August 5, 1949 in Will Book No. 392, page No. 508, Registrar of Wills, District of Columbia.
>
>>sons: Ray Alan Van Clief, Jr.
>>   Daniel Good Van Clief

1949 Deed August 19, 1949, recorded August 25, 1949 in Liber 9035 folio 164

>Daniel Good Van Clief
>Ray Alan Van Clief
>First and Merchants National Bank of Richmond
>   To
>The Government of Ireland
>
>"This Deed...by and between Daniel Good Van Clief and Ray Alan Van Clief, both residing at Esmont, Albermarle County, Virginia, and First and Merchants National Bank of Richmond ...Under the last Will and Testament of Margaret Good Van Clief, late of Esmont, Albermarle County, Virginia, acting pursuant to the power and authority to them granted by paragraph second of said will, parties of the first part, and the Government of Ireland, party of the second part...for and in consideration of Seventy-two Thousand Dollars ($72,000)..."
>
>Source: Recorder of Deeds, Washington, D.C.

C. Date of Erection:

The building was begun in June 1908 and completed in September 1909.

D. Building Permits

The applications for the following building permits were filed by the architect, contractor or owner's agent and provide significant data:

2234 Massachusetts Avenue, N.W.

No. 4046, June 18, 1908
Permit to build dwelling
    Owner: Mrs. Henrietta M. Halliday
    Architect: W. P. Cresson
    Builder: Frank L. Wagner
    Estimated cost: $40,000.

Filed with No. 4046, June 18, 1908
Application for Building Projection No. 72792, July 21, 1908
    "It is desired to extend the face of the basement wall below water table six inches beyond the building line, as shown by accompanying tracing and for the reason stated in the accompanying letter. It is also necessary to make a further projection at the main entrance of nine inches by a width of 15'-6" to carry pilasters about doorway, shown by front elevations submitted herewith."

No. 357, July 30, 1908
Permit to Repair or Reconstruct Building
    Owner: Mrs. E. C. Halliday
    Architect: William P. Cresson
    Contractor: Frank L. Wagner
    Cost of improvement: $100.
    "To extend face of basement wall below water table 6" beyond building line with a projection 9" X 15'-6" to carry pilasters."

No. 5635, June 6, 1911
Permit for Repairs, Alterations, etc.:
    Owner: A. J. Miller
    Architect: Boal & Brown
    Contractor: Langley
    Estimated cost: $3,000.
    Location: Lot 3, Square 2511
    "Change main stair, build partitions, brick up openings, cut openings, minor interior repairs. Structural features of building not disturbed. Change location of plumbing fixtures in one bath and in one basin. One new bath."

No. 6100, June 28, 1911
Permit for Repairs, Alterations, etc.
    Owner: A. J. Miller
    Architect: Boal & Brown
    Contractor: Langley
  *Address: 2236 Massachusetts Avenue, N.W.
    "Remove 13" brick wall on 2nd floor. Put in beam support and iron beams. Build bay windows in rear, one story high, fireproof: 3'-0" X 11'-0". Iron beams over openings as per plans on file."

  *Main floor plan filed with permit and the description of the building indicate that 2234 Massachusetts Avenue, N.W. is the same building. (See reproduction of floor plan.)

No. 4653, April 2, 1913
Permit for Repairs, Alterations, etc.:
    Owner: A. J. Miller
    Estimated cost: $500.
    "Iron and glass marquise to main entrance for Anna Jenness Miller."

Filed with No. 4653, April 2, 1913
Special Application for Building Projection
    One marquise: 6'-6" projection
               11'-5" width

No. 5557, May 19, 1913
Permit to install one electric passenger elevator: 3'4" X 3'4"
    Owner: Anna J. Miller
    Mechanic: Otis Elevator Company
    Cost: $2,450
    Location: South side of building

Source: D.C. Government: Department of Economic Development, Bureau of Licenses and Permits, Central Files.

E. Alterations and Additions:

The interior was extensively altered by Boal & Brown in 1911. (See Permits No. 5635 and No. 6100.) The main floor plan filed with Permit No. 6100 indicated the changes made to Cresson's original design. (See reproduction.)

The principal bedroom floor appears to have been remodeled after 1930.

F. Original Architect: William Penn Cresson, Washington, D.C.
Architect for Alterations (1911): Boal & Brown, Washington, D.C.

William Penn Cresson, the son of Dr. and Mrs. Hilbourne Thompson Cresson, was born in Claymont, Delaware on September 17, 1873. Cresson attended the University of Pennsylvania from 1895 to 1897 and then became a student at the École des Beaux Arts until 1902. In 1902 he studied at the École des Sciences Politiques.

Cresson came to Washington, D.C. in 1905 where he practiced architecture for two or three years. The city directories list "Wyeth & Cresson, architects" at 1517 H Street, N.W. in 1906 and 1907. In 1908 "Wm. P. Cresson" and "Nathan C. Wyeth" were listed separately, but still at 1517 H Street. Correspondence filed with the original building permit (No. 4046, June 18, 1908), was written under the following letterhead and signed by W. P. Cresson:

        Joint Offices of   McLean Building
        Nathan C. Wyeth   1517 H Street
        William P. Cresson   Washington, D.C.
        Architects   Telephone: Main 507

Mrs. E.C. Halliday's residence at 2234 Massachusetts Avenue was built in 1908 and 1909, but neither permits nor drawings indicate that Wyeth was involved in the design.

At various times in his life, Cresson was an architect, rancher, diplomat, author and professor of international law. In 1907 he left Washington to become a cattle rancher in Nevada for two years. His diplomatic career began in 1909 with his appointment as Secretary to the American Legation at Lima, Peru. Later posts included: Second Secretary to the American Embassy, London (1912-1913); Secretary to the American Legation at Quito, Ecuador (1913-1914); Secretary to the American Legation, Panama (1914-1915); Secretary to the American Embassy, Petrograd (1915-1917); and Secretary to the American Legation, Lisbon (1917).

During World War I, Cresson was commissioned as Lieutenant in the Air Service of the Signal Officer's Reserve Corps and subsequently promoted to Captain. After the war, he continued his service as a Major in the Reserve Officers Corps - as well as accepting a post as Assistant Professor of International Law at Princeton. He later became Fletcher Professor of International Law at Tufts College.

Cresson remained active in diplomatic affairs - serving as Secretary at the Conference on Limitation of Armament in Washington in 1921 and 1922; and Secretary at the Sixth Pan American Conference in Havana in 1928.

His writings include:

        "Persia, The Awakening East"
        "The Cossacks, Their History and Country"
        "The Holy Alliance"
        "Diplomatic Portraits"

In 1921 Cresson and Miss Margaret French, daughter of Daniel Chester French, sculptor, were married. They maintained homes in Washington, D.C. and Stockbridge, Massachusetts. Cresson died in Stockbridge on May 12th, 1932.

2234 Massachusetts Avenue, N.W.

Sources: Who Was Who in America 1897-1942: A Companion Volume to Who's Who in America, Vol. I, Chicago: The A. N. Marquis Co., 1942.

The New York Times, 5-13-32, 16:1 (obituary).

Theodore D. Boal (1867-1938), son of George Jack Boal, was born in Iowa City, Iowa. He attended Harvard University and was graduated from the University of Iowa. He then studied in Paris at the École des Beaux Arts.

Boal was listed under "Architects" in the Washington city directories from 1906 through 1909. From 1910 through 1916, the architectural firm of Boal & Brown was listed at 1725 H Street.

In 1916 Boal organized and financed the "Boal Troop", later designated Company A, 107th Machine Gun Battalion. The troop served on the Mexican border and then overseas. Col. Theodore Boal received the Croix de Guerre, the Distinguished Service Cross, and was an officer of the French Legion of Honor.

After World War I, he returned to his estate in the town of Boalsburg, Pennsylvania.

Source: The New York Times, 8-23-38, 17:4 (obituary).

Ward Brown (1877-1946) was born in San Francisco, California. He studied architecture at the Armour Institute in Chicago and the Atelier Paulin at the École des Beaux Arts, Paris - as well as other European schools.

Brown came to Washington in 1906 and continued his training under practicing architects. In 1910 he joined Theodore D. Boal to form Boal & Brown.

Boal & Brown carried out the extensive interior alterations of 2234 Massachusetts Avenue in 1911. Brown "designed the Netherlands Embassy and the Austrian...[Embassy] building, also a number of private residences in Washington and environs. In later years Mr. Brown made his home in Alexandria, Va., devoting his attention to the restoration of historic homes there and in Georgetown." (Biographical Dictionary of American Architects (Deceased))

Sources: Henry F. Withey and Elsie R. Withey, Biographical Dictionary of American Architects (Deceased), Los Angeles: New Age Publishing Co., 1956.

The Evening Star, 10-14-46, 2:8 (obituary).

2234 Massachusetts Avenue, N.W.

G. Known Plans, Drawings, Elevations, etc.:

Elevation on Massachusetts Avenue. Blueprint. Scale 1/4"=1'
Filed with Permit No. 4046, June 18, 1908
    "Residence for Mrs. E. C. Halliday. Sheridan Circle
    and Massachusetts Avenue, Washington, D.C.
    W. P. Cresson, Archt."
(see reproduction)

Projection plan. Ink on linen. Scale 1/4"=1'
Filed with Permit No. 4046, June 18, 1908
    "Residence for Mrs. E. C. Halliday. Sheridan Circle
    Massachusetts Ave., Washington, D.C.
    W. P. Cresson, Archt.
    1517 H St., N.W."
(see reproduction)

Plan of first floor. Blueprint. Scale 1/4"=1'
Filed with Permit No. 6100, June 28, 1911
    "Changes in Residence, Sheridan Circle & Mass. Ave.
    Boal & Brown, Archt.
    1725 H St., Washington, D.C."
(see reproduction)

Elevation and plan of marquise. Ink on linen. Scale 1/2"=1'
Filed with Permit No. 4653, April 2, 1913

H. Important Old Views: none found

I. Residents:

1. City and telephone directories list the following tenants:

    1909-1913 No listing
    1914-1916 Mrs. Anna Jenness Miller
    1917-1919 Arthur B. Campbell
    1920-1923 Mrs. Charlotte I. McDonald
    1924-1931 Vacant
    1932-1942 Charles M. Dick
    1943   Richard S. **R**heen
    1944   Mrs. Gordon Douglas
    1945-1946 No listing
    1947-1949 Mrs. Ray A. Van Clief
    1950   Irish Legation
    1951-1972 Embassy of Ireland, Chancery

2234 Massachusetts Avenue, N.W.

2. Biographies of the residents:

Henrietta M. Halliday, widow of Edward C. Halliday, was listed in the Washington city directories from 1906 through 1908 at 1814 N Street. Her husband, Edward C. Halliday, had been listed in the District of Columbia from 1890 through 1904 at the same address. He died sometime before June 7, 1905 when his will, as recorded in Will Book No. 61, page 228, was admitted to probate. The will states:

> I give and bequeath to my wife Henrietta M. Halliday the sum of One hundred thousand dollars...to be paid to her in lawful money of these United States as soon after my decease as circumstances may reasonably permit...I also give and devise to my said wife, her heirs and assign forever, the house and lot now owned and occupied by me, situate on the southerly side of N Street northwest between Connecticut Avenue and Nineteenth Street in the City of Washington, District of Columbia and known as...1814 N Street northwest, the lot being further indicated as number...(68) of E. C. Halliday's subdivision in Square...(139) as recorded in book...11 of subdivision page...191 Surveyor's Records, District of Columbia...

In May 1906 Mrs. Halliday purchased the Sheridan Circle lot on which 2234 Massachusetts Avenue was to be built; and in June 1908 "Mrs. Henrietta M. Halliday" was issued a permit to build a dwelling on her lot. Although the house was completed in 1909, Mrs. Halliday was never listed at her new address.

Mrs. Halliday owned other Massachusetts Avenue properties. In 1911 she bought The Wendell Mansion apartments from Anna Jenness Miller (Liber 3390, folio 480, Recorder of Deeds); and in 1922 she was deeded 2305 Massachusetts Avenue by Harry Wardman (Liber 4707, folio 249, Recorder of Deeds) - only to deed it back to him eight months later (Liber 4876, folio 27, Recorder of Deeds).

The Will of Henrietta M. Halliday, recorded in Will Book No. 116, page 24, was admitted to probate December 31, 1923. A letter filed with the Will valued Mrs. Halliday's estate at $1,930,870.57.

Anna Jenness Miller, widow of Conrad, purchased 2234 Massachusetts Avenue in 1911. In 1898 "Conrad Miller, publisher" was listed in the city directories at "Phelps c. LeRoy Place". This was the house which Thomas F. Walsh bought, completely furnished, in 1899 before construction of 2020 Massachusetts Avenue was begun. Evalyn Walsh McLean wrote:

301

> We called the house always, 'LeRoy and
> Phelps Place'...The house was three story
> yellow brick with tile roof...It had been
> the home of Mr. and Mrs. Conrad Jenness
> Miller; Conrad was a minor celebrity in
> Washington, a widely traveled lecturer...
> (<u>Father Struck It Rich</u>, p. 53)

In 1899 Conrad was listed at The Cairo, and from 1900 through 1909 he was not listed in city directories. Then, Annie J. Miller's name appeared separately in 1910. Her husband had apparently died sometime between 1900 and 1909, since she was eventually listed at 2234 Massachusetts Avenue in 1914 as "Anna Jenness Miller (widow of Conrad)".

Mrs. Anna Jenness Miller was an author and lecturer:

> For several years...[she] was proprietor and
> editor of the Jenness-Miller Monthly, a
> magazine published in New York and devoted
> to physical development and improved dress.
> Upon these topics she gave over eleven
> hundred lectures in the principal cities
> of the United States and Canada. Among her
> books may be mentioned Twixt Love and
> Marriage, Mother and Babe, How to Finish and
> Furnish a Home, Creating a Home, and the
> Philosopher of Driftwood. She also wrote the
> chapter on Dress for the revised Johnson's
> Encyclopedia...At the close of her platform
> work, Mrs. Jenness-Miller lived abroad for
> years, where she became interested in collecting
> paintings and curios. She has built many
> artistic houses. Her latest venture is Wendell
> Mansions, 2339 Massachusetts Avenue, where she
> resides now. (<u>American Biogarphical Directories,
> District of Columbia</u> 1908-1909)

Her several years abroad "collecting paintings and curios" probably included her work for Thomas F. Walsh, as Evalyn Walsh McLean related:

> My father had hired Mrs. Anna Jenness Miller
> to scout around and help my mother buy just
> what was needed for that house; it was a job
> that lasted several years...She even went abroad
> to get some choicer paintings and the bric-a-brac
> we needed...(<u>Father Struck It Rich</u>, p. 92)

In 1910 and 1911 Anna Jenness Miller lived at 2339 Massachusetts Avenue; and then after two years at 2117 Le Roy Place, N.W., she resided at 2234 Massachusetts Avenue from 1914 through 1916.

2234 Massachusetts Avenue, N.W.

Sources: <u>American Biographical Directories, District of Columbia</u>, 1908-1909, Washington, D.C.: The Potomac Press, 1908.

Evalyn Walsh McLean, with Boyden Sparkes, <u>Father Struck It Rich</u>, Boston: Little, Brown, and Company, 1936.

<u>Charlotte Jane Isabelle McDonald</u> (later the Marchioness of Huntley), the daughter of John F. Fallon, purchased 2234 Massachusetts Avenue in 1916. Her husband, James McDonald, had died January 13, 1915 in their home at 1701 22nd Street, N.W.. Mr. McDonald, a native of Scotland who came to the United States in 1840 at the age 15, had organized the European Branch of Standard Oil. For many years, he and his family lived in London where McDonald handled Standard Oil's European and Asian Affairs. Besides his wife, McDonald left a son, James, Jr., and a stepson, Arthur B. Campbell (Charlotte Jane Isabelle McDonald's son).

Source: <u>The New York Times</u>, 1-14-15, 11:4 (obituary).
<u>The Washington Post</u>, 1-14-15, 14:6 (obituary).

<u>Arthur B. Campbell</u> (1888-1954) served as a captain in the U. S. Army in World War I. From 1917 through 1919 his home was listed in the directories at 2234 Massachusetts Avenue. Later, after serving in the U. S. diplomatic service, he became a vice-president of Riggs National Bank of Washington.

Source: <u>The New York Times</u>, 7-23-54, 17:6 (obituary).

In 1922 Arthur Cambpell's mother, Mrs. McDonald, became the <u>Marchioness of Huntley</u>, the second wife of the 11th Marquess of Huntley. The Marchioness died in Petersburgh, England in May 1939.

She had sold her residence at 2234 Massachusetts Avenue to Harry Wardman and James D. Hobbs on March 1, 1926.

Source: <u>The New York Times</u>, 5-18-39, 25:2 (obituary).

<u>Harry Wardman</u> (1873-1938) speculated in real estate over much of northwest Washington. <u>The New York Times</u>, March 19, 1938 noted:

> There was a time, not more than ten years ago, when it was believed that Mr. Wardman was landlord to about one-tenth of all the private residents in Washington.

He bought "2234" in 1926 and, according to the directories, left it vacant through 1930 when it was sold again.

2234 Massachusetts Avenue, N.W.

Wardman, born in Yorkshire, England, came to America in 1893 "with 7 shillings" in his pocket. When he first arrived in Washington, D.C. in 1895, he worked as a carpenter. Noting the lack of housing for government employees, he started to build "plain, low priced apartment houses and simple private dwellings...and later larger apartments for more money and more sumptuous hotels." (The New York Times, 3-19-38)

Two of these "sumptuous hotels" were the Wardman Park and the Carlton. In 1916 construction began on the Wardman Park Hotel (now the Sheraton Park Hotel) on Woodley Road and Connecticut Avenue, N.W. Many thought the project would be a failure because a luxury hotel had never been built so far from the center of the city. The sceptics were proven wrong. In 1926 the Carlton Hotel was built on the site of H. H. Richardson's Anderson House at 16th and K Streets, N.W. The 250 room Carlton cost more than $3,000,000 to build.

Other Wardman apartments and hotels included:

Brighton Hotel	2123 California St., N.W.
The Cathedral Mansions	
Center:	3000 Connecticut Ave., N.W.
North:	3100 Connecticut Ave., N.W.
The Castleton Hotel:	1710 16th St., N.W.
The Conard (apartments)	1228 I St., N.W.
The Dresden (apartments)	2226 Connecticut Ave., N.W.
Hay-Adams Hotel	800 16th St., N.W.
The Highlands (apartments)	1914 Connecticut Ave., N.W.
The Roosevelt Hotel	16th St. between V and W St., N.W.
Stoneleigh Court (apartment-hotel)	Connecticut Ave. and L St., N.W.
Park Lane Hotel	London, England

At the height of its speculative success Wardman Real Estate Properties, Inc. owned property valued at $30,000,000. However, with the Depression, Wardman started to suffer severe losses and sold many of his larger holdings.

Sources: The Evening Star, 6-4-35, B1:1.
        The Evening Star, 3-19-38, 2:1 (obituary).
        The New York Times Magazine, "Another Dick Whittington Returns", by William Atherton DuPuy, 10-11-25 p. 9.
        The New York Times, 3-19-38, 15:3 (obituary).
        The Washington Post, 3-19-38, 1:2 (obituary).
        The Washington Post, Potomac, "The Washington Wardman Built", by Carl Bernstein, 2-16-69, pp. 23-32.
        The Washington Herald, 5-26-19, 6:5.
        The Washington Herald, 10-22-32, 1:3.
        The Washington Herald, 7-8-36, 11:1.
        The Washington Herald, 3-19-38, 1:2 (obituary).

2234 Massachusetts Avenue, N.W.

Garnett Crossan Dick (later Douglas), wife of C. Mathews Dick owned the house from 1930 until 1945. She was divorced from C. Mathews Dick in 1943, and remarried one month later to Gordon Douglas:

> Mrs. Dick of 2234 Massachusetts Avenue, N.W.... considered one of the District's best dressed hostesses, and Gordon Douglas, wealthy socialite and New York businesman, were married last week at the Arlington Court House...Mr. Douglas has entertained extensively at his home at Newport, R. I., and at Palm Beach, Fla. He met Mrs. Dick at Newport several years ago. (The Sunday Star, June 6, 1943)

Mrs. Dick had two sons - C. Mathews Dick, Jr. age 18 and Ronald Dick, age 15.

Source: The Sunday Star, 6-6-43, 6:5.

Mrs. Margaret Good Van Clief, widow of Ray Alan Van Clief, bought the residence in September 1945. Her husband was a landowner in Virginia and Newport, Rhode Island, and a well-known "industrialist, horse-breeder, and yachtsman."(The New York Times, 4-5-48) During World War II, Mr. Van Clief served as a special consultant to the War Manpower Commission. He died in June 1945.

Mrs. Van Clief died in April 1948 at the family estate "Nydrie", near Esmont, Virginia. She left two sons, Ray Alan and Daniel Good Van Clief, who sold 2234 Massachusetts Avenue to the Irish Republic in 1949.

Sources: The Evening Star, 6-29-45, 8:3 (Mr. Van Clief's obituary).
        The New York Times, 4-5-48, 21:4 (Mrs. Van Clief's obituary).
        The Washington Post, 4-5-48, B 2:6 (Mrs. Van Clief's obituary).

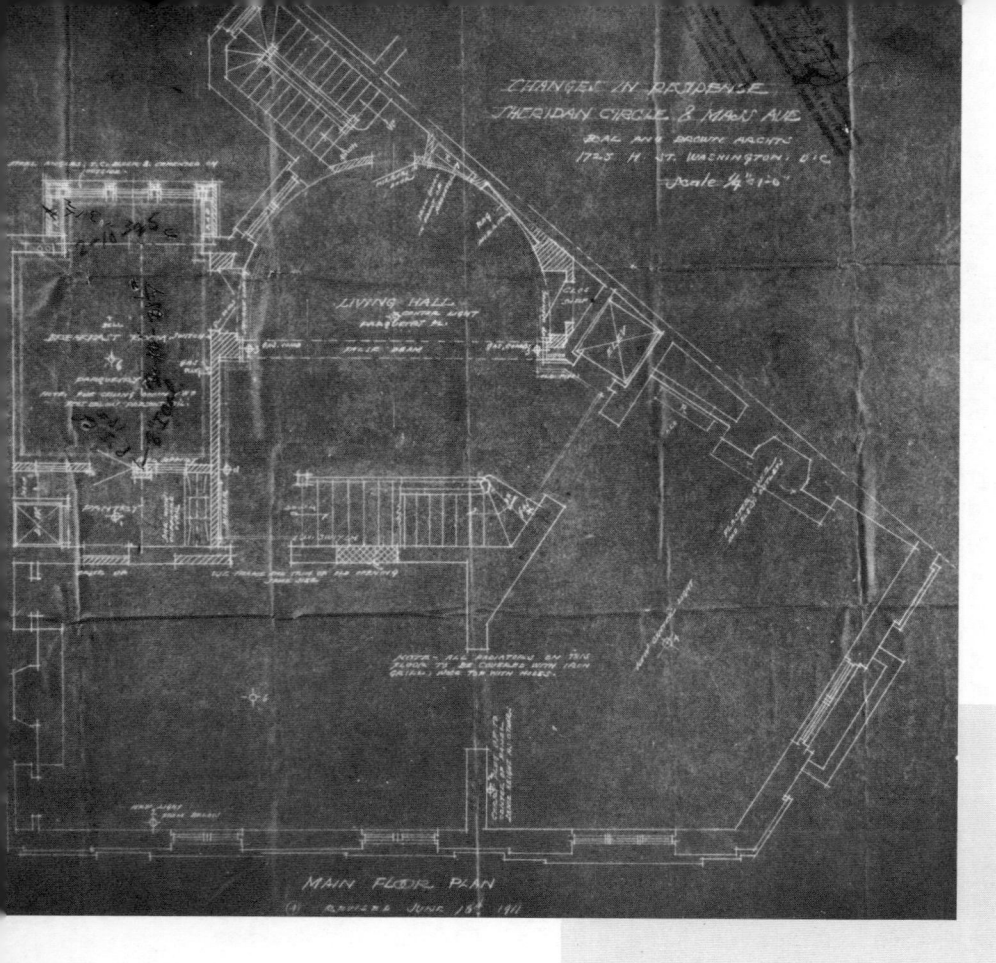

First Floor Plan
D.C. Government,
Bureau of Licenses and Permits

HABS photo
Boucher 1972

306

D.C. Government,
Bureau of Licenses
and Permits

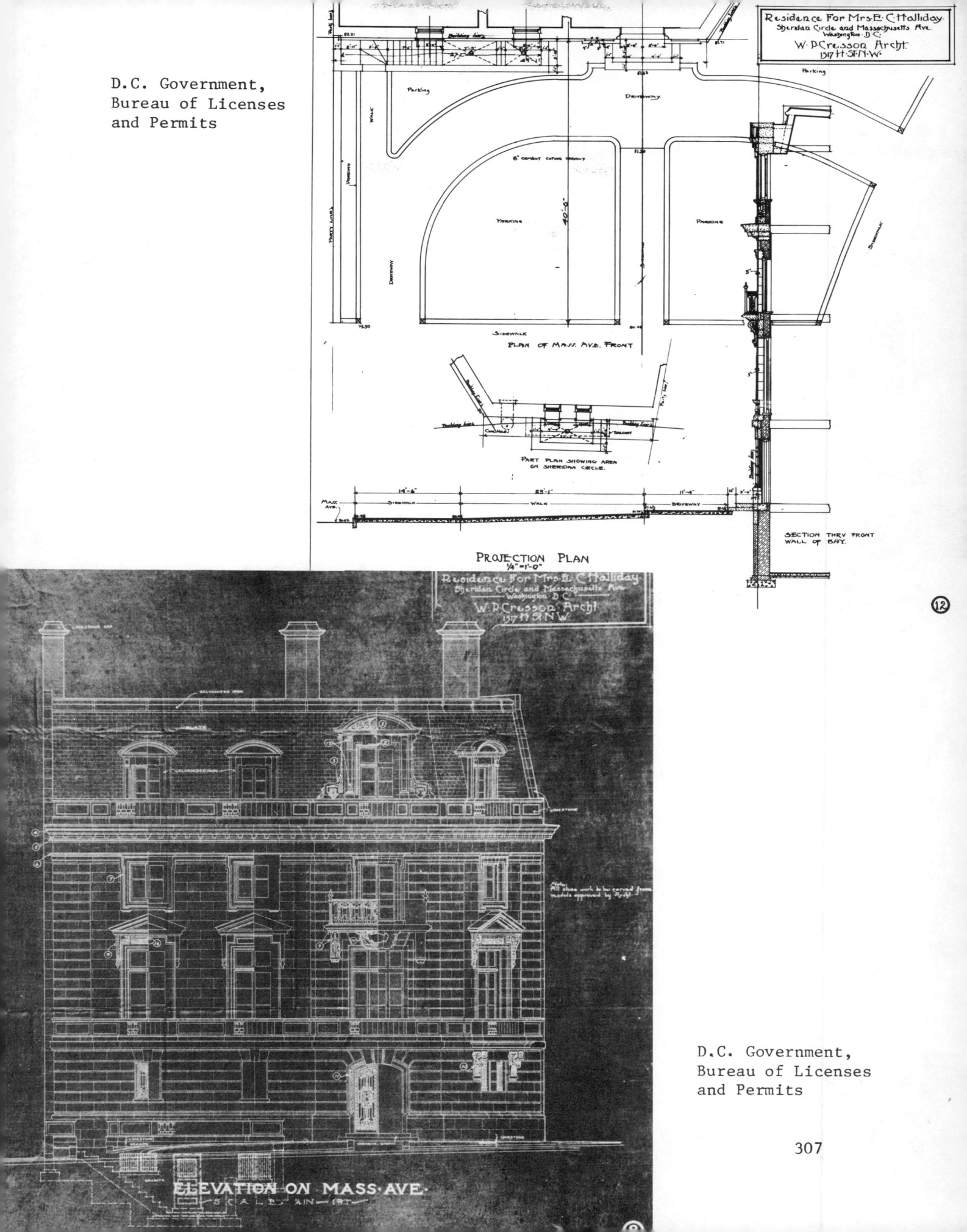

307

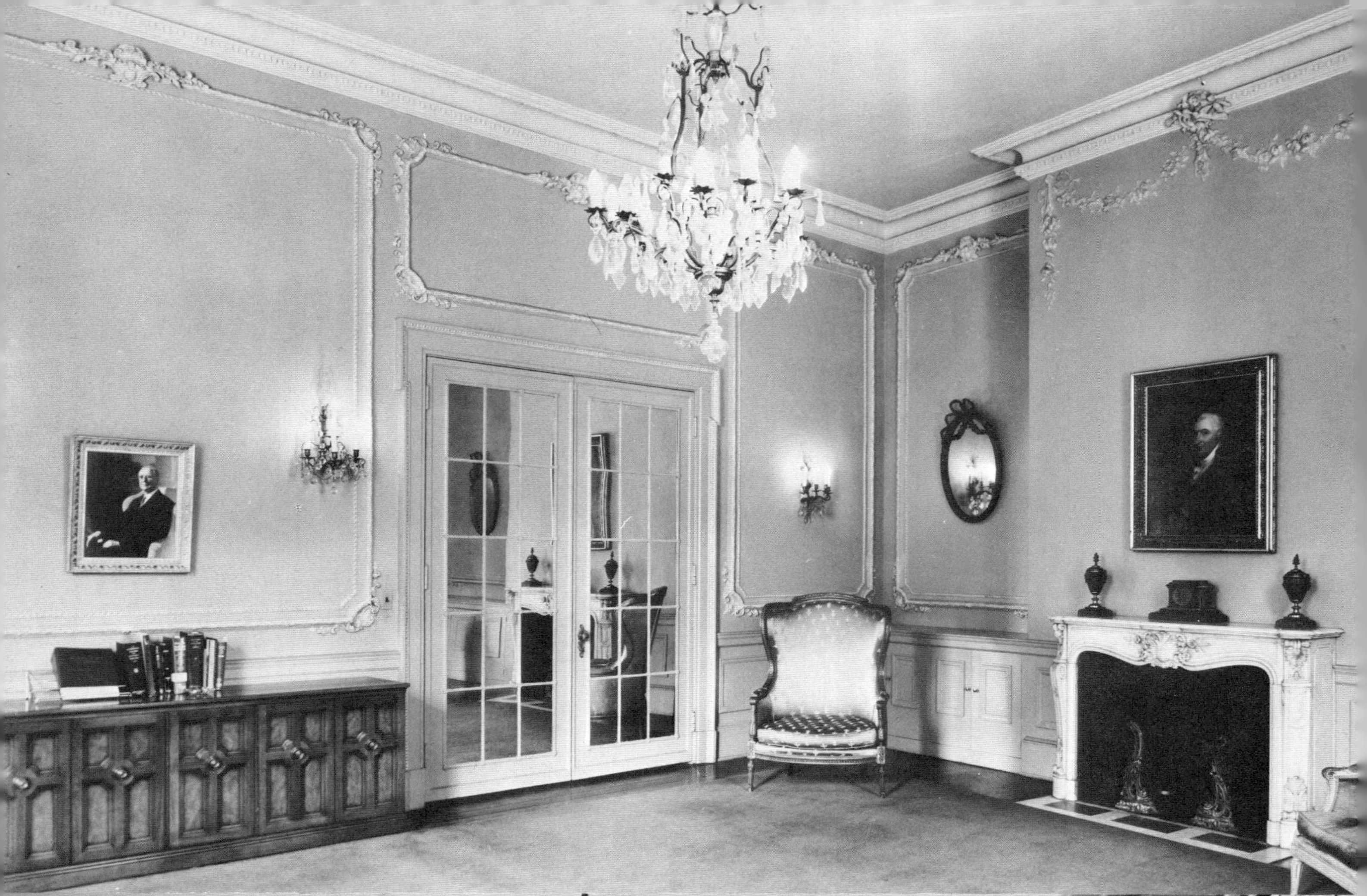

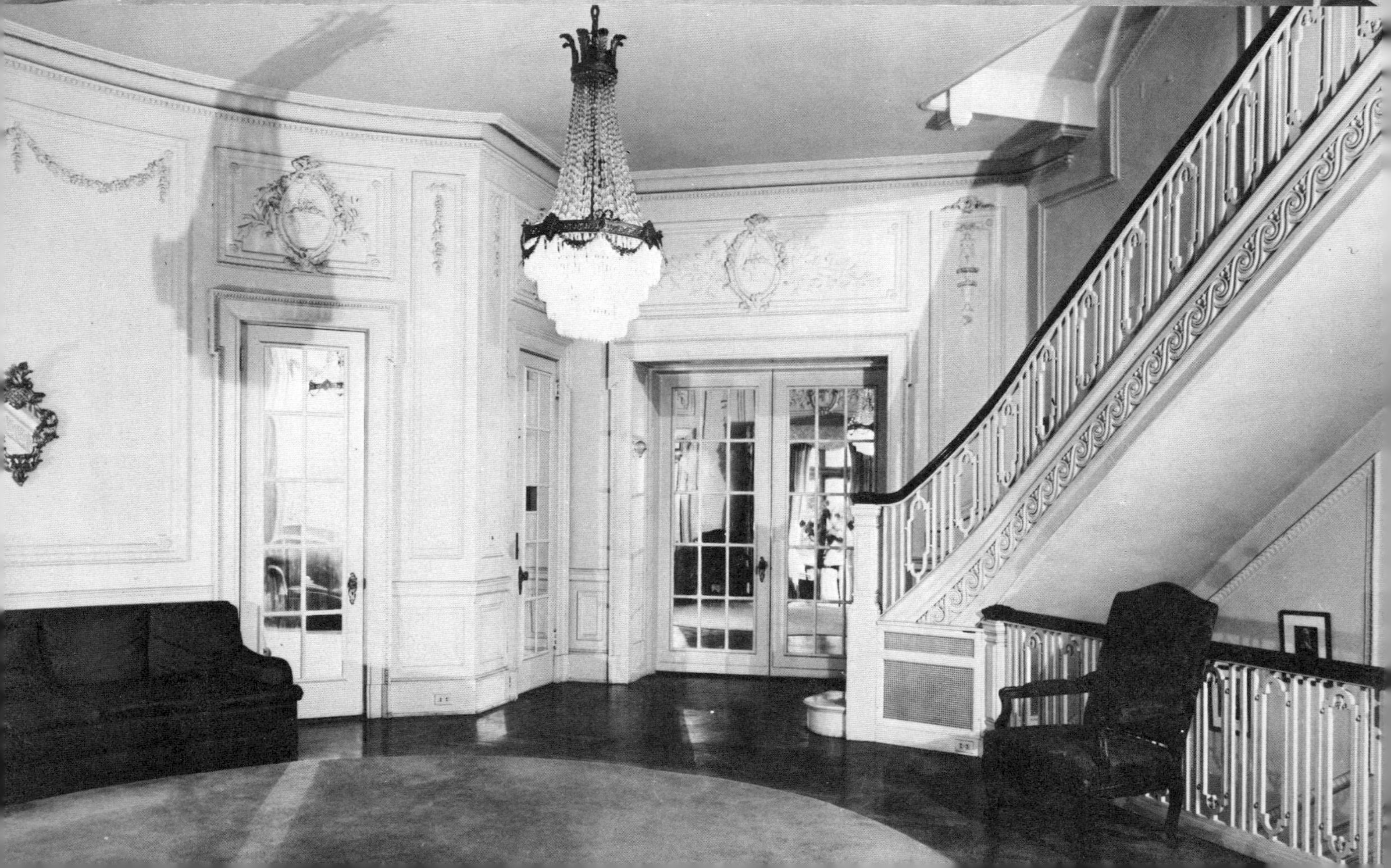

Opposite, Top
Drawing Room
(Ambassador's office)
CFA photo
Boucher 1970

Opposite, Below
Living Hall
CFA photo
Boucher 1970

Right
Detail over door
Dining Room
CFA photo
Boucher 1970

Below
Dining Room
CFA photo
Boucher 1970

2234 Massachusetts Avenue, N.W.

PART II. ARCHITECTURAL INFORMATION

    A. General Statement:

        1. Architectural character: This semidetached structure has a Louis XVI exterior with 18th century French and English interior details, and a polygonal plan.

        2. Condition: The exterior is well maintained. The interior (except for the main floor) was remodeled after 1930.

    B. Exterior Description:

        1. Overall dimensions: The three and one half story plus basement structure measures 58'-0" from sidewalk to roof ridge. Its plan is polygonal, having two major elevations (one on Massachusetts Avenue, the second on Sheridan Circle). The east party wall is 39'-0" long; the three bay north elevation (the entrance bay on Massachusetts Avenue broken forward slightly), 49'-9"; the one bay northwest elevation (Sheridan Circle), 23'-2"; the southwest party wall, 50'-0"; the one bay southeast elevation (which is broken forward 12'-0" by a 7'-6" south end service stair), 15'-6"; and the one bay south wall, 14'-0".

        2. Foundations: concrete footings and slab.

        3. Wall construction: The building, faced in tan limestone, has a smooth base capped by a torus and cavetto water table. The rusticated ground floor is separated from the first and second floors by a cyma and block string course which serves as base for a raised panel, false balustrade. The first and second floors are smooth limestone, except for the corners and the full height of the entrance bay, which are rusticated.

        4. Structure: concrete block and brick bearing walls.

        5. Mechanical: hot air, oil-burning furnace. Electric lighting. The iron and wood, 1200 lb. Otis passenger elevator was installed in 1913.

        6. Porches, stoops, bulkheads, etc.: At the northeast corner on Massachusetts Avenue, an urn baluster, limestone balustrade with panelled ends (see elevation drawing) encloses twelve granite risers which ascend east from the basement areaway to grade level.

            Approached from the avenue, the entrance stoop has two granite risers flanked by cheek walls with wrought iron panels and scrolls supporting a marquise canopy.

            At each first floor window, the false balustrade is interrupted

2234 Massachusetts Avenue, N.W.

by urn balusters, a panel of which breaks forward at the Sheridan Circle facade to form a balcony on concave consoles with guttae and swags.

At the head of the first floor window above the entrance, a shallow, limestone balcony with a decorative cast and wrought iron railing is supported by acanthus consoles.

7. **C**himneys: Visible from the street are three brick chimneys each with limestone cornice and cavetto cap (one at the east party wall, one at the southwest party wall and the last at the building mid-section).

8. Openings:

   a. Doorways and doors: The segmentally-arched street entrance has a recessed, glazed double door with decorative cast and wrought iron grilles; and a limestone architrave of oak leaf pulvination set within voussoirs and interrupted by the keystone.

   b. Windows: All windows are casement, those on the first floor having transoms.

   The ground floor windows are two-lights wide (except for the central north bay which is one-light in width) and have decorative wrought iron grilles, fillet and block sills, and keystones.

   The first floor French windows are two-lights wide, except for two bays (one over the entrance and the second on Sheridan Circle) which are three-lights in width. Each window has a talon architrave, guilloche frieze and acanthus consoles which support a pediment. The bay over the entrance has a pulvinated architrave, recessed within a cove, and an escutcheon keystone.

   The second floor windows and the French door over the entrance are two-lights wide, having crossette talon architraves with guttae at their bases.

9. Roof:

   a. Shape, covering: The slate mansard roof has limestone coping and a galvanized iron, pulvinated ridge cap with built-up flat roofing behind.

   b. Cornice, eaves: The limestone entablature has a fascia and talon architrave; a plain frieze; and an egg and dart, bracket, corona and cyma cornice. The entablature is capped by a panelled balustrade interrupted by urn balusters centered over each bay.

   c. Dormers, cupolas, towers: Each galvanized iron, casement

311

dormer has panelled pilasters capped by a frieze
broken forward to support a segmentally-arched pediment.
The exception is the limestone dormer over the entrance.
This opening has panelled pilasters flanked by decorative
block consoles and capped by a frieze broken forward over
either pilaster. Above the frieze is a segmentally-arched
pediment having a shell and spray tympanum.

C. Interior Description:

1. Floor plans: Entered by the north entrance vestibule (flanked by closets) the ground floor reception hall on Sheridan Circle gives access to two chambers on Massachusetts Avenue, as well as the main stair at the east and an oval sitting room at the southeast. The sitting room is approached by an elevator vestibule and terminated by the service stair. To the east of the main stair, service rooms connect the sitting room to the chambers on Massachusetts Avenue.

   The main stair ascends east to the first floor apsidal living hall. Immediately at the head, and to the left, is the dining room (north); while to the east are the pantry and the breakfast room, the latter having a bay window overlooking the rear court (south). Connected to the dining room, the drawing room on Sheridan Circle is at the west via the elevator vestibule. (See plan.)

2. Spaces:

   Entrance hall:

   a. Flooring: The marble floor has white squares with black insets at the corners.

   b. Baseboard: 6", wood painted cream, with cyma cap.

   c. Walls: plaster, painted.

   d. Cornice: cove.

   e. Ceiling: plaster painted white.

   f. Doorways and doors: All doors have fascia and cyma architraves. The beveled glass double door to the vestibule has decorative cast iron grilles, a rectangular transom and side lights. The convex double door to the sitting room is mirror-paned. The remaining single doors (one to the north rooms and one each to the closets, flanking the vestibule) are panelled.

   g. Hardware: bronze door handles and lock escutcheons.

2234 Massachusetts Avenue, N.W.

Stair:

The main stair ascends nine risers on a southeast curve and east eleven additional straight-run risers from the entrance hall to the first floor living hall. The second flight ascends twenty-four risers east to the second floor; the third proceeds to the dormer level. Each flight has a plaster soffit, painted wood risers and treads, a closed stringer with wave ornament, a wrought iron bar and panel banister, and an oak handrail. (See photograph.)

Living hall: (painted tan. See photograph.)

a. Flooring: oak, herringbone parquetry with cherry border.

b. Baseboard: 11", wood with bead and reed cap.

c. Dado: raised panels with cavetto moulding.

d. Chairrail: 3'-0" high, wood, fascia and cyma.

e. Walls: Panels are formed by applied cavetto leaf mouldings with floral drapes and pendants at the top.

f. Cornice: cyma, egg and dart, cove, leafy roll and cyma.

g. Ceiling: 13'-6" high, plaster painted white.

h. Doorways and doors: All doors are mirror-paned and have egg and dart, crossette architraves. The doors are capped by rosette indented panels centered by flower basket escutcheons with swags and sprays.

i. Hardware: gilded, rocaille door knobs and mortise lock escutcheons.

j. Lighting: The single chandelier has multiple tiers of crystal pendants hung from a bronze girdle of masks and swags attached by crystal prisms drapes to a bronze acanthus leaf crown.

Drawing room: (Ambassador's office; painted pale yellow. See photograph.)

a. Flooring: oak, herringbone parquetry.

b. Baseboard: 11", wood with bead and reed cap.

c. Dado: panels formed by applied cavetto moulding. Base cabinets to chairrail height flank the south wall chimney.

d. Chairrail: 3'-0" high, wood, fascia and cyma.

2234 Massachusetts Avenue, N.W.

e. Walls: Between each opening, over both doors and flanking the chimney, are applied, plaster, rocaille wall panels.

f. Cornice: cyma, egg and dart, cove, leafy roll and cyma.

g. Ceiling: 13'-6" high, plaster painted white.

h. Doorways and doors: mirror-paned double doors to living hall and dining room (sliding).

i. Hardware: gilded, rocaille door pulls, knobs and mortise lock escutcheons.

j. Lighting: There are six, four-light, brass sconces with crystal ball drops and finial. There is one, ten-light brass, rocaille chandelier with crystal prisms, leaf drops and pendant.

k. Heating: The south wall chimney has a grey marble hearth, with rectangular black marble insets, and a cast iron firebox with a wreath back panel and a lattice surround. The white marble mantle, in the Louis XV manner (4'-0" high by 1'-0" deep) has a curvilinear architrave with an acanthus leaf and floral key and flanking, splayed, acanthus consoles and caps. The overmantle has floral drapes and pendants centered by a bird and flower bouquet at the cornice.

Dining room: (painted green. See photographs.)

a. Flooring: oak, herringbone parquetry with cherry border.

b. Baseboard: 11", wood with bead and reed cap.

c. Dado: panels formed by applied cavetto mouldings.

d. Chairrail: 3'-0" high, wood, fascia and cyma.

e. Walls: The plaster walls have panels of applied ogee mouldings. Mirrors, set in bundled reed brass frames, flank the east wall chimney and the west wall door to the drawing room.

f. Cornice: cyma, egg and dart, cove and leafy roll.

g. Ceiling: 13'-6" high, plaster painted white. There is a pulvinated bay leaf border moulding punctuated by cornflower rosettes, and a similarly molded central panel with quarter-round indented corners.

h. Doorways and doors: There is a mirror-paned, sliding double door to the drawing room and a single mirror-paned door to the living hall. The crossette egg and dart archi-

2234 Massachusetts Avenue, N.W.

traves each have a guilloche frieze and enriched cornice, capped by a crossette panel which is centered by an oval plaque with sprays and swags. (See detail photograph.)

- i. Hardware: gilded, rocaille door pulls, knobs and mortise lock escutcheons.

- j. Lighting: **Each** mirror has a two-light, brass sconce. There is a six-light, brass, rocaille chandelier with crystal leaf drops and pendant.

- k. Heating: The east wall chimney has a marble hearth and cast iron firebox and surround. The white trimmed, green marble mantle, in the late Georgian manner (4'-6" high), has candelabra pilasters, a fascia and talon architrave, a frieze with central and terminal decorative plaques, and an egg and dart, corona and cyma shelf.

D. Site:

1. Setting and orientation: The building faces north on a lot measuring 52'-3" on the north (Massachusetts Avenue); 73'-7" on the east; 83'-11" on the south; and 27'-8" on the west (Sheridan Circle).

2. Enclosures: none.

3. Outbuildings: none.

4. Walks: The north stoop and basement entrance have concrete walks leading from a semicircular asphalt drive on Massachusetts Avenue.

5. Landscaping: There are basewood and ginko trees lining the street, with juniper bushes, a blue spruce, a Canadian whitewood, and grass bordering the building.

1606 23rd STREET, N.W., WASHINGTON, D.C.

View from Sheridan Circle
CFA photo
Boucher 1970

Location: 1606 23rd Street, N.W., Washington, D.C.;
                       on the west side of 23rd Street between
                       Sheridan Circle and Que Street.

Present Owner: Republic of Turkey

Present Occupant: Republic of Turkey

Present Use: Embassy

Statement of   This limestone structure reflects the more eclectic
Significance: variations which influenced beaux-arts neoclassicism.
                       With its size and setting on 23rd Street, the building
                       takes visual command of the eastern approach to Sheri-
                       dan Circle. The interiors are notable for the lavish
                       use of materials - especially the wood panelling, car-
                       ving and parquetry. The facilities include the original
                       indoor swimming pool.

PART I.   HISTORICAL INFORMATION

   A. Lot and Square:

   The building is located in Square 2507, lot 51 (formerly lots 1 and
   2 in Block 8 of "Kalorama Heights").

   B. Original and Subsequent Owners:

   The following chain of title to the property shows the owners of
   the present structure and of any known preceding structures on the
   site:

   1909   Deed January 21, 1909, recorded January 27, 1909 in
          Liber 3203 folio 381

          Agnes E. Platt
          Lulu Platt Hunt
          (joint tenants)
                To
          Edward H. Everett

          "This Deed made...by and between Agnes E. Platt and Lulu
          Platt Hunt, both of the City of Washington, in the District of
          of Columbia, parties of the first part, and Edward H. Everett
          of the same place, party of the second part...Lot...(1) in
          Block...(8) of Rodgers and Stellwagen, Trustees' subdivision
          of 'Kalorama Heights', as per plat recorded in the Office of
          the Surveyor for the District of Columbia, in Liber County 7
          at folio 34..."

1606 23rd Street, N.W.

1909   Deed January 26, 1909, recorded January 27, 1909 in
Liber 3203 folio 380

Edith P. Dickens
      To
Edward H. Everett

"...Lot...(2) in Block...(8) of Rodgers and Stellwagen, Trustees' subdivision of 'Kalorama Heights'..."

NOTE: February 7, 1910 Edward H. Everett combined lots 1 and 2, Block 8, "Kalorama Heights" into lot 51. Recorded in Subdivisions Liber 39 folio 19, Office of the Surveyor, District of Columbia.

1922   Deed December 5, 1922, recorded January 8, 1923 in
Liber 4802 folio 492

Edward H. Everett et ux,
Grace Burnap Everett
      To
Neenah Laub, unmarried

"This Deed...by and between Edward H. Everett and Grace Burnap Everett, his wife, of Bennington, Vermont, parties of the first part, and Neenah Laub, of the City of Washington, party of the second part..."

Lot 51 in Edward H. Everett's combination of lots in Block 8, "Kalorama Heights."

1922   Deed December 7, 1922, recorded January 8, 1923 in
Liber 4802 folio 492

Neenah Laub, unmarried
      To
Grace Burnap Everett

1936   Deed April 13, 1936, recorded May 1, 1936 in
Liber 6988 folio 53

Grace Burnap Everett
      To
Alyce Sternberg

"This Deed...by and between Grace Burnap Everett, of the District of Columbia, party of the first part; and Alyce Sternberg, of said District, party of the second part...Lot (51) in Edward H. Everett's combination of Lots...(1) and

1606 23rd Street, N.W.

   ...(2) in Block...(8), 'Kalorama Heights',...; reserving however for the party of the first part, her heirs and assigns, for the benefit of Lot...(3) in Square...(2507), a right of way for purpose of driveway and ingress and egress over the following part of said Lot...(51); beginning on the Northeasterly line of Water Side Drive at the most Westerly corner of said lot and running thence Northeasterly along the Northwesterly line thereof, 20 feet; thence Southeasterly to a point in the Northwesterly line of Water Side Drive, 20 feet Southeasterly from the point of beginning; thence Northwesterly along Water Side Drive, 20 feet to the point of beginning. Subject to a first Deed of Trust of $114,000.00 which the party of the second part agrees to assume..."

1936 Deed April 13, 1936, recorded May 1, 1936 in
   Liber 6988 folio 59

   Alyce Sternberg
     To
   Turkish Republic

   Lot 51 in Edward H. Everett's combination of lots 1 and 2 in Block 8, "Kalorama Heights."

   "...subject to right of way reserved unto Grace Burnap Everett, her heirs and assigns, by Deed dated April 13th, 1936, for the benefit of Lot...(3) in Square...(2507) for the purpose of driveway and ingress and egress over the following part of said Lot...(51)...[See Liber 6988 folio 53 above] subject to a first Deed of Trust of record in the sum of One hundred and fourteen thousand dollars ($114,000) and a second Deed of Trust of record in the sum of One hundred and thirty-four thousand dollars ($134,000) which the party hereto of the second part hereby assumes and agrees to pay, as is evidenced by the signature hereto of M. M. Ertegun, its Ambassador..."

   NOTE: Internal Revenue Stamp affixed: $144.

   Source: Recorder of Deeds, Washington, D.C.

C. Date of Erection:

The building was begun in August 1910 and completed in June 1915.

D. Building Permits:

The applications for the following building permits were filed by the architect, contractor or owner's agent and provide significant data:

1606 23rd Street, N.W.

No. 591, August 2, 1910
Permit for hoisting engine

No. 593, August 2, 1910
Permit to erect shed

No. 594, August 2, 1910
Permit to erect shed

No. 607, August 3, 1910
Permit to build dwelling
    Owner: E. H. Everett
    Architect: Geo. Oakley Totten, Jr.
    Builder: Geo. A. Fuller Co.
    Estimated cost: $150,000.
    Location: 2300 Mass. Ave.; lot 51, Square 2507

Filed with No. 607, August 3, 1910
Special Application for Projections Beyond Building Line, No. 89317, July 25, 1910
    Area: 4'-0" and 4'-6" projection
            20'-0"   width

    Base: 1'-2"   average projection
            3'-6"   height on Mass. Ave.

No. 3163, January 2, 1912
Permit for Elevator
    Owner: E. H. Everett
    Mechanic: Otis Elevator Co.
    Cost of installation: $2650.
    Dimensions: 3'-9 1/2" X 3'-0 1/2"

No. 2879, December 31, 1915
Permit to erect marquise
    Owner: E. H. Everett
    Architect: Geo. Oakley Totten, Jr.
    Contractor: Sterling Bronze Co.
    Estimated cost: $1500.

Filed with No. 2879, December 31, 1915
Special Application for Projection Beyond Building Line, May 25, 1915
    Marquise: 5'-6" projection
                  18'-0" width

Source: D.C. Government: Department of Economic Development, Bureau of Licenses and Permits, Central Files.

E. Alterations and Additions:

No significant changes have been made on the main floors.

1606 23rd Street, N.W.

F. Architect: George Oakley Totten, Jr., Washington, D.C.

Major George Oakley Totten, Jr. (1866-1939), the son of George Oakley Totten and Mary Elizabeth (Styles) Totten, was born in New York City. He attended public schools in Newark, New Jersey and the Newark Technical School. In 1891 he received his A.B. and in 1892 his A.M. from Columbia University. The Columbia McKim traveling fellowship, awarded to Totten in 1893, enabled him to study at the École des Beaux Arts in Paris from 1893 to 1895.

Totten moved to Washington in 1895 and became chief designer in the Office of the Supervising Architect, U.S. Treasury Department. His independent practice, opened in 1898, was first listed in the business directory in 1899 as the firm of Totten & Rogers, 801 19th Street, N.W. The residential directory of the same year lists his associate: "Laussat R. Rogers (Totten & Rogers), Philadelphia". Apparently, the firm Totten & Rogers continued until 1907 when Totten was listed separately in the business directory.

During 1908 Totten spent several months in Turkey, where he designed the American chancery and a pretentious residence for Prime Minister Issez Pasha. Sultan Abdul Hamid was impressed by Totten's work and asked him to design commercial structures for the Imperial government. Totten declined and returned to Washington. The Sultan then offered him the position of "private architect to the Sultan of Turkey", which he apparently accepted. However, Sultan Abdul Hamid's overthrow in 1909 for constitutional government terminated his plans. (The Evening Star, 9-25-37; and The Washington Post, 9-18-32)

Between 1897 and 1939, Totten served as an American delegate to the International Congress of Architects in Brussels (1897), Paris (1900), Madrid (1904), London (1906), Vienna (1908), Rome (1911) and Budapest (1931). During World War I, he was commissioned as a major in the U.S. Army Engineers Corps.

On August 22nd, 1921 Totten married Vichen von Post, a Swedish sculptress who had come to this country for a few months to exhibit her porcelain figurines. The Tottens were to have two sons: George Oakley and Gilbert von Post Totten.

George Oakley Totten, Jr., was a prolific designer of Washington buildings:

> He was the architect for many public buildings in the city and drew the plans for ten legation and embassy buildings...He also designed many private city and country dwellings in Washington, ...representing several styles of architecture. (The National Cyclopedia of American Biography)

> The most important personal force in [the] development [of 16th Street] was the late Mrs. John B. Henderson, widow of the United States Senator who built 'Henderson's Castle' [in 1888]. Between 1906 and 1929, under the architectural guidance of George Oakley Totten, Mrs. Henderson constructed nearly a dozen costly residences on or near Sixteenth Street, most of them in the Meridian Hill district and designed to house foreign embassies or legations. (Washington City and Capital, Federal Writer's Project)

Among these residences are: 2401, 2437, and 2535 15th Street, N.W.; and 2460, 2600, 2620 (destroyed), 2622, 2640, 2801, and 3149 16th Street, N.W. In the area of Massachusetts Avenue, N.W., he designed 1606 23rd Street, 2230, 2315 and 2349 Massachusetts Avenue. The "Embassy District" of Mrs. Henderson and George Oakley Totten has since lost its popular title to Massachusetts Avenue - although embassies and chanceries are still located in the 16th Street area. The interior and exterior detailing of these buildings represents a mixture of styles, which is characteristic of Totten's work - as a study of his buildings indicates.

Totten also designed and built a house, studio, and garden for himself at 2633 16th Street, N.W. (ca. 1921). Several years after the house and studio were completed, Totten reconstructed the B. H. Warder House on his 16th Street property. The Warder House had been designed by H. H. Richardson and built in the 1880's on K Street, N.W., between 15th and 16th Streets. It was later dismantled to make way for the Investment Building, which was completed in 1924. Totten bought and stored the house and then moved it to 2633 16th Street. (The Evening Star, 12-8-24)

Some of his works outside of Washington, D.C. were: The Post Office in Waterbury, Connecticut; the Newark, New Jersey, Post Office and Court Building (designed in association with William E. Lehman); a residence in Bennington, Vermont, for E. H. Everett; and residences in New Jersey. (The National Cyclopedia of American Biography)

Totten's only publication was a book, Maya Architecture (1926).

Sources: The National Cyclopedia of American Biography, Vol. XLI, New York: James T. White & Company, 1956, p. 496.

Who Was Who in America 1897-1942: A Companion Volume To Who's Who in America, Vol I, Chicago: The A. N. Marquis Co., 1942.

1606 23rd Street, N.W.

    Federal Writers' Project, American Guide Series, <u>Washington, City and Capital</u>, Washington, D.C.: U.S. Government Printing Office, 1937.

    Henry F. Withey and Elsie R. Withey, <u>Biographical Dictionary of American Architects (Deceased)</u>, Los Angeles: New Age Publishing Co., 1956.

    <u>Architectural Forum</u>, Vol LXX, No. 4 (April 1939), p. 54.

    <u>The American Architect</u>, Vol. C, No. 1863 (September 6, 1911), plates.

    "The House of George Oakley Totten", <u>The American Architect</u>, Vol. CXX, No. 2371 (July 6, 1921), pp. 1-7.

    <u>The Evening Star</u>, 12-8-24, 6:6.
    <u>The Evening Star</u>, 9-25-37, C 6:1.
    <u>The New York Times</u>, 2-3-39, 15:2 (obituary).
    <u>The Washington Post</u>, 9-18-32, 15:6.
    <u>The Washington Post</u>, 2-2-39, 28:1 (obituary).

G. Known Plans, Drawings, Elevations, etc.:

    Projection plan on Sheridan Circle. Ink on linen. Scale 1/4" = 1'
    Filed with Permit No. 607, August 3, 1910
        "Res. for E. H. Everett, Esq.
        23rd & Sheridan Circle"

    Elevation of projection. Ink on linen. Scale 1/2" = 1'
    Filed with Permit No. 607, August 3, 1910
        "Elevation of Base and Area or End of
        E. H. Everett Residence, Sheridan Circle"

H. Important Old Views:

    Exterior photograph ca. 1915. Herbert French Collection: Library of Congress, Prints and Photographs Division. (see reproduction)

    Photograph: view from across Rock Creek Park, ca. 1915.
    CFA photo file at National Archives. (see reproduction)

I. Residents:

1. City and telephone directories list the following tenants:

    1914-1924 No listing
    1925-1929 Edward H. Everett
    1930-1933 Grace B. Everett
    1934-1972 Turkish Embassy

2. Biographies of the residents:

Edward H. Everett, a native of Cleveland, was a multimillionaire industrialist and philanthropist who was maintaining residences in Washington, D.C., Bennington, Vermont, and Switzerland at the time of his death. His obituary in The Evening Star, April 29, 1929 noted:

> Mr. Everett was known as a pioneer in the glass industry in this country. In later years he acquired oil interests in Ohio and Texas. He was a former director of H. A. Hamilton & Co., and the Compair Corporation of Texas...[He] was president of The Orchards Co. of Bennington and president of the E. H. Everett Co., which includes oil, gas and sand industries in the Middle West. At one time he was a large stockholder of the Anheuser Busch Co. of St. Louis.

Everett and his first wife, Amy K. Everett (who is noted in the Deed-in-Trust recorded in Liber 3203, folio 382, January 27, 1909), purchased property on Sheridan Circle in 1909. Construction began at 1606 23rd Street in 1910. According to the daily reports of the building inspector filed with the building permits, piles were being driven for the foundation on August 5, 1910; and construction was 99% complete on June 4, 1915. After the house was finished, the tax assessment was $230,000 for improvements, and $50,800 for the ground. (General Tax Assessment Washington City 1917-1918) The original building permit estimated that the cost of the building would be $150,000.

The Sunday Star, September 9, 1956, gave a colorful impression of the building's interior, which has remained largely unchanged since its completion. The article mentions:

> The huge entrance hall of black and white marble;...the sweeping center staircase in the vast hallway;...the ballroom, with red velvet draperies and rich red and gold embroidered fabric above the dark paneling... the ornamental ceilings [which] enhance every room, and marble fireplaces carved in exquisite detail.
>
> On the floor above the ballroom is a roof garden, tiled and latticed...Below the first floor of the mansion is a swimming pool built by the Everetts, but for many years boarded over until discovered by the present Ambassador, Haydar Gork. Now they have reopened it and hope to repair it for future use.

1606 23rd Street, N.W.

> An ideal building for an embassy - it is well suited for large scale entertaining. One party for 3,000 guests was described in columns of space by society reporters in the '30's. The food was lavish, the orchestra stayed until 3 a.m., and 'footmen in mulberry livery, with white silk stockings and pumps with silver buckles were everywhere.'

City directories do not list Edward H. Everett or 1606 23rd Street until 1925. However, "Mr. Everett and his family moved into the palatial home at Sheridan Circle shortly before World War I. Mrs. [Amy K.] Everett died in 1917." (The Sunday Star, 9-9-56)

In 1919 Everett met Miss Grace Burnap at a tea arranged by Mrs. John B. Henderson. Miss Burnap and Mr. Everett were married in 1920 "and from then until Mr. Everett's death in 1929, their home was the scene of many musical parties featuring...singers from the Metropolitan Opera." (The Sunday Star, 9-9-56)

Everett was survived by his wife, Grace, and five children: the Countess Turri of Florence, Italy; Mrs. L. A. Wing of Great Neck, Long Island, N.Y.; Mrs. James K. Seldon of Andover, Mass.; and two minor children - Grace Everett and Sarah Everett. (The Evening Star, 4-29-29)

Sources: General Tax Assessment, Washington City 1917-1918, Squares 1303-3613, Vol. III, Washington, D.C.: William H. Manoque, 1918.

Who's Who in the Nation's Capital 1921-1922, Washington, D.C.: The Consolidated Publishing Company, 1922.

The Evening Star, 4-29-29, 9:3 (obituary).
The Sunday Star, 9-9-56, D 1:1.

Grace Everett occupied the house until fall of 1932. Then the Turkish Embassy, previously located at 1708 Massachusetts Avenue, leased the property while they searched for a permanent Embassy. (The Evening Star, 6-18-32)

> In the Turkish Embassy files...are a series of letters written by their Ambassador at that time, Mehmet Ertegun...The Ambassador...wrote his government that the choice was between the Everett home and a residence on Sixteenth Street. This was in 1934. [He wrote] 'While many embassies are now located on Sixteenth Street, it is said that this area is more and more losing its value. Massachusetts Avenue is gaining more prominence.' (The Sunday Star, 9-9-56)

1606 23rd Street, N.W.

The Turkish Republic purchased 1606 23rd Street in April 1936. Although the Star (9-9-56) wrote that Turkey paid "a reported $265,000," the deed indicated the value of the transaction was more - approximately $402,000. Turkey assumed two deeds-in-trust totaling $258,000. The $144 stamp tax levied on the transaction shows that an additional $144,000 was paid for the property. (The Internal Revenue Stamp Tax was imposed at the rate of $.50 per $500 and excluded assumed trusts.) The assessed value of the property in 1936 was $390,000 ($80,000 for the ground and $310,000 for improvements).

Sources: General Assessment, Washington, D.C. 1935-1936: Squares 1-2753, Vol. I, Washington, D.C.: Rufus S. Lusk, 1936.

The Evening Star, 6-18-32, B 2:1.
The Sunday Star, 9-9-56, D 1:1.
The Washington Post, 9-18-32, 15:6.

Herbert French Collection
Prints and Photographs Division, Library of Congress
Date unknown

CIRCLE

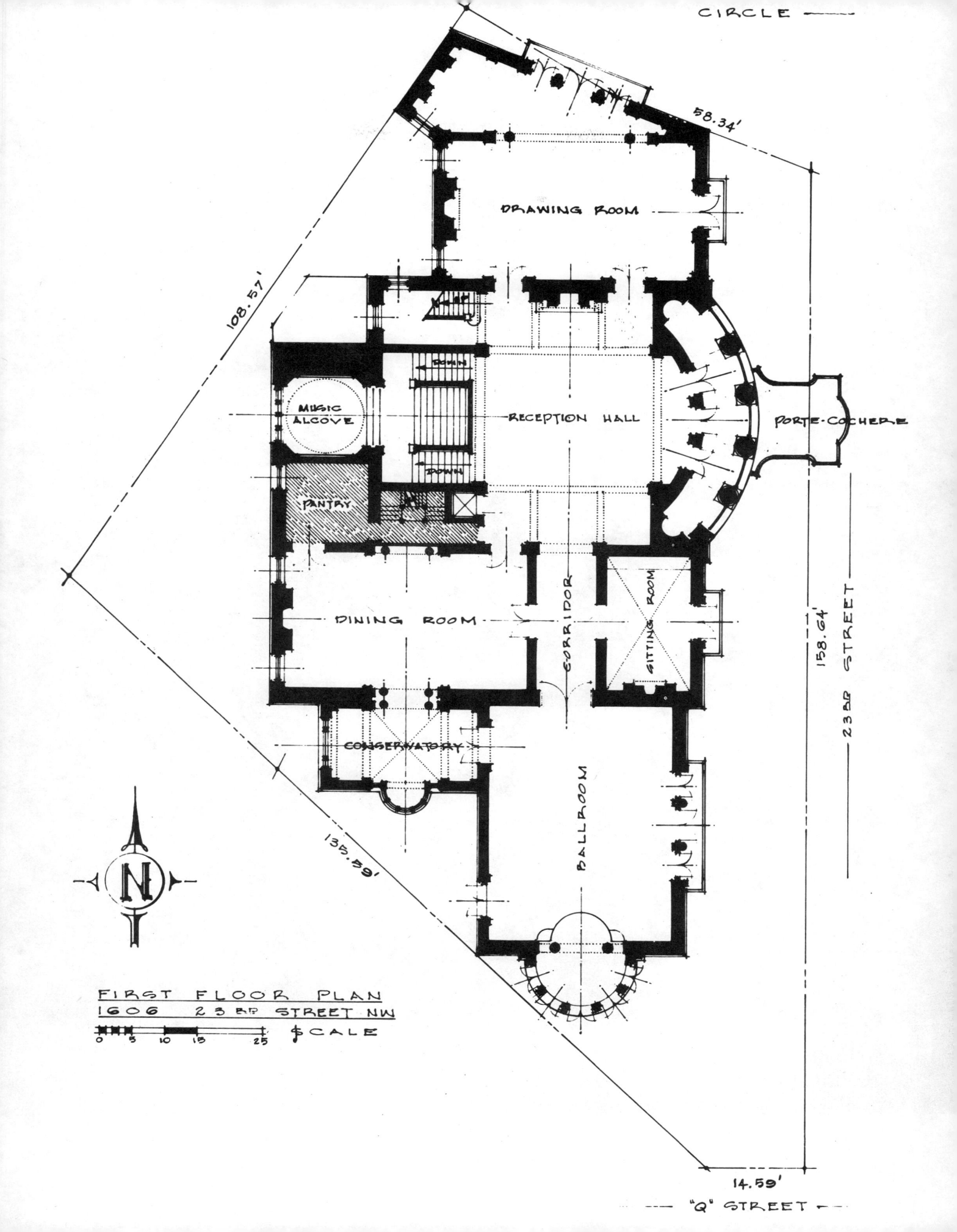

58.34'

DRAWING ROOM

108.57'

MUSIC ALCOVE

RECEPTION HALL

PORTE-COCHERE

PANTRY

158.64'

23RD STREET

DINING ROOM

CORRIDOR

SITTING ROOM

CONSERVATORY

BALLROOM

N

135.59'

FIRST FLOOR PLAN
1606 23RD STREET NW
SCALE 0 5 10 15 25

14.59'

"Q" STREET

View from across Rock Creek Park
CFA photo file at National Archives
ca. 1915

First Floor Sitting Room
CFA photo
Boucher 1970

First Floor Drawing Room
CFA photo
Boucher 1970

Opposite
First Floor
Reception Hall
CFA photo
Boucher 1970

Ground Floor Entrance Hall
CFA photo
Boucher 1970

332

Opposite
Reception Hall Detail
CFA photo
Boucher 1970

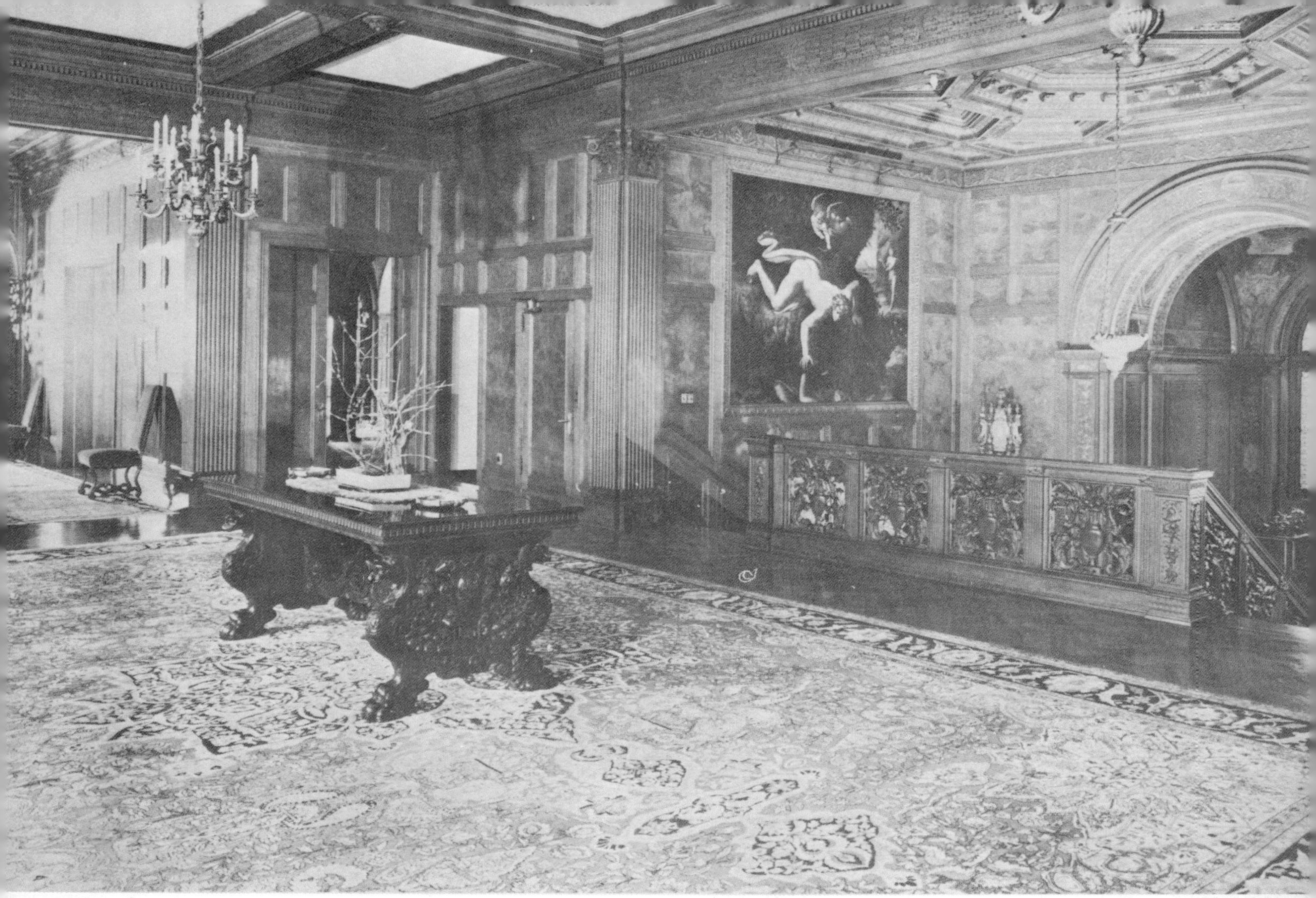

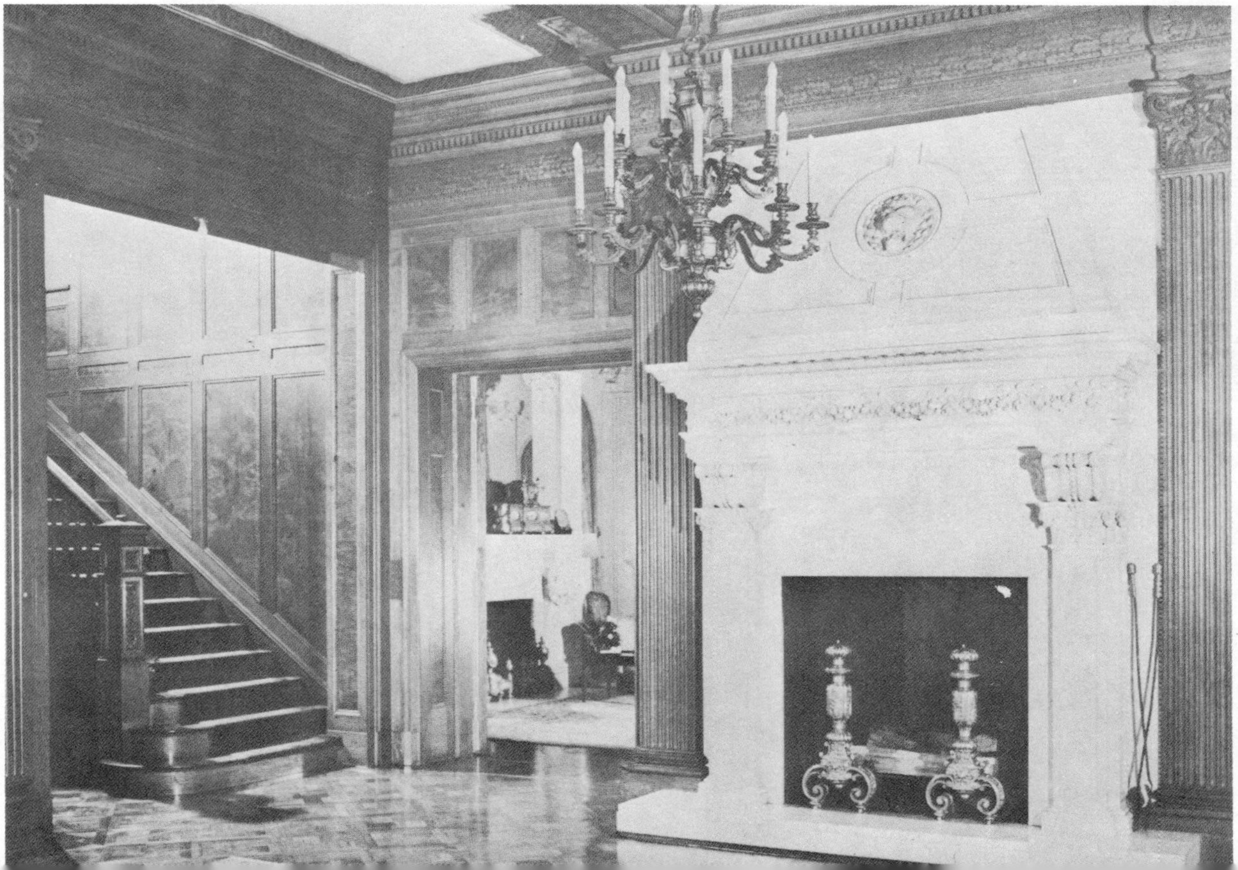

Ballroom toward Conservatory
CFA photo
Boucher, 1970

Opposite
Dining Room toward Conservatory
CFA photo
Boucher 1970

Detail Elevator Cab
CFA photo
Boucher 1970

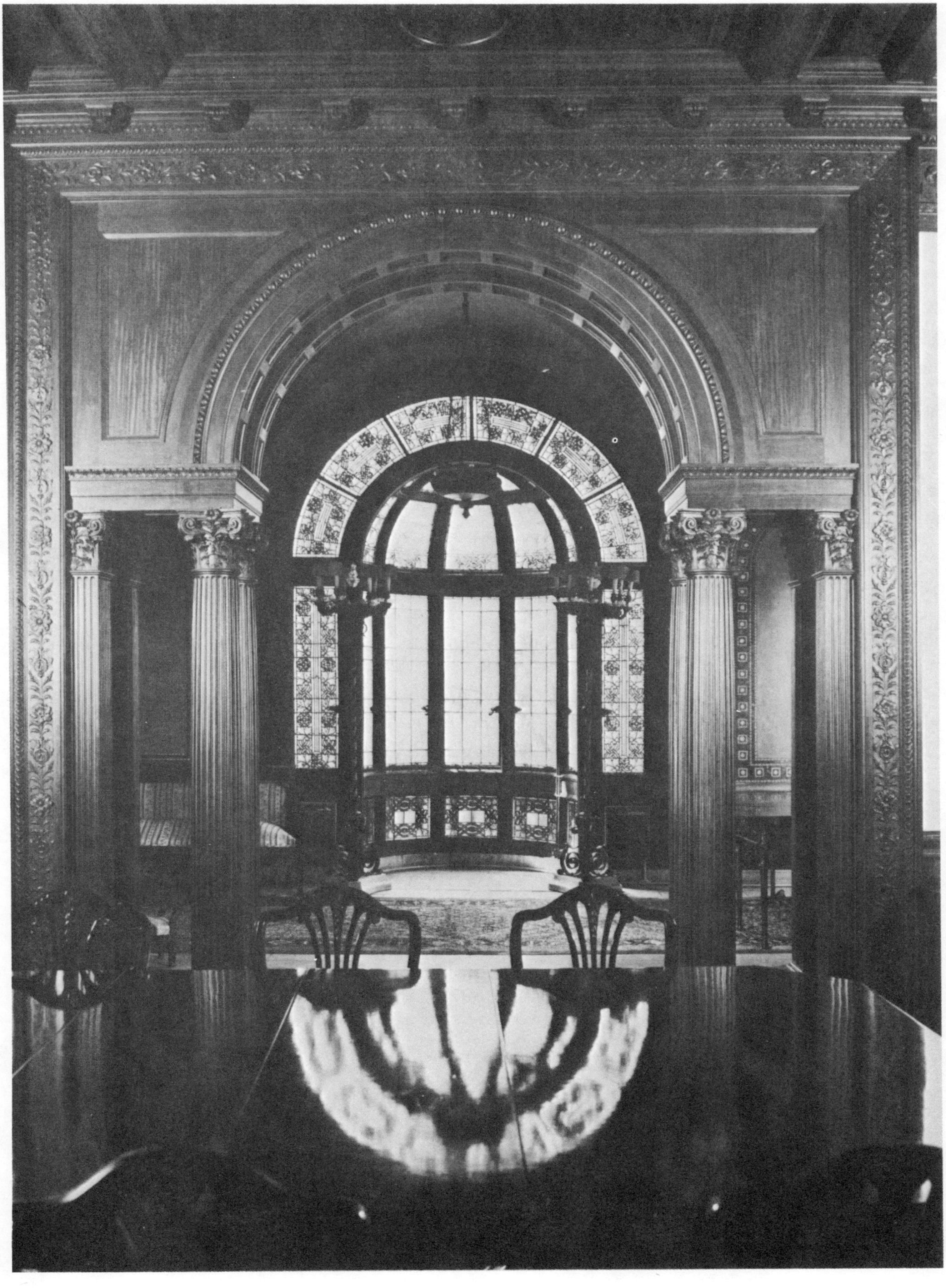

1606 23rd Street, N.W.

PART II. ARCHITECTURAL INFORMATION

    A. General Statement:

        1. Architectural character: This detached structure is eclectic, combining neoclassical elements of 18th century Europe with 15th century Italianate details.

        2. Condition: excellent.

    B. Exterior Description:

        1. Overall dimensions: The three story, plus basement and attic building has a two story ballroom wing at the south. From the sidewalk to the highest point of the roof is 61'-0". The east elevation of the main structure which measures 91'-6" on 23rd Street, has a 26'-6" south bay, a 38'-6" colonnaded entrance bow, and a 26'-6" north bay. The composite bay northeast elevation on Sheridan Circle is 42'-0" and forms an acute angle with the building. At the northwest is a 15'-0" party wall. A two bay (22'-3") section of the 90'-0" west wall breaks back 24'-6" to form the generally triangular northwest courtyard. Projecting from the 66'-3" south elevation is the 32'-0" wide southeast ballroom wing, its 39'-0" east elevation is recessed 2'-6" from the main facade. The southwest, first floor conservatory measures one bay (13'-6") at the west and one bay (24'-0") at the south.

        2. Foundations: concrete piles and slab.

        3. Wall construction: The limestone-faced building has a base with a prominent cavetto and torus water table which supports a rusticated ground floor. The rustication is capped by a plain frieze acting as ground floor window lintel. The frieze supports the cyma and corona base for a plain, false balustrade with cyma rail. The first and second floors are smoothly surfaced.

        4. Structure: brick bearing with steel roofing members.

        5. Mechanical: The building has a Syracuse, N.Y., E.C. Steam Heating System, patent #7607; 1910-11. The Camden, N.J., Webster Air Washer and Humidifier has a 1908 patent. The Otis passenger eleavator, in the rococo manner (see photograph), has a 1000 pound capacity. The lighting is electric and speaking tubes communicate between floors. The kitchen has a 7'-0" long, Vulcan, cast iron stove with hood.

        6. Porches, stoops, bulkheads, etc.: The ground floor entrance on 23rd Street has a granite stoop flanked by panelled limestone balustrades with pedestal stops. The pedestals support composite columns on decorative drums. The columns, with

1606 23rd Street, N.W.

candelabra composite pilasters buttressed by consoles, support cast iron lattice scrolls and lanterns, below a marquise with anthemion and palmette filigree and opaque glass panels.

The first floor, two story portico has fluted, composite columns and candelabra, composite pilasters. The north and south walls of the portico are interrupted at the first and second floors by shell niches with fillet and ovolo sills. Between the columns and pilasters are free-standing balustrades with turned balusters and volute rails. The portico ceiling is coffered.

The ground floor window heads are flanked by scrolled consoles which support first floor window balconies of turned balusters with end panels. The balconies carry the false balustrade lines.

The second floor windows have low, wrought iron balcony railings.

Over the south ballroom wing is a second floor limestone loggia. The loggia has a cyma reversa and running dog string course which supports a plain balustrade interrupted by projecting panels of turned balusters. The balustrade supports piers with rinceau panels below a wood, open-beamed trellis.

7. Chimneys: Behind the attic balustrade are limestone chimneys (one visible from "Q" Street) with moulded caps.

8. Openings:

    a. Doorways and doors: The 23rd Street entrance has a recessed, plate glass and bronze grille, double door and transom. The rinceau architrave is flanked by the marquise pilasters. The three French doors and transoms in the portico each have an anthemion and palmette architrave, capped by a plain frieze and joined by a common cornice of talon, corona and cyma mouldings.

    b. Windows: All ground floor windows are double-hung and protected by decorative, cast iron bar grilles.

    All first floor windows are casement. Each has a semi-circular transom, candelabra pilasters, fascia arch and rosette spandrels. Encasing this is an egg and dart moulding capped by a plain frieze and a talon, corona and cyma cornice. The exceptions are:

    (1.) the Sheridan Circle and south wing openings, each divided into triple casements by half-engaged Tuscan columns, and

(2.) the ballroom south elevation bow, which rests on the panelled false balustrade. The bow has five casement windows with transoms and candelabra mullions within an arabesque architrave.

All second floor windows are casement. Each is flanked by candelabra panels and supported on fillet and ovolo sills over scrolled brackets. The exceptions are:

(1.) the side-lighted windows flanking the entrance bow and

(2.) the plain, cased openings flanking the north elevation bay.

9. Roof:

   a. Shape, covering: The low-pitched, hipped roof is concealed behind the attic balustrade, the center of the roof is interrupted by a skylight which serves as an attic lightwell.

   b. Cornice, eaves: The building has a rinceau architrave, a plain frieze, and a dentil, modillion, corona and cyma cornice capped by an urn baluster balustrade. At the portico, the architrave is plain, and the frieze is interrupted by a decorative panel centered above each column.

   c. Dormers, cupolas, towers: South and west dormer windows are concealed behind the balustrade.

C. Interior Description:

1. Floor plans: On axis with the 23rd Street entrance is the ground floor vestibule, the entrance hall, the stair hall and the stair (music alcove) landing. The entrance hall is separated from flanking antehalls by columnar screens. Beyond the north antehall is the game room (Ambassador's office) on Sheridan Circle. Beyond the south antehall are the library, a service corridor and servants' rooms. The main stair is flanked by the enclosed family stair at the north and an elevator and the utility stair at the south.

The main stair gives access to the first floor reception hall and the 23rd Street portico. North of the reception hall is the double drawing room on Sheridan Circle. To the south, a corridor gives access to the east sitting room, west dining room and south ballroom. In the ell formed by the dining room and ballroom is the conservatory. (See plan.)

1606 23rd Street, N.W.

The south elevator and the service and family stairs ascend to the second floor. The master bedroom suite is at the south on the second floor and has access to the loggia above the ballroom. The attic contains a light-well with servants' quarters at the south and west, and storage at the east.

2. Spaces:

Entrance hall: (see photograph)

- a. Flooring: grey-veined, white marble with a green, red and yellow mosaic tile border. Under the columnar screens are mosaic panels.

- b. Baseboard: grey-veined, white marble with roll cap.

- c. Walls: plaster painted white, with panels formed by applied mouldings. Each screen has two, marble, flute and drum, Roman Doric columns in antis. Pilasters flank the north antehall chimney, the south antehall library door and the stair hall.

- d. Cornice: The full entablature has an anthemion architrave; triglyph and metope frieze with pattera; and an egg and dart, dentil and corona (with fret soffit) cornice.

    The architrave is interrupted by the pilasters and the frieze and cornice are carried across the columnar screens.

- e. Ceiling: plaster painted white.

- f. Doorways and doors: The plate glass vestibule door has a cast iron lattice grille with a scroll and medallion border, side lights, and a rectangular transom centered by an escutcheon symbolizing Turkey.

    The remaining doors are all natural wood with raised panels. The double doors to the library and flanking the north chimney have marble, fascia and cable architraves. The west wall, paired, single doors in either antehall have fascia and cyma architraves.

- g. Hardware: gold-plated, bundled-reed handles and mortise lock escutcheons.

- h. Lighting: The vestibule door is flanked by porcelain and alabaster candelabra in the Venetian manner. The antehalls each have two, three-light, baroque sconces.

- i. Heating: The north wall chimney has a grey marble mantle with tan marble, panelled pilasters which support acanthus consoles, a linen fold frieze and a gouge corona shelf.

1606 23rd Street, N.W.

The overmantle has a centered wreath with ribbons and escutcheon, flanked by pedestal and urn panels.

Library:

a. Flooring: diamond and square parquetry.

b. Baseboard: wood with cyma cap.

c. Dado: raised wood panels.

d. Chairrail: 3'-6" high, wood, cyma and bead.

e. Walls: plaster panels painted white and set in wood stiles and rails. Wood panels are above each door.

f. Cornice: wood with modillions.

g. Ceiling: plaster painted white.

h. Doorways and doors: pair of wood double doors with fascia and bead architraves.

i. Hardware: gold-plated, bundled reed handles and mortise lock escutcheons.

j. Heating: The south wall chimney has a white marble mantle with swag and bead consoles, a rinceau frieze and a cyma shelf.

Stair hall: (The stair hall is separated from the entrance hall by three, marble, convex risers with stair platform.)

a. Stairway: The oak stair ascends ten risers west to a hall-width landing. The stair returns and ascends on two parallel flights ten risers east to the first floor. At the west, and three risers above the midlanding, is the music alcove. The balustrades have carved urn panels framed by tuber sprays, birds and flowers. The newels have marquetry bases, bell and flower pendant panels and gouge frieze caps.

b. Wainscot: raised panels.

c. Walls: flat, burled walnut panels in oak stiles and rails. At the north and south walls are allegorical canvases set in palmette talon mouldings.

d. Cornice: The full entablature has a rope architrave, an anthemion and palmette frieze and a talon cornice.

e. Ceiling: Decoratively painted dropped beams with bosses form frescoed coffers within talon mouldings. The central octagon has a modillion surround.

f. Doorways and doors: Flanking the music alcove, candelabra pilasters support the semicircular archway having a painted anthemion and palmette frieze. The arch soffit has frescoed coffers flanked by fret bands.

g. Lighting: Flanking the first flight of risers on the ground floor are seven-light, bronze candelabrum. The music alcove archway is flanked by scroll and lantern, baroque sconces. Suspended from the octagonal ceiling coffer is a brass chain, alabaster bowl and pendant lamp with carved cherubs.

h. Music alcove: The floor has various woods in decorative parquetry. Each elevation has a single semicircular arch. The west wall is glazed, and the north and south wall fans are frescoed. The four, frescoed corner pilasters support a frescoed pendentive dome.

Secondary stairs:

The family stair ascends from the basement to the first floor on marble treads and risers, with iron balusters and a brass railing. From the first floor the stair ascends fifteen risers west to the first landing and returns to continue the ascent east to the second floor. This flight has wood stringer, risers and treads with turned balusters and a decoratively panelled newel. The newel has a rosette frieze and a gouge cap.

The modern service stair from the basement to the ground floor is metal. The remaining half-turn flights are wood.

Reception hall: (south corridor similarly treated. See photographs.)

a. Flooring: quadrant basket weave within lattice parquetry.

b. Baseboard: 8", wood.

c. Walls: flat, burled walnut panels in oak stiles and rails. Fluted, wood, composite pilasters flank the west stair hall, the east portico bow, the south corridor and the north wall chimney.

d. Cornice: The full entablature has a wood, fascia and talon architrave, a pulvinated bundled oak leaf frieze, and a dentil, cyma, corona, talon and cyma cornice.

e. Ceiling: 14'-0" high, plaster painted white. False beams with fret soffits and crossing bosses divide the ceiling into bays. Above dentil height, the cornice is carried along the beams. The plaster bays are bordered by fresco.

f. Doorways and doors: All doors have burled walnut panels. The recessed, double doors to the dining room, the sitting room and drawing room have fascia and cyma architraves. The single doors to the elevator and service hall are defined by the stiles and rails of the walls.

g. Hardware: gold-plated, leaf and finial handles and mortise lock escutcheons.

h. Lighting: There are two, double-tiered, sixteen-light, bronze, baroque chandeliers.

i. Heating: The north wall chimney has a white marble, 6" **high** hearth. The white marble mantle (6'-0" wide by 7'-0" high) has candelabra composite pilasters which support beaded consoles. The consoles flank an escutcheon and griffin rinceau frieze, and support a talon architrave, a fruit swag and ribbon frieze, and a cyma and talon shelf. The panelled overmantle hood is centered by a lion mask.

Drawing room: (designed as two spaces; a south rectangle and a north triangle. See photograph.)

a. Flooring: quadrant basket weave within diagonal lattice. A columnar screen divides the room into two spaces.

b. Baseboard: 9", painted white with bead cap.

c. Walls: plaster painted white and divided into bays and openings by fluted composite pilasters. Fluted composite columns in antis separate the rectangular space from the triangular area overlooking Sheridan Circle. The west chimney wall breaks forward in either space.

d. Cornice: The full entablature has a fascia and talon architrave; a palmette and urn rinceau frieze; and an egg and dart, dentil, talon, corona and talon cornice. The entablature is carried across the columnar screen.

e. Ceiling: plaster painted white.

f. Doorways and doors: The two south wall double doors have egg and dart architraves.

g. Windows: The semicircular-arched rinceau window surrounds, each within an egg and dart moulding, have recesses for drapes.

h. Hardware: gold-plated, leaf and finial handles and mortise lock escutcheons.

i. Lighting: There are two, three-light, brass and crystal pendant sconces. There are two, single tier, ten-light,

1606 23rd Street, N.W.

       brass, crystal pendant and drape chandeliers, each with a five-light crown.

  j. Heating: There are two, west wall, white marble chimney mantles, both 5'-0" high. The main drawing room mantle has lion foot, bead and drape consoles, which flank a plain frieze and support a fascia and bead architrave, and a lattice corona and talon shelf. The second mantle has candelabra pilasters which support a plain frieze and a corona and cyma shelf.

Sitting room: (see photograph)

  a. Flooring: quadrant basket weave separated and bisected by grid and lattice parquetry.

  b. Baseboard: 9", wood with cyma cap.

  c. Walls: plaster painted white. The north wall has a three bay china cupboard. Each bay of prism panes is separated by wood, candelabra, composite pilasters. Flanking the door and window are fluted composite pilasters. The south chimney wall breaks forward.

  d. Cornice: The full entablature has a wood, fascia architrave; a swag and ribbon frieze; and an egg and dart, corona, talon and cavetto cornice.

  e. Ceiling: plaster painted white and vaulted. A rinceau fresco is at the base, and the rectangular central panel is painted in the Pompeiian manner. The ceiling cove is bisected by a vault over the east window.

  f. Doorways and doors: The double door to the corridor has a fascia and cyma architrave.

  g. Lighting: brass chandelier.

  h. Heating: The south wall chimney has a black-veined, white marble hearth and mantle. The firebox is flanked by candelabra pilasters with modillion caps which support a beaded architrave; a prominent, three panel, wreath and flambeau frieze with candelabra terminal panels; and a talon, corona and cyma shelf. The mantle is framed by wood, candelabra, composite pilasters and the full entablature which breaks forward with the chimney wall.

Dining room: (see photograph)

  a. Flooring: various woods set in squares of herringbone parquetry.

  b. Baseboard: 9", wood with cyma cap.

c. Dado: raised wood panels in bead mouldings. The dado serves as base for a flush buffet with the serving shelf recessed into the north wall.

d. Chairrail: 3'-0" wood, bead and cyma.

e. Walls: plaster painted white. The north wall buffet serving shelf intersects a wood, Venetian arch of composite columns. The composite columns and pilasters support a fascia and talon architrave; a semicircular arch with an egg and dart surround and coffered soffit; and rinceau spandrels.

f. Cornice: The full entablature has a wood, talon architrave; rinceau frieze; and an egg and dart cornice with alternating modillion and guilloche mouldings.

g. Ceiling: raised wood panels separated by panelled beams.

h. Doorways and doors: The three sets of wood, double doors, one each to the reception hall, corridor and northwest pantry, all have a floral frieze architrave. The south wall is interrupted by a Venetian arch (similar to the buffet) which gives access to the conservatory. The fluted, paired, Corinthian columns support a fascia and talon architrave; a semicircular arch with an egg and dart surround and a coffered soffit; plain spandrels; and a floral frieze and guilloche surround (which interrupts the room entablature).

i. Hardware: gold-plated, rocaille door handles.

j. Lighting: There are two, gilded wood and plaster, baroque candelabra.

k. Heating: The west wall chimney has a maroon-veined, tan marble mantle, 7'-0" high. The firebox has flanking Corinthian columns which support a rinceau frieze broken forward as consoles over both columns. Fluted pilasters separate the overmantle into three bays of shell niches.

Ballroom: (Flanking the south wall bow are curved risers which give access to a dais. Both flights have ornamental console balustrades. The dais has two, fluted, composite columns which support the entablature carried across as a beam. See photograph.)

a. Flooring: beaket weave within lattice parquetry.

b. Baseboard: 10", wood with roll and cyma cap.

c. Wainscot: 8'-0" high, wood. There are three rows of

raised panels with painted cyma mouldings above which are gold on blue, rinceau panels separated by diminuitive consoles. A talon cornice caps the wainscot. The west wall has a built-in mirror, with flanking columns, in the 15th century Italianate manner.

d. Walls: gold thread damask in Persian manner.

e. Ceiling: Nine plaster panels (painted white) are framed by gold and blue, rinceau-panelled, dropped beams. The beams are bordered by gouge, alternating modillions and pattera, and talon mouldings.

f. Doorways and doors: The upper section of the raised panel double door to the corridor is pierced with carved rinceau. With the door closed, the carving forms one half of a circular motif; the upper half enclosed by the semicircular arch of the cased opening. The door is flanked by half-engaged, composite columns which support the coffered soffit and arch mouldings.

g. Lighting: There are eight, three-light, cherub and pendant, gilded plaster, baroque sconces.

Conservatory:

a. Flooring: grey-veined, white marble.

b. Baseboard: 8", limestone.

c. Wainscot: 2'-6" high, blue and green, glazed tiles.

d. Walls: semicircular-arched limestone bays bordered by mosaic squares and flanked by rinceau panelled pilasters.

e. Ceiling: intersected barrel vault of plaster with mosaic borders.

f. Doorways and doors: The semicircular-headed, cased opening to the ballroom has a cast iron double gate of acanthus sprays and bronze, floral and tendril applique.

g. Windows: The southwall, leaded glass oriole has a grape and basket border and quarter-spherical glazed dome. The semicircular arch at the west wall has stained glass.

h. Lighting: There are two, eight-light, iron, bronze and glass candelabra, each supported on a marble base. Centered in the ceiling is a hanging, acanthus leaf, alabaster bowl and pendant lamp.

1606 23rd Street, N.W.

D. Site:

1. Setting and orientation: The building faces east on a lot measuring 158'-8" on 23rd Street; 14'-6" on the south (Q Street); 135'-6" on the southwest (Rock Creek Park); 108'-6" on the west; and 58'-4" on the north (Sheridan Circle).

2. Enclosures: The land bordering the streets is built up to form a platform enclosed by a limestone retaining wall. The wall is capped by a panelled balustrade interrupted by projecting panels of urn balusters.

3. Outbuildings: none.

4. Walks: Seven limestone risers with cheek walls ascend from the 23rd Street sidewalk to the semicircular concrete drive and stoop.

5. Landscaping: Within the balustrade border the flat terrace is planted with hemlock, azaleas, dogwood, English ivy, northern magnolia, and sod. Massachusetts Avenue and 23rd Street are lined by elms, maples and oaks.

2253 R STREET, N.W., WASHINGTON, D.C.

CFA photo
Boucher 1970

Address: 2253 R Street, N.W., Washington, D.C.

Significance: This building, created within an 18th century Mediterranean context, is an example of the smaller, less expensive residence with a simple, open plan.

Present Owner: Philippine Embassy
Present Use: Embassy residence
Lot and Square: Square 2516, lot 45 (formerly lot 11 and part of lot 10 in Block 11, "Kalorama Heights")

HISTORICAL AND ARCHITECTURAL INFORMATION

Original Owner: Mrs. Emma S. Fitzhugh (1903-1929)
Original Use: Residence
Date of Erection: 1904
Architect: Wood, Donn and Deming, Washington, D.C.
Builder: William P. Lipscomb
Estimated cost: $38,000.

Subsequent Owners:

Fred A. Britten and Alma H. Britten, his wife (1929-1946)
Joaquin M. Elizalde, of the Republic of the Philippines (1946-1949)
The Republic of the Philippines (1949-   )

City and Telephone Directories List:

1908-1909	Charles L. Fitzhugh
1912	Charles L. Fitzhugh
1913	Stephen L. H. Slocum
1914	William Fitzhugh
1915-1918	Charles L. Fitzhugh
1919	No listing
1920-1924	Charles L. Fitzhugh
1925	Vacant
1926	Adolph C. Miller
1927	Sherman Flint
1928-1929	Czecho-Slovakian Legation
1930	Vacant
1931	Charles E. Hughes
1932-1946	Fred A. Britten
1947-1953	No listing found
1954-1972	Embassy of the Philippines

Known Plans, Drawings, Elevations, etc.: none found.

Important Old Views: none found.

2253 R Street, N.W.

Building Dimensions:

    Stories: 3 plus basement

    Height: 47'-0" to roof ridge

    Bays: 3 bays on R Street
             5 bays at east elevation
             3 bays at north elevation
             4 bays at west elevation

    Widths: 58'-3" on R Street
             57'-3" on north elevation
             64'-1" in depth

Lot Dimensions:

    100'-0" on south (R Street)
    100'-0" on north
     97'-6" on east and west

Major Alterations:

    The ground floor northwest chamber was converted to a family room by the present owners.

Opposite
Entrance Hall
CFA photo
Boucher 1970

Stair Hall
CFA photo
Boucher 1970

Rear Drawing Room
CFA photo
Boucher 1970

Front Drawing Room
CFA photo
Boucher 1970

2301 MASSACHUSETTS AVENUE, N.W., WASHINGTON, D.C.

CFA photo
Boucher 1970

Location: 2301 Massachusetts Avenue, N.W., Washington, D.C.;
                    on the north side of Massachusetts Avenue at its
                    intersection with R Street and Sheridan Circle.

Present Owner: Arab Republic of Egypt

Present Occupant: Arab Republic of Egypt

Present Use: Residence of the Minister Plenipotentiary

Statement of   The detached, stucco and limestone residence, in the
Significance: 18th century Roman revival manner, is significant for its
                    plan, spatial composition, and use of detail and material.
                    The pie-shaped site faces across the west end of Sheridan
                    Circle and the intersection of Massachusetts Avenue and
                    R Street. This shape is reflected in the convex facade
                    of the building and in its spatial sequences. The in-
                    terior spaces on the ground floor contract toward the
                    public stair at the rear and on the first floor expand
                    outward from the stair to the street facade. The remark-
                    able interior plasterwork is a foil for the sobriety of
                    the exterior treatment.

PART I. HISTORICAL INFORMATION

   A. Lot and Square:

   The building is located in Square 2516, lot 62 (formerly lot 57,
   which was made up of original lots 12 and 13 in Block 11, "Kalorama
   Heights"). Lot 61, Square 2516 (formerly part of original lot 21
   in Block 11, "Kalorama Heights") is also included in the property.

   B. Original and Subsequent Owners:

   The following chain of title to the property shows the owners of
   the present structure and of any known preceding structures on the
   site.

   1903 Deed April 21, 1903, recorded May 21, 1903 in
         Liber 2730 folio 332

         Wickliffe E. Mallory et ux, Rosena
         William F. Hunter et ux, Elizabeth F.
             To
         Margaret K. C. Beale

         "...Lot...(12) in Block...(11) 'Kalorama Heights' as per plat

2301 Massachusetts Avenue, N.W.

recorded in Liber County # 7 folio 34, of the Land Records of the Office of the Surveyor of the District of Columbia..."

1905   Deed December 21, 1905, recorded December 23, 1905 in Liber 2935 folio 225

R. Golden Donaldson et ux
    To
Charles S. Hillyer

"This Deed...by and between R. Golden Donaldson and Antoinette C. Donaldson, his wife, parties of the first part, and Charles S. Hillyer, all of the District of Columbia, party of the second part. Witnesseth, That in consideration of Seven thousand five hundred Dollars, the parties of the first part do grant unto the party of the second part, in fee simple...Lot...(13) in Block...(11) of 'Kalorama Heights' a subdivision of part of Widows Mite, 'Pretty Prospect' as said subdivision is recorded in the Office of the Surveyor of the District of Columbia in County Book 7 page 34..."

1905   Deed December 22, 1905, recorded December 23, 1905 in Liber 2935 folio 226

Charles S. Hillyer et ux
    To
Margaret K. C. Beale

Lot 13, Block 11, "Kalorama Heights."

NOTE: April 11, 1907 Margaret K. C. Beale combined lots 12 and 13, Block 11, "Kalorama Heights" into lot 57. Recorded in County Book 22 folio 123, Office of the Surveyor, District of Columbia.

1907   Deed April 25, 1907, recorded April 25, 1907 in Liber 3075 folio 195

Margaret K. C. Beale
    To
Charles S. Hillyer

"This Deed...Witnesseth, That Margaret K. C. Beale, of the District of Columbia, acting herein in relation to her sole and separate estate, party hereto of the first part, in consideration of Ten (10) Dollars, does hereby grant unto Charles S. Hillyer,...Party of the second part in fee simple,...Lot ...(57) in Margaret K. C. Beale's subdivision of Lots in Block ...(11) 'Kalorama Heights'..."

1907   Deed April 29, 1907, recorded April 29, 1907 in
       Liber 3078 folio 140

       Charles S. Hillyer et ux
            To
       Joseph Beale

       Lot 57, Block 11, "Kalorama Heights".

       NOTE: March 30, 1909 Joseph Beale subdivided part of lot 21
              and all of lot 57, Block 11, "Kalorama Heights" into
              lots 61 and 62. Recorded in Subdivisions, Book 35
              folio 89, Office of the Surveyor, District of Columbia.

1916   Deed January 7, 1916, recorded January 7, 1916 in
       Liber 3848 folio 338

       Joseph Beale
            To
       Margaret K. C. Beale

       "This Deed...by and between Joseph Beale, of the District of
       Columbia, party of the first part, and Margaret K. C. Beale,
       of the District of Columbia, wife of said Joseph Beale, party
       of the second part...for and in consideration of his natural
       love and affection, and the sum of Ten (10) Dollars to him
       paid by said party of the second part, in fee simple,...Lots
       ...(61) and ...(62) in the Subdivision made by Joseph Beale of
       Lots in Block...(11), 'Kalorama Heights', (now known as Square
       2516), as per plat of said subdivision recorded in Liber No.
       35 folio 89 of the Records of the Office of the Surveyor of
       the District of Columbia..."

1928   Deed November 19, 1928, recorded November 27, 1928 in
       Liber 6256 folio 65

       Margaret K. C. Beale
            To
       The Royal Government of Egypt

       "Witnesseth that for and in consideration of the sum of
       $150,000 the said party of the first part...does grant unto
       the said party of the second part...Lot...(61) and...(62) in
       Joseph Beale's Subdivision of lots in Block...(11), 'Kalorama
       Heights'..."

       Source: Recorder of Deeds, Washington, D.C.

C. Date of Erection:

    The building was begun in April 1907 and completed in 1909.

D. Building Permits:

The applications for the following building permits were filed by the architect, contractor or owner's agent and provide significant data:

No. 3327, April 23, 1907
Permit to build dwelling
    Owner: Mrs. Joseph Beale
    Architect: Glenn Brown
    Builder: John H. Nolan
    Estimated cost: $70,000.

Filed with No. 3327, April 23, 1907
Application for Building Projection, No. 64872
    "Bay windows": 5'-0" projection
                        15'-0" width

    "Porch, open": 3'-0" projection
                        7'-0" width

No. 4009, June 14, 1907
Permit for Repairs, Alterations, etc.
    Owner: Mrs. Joseph Beale
    Architect: Glenn Brown
    Contractor: John H. Nolan
    "To project the base and water table 7" beyond the building line, for a width of 2'-0"."

No. 2230, December 10, 1908
Permit to Repair or Reconstruct Building
    Architect: Glenn Brown & Bedford Brown
    Contractor: John H. Nolan
    "Build brick fence along east side of lot line - 80'-0" long X 7'-9" high. Stuccoed on house side."

Source: D. C. Government: Department of Economic Development, Bureau of Licenses and Permits, Central Files.

E. Alterations and Additions:

Interior walls have been removed between the ground floor east rooms which originally included the ladies' reception room, man's room, servants' hall, and kitchen. This area is now used as a museum.

The east wall chimney mantle in the kitchen has been removed, and the kitchen moved to the basement.

A curvilinear design for the vestibule and hall was not executed. (See reproduction of plan which is filed with Permit No. 4009, June 14, 1907.)

2301 Massachusetts Avenue, N.W.

F. Architect: Glenn Brown, Washington, D.C.

Glenn Brown (1854-1932), son of Bedford Brown II, was born in Fauquier County, Virginia. After the Civil War his family moved to Washington. He studied at Washington and Lee University, received his M.A. from George Washington University and completed a special architectural course at the Massachusetts Institute of Technology. (Who Was Who in America 1897-1942; Biographical Dictionary of American Architects (Deceased)) On February 1, 1876 Glenn Brown and the former Mary Ella Chapman were married. They were to have two sons: Glenn M. and Bedford III.

In 1879 Glenn Brown was first listed as an architect in the Washington city directory, and in 1887 he was made a Fellow of the American Institute of Architects. From 1899 to 1913 he served as Secretary Treasurer of the AIA. During this period Brown was active in the AIA's efforts to encourage the Federal Government to employ private architects to design Federal buildings. He also promoted the creation of the predecessor of the National Fine Arts Commission.

> On January 11, 1909, a committee of the American Institute of Architects appealed to President Roosevelt for the establishment of a Bureau of Fine Arts to advise as to plans and designs of all future public works of architecture, paintings, sculpture, parks, bridges, or other works of which the art of design forms an integral part. As an initiatory step the committee, of which Cass Gilbert was chairman and Glenn Brown secretary, suggested that the President designate a Council of the Fine Arts, which could exercise advisory functions when called upon...(Washington the National Capital, H. P. Caemmerer, p. 105.)

From 1921 to 1926 Brown was architect for the U.S. Marine Corps, Quantico, Virginia.

Glenn Brown's writings varied from historical to technical.

Water Closets - A Historical, Mechanical and Sanitary Treatise (1884)
Healthy Foundations for Houses (1885)
Trap Syphonage (1886)
History of the United States Capitol, 2 volumes (1900)
Papers Relating to the Improvement of the City of Washington (1901) (compiled by Glenn Brown)
The Octagon (1915)
Personal Recollections of Charles F. McKim (1916)
Roosevelt and the Fine Arts (1919)
Memories of Washington City 1860-1930
European and Japanese Gardens (1902), Glenn Brown, editor
Frank D. Millet and Augustus Saint Gaudens, memorial volume (1913), Glenn Brown, editor

"Maintaining an office in the capital city for many years, Mr. Brown received commissions to design both public and private buildings, restored the old Pohick Church and Gunston Hall in Fairfax County, Va., and in association with his son, Bedford Brown, designed the Dumbarton Bridge in Washington (1914)" which takes Que Street, N.W. across Rock Creek Park. (Biographical Dictionary of American Architects (Deceased)) Better known as the "Buffalo Bridge", Dumbarton Bridge is flanked at each end by a pair of large bronze bison, designed by A. Phimister Proctor.

Three residences of various stylistic influences are known to have been designed by Glenn Brown: 927 Massachusetts Avenue, N.W. (1881); 1732 Massachusetts Avenue, N.W. (1889) and its library addition (1909); and 2301 Massachusetts Avenue, N.W. (1909).

Sources: H. P. Caemmerer, Washington the National Capital, Washington: The United States Government Printing Office, 1932.

Henry F. Withey and Elsie R. Withey, Biographical Dictionary of American Architects (Deceased), Los Angeles: New Age Publishing Co., 1956.

Who Was Who in America 1897-1942: A Companion Volume to Who's Who in America, Vol. I, Chicago: The A. N. Marquis Company, 1942.

American Architect, Vol. 141, No. 2608 (June 1932), p. 44.

The Washington Post, 4-23-32, 5:5 (obituary).

G. Known Plans, Drawings, Elevations, etc.:

Front elevation. Blueprint. Scale 1/4" = 1'
Filed with Permit No. 3327, April 23, 1907
    "Beale House, Washington, D.C.
    Glenn Brown, Architect
    February 21, 1906"
(see reproduction)

Ground floor plan. Blueprint. Scale 1/4" = 1'
Filed with Permit No. 4009, June 14, 1907
    "Residence for Mr. Joseph Beale, Massachusetts Avenue
    and R Street, Washington, D.C.
    Glenn Brown, Architect
    806 17th Street
    Washington, D.C."
(see reproduction)

Projection plan. Ink on linen. Scale 1/8" = 1'
Filed with Permit No. 3327, April 23, 1907
    "Residence for Mrs. Joseph Beale
    Glenn Brown, Architect"

2301 Massachusetts Avenue, N.W.

H. Important Old Views: none found.

I. Residents:

   1. City and telephone directories list the following tenants:

1909	Beale, Jos., real est. 808 17th n.w.
	home: 2301 Mass. Ave. n.w.
1910-1912	Beale, Jos., real. est., 2301 Mass. Ave. n.w.
1913-1917	Beale, Jos., 2301 Mass. Ave.
1918-1929	Vacant
1930-1946	Egyptian Legation
1947-1969	Egyptian Embassy
1970	Not listed
1971-1972	Indian Embassy (U.A.R. Interests Section)

   2. The following residents were included in volumes of <u>The Elite List: A Compilation of Selected Names of Residents of Washington City, D.C. and Ladies Shopping Guide</u>:

      1910-1918 Mr. and Mrs. Joseph Beale and daughter (Miss A. Waller Beale)

   3. Biographies of the residents:

      Little biographical material has been found on Joseph Beale or his wife, Margaret K. C. Beale. However, city directories and <u>The Elite Lists</u> provide several clues. Joseph Beale was first listed in the city directories in 1899 at 2023 Hillyer Place, N.W. From 1900 to 1903 he was listed at 2012 Massachusetts Avenue, N.W. and from 1904 to 1908 at 2026 Columbia Road, N.W. The following listings indicate his occupation and address during these years:

      <u>City Directories</u>

1902	Joseph Beale, agent, 2012 Mass. Ave. N.W.
1903	Joseph Beale, marine eng, 808 17th St. N.W.
	home: 2012 Mass. Ave. N.W.
1904-1906	Joseph Beale, real estate, 2026 Columbia Rd. N.W.
1907	Joseph Beale, U.S.N. 2026 Columbia Rd. N.W.

      <u>Elite Lists</u>

1900-1903	Joseph Beale, Lieut. and Mrs. 2012 Mass. Ave. N.W.
1905	Joseph Beale, Lieut. and Mrs. 2026 Columbia Rd. N.W.

      The only listing for Margaret K. C. Beale between 1918 and 1936 was: "1922-1923 M. K. C. Beale, Mrs., res. Wardman Park Hotel."

2301 Massachusetts Avenue N.W.

Her obituary in The Evening Star, January 10, 1936 reported that Mrs. Margaret K. C. Beale of 1712 Twenty-second Street, N.W. had died on January 1st in Atlantic City, N.J. She left an estate of $400,000. to her daughter, Mrs. Atala Waller Beale Pankoke of Chicago. In the event of her daughter's death, the estate was to go to Margaret K. C. Beale's two sons: DeCoursey Fales and Halliburton Fales.

Source: The Evening Star, 1-10-36, 10:1 (obituary).

Opposite
CFA photo
Alexander 1971

Below
D.C. Government,
Bureau of Licenses
and Permits

Ground Floor Plan
D.C. Government,
Bureau of Licenses
and Permits

Opposite
Detail Entrance Stoop
CFA photo
Alexander 1971

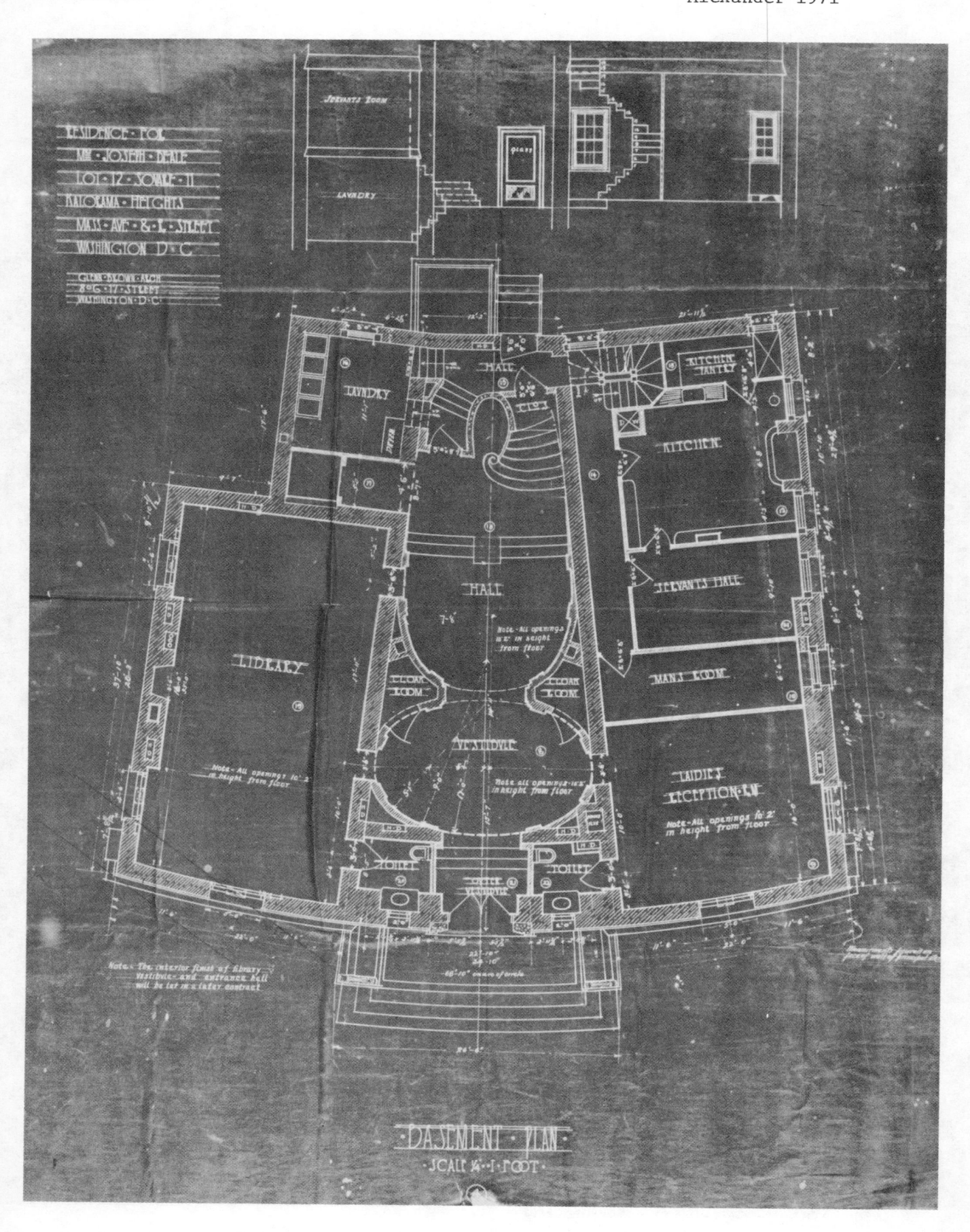

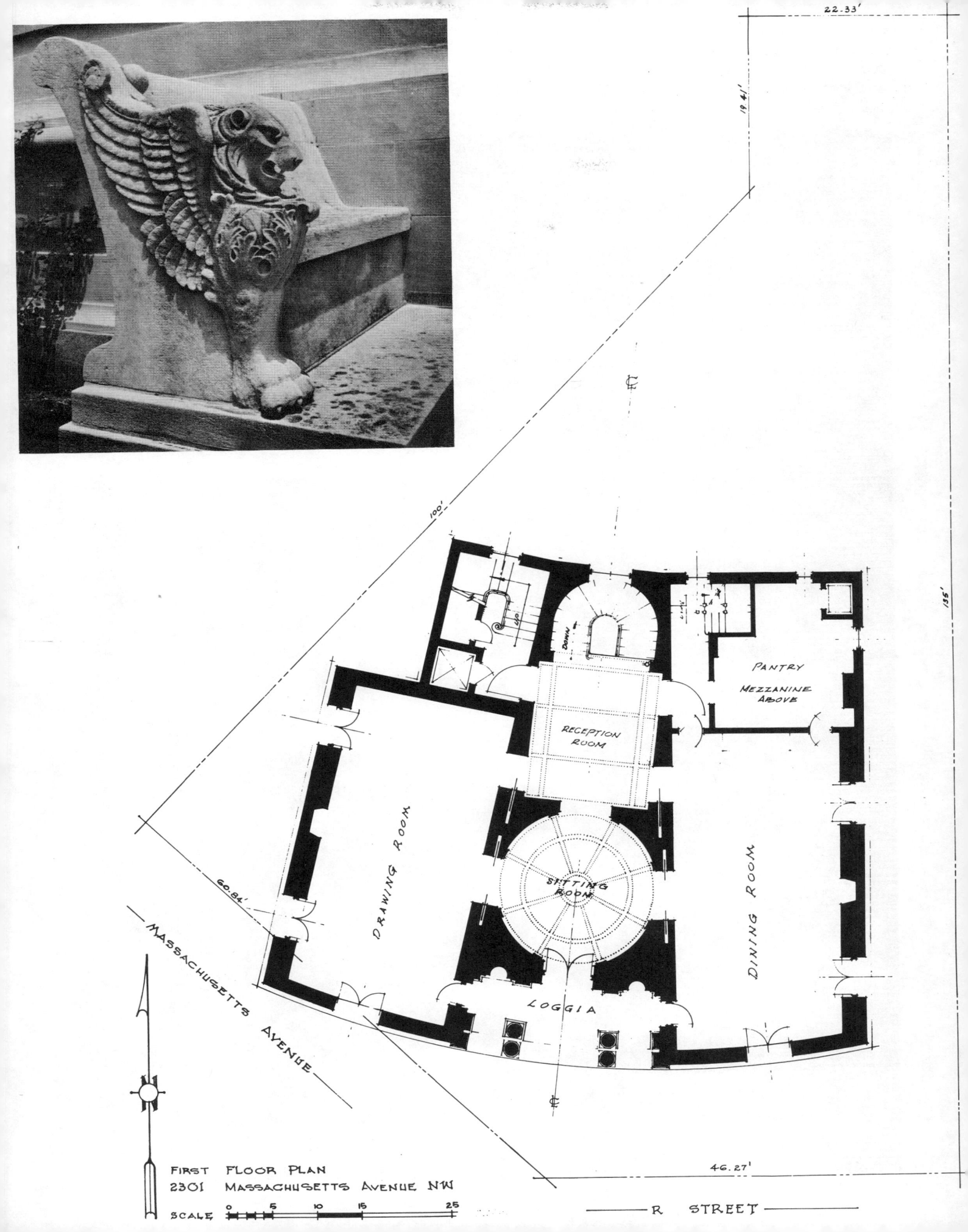

FIRST FLOOR PLAN
2301 MASSACHUSETTS AVENUE NW
SCALE 0 5 10 15 25

DRAWING ROOM
RECEPTION ROOM
PANTRY
MEZZANINE ABOVE
SITTING ROOM
DINING ROOM
LOGGIA

MASSACHUSETTS AVENUE
R STREET

Reception Room
CFA photo
Alexander 1971

Sitting Room
CFA photo
Alexander 1971

Detail Sitting Room Ceiling
CFA photo
Alexander 1971

Detail Sitting Room Walls
CFA photo
Alexander 1971

Sitting Room into Drawing Room
CFA photo
Alexander 1971

Drawing Room
CFA photo
Alexander 1971

Dining Room
CFA photo
Alexander 1971

Below
Detail Cornice
Drawing Room
CFA photo
Alexander 1971

2301 Massachusetts Avenue, N.W.

PART II. ARCHITECTURAL INFORMATION

    A. General Statement:

        1. Architectural character: This detached structure, with rich interior plaster details, is in the 18th century Roman revival manner.

        2. Condition: well maintained.

    B. Exterior Description:

        1. Overall dimensions: The four story plus basement structure measures 63'-1" from sidewalk to parapet cap. All elevations are three bays wide: the convex Sheridan Circle elevation 68'-10", with a tripartite central bay; the concave rear elevation 44'-8"; and the east and west elevations approximately 55'-4".

        2. Foundations: concrete footings and slab.

        3. Wall construction: Except for the exposed brick rear elevation, the wall surfaces are stucco with limestone decorative details. The base rustication has a torus and cavetto water table which serves as ground floor window sill. Above the rusticated ground floor, a block string course acts as first floor window sill and balustrade cap for the Venetian loggia. The first and second floor stuccoed walls have corner quoines. The third floor is a full entablature. The window bays within the "frieze" are separated by incised panels.

        4. Structure: brick bearing walls with steel roofing members.

        5. Mechanical: The building has a steam and hot water heating system, an Otis passenger elevator, and electric lighting.

        6. Porches, stoops, bulkheads, etc.: The R Street entrance stoop has four limestone risers. The torus water table is interrupted by benches which flank the stoop. The benches, set perpendicular to the building wall, are terminated by griffin arm rests.

        The two story Venetian loggia has pairs of stone columns. The inner columns and pilasters, including those flanking the central door, rest on pedestals above a quarry tile floor. Flanking the central door are shell niches. The loggia entablature is plain. The arch has an acanthus keystone, a rosette-coffered soffit and incised spandrel panels.

        At the north (rear), a stair descends to the basement, and a stoop of five risers leads up to the northeast service entrance (formerly the kitchen).

7. Chimneys: Flush with the structure wall above the cornice are single east and west wall chimneys with plain limestone caps.

8. Openings:

    a. Doorways and doors: The wood, double door entrance with transom has a crossette, fascia and bead, limestone architrave with scroll consoles which flank a plain frieze and dentil course and support a bracket and cyma cornice.

    Glazed doors enter onto the loggia from the east and west. The central casement and transom door at the north has a plain Ionic architrave.

    b. Windows: All windows are casement, except for those of the service rooms. The main first floor windows have transoms.

    The ground floor windows have flat voussoir arches and wrought iron, stylized lattice grilles. Each, main, first floor window has an Ionic architrave with a plain frieze and a cyma cornice. The cornice of either bay flanking the loggia is supported by scroll consoles. The central second floor window is located over the loggia door. The end bays each have a crossette architrave and sill brackets supported by the first floor window cornices. The remaining second floor windows have plain architraves. The third floor end bays are set within recessed panels. The central bay of the third floor facade is separated into three window sections by panelled Tuscan pilasters.

9. Roof:

    a. Shape, covering: built-up flat roofing, skylight at center.

    b. Cornice, eaves: ovolo, guttae bracket and cyma cornice capped by panelled parapet.

    c. Dormers, cupolas, towers: none.

C. Interior Description:

1. Floor plans: On axis with the street entrance are the ground floor vestibule (flanked by lavatories accessible from the library and museum), the trapezoidal entrance hall (approached by three risers within the vestibule), and the apsidal stair hall (approached by three risers from the entrance hall). The west library and east museum (refer to "Alterations and Additions" under Part I) flank the entrance hall. Flanking the stair are the northeast service rooms and utility stair, and the northwest elevator. (See plan.)

2301 Massachusetts Avenue, N.W.

The apsidal stair ascends only to the first floor where it is on axis with the rectangular reception room, the circular sitting room and the convex Venetian loggia. Flanking all three spaces are the west drawing room and the east dining room. The stair is flanked on the east by a butler's pantry and stair with musicians' mezzanine, and on the west by the family stair and elevator. (See plan.)

Both the family and service stairs ascend to the second and third floors. The second floor has a skylighted foyer with peripheral bedroom suites. The third floor has additional bedrooms and servants' quarters.

2. Spaces:

Entrance hall: (trapezoidal)

a. Flooring: carpeted.

b. Baseboard: 1'-8", wood with double plinth.

c. Walls: plaster, recessed panels.

d. Ceiling: 11'-0" high, plaster painted white.

e. Doorways and doors: All dcorways have 10" double fascia architraves; the vestibule double door has crossettes.

Museum: (formerly the ladies' lounge, man's room, servants' hall and kitchen: walls removed.)

a. Flooring: 2" regular hardwood, except for basket weave parquetry in the former southeast ladies' reception room.

b. Walls: plaster.

c. Ceiling: 12'-0" high, plaster painted white.

Library:

a. Flooring: carpeted.

b. Walls: wood panelled; north and south wall built-in bookcases with glass doors.

c. Cornice: 4" dentils, cyma.

d. Ceiling: 12'-0" high, plaster painted white. The recessed central section has a 2'-0" wide wood border with a 5" cyma moulding.

e. Doorways and doors: door and window surrounds formed by wall panelling.

2301 Massachusetts Avenue, N.W.

f. Hardware: brass knobs and handles.

g. Lighting: There is an eleven-light (exposed bulb), double sunburst, gilded ceiling fixture.

h. Heating: The west wall chimney firebox has a fire tile lining. The limestone mantle, in the 15th century Italian manner (6'-0" wide by 7'-2" high) has plinths which support candelabra pilasters of paired dolphins, cherub, fountain and lamp; a plain architrave; a frieze with centered escutcheon flanked by rinceau-tailed griffins, cherubs and ribbon-rounded mantle ends; and a dentil and cyma shelf.

Stair hall: The three marble risers from the entrance hall and their landing are flanked by panelled, paired pilasters. Flaired at the bottom, twenty-one risers ascend around the stair well to the first floor. The stringer, risers and treads are grey granite. The black-enamelled double balusters have gilded leaves; the round handrail is bound in blue velvet; and the spiral newel is capped by a brass rosette and crystal prism finial.

a. Baseboard: At the first floor, a plain grey granite frieze, which reflects the floor thickness, is carried around the stair wall. The frieze is capped by the continuation of the 8", first floor, marble baseboard. The baseboard serves as sill for a stair window.

b. Walls: plaster. The stair and foyer are separated by panelled, paired pilasters which support a transverse beam.

c. Cornice: gouge and rosette frieze with bead and egg and dart mouldings below a modern light cove.

d. Ceiling: The shallow, quarter-spherical ceiling has plaster vault ribs of fruit, flower and oak leaf applique with crossing bosses. The coffers are lined by gouge, egg and dart, dentil and talon mouldings.

e. Lighting: an alabaster, cornucopia rinceau relief, hanging lamp.

Reception room: (see photograph)

a. Flooring: primary and secondary diagonally opposed lattice parquetry.

b. Baseboard: 8", marble.

c. Walls: plaster.

d. Cornice: gouge and rosette frieze with bead and egg and dart mouldings below a modern light cove.

2301 Massachusetts Avenue, N.W.

   e. Ceiling: The 15'-9" high, elliptical ceiling has plaster barrel vault ribs of fruit, flower and oak leaf applique with crossing bosses. Lined by gouge, egg and dart, dentil and talon mouldings, there are three central coffers flanked by six smaller coffers.

   f. Doorways and doors: The 8'-4" high by 4'-4" wide doors have double fascia (8") architraves. The exception is the cased opening of the sitting room (10'-8" high by 6'-0" wide) with a talon and egg and dart architrave interrupting the wall frieze and cornice.

   g. Hardware: brass pulls and knobs.

Sitting room: (circular. See photographs.)

   a. Flooring: herringbone parquetry.

   b. Baseboard: 8", marble.

   c. Walls: Wood, fluted, Corinthian pilasters on 8" marble bases flank all four openings. Between each opening is an urn, cornucopia, mask, flambeau and cherub, plaster rinceau panel. Each panel has an egg and dart, fascia and anthemion and palmette frame within a fruit and ribbon, swag and pendant surround. (See detail photograph)

   d. Cornice: plaster, anthemion and palmette frieze behind a modern light cove.

   e. Ceiling: The 14'-6" high, plaster ceiling is a shallow dome of three concentric circles divided by eight, radiating, decorative ribs. At the center is a rosette and acanthus leaf medallion surrounded by palmette. Each of the inner ring rinceau panels has an eagle standard and wreath. The outer ring panels are divided into three coffers of mask, basket and palmette rinceau. (See detail photograph)

   f. Doorways and doors: All openings are 10'-8" high by 6'-0" wide. The double door to the loggia is glazed; the dining and drawing room double doors are sliding.

   g. Lighting: Between each pilaster and panel is a two-light, flambeau, urn and drape, brass sconce.

Dining room: (painted white. See photograph.)

   a. Flooring: primary and secondary diagonally opposed lattice parquetry.

   b. Baseboard: 8", marble.

2301 Massachusetts Avenue, N.W.

c. Walls: plaster. A marble, paired console buffet is centered at the north wall. Over the buffet is a talon-framed mirror which interrupts the wall architrave. Above the mirror the wall entablature frieze is pierced by an orchestra grille.

d. Cornice: The full entablature is plaster, approximately 3'-6" high, having:

(1.) an egg and dart and acanthus fascia architrave;
(2.) a frieze with alternating floral rinceau and plain panels bordered by egg and dart (the plain panels flanked by fruit pendants); and
(3.) a cornice of talon (interrupted by lion masks over each plain panel), brackets, wave corona (with Greek key soffit), egg and dart, dentil and talon mouldings.

The cornice extends 1'-6" to form north and south coffers. At the north wall, the pierced lattice of the orchestra mezzanine grille is centered by a harp with leaf sprays.

e. Ceiling: 15'-9" high, plaster painted white.

f. Doorways and doors: Both the 8'-4" high, 2'-10" wide, glazed loggia door and the 4'-4" wide, sliding foyer door have double fascia architraves. The 10'-8" high by 6'-0" wide, sliding double door to the sitting room has a talon architrave which interrupts the wall architrave.

g. Lighting: There are eight, six-light, silver-plated escutcheon sconces.

h. Heating: The east wall chimney has a cast iron firebox in a lattice motif. The white marble mantle (6'-6" wide by 4'-10" high) has an egg and dart surround and flanking plinths which support lion head and paw console terms below a fascia and talon architrave, and an egg and dart, corona and talon shelf.

Drawing room: (painted white. See photographs.)

a. Flooring: primary and secondary diagonally opposed lattice parquetry.

b. Baseboard: 8", marble

c. Walls: plaster.

d. Cornice: The full entablature is plaster, approximately 3'-6" high. It has an egg and dart and acanthus fascia architrave; a frieze of alternating egg and dart-bordered rinceau panels separated by lion mask with fruit pendants; and a talon, dentil, egg and dart, corona and talon cornice. (See detail photograph.)

2301 Massachusetts Avenue, N.W.

    e. Ceiling: The 15'-9" high, plaster ceiling has a border of guilloche recessed between two parallel, pulvinated bay leaf beams with gouge sides. The beams form corner coffers with pattera at their intersections. Around the plain central panel is a border of acanthus modillions and talon. Centered in the ceiling is a palm leaf fixture medallion.

    f. Doorways and doors: The 8'-4" high, 2'-10" wide glazed loggia door and the 4'-4" wide sliding foyer door have double fascia architraves. The 10'-8" high by 6'-6" wide, sliding double door to the sitting room has a talon architrave which interrupts the wall architrave.

    g. Lighting: There are two, Empire, standing candelabra each with a ram's head, griffin and anthemion-cornucopia pedestal which supports a bulbous bowl with a fluted shaft capped by a brass and crystal pendant, twelve-light candelabrum. Flanking the sitting room door are two brass and crystal sconces, which are similar in design to the candelabra. There is a tear drop, 5'-0" high, eighteen-light chandelier with brass bowl ribs, girdle, arms and acanthus crown, and crystal prism drapes.

    h. Heating: The west wall chimney has a cast iron firebox in a lattice motif. The white marble mantle (6'-6" wide by 4'-10" high) has a fascia and egg and dart surround and moulded plinths which support draped female terms below a fascia and talon architrave, and an egg and dart, corona and talon shelf. The overmantle moulded mirror frame interrupts the wall architrave.

D. Site:

1. Setting and orientation: Facing the west end of Sheridan Circle, the lot measures 46'-3" on R Street, 60'-10" on Massachusetts Avenue, 11'-0" on the west and 135'-0" on the east. A separate garage and garden stair form a rectangular north addition, 19'-5" deep by 22'-4" wide.

2. Enclosures: retaining walls at rear.

3. Outbuildings: The single space garage has a Roman clerestory window which gives interior light from above the car entrance. Its roof terrace is edged by a pierced balustrade. Attached to the garage east wall is a concrete stair, with a closed banister, which ascends to the terrace and Decatur Street.

4. Walks: The rear courtyard and semielliptical entrance drive are concrete. From the R Street sidewalk three risers ascend to the drive and entry on axis with the entrance stoop. The drive and sidewalk have limestone curbing.

5. Landscaping: hedges along driveway; boxwood, roses, ivy, grass and tree at west.

2306 MASSACHUSETTS AVENUE, N.W., WASHINGTON, D.C.

CFA photo
Boucher, 1970

Address: 2306 Massachusetts Avenue, N.W., Washington, D.C.

Significance: This building, which includes studio and stage facilities, was designed as a private cultural center for artistic pursuits and informal entertaining.

Present Owner: Smithsonian Institution
Present Use: Offices
Lot and Square: Square 2507, lots 4 and 5 (formerly in Block 8, "Kalorama Heights")

HISTORICAL AND ARCHITECTURAL INFORMATION

Original Owner: Alice P. Barney (1901-1931) *
Original Use: Studio house
Date of Erection: 1902
Architect: Waddy B. Wood, Washington, D.C.
Builder: Charles A. Langley
Estimated cost: $18,000.

Subsequent Owners:

    Natalie Clifford Barney and Laura A. Dreyfus-Barney (1931-1963)
    Smithsonian Institution (1963-   )

City and Telephone Directories List:

1904-1907	Alice P. Barney
1908-1911	No listing found
1912-1914	Christian D. Hemmick
1915	John J. White
1916-1917	Christian D. Hemmick
1918-1919	Mark Requa
1920	C. F. Cramer
1921-1923	Harold Walker
1924	No listing
1925-1926	Peruvian Embassy
1927	Vacant
1928	Vivian Spencer
1929-1930	Laurence Wilder
1931	Alice P. Barney
1932-1933	D. Laura Barney
1934	William M. Cheeks
1935	Vacant
1936-1938	Columbian Legation

---

* Lot 4 was purchased in 1901 and lot 5 in 1903.

1939-1940	National Capital Film Laboratories, Inc.
1941	Vacant
1942-1943	Sir Vivian Gabriel
1944-1947	No listing found
1948	Natalie C. Barney
1949-1953	No listing found
1954-1961	Vacant
1962-1970	American Association of Museums
1971-1972	Smithsonian Institution

Known Plans, Drawings, Elevations, etc.:

Front elevation. Blueprint. Scale 1/4" = 1'
Filed with Permit No. 172, July 26, 1902
    "Studio for Mrs. A. C. Barney
     Waddy B. Wood, Architect
     808 17th Street, N.W."
(see reproduction)

Floor plans of basement, first, second, third, fourth and fifth floors.
Blueline prints. Scale 1/4" = 1'
Drawn for Smithsonian Institution

Important Old Views:

Photograph: exterior view from Sheridan Circle
The Architectural Annual, Washington, D.C., published by
The Architectural League of America, 1906.

Photograph: exterior view from Sheridan Circle
National Collection of Fine Arts, Smithsonian Institution
Date: before 1911
(see reproduction)

Photograph: 3rd floor studio
National Collection of Fine Arts, Smithsonian Institution
Date: 1904
(see reproduction)

Building Dimensions:

Stories: 4 and 1/2 plus basement

Height: 53'-0" to roof ridge

Bays: 3 bay elevation on Mass. Ave.

Widths: 33'-0" on Mass. Ave.
        40'-0" at west elevation
        60'-6" in depth

2306 Massachusetts Avenue, N.W.

Site Dimensions:

    60'-9" on northeast (Mass. Ave.)
   122'-9" on northwest
   101'-4" on southwest (Rock Creek Park)
   105'-0" on southeast

Major Alterations:

In 1911 a detached garage was added at the rear of the property to the west. At that time, the decorative garden wall flanking the driveway entrance may have been constructed. At a later date, a shallow dormer was installed over the left bay on the fifth floor.

Third Floor Studio, 1904
Courtesy of National Collection of Fine Arts
Smithsonian Institution

383

Before 1911
Courtesy of National Collection of Fine Arts
Smithsonian Institution

D.C. Government, Bureau of Licenses and Permits

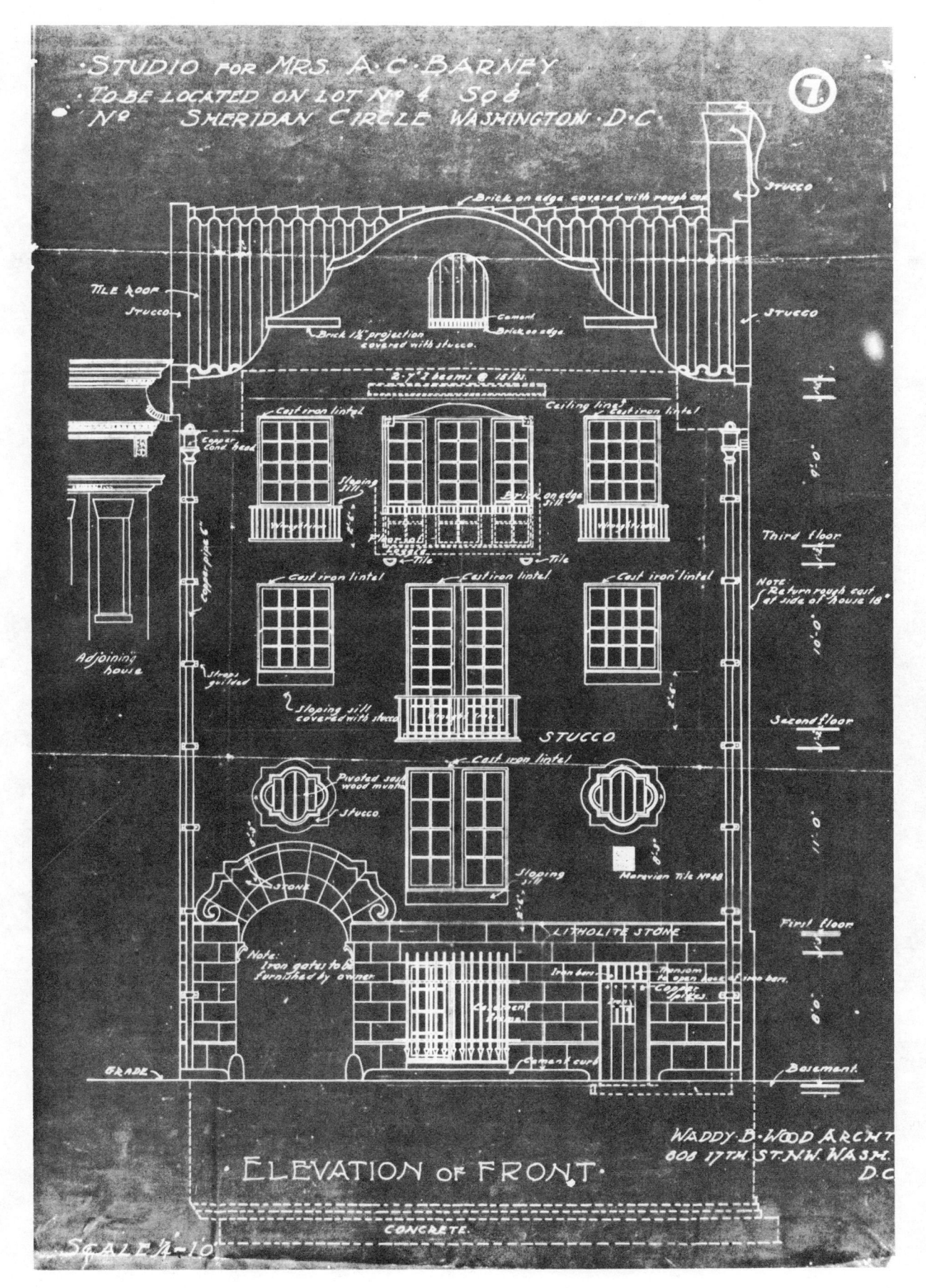

Third Floor Studio, ca. 1963
Courtesy of National Collection of Fine Arts
Smithsonian Institution

Third Floor Studio, ca. 1963
Courtesy of National Collection of Fine Arts
Smithsonian Institution

2311 MASSACHUSETTS AVENUE, N.W., WASHINGTON, D.C.

CFA photo
Boucher 1970

Location: 2311 Massachusetts Avenue, N.W., Washington, D.C.; on the north side of Massachusetts Avenue and approximately 230 feet west of Sheridan Circle.

Present Owner: Republic of China

Present Occupant: Republic of China

Present Use: Chancery

Statement of Significance: Originally a private residence, this semidetached building was designed in the 18th century French manner. Finely crafted academic details are combined to form a scheme that is harmonious and crisply delineated.

PART I. HISTORICAL INFORMATION

A. Lot and Square:

The building is located in Square 2516, lot 63 (formerly lots 17 and 18, and part of 21 in Block 11, "Kalorama Heights").

B. Original and Subsequent Owners:

The following chain of title to the property shows the owners of the present structure and of any known preceding structure on the site:

1908 Deed November 27, 1908, recorded December 2, 1908 in Liber 3186 folio 241

Potomac Realty Co.
    To
Gibson Fahnestock

Lots 17 and 18 in Block 11, "Kalorama Heights."
"This Deed...by and between The Potomac Realty Company, a body corporate duly incorporated under the laws in force in the State of New Jersey...party hereto of the first part, and Gibson Fahnestock of the District of Columbia, party hereto of the second part..."

NOTE: April 16, 1909 Gibson Fahnestock combined lots 17, 18 and the West 18.25 feet of lot 21 (of subdivision by Rodgers and Stellwagen Trustees recorded in County Book 7, page 34), Block 11, "Kalorama Heights" into lot 63. Recorded in Subdivisions Liber 35, folio 126, Office of the Surveyor, District of Columbia. (Nathan C. Wyeth also signed the recorded combination.)

Will of Gibson Fahnestock was recorded April 26, 1917 in Will Book No. 93, page No. 13, Registrar of Wills, District of Columbia. The will stated:

"I, Gibson Fahnestock, of Newport, Rhode Island,... give, devise and bequeath unto my wife, Carolyn Snowden Fahnestock, my house and premises at Newport, also my house and premises at Washington, D.C...."

1909 Deed March 23, 1909, recorded March 24, 1909 in Liber 3221 folio 223

Joseph Beale et ux, Margaret K. C.
        To
Gibson Fahnestock

Part of lot 21 in Block 11, "Kalorama Heights."
"...Beginning for the same at a point in Decatur Place at the northwest corner of said lot and running thence south along the dividing line between said lot...(21) and lot... (18) in said subdivision...12.06 feet to the northwesterly corner of lot...(17) in said subdivision; thence southeast along the line between lots...(21) and...(17)...25 feet to the northeasterly corner of said lot...(17); thence north at right angles to Decatur Place...29.15 feet to the south line of...Decatur Place; thence west...18.25 feet to the point of beginning..."

1938 Quit-Claim-Deed September 30, 1938, recorded November 17, 1938 Liber 7289 folio 398

Snowden Fahnestock et ux
Gibson Fahnestock (son) et ux
Margaret Fahnestock Drummond-Wolff et vir
        To
The Montpelier Corporation

"This Deed...by and between Snowden Fahnestock and Gibson Fahnestock, both of the City and County of Newport in the State of Rhode Island, and Margaret Drummond-Wolff, of London, England, parties of the first part, and The Montpelier Corporation, a corporation organized and existing under the laws of the State of Rhode Island and located in Newport, party of the second part...Lots...(17) and...(18) in Block... (11), 'Kalorama Heights'...said premises having been devised to these Grantors by...the Will of Carolyn S. Fahnestock, late

2311 Massachusetts Avenue, N.W.

of Newport, Rhode Island, deceased..."

1943   Deed April 6, 1943, recorded April 12, 1943 in
Liber 7847 folio 557

The Montpelier Corporation
          To
The National Government of the
Republic of China

"...for and in consideration of the sum of Seventy-five thousand Dollars..."

Source: Recorder of Deeds, Washington, D.C.

C. Date of Erection:

The building was begun in July 1909 and completed in November 1910.

D. Building Permits:

The applications for the following building permits were filed by the architect, contractor or owner's agent and provide significant data:

No. 22, July 2, 1909
Permit to build dwelling
    Owner: Gibson Fahnestock
    Architect: Nathan Wyeth
    Builder: George A. Fuller Co.
    Estimated cost: $150,000.

No. 2084, September 27, 1909
Permit to erect passenger elevator
    Owner: Gibson Fahnestock
    Mechanic: Otis Elevator Company
    Estimated cost: $3000.
    Location: "Side, near center"

No. 558, August 1, 1910
Permit to build retaining wall at rear of building
    Owner: Gibson Fahnestock
    Architect: N. C. Wyeth
    Estimated cost: $800.

No. 1772, October 8, 1910
Permit to erect iron marquise
    Owner: Gibson Fahnestock
    Architect: N. C. Wyeth

2311 Massachusetts Avenue, N.W.

       Builder: George A. Fuller Co
       Estimated cost: $550.

   Source: D. C. Government: Department of Economic Development, Bureau of Licenses and Permits, Central Files.

E. Alterations and Additions:

The building permits available do not indicate any significant changes to the residence - though the owners have partitioned the original drawing and dining rooms for office space.

F. Architect: Nathan C. Wyeth, Washington, D.C.

Nathan Corwith Wyeth (1870 - 1963) was graduated from the art school of the New York Metropolitian Museum of Art in 1889. He then spent ten years studying at the École des Beaux Arts in Paris. After one year (1899-1900) as a designer with the Washington office of Carrère and Hastings, Wyeth joined the Office of the Supervising Architect, Treasury Department.

From 1904 through 1905, he was chief designer for the Architect of the Capitol. There is evidence that Wyeth was involved in the design of the "old" Senate Office Building and the Cannon Office Building at the time. A photograph of a rendering of the "Terraces, Balustrades, and Approaches, Senate Office Building" indicates "Wyeth and Sullivan, Consulting Architects". Another rendering, "Office Building, House of Representatives, Washington, D.C.: B Street Elevation", is signed by Wyeth. Unfortunately, neither rendering is dated. (Files of the Commission of Fine Arts)

From 1905 to 1919 Wyeth maintained a private practice, during which time he "designed many of the city's most gracious homes that sheltered the city's most prominent people and entertained its most sparkling society under chandeliers and carved panelling that matched elegant exteriors." (Mrs. Nathan C. Wyeth, The Sunday Star, 12-13-70) He also designed the Battleship Maine Monument in Arlington Cemetery, the Tidal Basin Bridge, Key Bridge, the Old Emergency Hospital and Columbia Hospital.

During World War I, Mr. Wyeth, as a major in the construction division of the Office of the Surgeon General, designed hospitals. After the war, he became ill and spent several years recuperating in Switzerland. He returned to Washington to open his practice again, only to lose it during the stock market crash six years later.

From 1934 until his retirement in 1946, Wyeth was the Municipal Architect of the District of Columbia. Some of the public buildings he designed were: The Municipal Center; The Recorder

2311 Massachusetts Avenue, N.W.

of Deeds Building; the Georgetown Branch of the Public Library; Woodrow Wilson High School; and the National Guard Armory.

Sources: The New York Times, 9-3-63, 33:2 (obituary).
        The Sunday Star, 12-30-70, F 1:1, "Architect's Widow Recalls the Past."
        The Washington Post, 8-31-63, B 3:1 (obituary).

G. Known Plans, Drawings, Elevations, etc.:

Elevation of retaining wall. Blueprint. Scale 1/4" = 1'
Filed with Permit No. 558, August 1, 1910

Projection plan of marquise. Ink on linen.
Filed with Permit No. 1772, October 8, 1910
    "Res. for Gibson Fahnestock, Esq.
    N. C. Wyeth, Arch't
    Washington, D.C."

Plan of marquise: side elevation of marquise; partial front elevation; plan showing location of gateway; side elevation of gateway showing stiffening rod. Blueprint (1).
    "Exterior Ironwork
    Res. for Gibson Fahnestock, Esq.
    3-16-10 "

H. Important Old Views: none found

I. Residents:

1. City and telephone directories list the following tenants:

1911	Gibson Fahnestock
1912	No listing
1913	Gibson Fahnestock
1914	No listing
1915-1917	Gibson Fahnestock
1918-1919	Mrs. Gibson Fahnestock
1920-1930	Caroline S. Fahnestock
1931	Vacant
1932-1934	Gibson Fahnestock [son]
1935-1937	Carolyn S. Fahnestock
1938-1941	Vacant
1942	Snowden Fahnestock
1943	China Defense Supplies, Inc.
1944-1947	Chinese Embassy, Supply Commission
1948	Universal Trading Corp.
1949-1951	Chinese Embassy, Commercial Counselor's Office
1952-1972	Chinese Embassy, Chancery

2. Biographies of residents:

Gibson Fahnestock was the son of Harris Fahnestock, president of the First National Bank of New York. Gibson worked in the bank for several years and then retired. However, he was to remain a prominent New York and, later, Washington financier. For many years after his retirement, he and his family lived in Rome and on his estate on the Riviera.

After the Fahnestocks came to Washington, they divided their time between their residence here and their summer home in Newport, R. I. Gibson Fahnestock was first listed in the city directories at the New Willard in 1906. His name appears again from 1908 through 1910 at 1812 I Street, N.W. During this period he purchased land and built a house at 2311 Massachusetts Avenue, N.W.

Fahnestock died in March 1917 leaving his wife, Carolyn, and three children: Gibson, Snowden A., and Margaret.

Source: The Evening Star, 3-2-17, 7:7 (obituary).

Carolyn Snowden Andrews Fahnestock (1862-1937), widow of Gibson, was the daughter of General Richard Snowden Andrews (of the Confederate Army) and of the former Mary Katherine Lee, of Baltimore. "Prominent in the social circles of Washington, New York, and Newport, Mrs. Fahnestock was active all her life in philantropic, religious and patriotic movements. During the World War, she was a leader in the Red Cross and other relief activities and a founder of the Women's Naval Service and the National Service Schools for Women." (The New York Times, 10-19-37) At the time of her death in 1937, she was vice-president of the Home for Incurables, located at 2025 Massachusetts Avenue, N.W.

Mrs. Fahnestock died at the age of 75 while staying at the Sulgrave Club (1801 Massachusetts Avenue, N.W.) and waiting for her home at 2311 Massachusetts Avenue to be opened "for the season." Her three children were living at the time of her death: Col. Snowden A. Fahnestock, of Washington, D.C.; Gibson Fahnestock, who was living in China; and Mrs. Henry Drummond-Wolf, of London, England.

Sources: The National Cyclopedia of American Biography, Vol. XXX, New York: James T. White & Company, 1943, p. 553.

The Evening Star, 10-19-37, 12:4 (obituary).
The New York Times, 10-19-37, 25:3 (obituary).
The Washington Daily News, 10-19-37, 11:1 (obituary).
The Washington Post, 10-19-37, 26:2 (obituary).
The Washington Post, 10-24-37, S 4:5.

2311 Massachusetts Avenue, N.W.

Gibson Fahnestock (son) and his wife lived in Washington and New York, and at one point had a home in France. City directories place them at 2311 Massachusetts Avenue from 1932 through 1934. They were living in Manila, P.I. when the Japanese invaded in 1941. Both were placed in concentration camps. In June 1942, Mrs. Fahnestock was released because of bad health. Though Mr. Fahnestock was still imprisoned at the time of his wife's death, continued research has not revealed anything beyond his imprisonment.

Source: The New York Times, 10-9-42, 22:3 (obituary, Mrs. Fahnestock).

Col. Snowden Andrews Fahnestock (1886-1962), the second son of Gibson and Carolyn Fahnestock, was listed as a resident in 1942 - one year before the sale of the house to the Republic of China.

Col. Fahnestock was a veteran of the two World Wars, serving in the United States Army Reserve from 1917 to 1946. During World War I, he was in the first Battalion, 308th Infantry, 77th Division and received the rank of major, the Purple Heart, and the French Croix de Guerre. He served as a Colonel in Intelligence at the Pentagon during the Second World War.

After World War I, Fahnestock was an "officer in many corporations, and was a director of the First National Bank of New York City until resigning in 1942 for war duty. The bank has since merged with National City Bank." (The Evening Star, 11-11-62)

Col. Fahnestock married Elizabeth Bertron in 1910. After their divorce in 1925, he married Helen Morgan Moran. Their well-publicized divorce was granted in 1935. He was remarried in 1936 to the former Mrs. Beatrice Beck Tuck.

Sources: The Evening Star, 1-4-35, B 1:1.
         The Evening Star, 1-11-35, 3:2.
         The Evening Star, 10-8-35, B 1:5.
         The Evening Star, 11-30-35, 1:2 (obituary, Mrs. Helen Fahnestock).
         The Evening Star, 11-11-62, B 7:1 (obituray, Col. Fahnestock).
         The New York Times, 11-11-62, 88:7 (obituary, Col. Fahnestock).

CFA photo
Boucher 1970

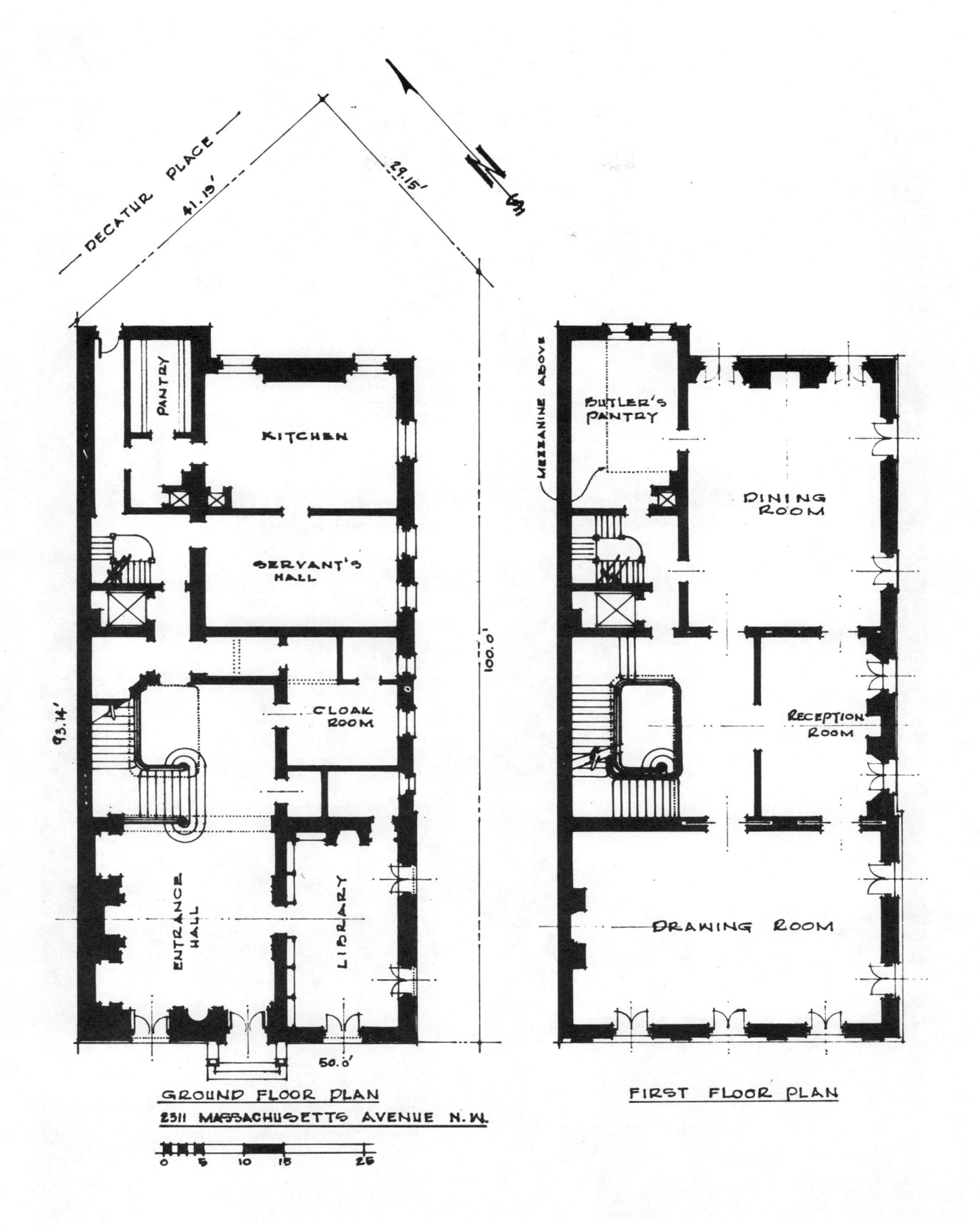

GROUND FLOOR PLAN
2311 MASSACHUSETTS AVENUE N.W.

FIRST FLOOR PLAN

400

Stair Hall
CFA photo
Boucher 1970

Opposite
Detail Entrance Hall
CFA photo
Boucher 1970

2311 Massachusetts Avenue, N.W.

PART II. ARCHITECTURAL INFORMATION

    A. General Statement:

        1. Architectural character: This semidetached structure has Louis XVI exterior and interior details.

        2. Condition: good, primarily original, some interior remodeling and partitioning.

    B. Exterior Description:

        1. Overall dimensions: The three and one half story plus basement and attic structure is 70'-0" from sidewalk to roof ridge. It measures 42'-0" across the three bay south (Massachusetts Avenue) and north elevations; 88'-6" along the six bay (first floor) east elevation; and 92'-6" along the west party wall.

        2. Foundations: concrete footings and slab.

        3. Wall construction: The walls are tan Roman brick, except for the south elevation and the first two east elevation bays which are limestone. The building base is capped by a block water table acting as window sill for the rusticated ground floor. An entablature string course (with a fascia and roll architrave; a plain frieze; and a cyma, corona and roll cornice) acts as base for the range-coursed first and second floors, the bays of which are separated by two story, fluted, Corinthian pilasters on pedestals.

        4. Structure: brick bearing walls with steel structural members.

        5. Mechanical: The building has hot air, in-wall ducts and registers. The electric lighting is combined with a gas system in the service areas. The passenger elevator is by Otis.

        6. Porches, stoops, bulkheads, etc.: Three granite risers ascend to a 12'-6" wide stoop flanked by panelled limestone balustrades having acanthus console terminals and block caps turned from the building water table. The caps support cast iron side panels and scrolls below a decorative marquise with guilloche frieze.

        Each first floor window has a shallow, decorative cast iron, rocaille railing centered by a wreath. At the north elevation, brick retaining walls enclose granite risers, which descend to the basement.

2311 Massachusetts Avenue, N.W.

7. Chimneys: Visible from ground level are three chimneys. The east and west walls each have one of Roman brick with a limestone cap, while the west wall has one of limestone, capped by a full entablature.

8. Openings:

    a. Doorways and doors: The original entrance door has been replaced. The crossette, double fascia, and egg and dart limestone architrave has an acanthus scroll keystone with foliate sprays.

    b. Windows: All windows are casement, two-lights in width. The ground floor has decorative wrought iron grilles. The floor length first floor bays have transoms.

    Each first floor bay has a guilloche frieze within a crossette limestone architrave on a raised ground. The dentil cap and frieze are flanked by acanthus consoles which support a cyma cornice. Each second floor bay has a scrolled keystone and spray, crossette architrave on a raised ground. Each architrave interrupts the building entablature.

9. Roof:

    a. Shape, covering: A false parapet supports the slate, mansard roof, which has a copper egg and dart gutter, bead flashing and a pulvinated egg and dart ridge cap with built-up flat roofing behind.

    b. Cornice, eaves: The full Corinthian entablature is limestone. The fascia architrave, plain frieze, and dentil and egg and dart cornice mouldings are broken forward over each pilaster. The false parapet is panelled.

    c. Dormers, cupolas, towers: Interrupting the false parapet are limestone third floor dormers having panelled strips flanked by angular consoles and capped by bracket scrolls. The bracket scrolls flank a guilloche frieze and keystone, and support a segmentally-arched pediment. Centered over each bay is a wood, fourth floor dormer with a segmentally-arched pediment.

C. Interior Description:

1. Floor plans: The ground floor entrance and vestibule give access to the entrance hall, which is followed by the stair hall and service area. East of the vestibule and entrance hall is the library; east of the stair hall is a cloak room and lavatory. (See plan.)

    The main stair ascends along the west wall to the first floor hall with the drawing room (on Massachusetts Avenue) to its south and the dining room to the north. Both are connected by the reception room to the east. West of the dining room is the service area. (See plan.)

The second and third floors have major bedrooms and baths. The fourth floor contains servants' quarters.

2. Spaces: (The drawing and dining rooms were not available for inspection.)

Entrance hall: (see photograph)

a. Flooring: limestone blocks, two feet square, laid diagonally. Carpeted.

b. Baseboard: 6" limestone.

c. Walls: tan limestone. Set in bead and ogee mouldings are single raised panels with corner rosettes. Flanking the library door are paired and panelled pilasters with acanthus leaf and gouge capitals. Single pilasters of similar design frame rectangular niches flanking the west chimney wall. The niches contain built-in limestone benches on acanthus consoles. Between the entrance door and west bay is a shell niche. Pilaster piers of similar design to the above frame the stair hall.

d. Cornice: The wood cornice (painted white), of fascia, astragal, cyma and bracket courses, is carried across the piers.

e. Ceiling: 11'-0" high, plaster painted white.

f. Doorways and doors: Each leaf of the beveled glass double door entrance has a decorative tulip, lattice and rosette cast iron grille.

The oak, double door to the library has three raised panels in a cyma moulding.

Both doors have a limestone scroll with foliate sprays.

g. Hardware: brass door locks and bundled-reed handles.

h. Lighting: There are six, two-light, triglyph and urn, brass sconces with reeded arms holding opaque glass light bowls.

i. Heating: The west wall, limestone chimney mantle has pilasters with oak leaf panels and acanthus console caps which flank a rinceau frieze and support a shelf and raised panel hood. (See photograph.)

2311 Massachusetts Avenue, N.W.

Library: (dry-wall partitioning)

a. Flooring: basket weave parquetry.

b. Baseboard: 8", oak with cyma cap.

c. Dado: oak, flat panels in cyma moulding.

d. Chairrail: 3'-0" high, oak with fascia and cyma.

e. Walls: oak. Flat panels in cyma moulding. The windows are flanked by rosette-centered, panelled pilasters on pedestals with acanthus leaf capitals. At the west wall and flanking the left side of the north chimney are walnut cabinets which support built-in bookshelves.

f. Cornice: plaster; fascia, cyma and corona with fret soffit.

g. Ceiling: 11'-0" high, plaster painted white.

h. Doorways and doors: The oak double door to the entrance hall has three raised panels in cyma mouldings within a cyma and double fascia architrave. East of the mantle, a door leads through a short antehall to the lavatory.

i. Hardware: brass door knobs and reeded handles.

j. Lighting: There are two, three-light, bronze sconces with swags.

k. Heating: The north wall, grey marble (4'-0" high) chimney mantle (in the French Baroque manner) has an adapted bolection surround between cyma and ogee mouldings.

Stair hall: (see photographs)

a. Flooring: limestone blocks, two feet square, laid diagonally. Carpeted.

b. Baseboard: 6", limestone.

c. Walls: limestone. Raised panels are set in bead and ogee mouldings. A pilaster with acanthus scroll cap flanks the stair well at the north wall.

d. Cornice: wood painted white; three fascia and bead courses with cyma.

e. Ceiling: 11'-0" high, plaster painted white.

f. Doorways and doors: The single oak doors to the east closet

2311 Massachusetts Avenue, N.W.

and lavatory both have three raised panels in cyma mouldings, and plain limestone keystones. The doorway to the north service area has an acanthus scroll keystone with foliate sprays. The keystone interrupts a raised panel with corner rosettes in an ogee moulding.

g. Hardware: brass door locks and reeded handles.

h. Lighting: The stair landings are lighted by single, two-light, triglyph and urn, brass sconces with reeded arms and opaque glass light bowls.

i. Heating: Beneath the stair stringer is a hot air register with a Greek key and link, brass grille and a limestone voussoir lintel.

j. Stair: The main stair ascends nine risers west to the first landing (the first three treads of which are terminated in concentric semicircles), twelve risers north to the second landing, and three risers east to the first floor hall. The risers, treads and closed stringers are limestone. The stringers begin on the third tread from the ground floor. The decorative cast iron banister has alternating oval guilloche and decorative panels between urn finials. The handrail is wood. (See photograph.)

Reception room: (painted grey)

a. Flooring: decorative parquetry with fret border.

b. Baseboard: 6", wood with cyma cap.

c. Dado: flush, plaster panels with incised border.

d. Chairrail: 3'-0" high, wood with fascia and cyma.

e. Walls: flush, plaster panels with incised border and ribbon-roll moulding.

f. Cornice: plaster; bead, acanthus frieze and talon.

g. Ceiling: 14'-6" high, plaster; cove ending in two block courses.

h. Doorways and doors: The three-panelled double doors to the west stair hall, the south drawing room and the north dining room all have a crossette architrave capped by an urn and rinceau frieze. The architrave and frieze are framed within a talon moulding. The frieze is flanked by consoles supporting an egg and dart, and corona cornice.

i. Hardware: brass. The stair hall door has urn and rinceau, rectangular rim locks, reeded handles, and acorn finial

2311 Massachusetts Avenue, N.W.

and pendant hinges. The windows have acanthus, drapery tie-backs and lock rods with rosette knobs.

j. Lighting: There are four, three-light, brass sconces, the lights held by a central cherub and flanking griffins.

k. Heating: The east wall chimney has a white marble hearth and a decorative cast iron firebox. The white marble 3'-0" high mantle (in the Georgian manner) has yellow marble trim. Beaded consoles support a bead architrave, a wreath and spray frieze broken forward over either console, and a corona and cyma shelf.

D. Site:

1. Setting and orientation: The building faces south on a pentagonal lot measuring 50'-0" on the south (Massachusetts Avenue); 93'-2" on the west (party wall); 41'-3" on the northwest (Decatur Place); 29'-2" on the northeast; and 100'-0" on the east.

2. Enclosures: A granite, southwest retaining wall is capped by a panelled limestone balustrade with a console terminal. A decorative cast iron, east wall gateway has a guilloche frieze and ogee pediment centered by a wreath with sprays and ribbon. The gate connects to a brick wall capped by a wrought iron fence which marks the east property line. Brick retaining walls with wrought iron railings enclose the north and west property lines (an iron stair to Decatur Place has been removed).

3. Outbuildings: none.

4. Walks: brick-paved north court and semicircular concrete entrance drive with granite curbing.

5. Landscaping: grass and single evergreen.

2315 MASSACHUSETTS AVENUE, N.W., WASHINGTON, D.C.

CFA photo
Boucher 1970

Address: 2315 Massachusetts Avenue, N.W., Washington, D.C.

Significance: This stucco building, with conglomerate 18th century, limestone and terra-cotta details, is a visual accent to an acute-angled street corner. Its plan terminates with a round tower which defines the lot shape and acts as a period set at the end of an important residential block.

Present Owner: Pakistan
Present Use: Chancery
Lot and Square: Square 2517, lot 60 (formerly lots 19 and 20 in Block 11, "Kalorama Heights").

HISTORICAL AND ARCHITECTURAL INFORMATION

Original Owner: Mrs. F. B. Moran, also known as Jane W. B. Moran (1908-1938)
Original Use: Residence
Date of Erection: 1909
Architect: George Oakley Totten, Jr., Washington, D.C.
Builder: Arthur Cowsill
Estimated cost: $62,000.

Subsequent Owners:

Eleanor Berger McConihe and Arabella A. Macfarland (1938-1940)
Eleanor B. McConihe and James O'Donnell, and his wife Alice (1940-1944)
Hebrew National Liberation Fund, Inc. (1944-1950)
Government of Pakistan (1950-   )

City and Telephone Directories List:

1911	Francis B. Moran
1912-1913	John Hays Hammond, mining expert
1914-1917	Francis B. Moran
1918	Lord Reading
1919	Vacant
1920	J. W. B. Moran
1921	Francis Moran
1922	Vacant
1923-1924	Francis B. Moran
1925	Vacant
1926-1927	Francis B. Moran
1928-1933	Vacant
1934	Djalah Ghaffer Khan
1935	Persian Legation
1936-1937	Iranian Legation
1938-1939	Vacant

2315 Massachusetts Avenue, N.W.

    1940-1943   Iranian Legation
    1944   No listing found
    1945-1949   Hebrew Committee of National Liberation
                      American League for a Free Palestine
    1950   No listing found
    1951-1972   Embassy of Pakistan, chancery

The following residents were included in the <u>Elite List: A Compilation of Selected Names of Residents of Washington City, D.C. and Ladies Shopping Guide</u>:

    1913   Mr. and Mrs. John Hays Hammond
    1914-1917   Mrs. Francis Berger Moran
    1918   Sir and Lady Crawford
    1927   Mrs. Francis Berger Moran
    1929   Mrs. Francis Berger Moran

Known Plans, Drawings, Elevations, etc.:

    Projection and site plan. Ink on linen. Scale 1/8" = 1'
    Filed with Permit No. 953, September 10, 1908
    (see reproduction)

    Front elevation. Blueprint. Scale 1/4" = 1'
    Filed with Permit No. 953, September 10, 1908
        "Residence for Mrs. F. B. Moran
          Mass. Ave. & Decatur Street
          George Oakley Totten, Jr., Architect
          808 17th St. N.W., Washington, D.C."
    (see reproduction)

    North elevation. Blueprint. Scale 1/4" = 1'
    Filed with Permit No. 953, September 10, 1908
        "Residence for Mrs. F. B. Moran
          Mass. Ave. & Decatur Street
          George Oakley Totten, Jr., Architect"
    (see reproduction)

    Plan of first story.
    <u>The American Architect</u>, Vol CVIII (August 11, 1915), plates.
    (see reproduction)

Important Old Views:

    Photographs: exterior view, gallery, entrance hall, and music room.
    <u>The American Architect</u>, Vol CVIII (August 11, 1915), plates.
    (See reproduction of music room.)

Building Dimensions:

    Stories: 3 and 1/2 plus attic and basement

2315 Massachusetts Avenue, N.W.

Height: 60'-0" to roof ridge

Bays: 3 bays on Massachusetts Avenue
3 bay tower on corner of Mass. Ave. and Decatur Place
5 bays on Decatur Place

Widths: 80'-0" on Massachusetts Avenue
86'-0" on Decatur Place
70'-0" along east party wall

Site Dimensions:

  99'-6" on south (Mass. Ave.)
136'-5" on northwest (Decatur Place)
  93'-2" on east

Major Alterations:

The doorway from the music room to the conservatory has been altered.

The garage door beneath the conservatory has been replaced with double-hung windows.

Detail Conservatory
CFA photo
Alexander 1971

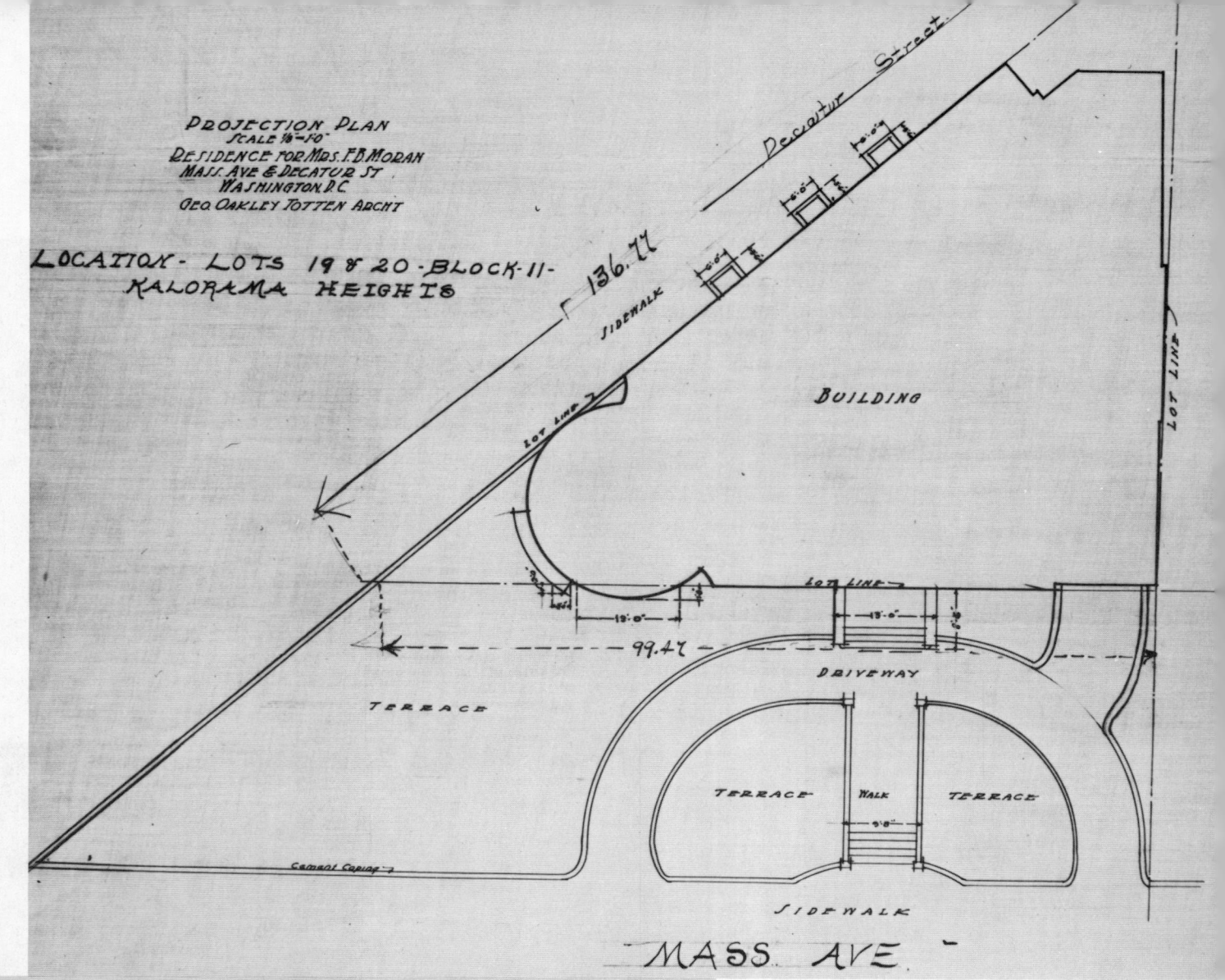

PROJECTION PLAN
SCALE ⅛"=1'-0"
RESIDENCE FOR MRS. F.B. MORAN
MASS. AVE & DECATUR ST
WASHINGTON D.C.
GEO. OAKLEY TOTTEN ARCH'T

LOCATION - LOTS 19 & 20 - BLOCK - 11 -
KALORAMA HEIGHTS

Decatur Street

136.77

SIDEWALK

LOT LINE

BUILDING

LOT LINE

LOT LINE

19'-0"

99.47

TERRACE

DRIVEWAY

TERRACE   WALK   TERRACE

Cement Coping

SIDEWALK

MASS AVE

THE AMERICAN ARCHITECT
VOL. CVIII, NO. 2068 — AUGUST 11, 1915

PLAN OF FIRST STORY

HOUSE OF MRS. F. B. MORAN, WASHINGTON, D. C.
MR. GEORGE OAKLEY TOTTEN, ARCHITECT

Site Plan
D.C. Government
Bureau of Licenses and Permits

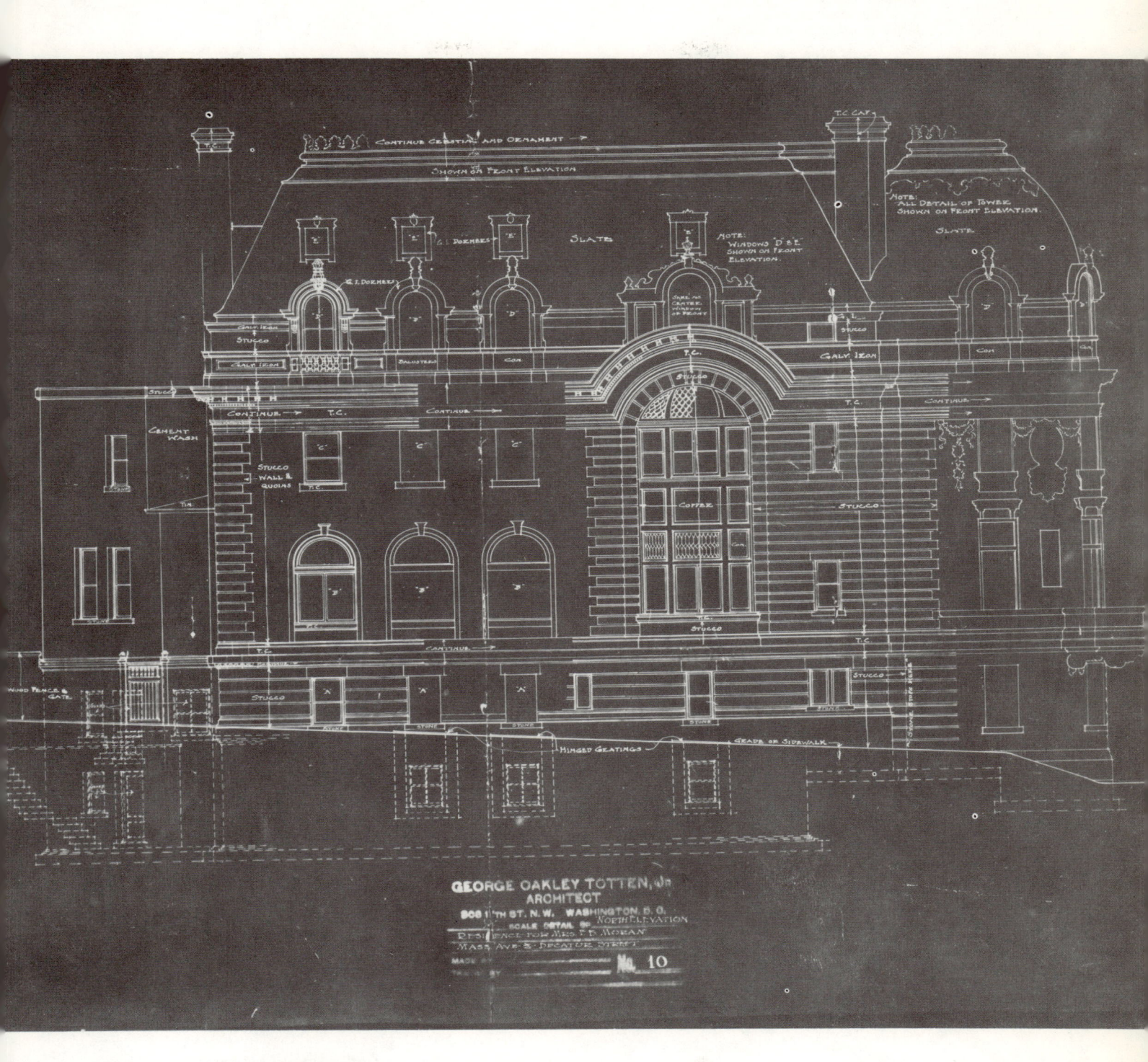

Decatur Street Elevation
D.C. Government
Bureau of Licenses and Permits

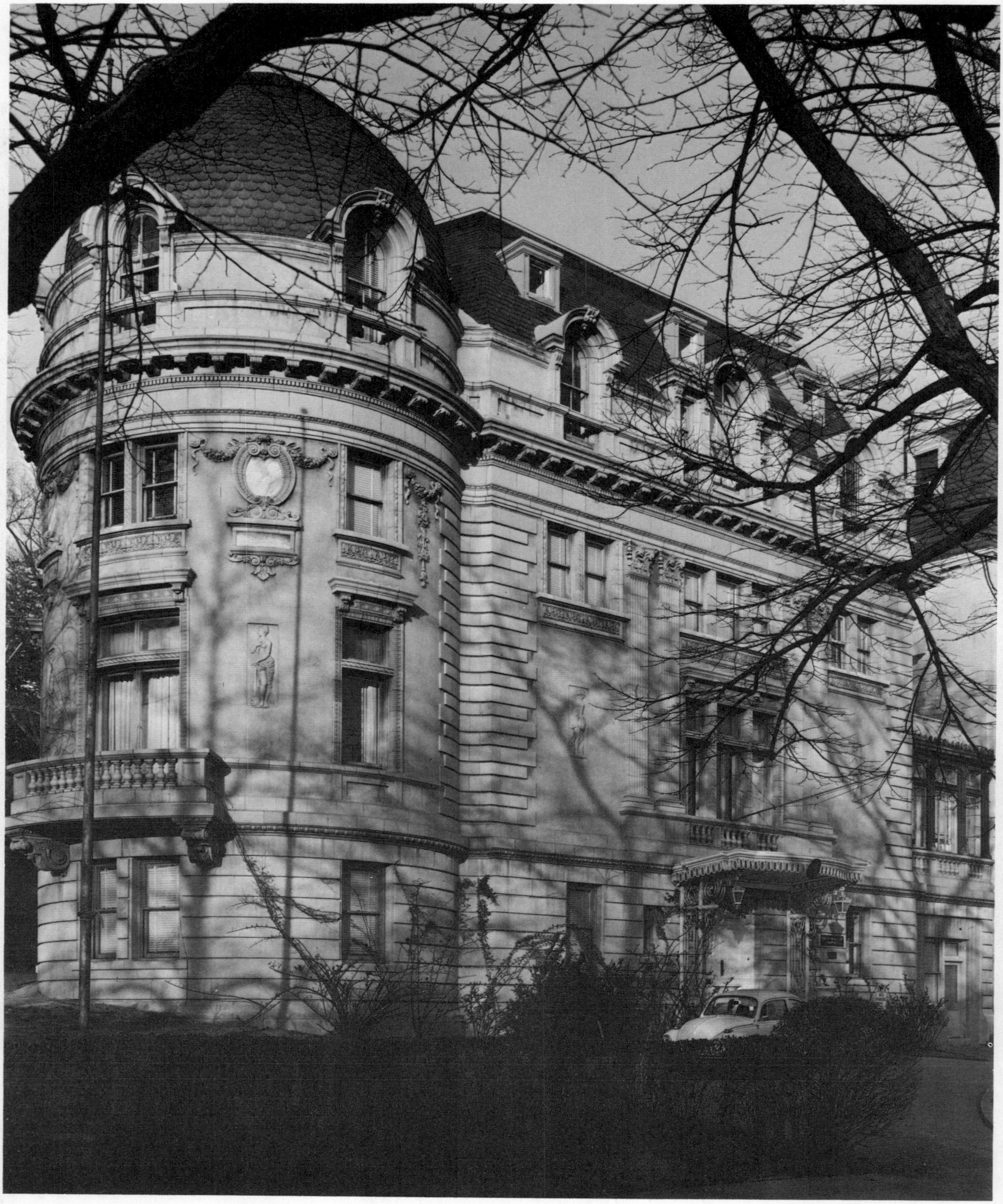

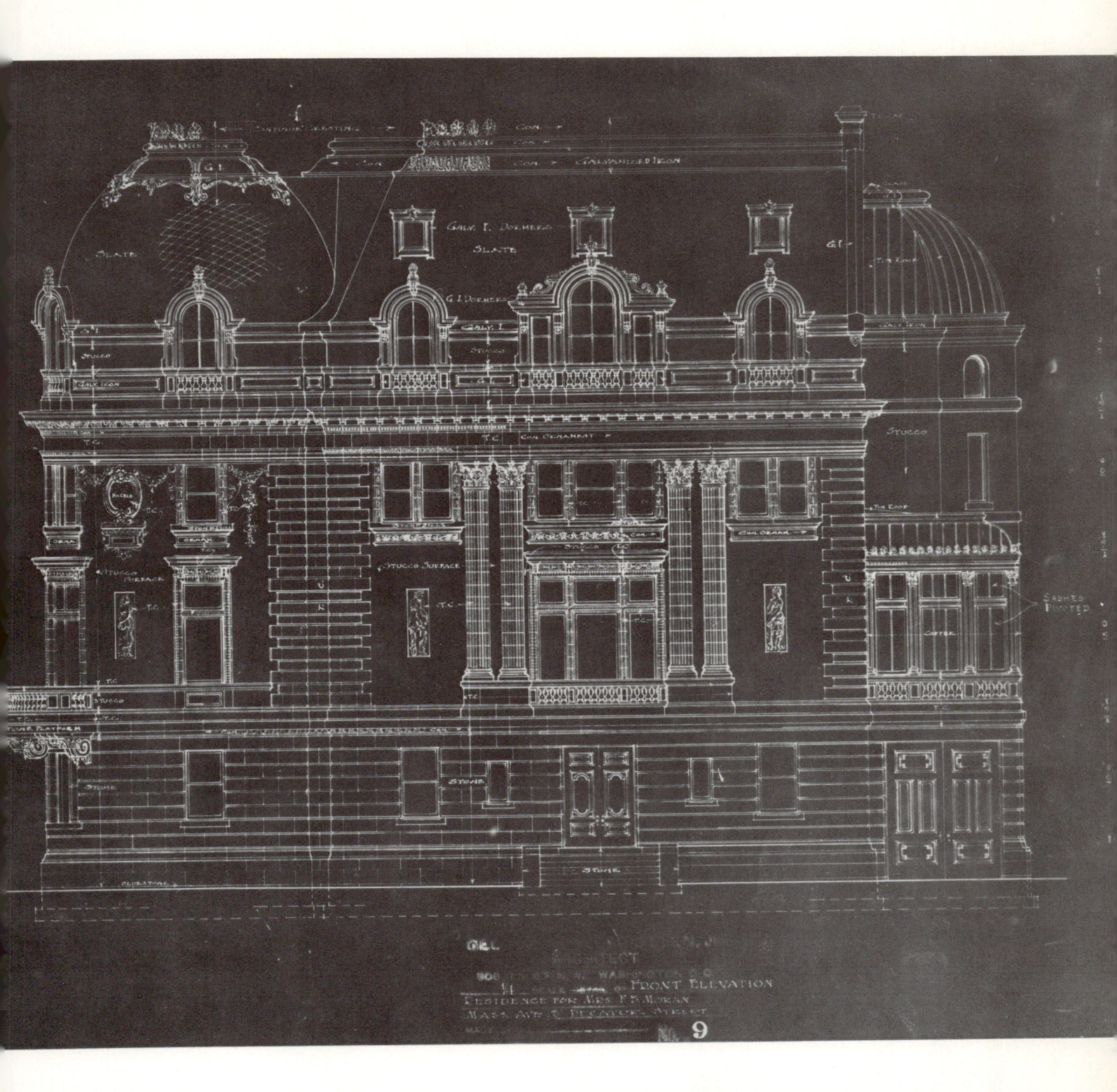

Opposite
CFA photo
Boucher 1970

Massachusetts Avenue Elevation
D.C. Government
Bureau of Licenses and Permits

MUSIC ROOM

HOUSE OF MRS. F. B. MORAN, WASHINGTON, D. C.

MR. GEORGE OAKLEY TOTTEN, ARCHITECT

Music Room
The American Architect
11 August 1915, Volume 108

2349 MASSACHUSETTS AVENUE, N.W., WASHINGTON, D.C.

CFA photo
Boucher 1970

Location: 2349 Massachusetts Avenue, N.W., Washington, D.C.; on the northeast corner of Massachusetts Avenue and 24th Street.

Present Owner: Federal Republic of Cameroon

Present Occupant: Federal Republic of Cameroon

Present Use: Chancery

Statement of Significance: This detached limestone residence, in the early 16th century French manner, is important for three reasons: its prime location, its commanding scale in relation to the adjacent avenue and its exuberant style. The building occupies a site bordered by two streets and an avenue. Its dominant scale is created by the structure's volume and height, and the prominent round tower on the corner of Massachusetts Avenue and 24th Street. Its picturesque Gothic detail has a vitality which is lacking in the less dramatic structures nearby.

PART I. HISTORICAL INFORMATION

    A. Lot and Square:

    The building is located in Square 2517, lots 807 and 808 (formerly lots 18 and 19; and parts of lots 20 and 21 in Block 12, "Kalorama Heights" - all of which were later combined to form lot 33); and lots 813 and 815 (formerly parts of lots 20 and 21).

    B. Original and Subsequent Owners:

    The following chain of title to the property shows the owners of the present structure and of any known preceding structures on the site:

    1906 Deed April 27, 1906, recorded May 3, 1906 in Liber 3000 folio 307

          Louisa D. Lovett, unmarried
               To
          Christian Hauge

          "This Deed...by and between Louisa D. Lovett, unmarried of the City of Philadelphia, State of Pennsylvania, party of the first part, and Christian Hauge, Envoy Extraordinary and Minister Plenipotentiary of the Kingdom of Norway, party of

421

2349 Massachusetts Avenue, N.W.

the second part...Lot...(18) in Block...(12) 'Kalorama Heights' as per plat recorded in County Book 7 page 34 of the Records of the Officer of the Surveyor of the District of Columbia..."

1906 Deed April 27, 1906, recorded May 3, 1906 in Liber 3000 folio 311

Charlotte E. Lovett, unmarried
    To
Christian Hauge

"All of Lot...(19) and parts of Lots...(20) and...(21) Block...(12) 'Kalorama Heights'...Said Lot...(20) being contained within the following metes and bounds: Beginning at the Southwest Corner of said Lot and running thence East along the South line of said Lot...117.8' to the Southeast corner of said Lot, thence North along the rear line of said Lot...25', thence West along the North line of said Lot... 5', thence South parallel with the East line of said Lot... 15' and thence West parallel with the South line of said Lot...112.8' to twenty fourth Street and thence South...5' to the place of beginning. And said part of Lot...(21) being contained within the following metes and bounds. Beginning at the Northeast corner of said Lot and running thence West along the North line of said Lot...5', thence South parallel with the East line of said Lot...25' to the South line of said Lot, thence East along said South line... 5' to the Southeast corner of said Lot and thence North along the rear line of said Lot...25' to the place of beginning..."

NOTE: June 18, 1906 Christian Hauge combined lots 18 and 19 and parts of lots 20 and 21, Block 12, "Kalorama Heights" into lot 33. Recorded in County Book 22 folio 12, Office of the Surveyor, District of Columbia.

The Will of Christian Hauge was recorded in Will Book No. 68, page 534 and admitted to probate April 29, 1908, Registrar of Wills, District of Columbia. The will stated:

"I give, devise and bequeath all of my estate, both real and personal, and wheresoever situated, of which I may die seized, possessed or entitled to my wife, Louise Todd Hauge..."

The Will of Louise Todd Hauge was recorded September 6, 1927 in Will Book No. 134, page 285, Registrar of Wills, District of Columbia. The will stated:

"I bequeath unto my brother, James Ross Todd, all of my household and personal effects of every description,

2349 Massachusetts Avenue, N.W.

> kind and wheresoever situated...I devise unto my brother, James Ross Todd, my residence and the lot adjoining the same, situated on Massachusetts Avenue in the City of Washington in the District of Columbia and all other real estate wheresoever situated of which I may die possessed..."

1927 Deed September 12, 1927, recorded September 12, 1927 in Liber 5992 folio 89

James Ross Todd et ux,
Margaret M. Todd
    To
Louise Todd Gilbert

"James Ross Todd, devisee under the last will of Louise Todd Hauge, deceased, and Margaret M. Todd, his wife, parties of the first part, and Louise Todd Gilbert, party hereto of the second part..." All of lots 18 and 19 and parts of lots 20 and 21 in Block 12, "Kalorama Heights", "...a subdivision of part of 'Widow's Mite' and 'Pretty Prospect'...now embraced in Lot...(33) in Chr. Hauge's (Minister of Norway), Combination of said lots and parts of lots in said Block... (12) 'Kalorama Heights', as per plat of said Combination recorded in Liber County No. 22 folio 12 of the Records of the Office of the Surveyor of the District of Columbia..."

1929 Deed March 25, 1929, recorded April 11, 1929 in Liber 6308 folio 480

Louise Todd Gilbert
    To
Estelle R. Wands

1929 Deed April 11, 1929, recorded April 11, 1929 in Liber 6308 folio 496

Estelle R. Wands
    To
Czechoslovak Republic

"Subject to a certain deed of trust for One hundred and sixty-five thousand dollars ($165,000) dated April 11, 1929...which the said party hereto of the second part assumes and agrees to pay..."

1972 Deed January 12, 1972, recorded January 12, 1972 in Liber 13304 folio 111

2349 Massachusetts Avenue, N.W.

        Czechoslovak Socialist Republic
                  To
     Republique Federale du Cameroon

     "...Parts of Lots...(20) and...(21) in Block...(12) 'Kalo-rama Heights', as per plat recorded in Liber County 7, folio 34 of the Records of the Office of the Surveyor for the District of Columbia...and Lot...(33) in Chr. Hauge's combination of lots and parts of lots in Block...(12), as per plat recorded in Liber County 22 at folio 12 of the aforesaid Surveyor's Office..."

     "Note: At the date hereof the above described land is designated on the Records of the Assessor for the District of Columbia for assessment and taxation purposes as lots numbered...(807),...(808),...(813), and...(815) in Square...(2517). Known as premises 2349 Massachusetts Avenue, N.W..."

     Source: Recorder of Deeds, Washington, D.C.

C. Date of Erection:

The building was begun in June 1906 and completed in May 1907.

D. Building Permits:

The applications for the following building permits were filed by the architect, contractor or owner's agent and provide significant data:

No. 3563, June 22, 1906
Permit to build dwelling
    Owner: Christian Hauge
    Architect: George O. Totten, Jr.
    Builder: John McGregor
    Estimated cost: $50,000.

Filed with No. 3563, June 22, 1906
Application for Building Projections, No. 59821, June 15, 1906
    Circular bay windows: 1'-6" projection
                         1'-9" wide

    Corner tower: 1'-6" projection
                10'-6" on each street

    Main steps: 7'-0" projection
           14'-0" wide

No. 2588, February 26, 1907
Permit to Repair or Reconstruct Building
    "Build one extension for rear service stairs 5' X 5'-6" of

2349 Massachusetts Avenue, N.W.

mansard type - covered with Galv. iron with tin roof. Build a rear addition to kitchen 19' X 6'-9". One story and cellar. Tin roof."

No. 1651, November 15, 1907
Permit to Repair or Reconstruct Building
"Excavate in boiler room for depth of 5'-6". Pit to be 8 X 12 feet. Underpin side walls."

No. 2895, October 12, 1921
Permit to Repair or Reconstruct Building
"Cut north wall for two french casement windows 3'-6" X 8' on first floor leading from music room to lot on the north owned by Madame Hauge."

No. 136561, October 1, 1930
Permit to repair balcony over entrance

No. 160727, February 13, 1933
Permit to Repair or Reconstruct Building
    Owner: Czechoslovak Legation
    Value of improvement: $2000.
    "Repair fire damage, floors, partitions, roof rafters."

No. 172683, July 3, 1934
Permit to Build
    Owner: Legation of Czechoslovakia
    Designer: Smith Bowman, Jr.
    Builder: Bowman & Tyson
    Location: Lot 813, 815 in Square 2517
    "Build one story brick and limestone building for Legation offices."

Filed with No. 172683, July 3, 1934
Special Application for Projection Beyond Building Line
    Entrance steps: Distance beyond building line: 4'-0"
                    Width: 10'-0"

    Marquise: Distance beyond building line: 3'-0"
              Width: 8'-0"

Source: D.C. Government: Department of Economic Development, Bureau of Licenses and Permits, Central Files.

E. Alterations and Additions:

Fire damage to the upper floors necessitated repairs to floors, partitions and roof in 1933.

Building permits indicate that the northwest addition of one story and basement was constructed for offices in 1934.

The architectural survey of this building was completed after the

2349 Massachusetts Avenue, N.W.

Czechoslovakian Embassy was moved in 1969. The first floor library had been partitioned.

Since the Federal Republic of Cameroon purchased the residence in January 1972, the interior has been renovated and redecorated. The chandeliers and canvas wall paintings were restored; and fluorescent lighting for offices and a new heating system installed. No significant changes were made in the main floor plans.

F. Architect: George Oakley Totten, Jr.

See biography of George Oakley Totten, Jr. under 1606 23rd Street.

G. Known Plans, Drawings, Elevations, etc.:

Plan showing projections. Ink on linen. Scale 1/4" = 1'
Filed with Permit No. 3563, June 22, 1906
  "Residence for Hon. Christian Hauge,
   N.E. Corner 24th St. and Mass. Ave.
   Geo. Oakley Totten, Jr., Architect"

Ground and first floor plans.
The Architectural Annual, Washington, D.C.: published by The Architectural League of America, 1907. (see reproductions)

H. Important Old Views:

Photographs: entrance hall with staircase; dining room; two of the salon (drawing room); library; bedroom; and exterior view. Photographs by Harris & Ewing, Washington, D.C.
The Mayflower's Log, Vol. III, No. 8 (October 1927), pp. 17-20.

Photographs: library; dining room; drawing room; and main staircase from ground floor. The photos are not dated, but were taken for the Czechoslovakian Legation and therefore date after 1930. Files of the Czechoslovakian Legation. (see reproductions)

Photographs: drawing room; dining room; library; main staircase; and exterior view.
The Sunday Star, August 5, 1945, Gravure Section.

Photographs: exterior view; details of balconies and main entrance.
The Architectural Annual, Washington, D.C.: published by The Architectural League of America, 1907. (see reproductions)

I. Residents:

   1. City and telephone directories list the following tenants:

2349 Massachusetts Avenue, N.W.

```
1912-1916   Mrs. C. L. Hauge
1917-1918   Mrs. Christian Hauge
1919-1927   Louise C. Hauge
1928-1929   Vacant
1930-1943   Czechoslovakian Legation
1944-1947   Czechoslovak Embassy
1948-1969   Czechoslovakian Embassy
1970-1971   Vacant
1972        Embassy of the Federal Republic of Cameroon, Chancery
```

2. Biographies of the residents:

Christian Hauge, born in Christiana, Norway in April 1862, began his diplomatic career in 1889 as an attaché to the legation of Norway and Sweden at London. He then served as attaché in Paris and Berlin; and as acting first secretary in the legations at Paris, Copenhagen, Berlin, and St. Petersburg.

Hauge came to Washington, D.C. in 1901 as Secretary of the Legation for Norway and Sweden. When Norway peacefully gained independence from Sweden in 1905, Christian Hauge became Norway's first minister to the United States.

> He was well-known socially here [Washington, D.C.] and in New York and also in Bar Harbor which was the summer home of the Sweden-Norway Legation for years. It was at Bar Harbor that he met his wife, formerly Mrs. Frederick Joy [née Louise Grundy Todd] of Louisville, Ky., a widow of large means. Their marriage took place about three years ago, [1904] and from that time until last summer they entertained very extensively. (The New York Times, 12-20-07)

In 1906 George Oakley Totten, Jr., designed 2349 Massachusetts Avenue, which according to floor plans published in the 1907 Architectural Annual was to serve as a residence and legation offices for Christian Hauge. (See reproductions.) The house was completed in June 1907. In November, Mr. and Mrs. Hauge left Washington for a three month vacation in London, Paris and Norway. They visited Paris " for the express purpose of selecting furnishings and decorations for their new home on Massachusetts Avenue." (The Washington Post, 12-20-07) One month later, Christian Hauge died on a snowshoeing trip near Christiana, Norway.

Mrs. Hauge returned to Washington and lived in the new residence on Massachusetts Avenue. Thus, the intended legation "became instead the home of Madame Hauge during the years of her social prominence, and the scene of much of Washington's most brilliant entertaining". (The Mayflower's Log, October 1927) Upon her death in 1927, the house was left to her brother James Ross Todd of Louisville, Kentucky.

2349 Massachusetts Avenue, N.W.

The building remained vacant for two years until the Todds sold it to the Czechoslovak Republic for about $250,000 (according to an article in The Evening Star, 3-16-29). Deeds indicate that the Czechoslovakian government assumed a deed of trust for $165,000, which does not eliminate the possibility that more money was involved in the transaction. The house served as the Czechoslovakian Embassy, even through World War II when the ambassador refused to surrender it to the Nazi German government. In September 1969 the Embassy was moved to 2612 Tilden Street, N.W., and the Massachusetts Avenue building was left vacant until sold in January 1972 to the Federal Republic of Cameroon. The Cameroon government spent an estimated $500,000 for the property and the renovation and redecoration of the residence. (The Evening Star, 3-23-72.)

Sources: "Homes of Interest in an around Washington", The Mayflower's Log, Vol. III, No. 8 (October 1927), pp. 17-20.

The Evening Star, 12-20-07, 15:4 (obituary).
The Evening Star, 1-29-33, 5:1.
The Evening Star, 3-29-29, 17:1.
The Evening Star, 3-23-72, D 3:5.
The New York Times, 12-20-07, 11:5 (obituary).
The Sunday Star, 8-5-45, Gravure Section, p. 2.
The Washington Herald, 1-29-33, 3:1.
The Washington Post, 12-20-07, 1:2 (obituary).
The Washington Post, 1-29-33, M 2:1.
The Washington Post, 3-17-39, 1:6.

Published in
The Architectural Annual
1907

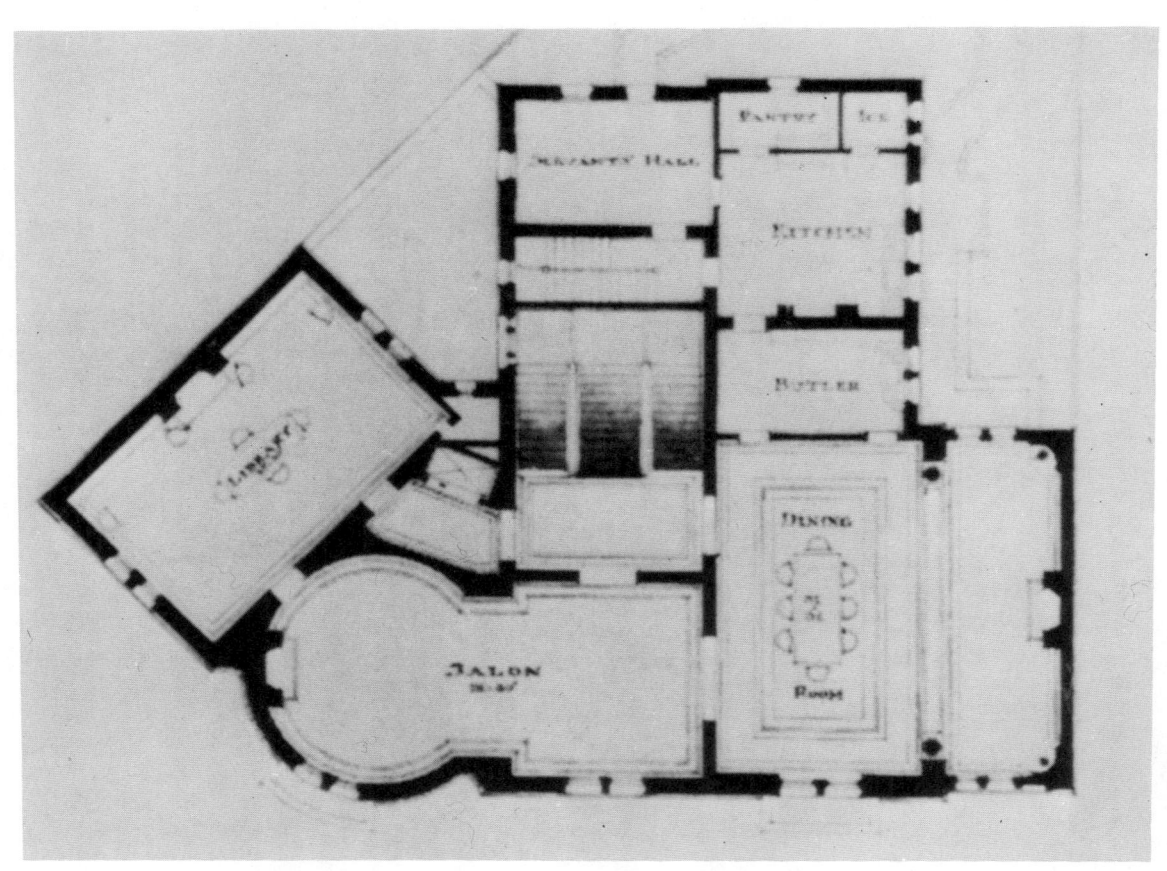

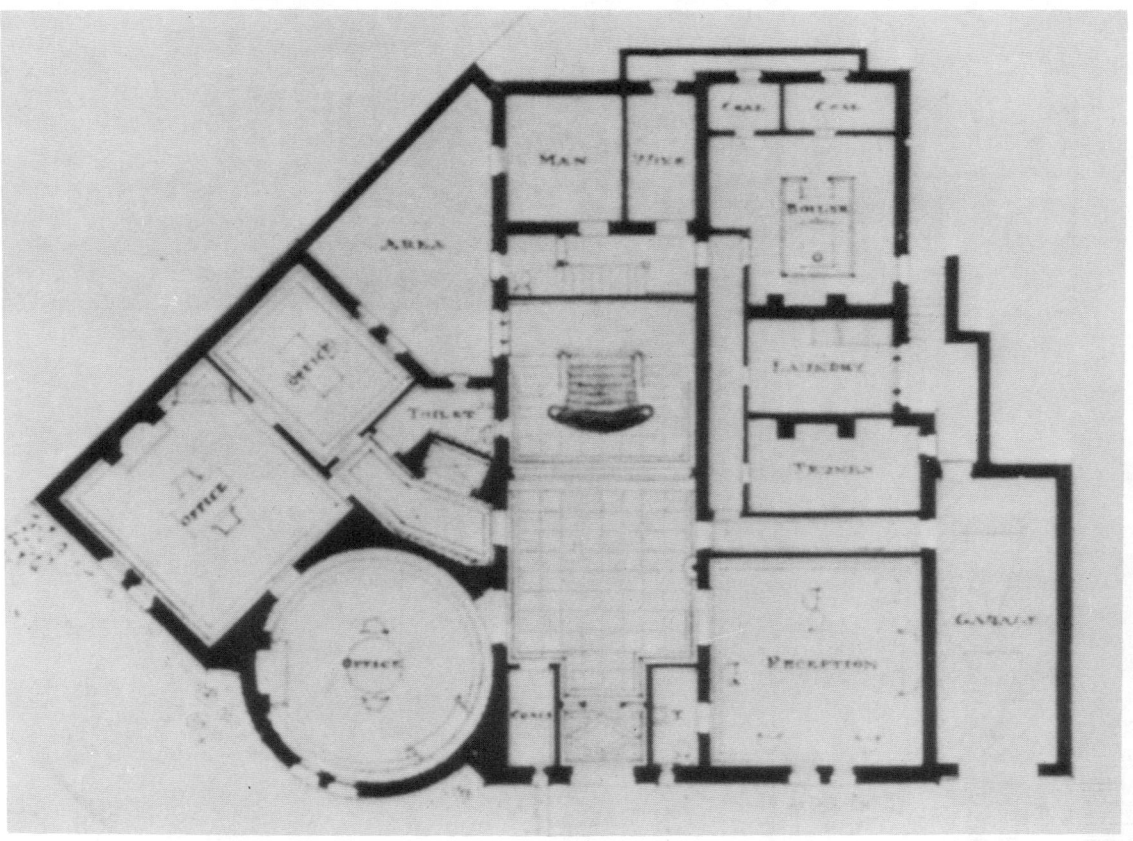

Top: first floor plan
Bottom: ground floor plan
The Architectural Annual, 1907

429

CFA photo
Boucher 1970

Fountain
Entrance Hall
CFA photo
Boucher 1970

FIRST FLOOR PLAN
2340 MASSACHUSETTS AVENUE NW

Detail
Overdoor and Cornice
First Floor Hall
CFA photo
Boucher 1970

Stair at Ground Floor
Photo after 1929
Courtesy of the Czechoslovak
Socialist Republic

Library
Photo after 1929
Courtesy of the Czechoslovak
Socialist Republic

Library Mantle
CFA photo
Boucher 1970

433

Drawing Room
Photo after 1929
Courtesy of the
Czechoslovak Socialist
Republic

Drawing Room
CFA photo
Boucher 1970

Dining Room
CFA photo
Boucher 1970

Dining Room
Photo after 1929
Courtesy of the
Czechoslovak Socialist
Republic

PART II. ARCHITECTURAL INFORMATION

    A. General Statement:

        1. Architectural character: This detached structure, in the early 16th century French Renaissance manner (including the single story 1934 addition), has Louis XV and neo-classical interior details.

        2. Condition: well maintained, with some interior remodeling.

    B. Exterior Description:

        1. Overall dimensions: Including its two story, 30'-0" deep east wing, the three and one half story structure measures 67'-9" in three bays along Massachusetts Avenue and 36'-8" along its single bay 24th Street elevation. The building depth, perpendicular to the avenue, is 65'-8". The height of its single bay, circular tower is 65'-0". The one story, northwest addition measures 40'-0" on 24th Street and 33'-9" on S Street.

        2. Foundations: concrete footings and slab (on grade).

        3. Wall construction: The smooth limestone street elevations are supported by a limestone base with a torus and cavetto water table. The first floor windows rest on a plain, false balustrade, the lines of which are carried around the addition. The low third floor walls are set back to allow for a parapet. The third floor window heads break into the roof with the effect of dormers.

        4. Structure: brick bearing walls with steel roof and floor members.

        5. Mechanical: The building is heated by an American Radiator Company, Ideal Oil Burning Furnace. The Shannon Manufacturing Company Clothes Dryer has a 1907 patent. The elevator is by Otis; the lighting electric. (The above list is as of 1970.)

        6. Porches, stoops, bulkheads, etc.: Four limestone risers ascend to the Massachusetts Avenue entrance. The risers are flanked by cheek walls which support cast iron, decorative bar panels, with ornamental scrolls and lanterns. Above the scrolls is a curvilinear marquise with shield fringe, filigree caps and opaque glass panels. The 24th Street entrance to the northwest addition has a similar canopy on braces over a limestone stoop.

            Limestone balconies with quatrefoil and crocket dados break forward from the false balustrade at both the tower bay and the central bay on Massachusetts Avenue. The balconies are supported on corbel brackets which flank the ground floor window transoms. Though flush with the wall, the false balustrade is similarly pierced at the east wing and over the entrance on 24th Street.

Above the Massachusetts Avenue entrance, the second floor bay has a limestone balcony with bead, diaper and egg and dart mouldings. The turned baluster dado has chamfered sides.

7. Chimneys: Three limestone chimneys are visible from the street. Though ornamental, the east chimney has a cusped panel flanked by panelled blocks. The inner face of the chimney acts as guard for a decorative iron roof crest. The northwest gable has a plain, limestone-capped chimney. The third chimney, set diagonally to the west side of the circular tower, has a beaded corner shaft with cyma string course, cusped frieze, cyma cornice and hipped cap. A fourth chimney (brick) ventilates the northeast service facilities.

8. Openings:

   a. Doorways and doors: The double door entrance on Massachusetts Avenue is plate glass and replaces a single, eight-light door which had both side lights and transom. The limestone hood moulding is flanked by the marquise side panels.

   The double door of the ground floor garage in the east wing has a hood moulding and cast iron, fleur-de-lis and decorative bar gates.

   b. Windows: All windows have cross sashes except for:

   (1.) the narrow windows flanking the entrance door;

   (2.) the first floor tripartite casement window over the garage door; and

   (3.) the second floor balcony window which has a tripartite sash and a three-point-arched transom within a cable architrave. The architrave is flanked by three-quarter-engaged, diaper shaft columns with stiff leaf capitals which support a section, broken forward, of the building cornice and parapet.

   Each ground floor window has a beaded fillet and block sill, a hood moulding and a decorative cast iron grille. The first floor windows have a reed and ribbon architrave capped by a pendant stop hood moulding. The second floor windows have a beaded fillet and block sill, with the parapet base acting as lintel.

9. Roof:

   a. Shape, covering: The gabled, slate roof has a cast iron, arabesque crest. The gutter is copper and the east bay terrace is gravel and asphalt.

   b. Cornice, eaves: The east wing first floor bay is capped by a turned baluster balustrade with panelled end blocks.

   On Massachusetts Avenue and 24th Street, the trefoil arclette frieze is interrupted by the second floor window transoms and, at the tower, by corbel brackets. Above the frieze is a fascia, cavetto, coved corona, roll and cyma cornice which supports the trefoil, quatrefoil and roundel balustrade parapet.

   The roof springs from the cyma, cove and corona cornice at third floor transom height.

   c. Dormers, cupolas, towers: The tower has a slate conical roof capped by a decorative, copper crocket and weather vane finial.

   The cross sash dormer of the tower has a lancet-arched hood moulding within a gable with crockets. Flanking and linked to the gable by tracery are shafts with finials. The design is similar for the smaller outer bays. Between each third floor bay, the attic level has a diminuitive, wood dormer with gable and finial.

C. Interior Description:

1. Floor plans: The main stair is on axis with the southwest vestibule and entrance hall. Closets, with access from the hall, flank the vestibule. The east salon and west lounge flank the entrance hall. Beyond the lounge is the reception room and the addition. To the northeast, a corridor links the entrance hall to the furnace and storage rooms. At the northwest a second corridor gives access to the elevator and reception room.

   From the main stair, the first floor foyer gives access to the east dining room, the south drawing room and the west library. The east bay of the two bay dining room is over the garage. The shorter dimension is punctuated by fluted Ionic columns. The drawing room west bay is formed by the tower. The west elevator corridor leads to the library. All three rooms are connected by way of the drawing room. The dining room gives access to the pantry, the kitchen and the service stairs at the northeast. (See plan.)

Both the main stair and the servants' stair ascend to
the second and third floors, which are arranged in bedroom
suites and northeast servants' quarters.

2. Spaces:

Entrance hall:

a. Flooring: grey mosaic tile within black fret border.

b. Baseboard: 9", grey marble.

c. Walls: plaster painted white, applied mouldings. The east wall marble fountain has an acanthus and shell console which supports a cherub, escutcheon and spray basin. Over the decoratively carved splash board is a triangular frieze with satyr's mask and spout, cherubs and scrolls. (See detail photograph.)

d. Cornice: egg and dart, ogee, terminated at north by main stair.

e. Ceiling: plaster painted white.

f. Doorways and doors: The double doors at the south and the single doors at the north all have raised panels and rinceau frieze caps within bead architraves. The west door to the lounge is convex.

g. Lighting: There are two, standing, gilded wood, baroque candelabra and one, two-tier, brass and crystal pendant, rocaille chandelier.

The elevator corridor has a two-armed, gilded rinceau sconce.

East salon:

a. Flooring: 2", common hardwood.

b. Baseboard: 8", wood with cyma cap.

c. Walls: plaster painted white.

d. Ceiling: plaster painted white.

e. Doorways and doors: bead architraves.

West lounge:

a. Flooring: 2", common hardwood.

b. Baseboard: 8", wood with cyma cap.

2349 Massachusetts Avenue, N.W.

    c. Walls: plaster painted white.

    d. Ceiling: plaster painted white.

    e. Doorways and doors: bead architraves.

    f. Lighting: one, two-tiered, brass and crystal pendant, rocaille chandelier.

    g. Heating: The west wall chimney has a maroon marble hearth and a cast iron lattice firebox. The white-veined, purple marble mantle (4'-6" wide by 4'-0" high) has stylized composite pilasters which support an ogee shelf centered by an escutcheon with leaf sprays.

Reception room:

    a. Flooring: black and white foot square marble tiles.

    b. Baseboard: 8", wood with cyma cap.

    c. Chairrail: 2'-6" high, wood.

    d. Walls: raised wood panels, painted.

    e. Heating: The northwest wall chimney has a cast iron fleur-de-lis firebox and white marble mantle, 4'-6" high, with diminuitive consoles supporting a three panel cherub frieze and cyma shelf.

Stair:

Separating the entrance hall from the stair at the north are three marble risers terminated by panelled composite pilasters on a grey and black mosaic platform, centered by a panel of Chinese calligraphy. The stair ascends north eight, flaired and convex, white marble risers to a landing and divides into two flanking ascents eleven risers south. The closed marble stringer has a plaster soffit, centered by a panel and wreath. The cast iron, gouge, and wave railing has a wood handrail with brass finials and four inch square newels buttressed by console scrolls and rosettes. The remaining flights above the first floor are wood.

    a. Baseboard: 9", marble.

    b. Walls: plaster painted white.

Foyer:

    a. Flooring: grey marble.

    b. Baseboard: 9", grey marble with wood at the south wall.

2349 Massachusetts Avenue, N.W.

   c. Walls: plaster painted white, with panels formed by
      applied mouldings.

   d. Cornice: acanthus cove and talon.

   e. Ceiling: plaster painted white.

   f. Doorways and doors: All doors, including the recessed door
      to the dining room, the sliding double door to the drawing
      room, and the single door to the elevator corridor, have
      raised panels and bead and fascia architraves, capped by
      rinceau panels. (See detail photograph.)

Dining room: (see photographs)

   a. Flooring: quadrant basket weave within lattice parquetry.

   b. Baseboard: 6", wood with bead cap.

   c. Dado: raised wood panels. Flanking the east chimney are
      paired consoles which support marble counters with splash
      boards. At the north wall is a built-in buffet with paired,
      guilloche-panelled consoles which support a purple marble
      counter.

   d. Walls: Flanking the east chimney are decorative twining-
      leaf panels. Over either buffet is a canvas in the neo-
      classical manner framed by talon. At the northeast and
      southeast corners of the room are semicircular-arched niches
      each with a marble, console-supported basin and leafy
      scroll keystone. Flanking the west doors are curvilinear
      raised panels with decorative spandrels. The northwest
      and southwest corners of the room are rounded by decorative
      twining-leaf panels.

   e. Cornice: tulip, egg and dart, fret dentils, corona with
      palmette soffit, and leaf pulvination.

   f. Ceiling: plaster painted white.

   g. Doorways and doors: All doors have rosette-indented, flush
      panels and a decorative lock rail. Two double doors at the
      west wall are each capped by an urn and floral canvas within
      a three-point arch. (The double door on the right is false,
      only the center opens to the foyer.) The pulvinated bay leaf
      architrave has an acanthus keystone with sprays and flush-
      panelled rosette spandrels.

      Both service doors at the north wall have a guilloche
      architrave, at the head of which scroll consoles, capped by
      an egg and dart cornice, flank a guilloche panel. The cornice
      supports a canvas lunette having ribbon and fruit pendants.

2349 Massachusetts Avenue, N.W.

h. Hardware: brass, baroque knobs and plain pulls.

i. Lighting: There are four, three-light, ramshead and leaf, gilded brass, baroque sconces. There is one four-light, urn, spike and swag rocaille sconce at the west wall.

j. Heating: The east wall chimney has a purple marble hearth with green rectangular insets, and a cast iron firebox with a wreath, arrow and ribbon back panel, concave rinceau side panels, and a ring, ribbon and swag surround. The white and grey-veined, purple marble mantle (5'-0" wide by 4'-0" high) has plain panels and a gouge and floral spray frieze broken forward in pod, ribbon and ring over either panel and capped by a cavetto cornice. The overmantle has a three-point-arched, rocaille mirror within a pulvinated moulding capped by swags and ribbons.

Drawing room: (see photographs)

a. Flooring: quadrant basket weave within lattice parquetry.

b. Baseboard: 9", wood, painted.

c. Dado: raised wood panels, painted.

d. Chairrail: 2'-6" high, flush rinceau rail.

e. Walls: Paired pilasters separate the circular and square areas of the room. The chimney and major openings are flanked by fluted, tulip stop, Ionic pilasters on baseboard plinths. Flanking the dining room door, and between the paired pilasters, gilded consoles support swag and gouge, marble-topped tables below mirrors with ribbon capped semi-circular arches on impost blocks.

f. Cornice: acanthus cove, talon.

g. Ceiling: plaster painted white.

h. Doorways and doors: There are three, sliding double doors with rosette indented panels. The foyer and dining room doors have flanking post and block architraves, capped by a three-point-arched rocaille mirror, with an acanthus keystone and ribbon. The library door has a pulvinated architrave capped by a floral canvas panel.

i. Hardware: brass pulls.

j. Lighting: Flanking the west chimney mantle are three-light, gilded brass, flambeau and swag sconces. The mirrors between the paired pilasters have a one tier, four-light, brass and crystal bead and pendant, tear-drop sconce. There are two, double tier, alternating eight-light and crystal finial chandeliers, with crystal pendants and beads.

2349 Massachusetts Avenue, N.W.

    k. Heating: The west wall chimney has a grey marble hearth with blue-veined, white marble insets; a cast iron firebox with a swag and musical instrument back panel; and a concave, guilloche and central rosette surround. The dark-veined, grey marble mantle (5'-0" wide by 3'-6" high) has acanthus and gilded rope consoles and a mask frieze of griffins and floral rinceau applique in brass. The overmantle mirror has flanking post panels and blocks below a semicircular arch in a false perspective, chrysanthemum panel surround. The surround is interrupted by a ribbon cap with sunflower and frond spandrels.

Library: (partitioned. See photographs.)

    a. Flooring: 2" common hardwood within basket weave border.

    b. Baseboard: 9", wood with cyma cap, painted.

    c. Walls: painted white over flock paper.

    d. Cornice: egg and dart, prominent cyma.

    e. Ceiling: plaster painted white (decorative plaster removed).

    f. Heating: The northwest wall chimney has a glazed tile hearth and a cast iron firebox with an escutcheon and ribbon pack panel. The tan and cream alabaster mantle in the 15th century Italianate manner (5'-6" wide by 6'-6" high), has flanking "forget-me-not" plinths which support candelabra pilasters of dragons, cherubs, snakes, flambeau and mythical animals. The acanthus leaf, cherub, and griffin capitals support a fascia and talon architrave; a griffin and leaf, rinceau frieze; and an egg and dart, "forget-me-not" and talon shelf. (See detail photographs.)

D. Site:

1. Setting and orientation: The building faces southwest on a pentagonal lot measuring 67'-9" on Massachusetts Avenue (south); 76'-8" on 24th Street (west); 117'-9" on S Street (north); 50'-0" on the east; and 100'-0" on the southeast. The building overlooks Robert Emmet park on the west.

2. Enclosures: none.

3. Outbuildings: the 1934 single story northwest addition.

4. Walks: On axis with the entrance stoop, three limestone risers ascend from the Massachusetts Avenue sidewalk over a wedge of grass to the circular concrete drive. A concrete walk leads

from 24th Street, across a grass border, to the west addition entrance.

5. Landscaping: grass planted with blue spruce, boxwood and yucca plants (as of 1970).

2370 MASSACHUSETTS AVENUE, N.W., WASHINGTON, D.C.

CFA photo
Boucher 1970

Address: 2370 Massachusetts Avenue, N.W., Washington, D.C.

Significance: This detached and unaltered dwelling of the late Beaux-Arts period was designed with an informal treatment of spaces in the manner of a Jacobean country home.

Present Owner: Rev. James B. Davis
Present Use: Residence
Lot and Square: Square 2507, lot 829 (formerly 814 and 822). Lot 814 was previously lots 38 and 39; and lot 822 was previously lot 40.

HISTORICAL AND ARCHITECTURAL INFORMATION

Original Owner: Alice W. B. Stanley* (1923-1972)**
Original Use: Residence
Date of Erection: 1930
Architects: Smith and Edwards, Washington, D.C.
Builder: Harry F. Boryer
Estimated cost: $90,000.

Subsequent Owner:

   Rev. James B. Davis (1972-   )

City and Telephone Directories List:

   1932-1940   Arthur C. Stanley
   1941-1948   Mrs. Alice B. Stanley
   1949   No listing found
   1950-1953   Camp Stanley, physician
   1954-1972   Rev. James B. Davis

Known Plans, Drawings, Elevations, etc.: none found.

Important Old Views: none found.

Building Dimensions:

   Stories: 3 plus basement and attic

   Height: 53'-0" to roof ridge

_____

* Alice W. B. Stanley was the wife of Arthur Camp Stanley, who died in 1940. Mrs. Stanley later married Rev. James B. Davis. Mrs. Davis died June 26, 1972.
** According to Deeds, Alice W. B. Stanley acquired lot 40 in 1923 and final title to lots 38 and 39 in 1932.

2370 Massachusetts Avenue, N.W.

Bays: 4 composite bays on Massachusetts Avenue

Widths: main block 55'-0" on Mass. Ave.
41'-0" in depth

rear service wing 38'-6" at south (Rock Creek Park)
25'-0" in depth

Site Dimensions:

65'-9" on north (Mass. Ave.)
65'-9" on south (Rock Creek Park)
100'-0" on east and west

Major Alterations:

No significant changes have been made.

Detail Entrance Stair Hall
CFA photo 1973

Detail Entrance
CFA photo
Alexander 1971

Dining Room
CFA photo 1973

Typical Interior Door
CFA photo 1973

2516 MASSACHUSETTS AVENUE, N.W., WASHINGTON, D.C.

CFA Files

Address: 2516 Massachusetts Avenue, N.W., Washington, D.C.

Significance: This building, in the Georgian manner, was designed as an embassy. It exemplifies the last stage of beaux-arts influence in Washington and is one of the few full-scale, formal estates in the city. The estate includes the house and its dependencies (with a tea house, two chancery buildings and recreational facilities). The landscaping complements Rock Creek Park.

Present Owner: Japan
Present Use: Embassy residence
Lot and Square: Square 2500, lots 851, 852 and 853 (formerly lots 8-16 and 35-43); and lots 871, 873 and 874.

HISTORICAL AND ARCHITECTURAL INFORMATION

Original Owner: Japan
Original Use: Embassy residence
Date of Erection: 1931
Architects: Delano and Aldrich, New York
Builder: unknown *
Estimated cost: $500,000. **

Subsequent Owners: none.

City and Telephone Directories List:

    1932-1941   Japanese Embassy
    1942-1948   Japanese Embassy (closed)
    1949-1953   No listing found
    1954-1972   Japanese Embassy

Known Plans, Drawings, Elevations, etc.: none found.

Important Old Views: none found.

Building Dimensions:

    Stories: 2 and 1/2 plus two basement levels

    Height: approx. 31'-0" to eaves

---

* Japan, as a foreign government, was not required to file for D.C. building permits.
** Federal Writers' Project, Washington, City and Capital (Washington, D.C.: Government Printing Office, 1937), p. 689.

2516 Massachusetts Avenue, N.W.

Bays: 7 bays on Mass. Ave.
6 bays at east (south bay, 1 story)
6 bays at south
5 bays at west

Widths: 98'-10" on Mass. Ave.
78'- 9" at east (last bay extends 16'-0" beyond south elevation)
99'- 0" at south (Rock Creek Park)
62'- 9" at west

Site Dimensions:

450'-0" on north
275'-0" on east
450'-0" on south
275'-0" on west

Major Alterations:

No significant changes have been made.

Detail Stair Hall
CFA photo
Alexander 1971

CFA photo
Alexander 1971

CFA photo
Alexander 1971

ARCHITECTURAL BIBLIOGRAPHY

Russell Sturgis. *Dictionary of Architecture and Building*. 3 Vols. New York and London, 1902. Book Tower, Detroit: Reprinted by Gale Research Company, 1966.

John Fleming, Hugh Honour and Nikolaus Pevsner. *The Penguin Dictionary of Architecture*. Baltimore: Penguin Books, Inc., 1967.

Franz Sales Meyer. *Meyer's Handbook of Ornament - Geometrical and Floral*. Pelham (New York): Bridgman Publishers, 1928.

Nikolaus Pevsner. *An Outline of European Architecture*. Baltimore: Penguin Books, 1960.

Sir Banister Fletcher. *A History of Architecture - On the Comparative Method*. Revised by R.A. Cordingley, New York: Charles Scribner's Sons, 1961.

Alexander Speltz. *The Styles of Ornament*. New York: Dover Publications, Inc., 1959.

ILLUSTRATED ARCHITECTURAL GLOSSARY

Selected Terms

GREEK DORIC ORDER:

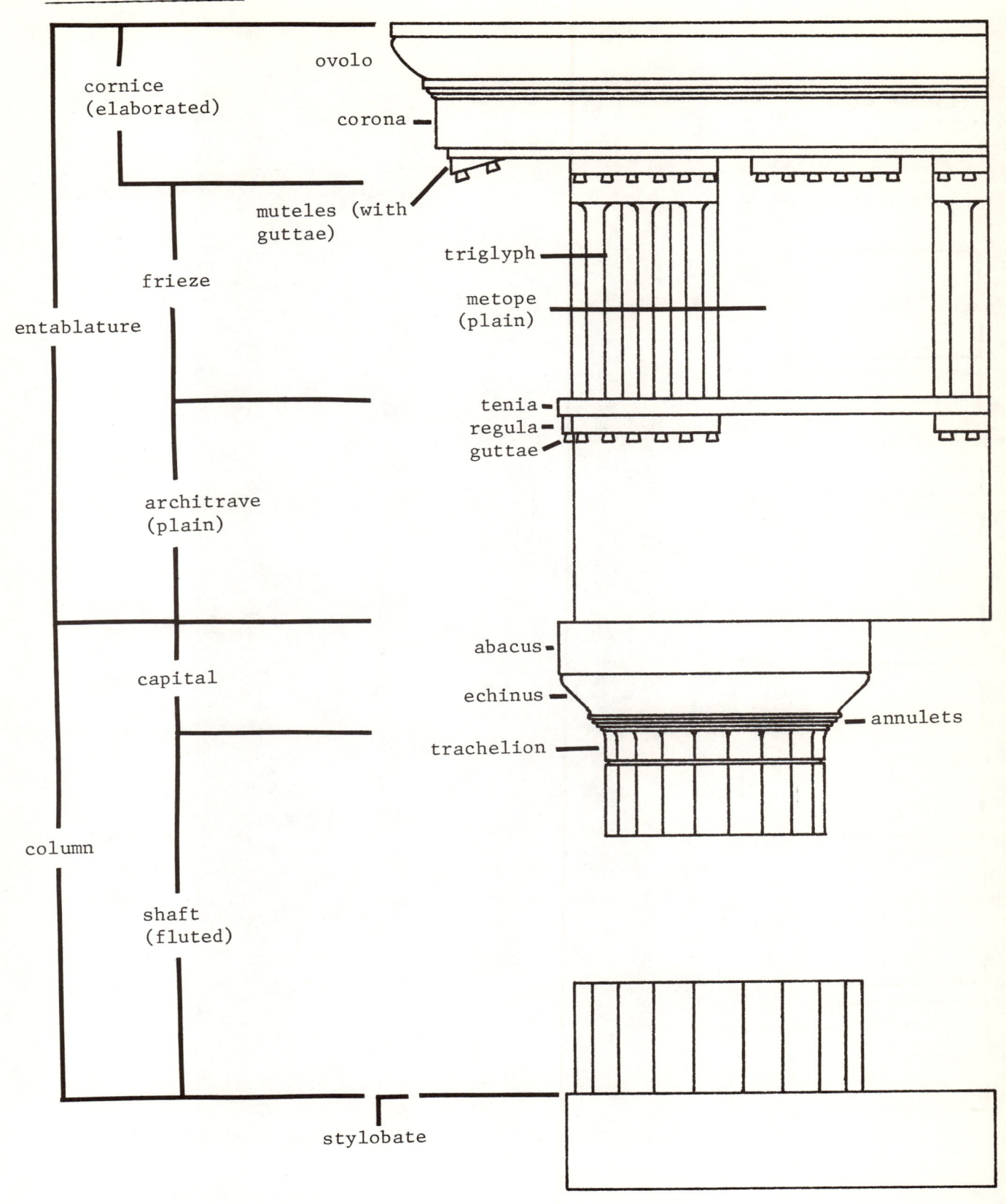

- entablature
  - cornice (elaborated)
    - ovolo
    - corona
    - muteles (with guttae)
  - frieze
    - triglyph
    - metope (plain)
    - tenia
    - regula
    - guttae
  - architrave (plain)
- column
  - capital
    - abacus
    - echinus
    - annulets
    - trachelion
  - shaft (fluted)
- stylobate

461

BUILDING ELEVATION:

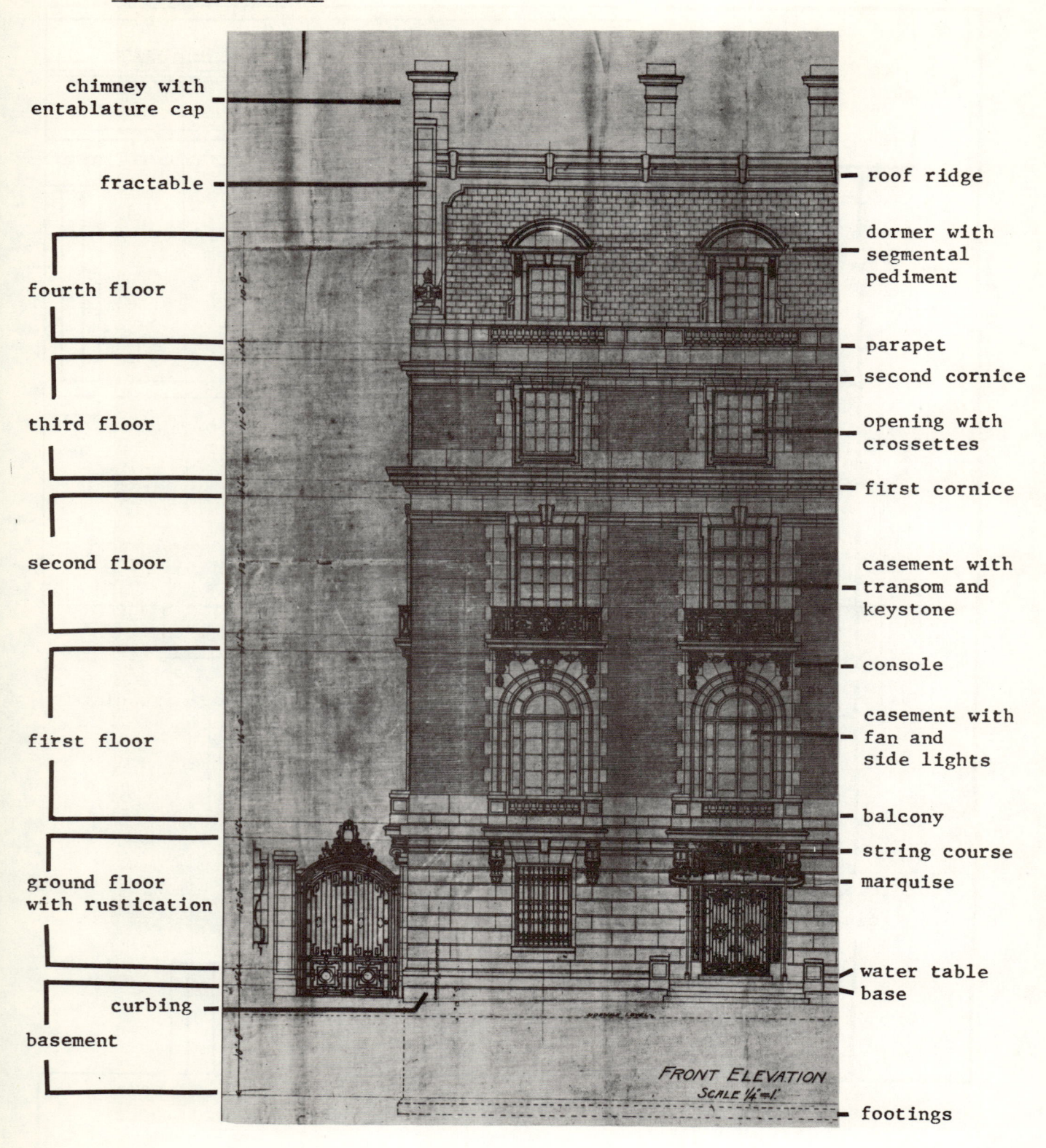

- chimney with entablature cap
- fractable
- fourth floor
- third floor
- second floor
- first floor
- ground floor with rustication
- curbing
- basement

- roof ridge
- dormer with segmental pediment
- parapet
- second cornice
- opening with crossettes
- first cornice
- casement with transom and keystone
- console
- casement with fan and side lights
- balcony
- string course
- marquise
- water table base
- footings

1746 Massachusetts Avenue, N.W. (detail)

RESIDENCE FOR CLARENCE MOORE, ESQ., WASHINGTON, D. C.

J. H. de Sibour, *Architect*

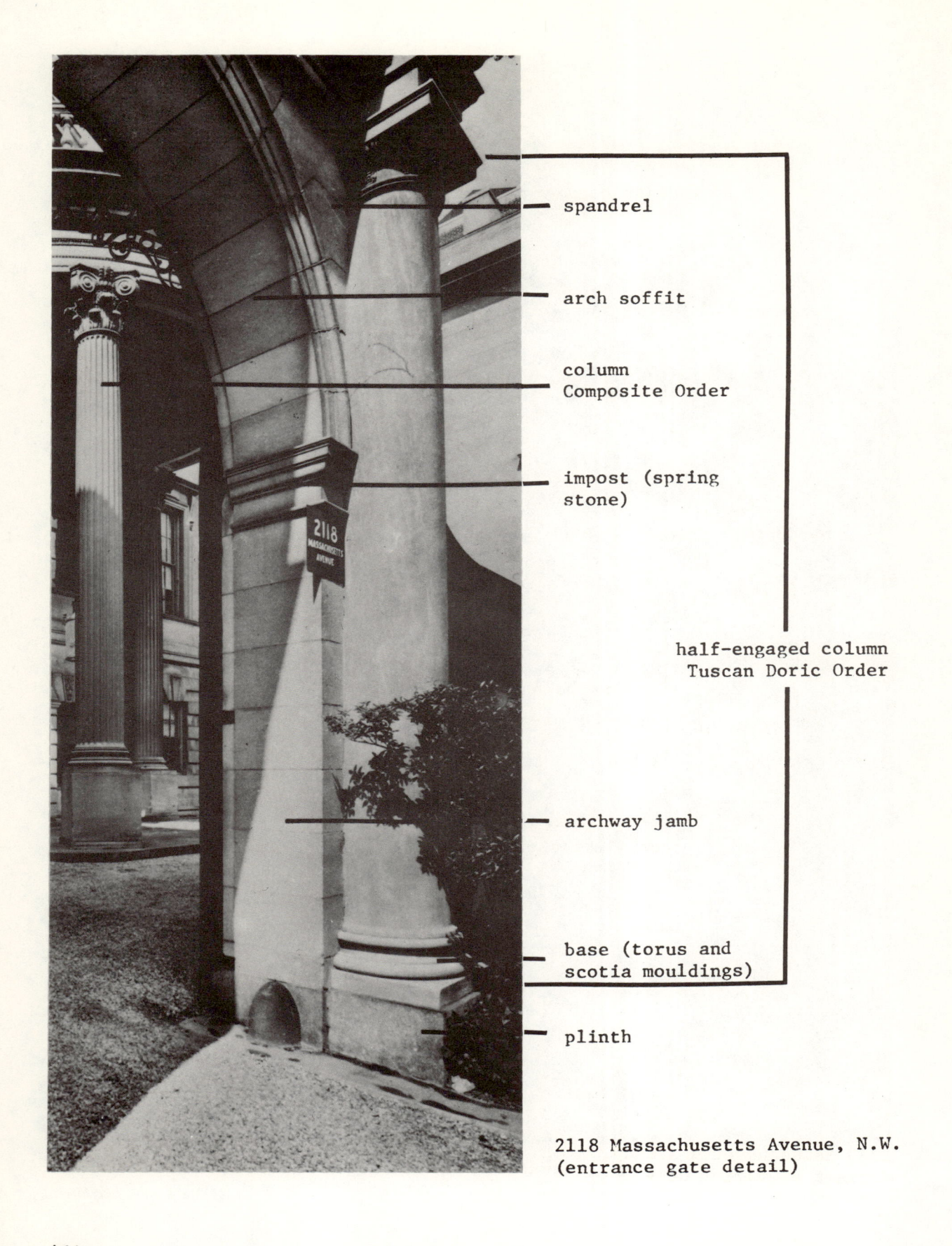

- spandrel
- arch soffit
- column Composite Order
- impost (spring stone)
- half-engaged column Tuscan Doric Order
- archway jamb
- base (torus and scotia mouldings)
- plinth

2118 Massachusetts Avenue, N.W.
(entrance gate detail)

spire with crockets

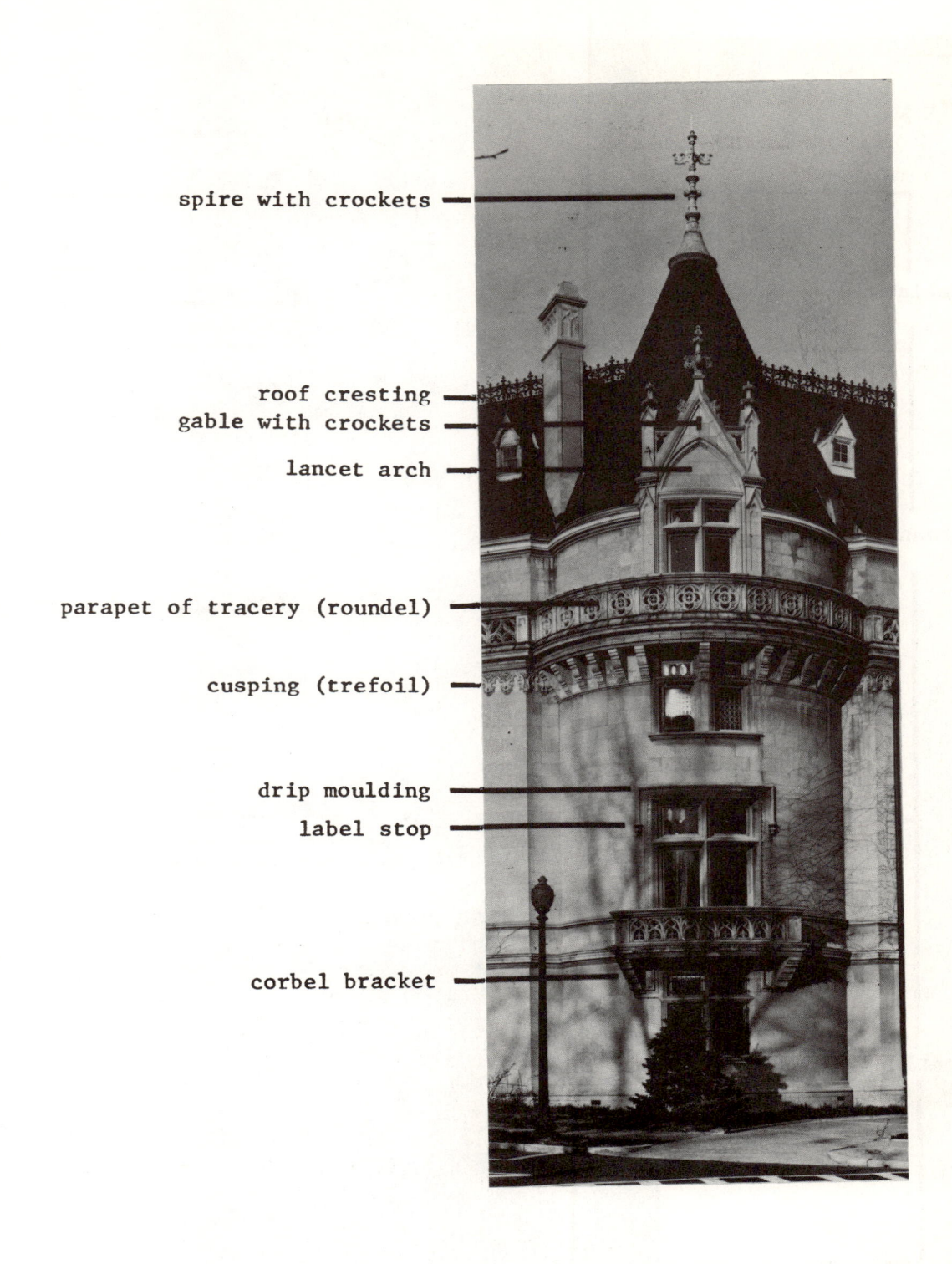

roof cresting
gable with crockets
lancet arch

parapet of tracery (roundel)

cusping (trefoil)

drip moulding
label stop

corbel bracket

2349 Massachusetts Avenue, N.W.
(street elevation detail)

MANTLE:

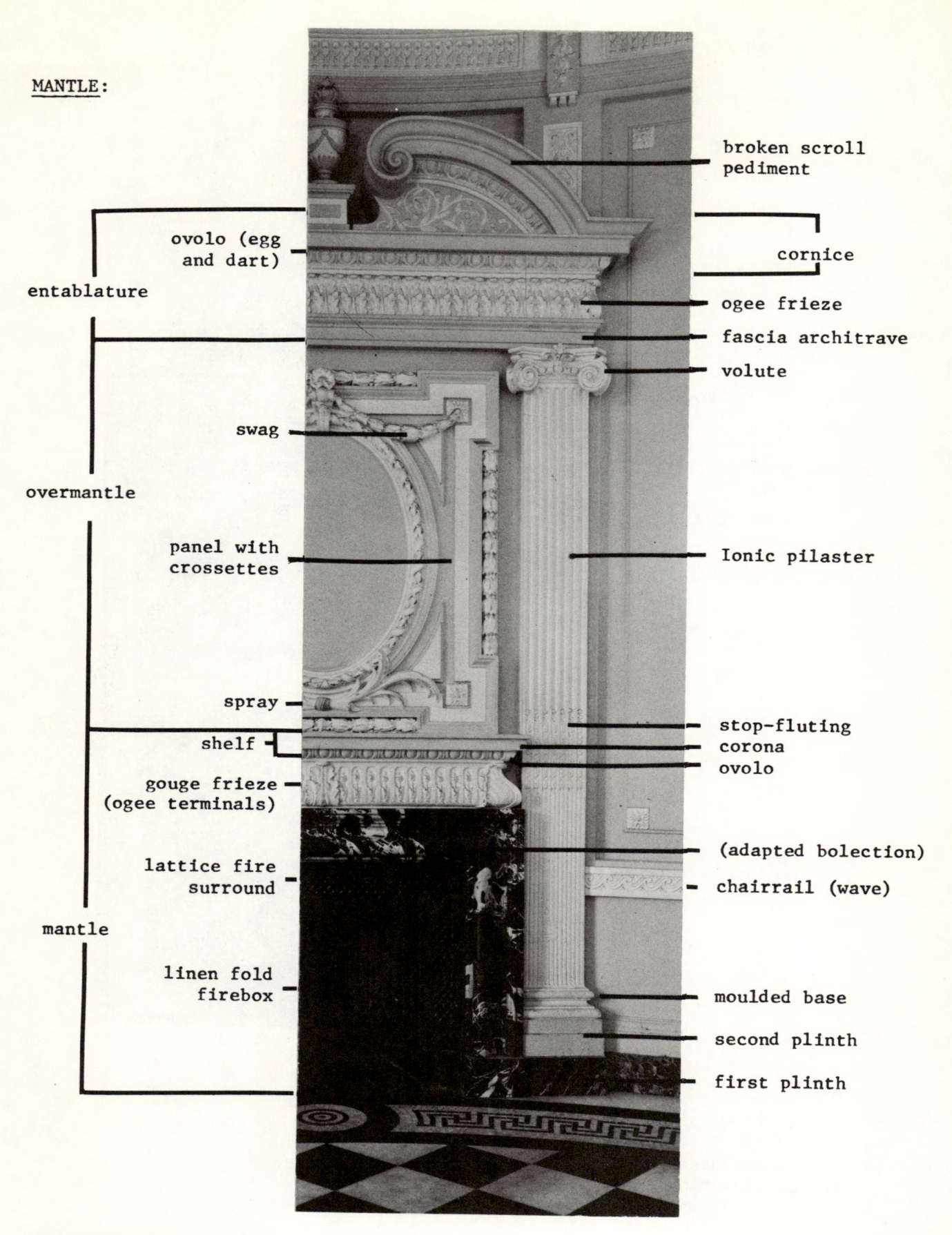

- entablature
  - ovolo (egg and dart)
  - broken scroll pediment
  - cornice
  - ogee frieze
  - fascia architrave
  - volute
- overmantle
  - swag
  - panel with crossettes
  - Ionic pilaster
  - spray
  - stop-fluting
  - shelf
  - corona
  - ovolo
- mantle
  - gouge frieze (ogee terminals)
  - (adapted bolection)
  - lattice fire surround
  - chairrail (wave)
  - linen fold firebox
  - moulded base
  - second plinth
  - first plinth

1785 Massachusetts Avenue, N.W.
(entrance lobby detail)

ARCHITECTURAL DETAILS:

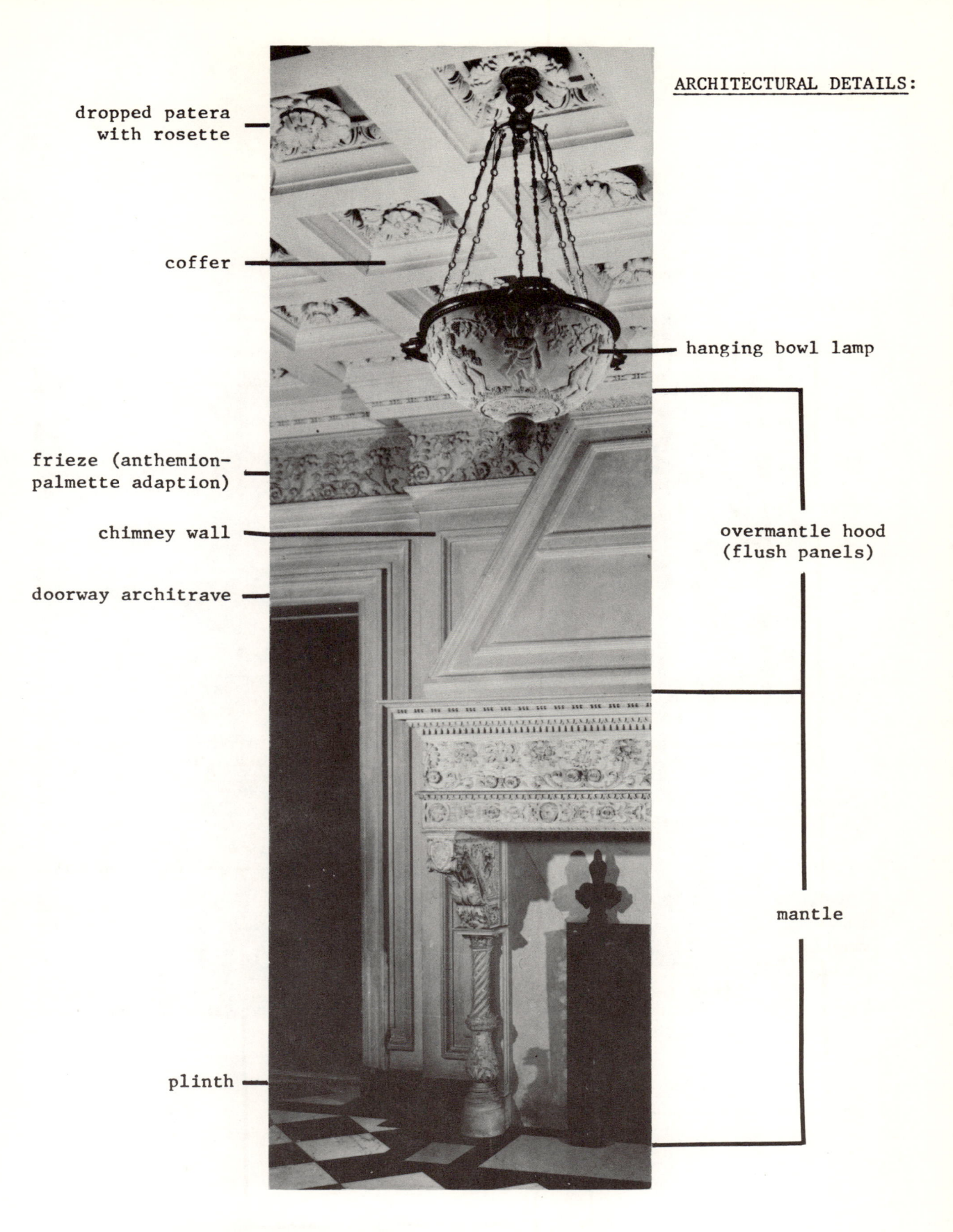

dropped patera with rosette

coffer

hanging bowl lamp

frieze (anthemion-palmette adaption)

chimney wall

doorway architrave

overmantle hood (flush panels)

mantle

plinth

1746 Massachusetts Avenue, N.W.
(stair hall detail)

467

ARCHITECTURAL DETAILS:

- pilaster
- lip (gadroon)
- ormolu mount
- torus (ribbon enrichment)
- crossette architrave
- bolection
- torus (garland enrichment)
- chairrail
- (panelled) dado
- base
- (baseboard) plinth
- pedestal
- hearth (marble insets)
- parquetry (basket weave)

2020 Massachusetts Avenue, N.W. (entrance room detail)

MOULDINGS:

corona
modillion (acanthus)
talon (enriched cyma reversa)
gouge
fascia (acanthus enrichment)
ovolo (egg and dart enrichment)
astragal (bead and reel)
rinceau panel
guilloche
pulvination (bundled bay leaf)
corona
dentils
pendant
fascia
fascia (enriched)

2301 Massachusetts Avenue, N.W. (drawing room detail)

STAIR:

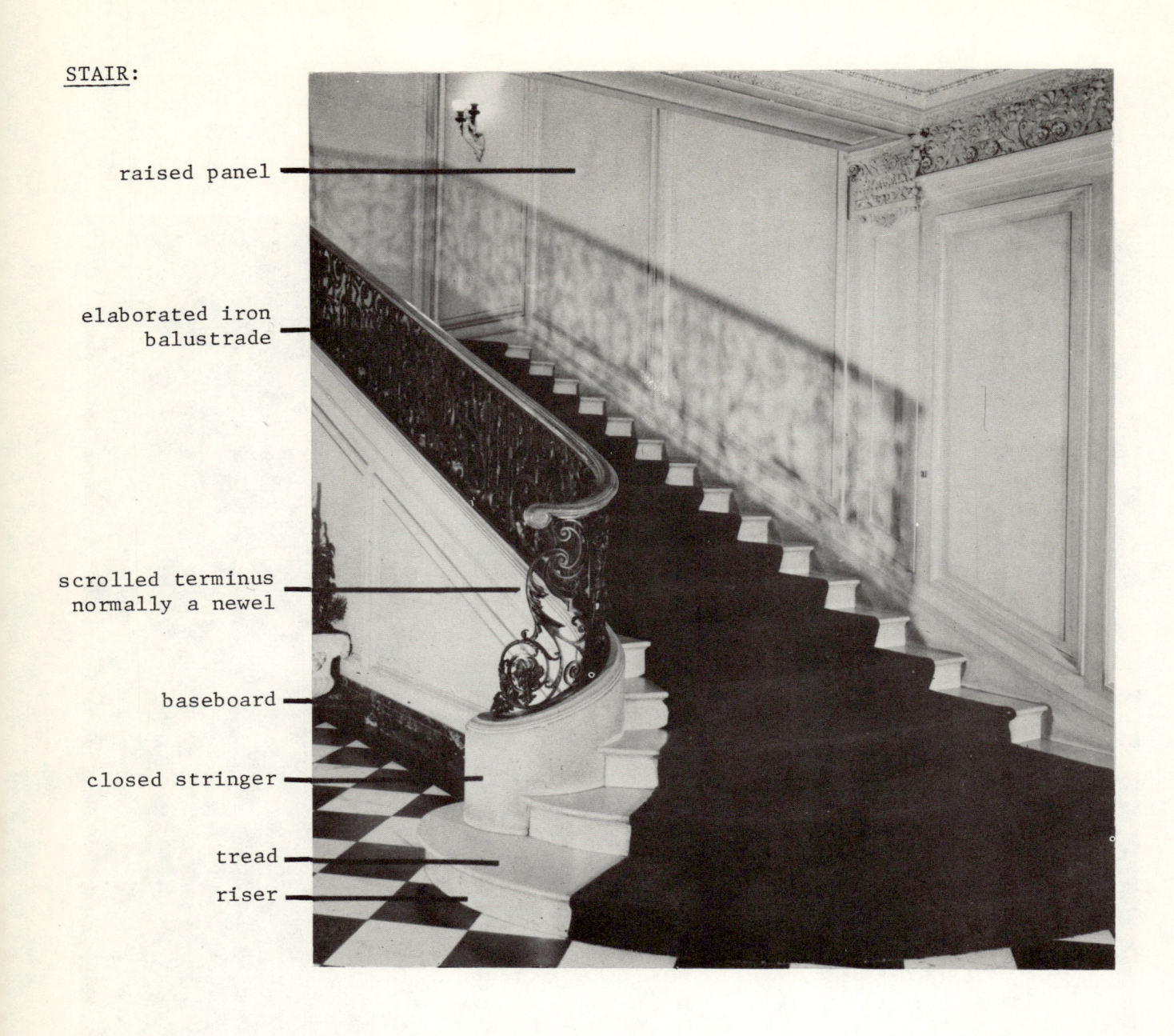

- raised panel
- elaborated iron balustrade
- scrolled terminus normally a newel
- baseboard
- closed stringer
- tread
- riser

1746 Massachusetts Avenue, N.W.
(stair hall detail)

COVER CREDITS:

Decatur Place and Massachusetts Avenue, Northwest
Foreground 2315 Massachusetts Avenue
Erected 1909
George Oakley Totten, Jr., Architect
CFA photo
Boucher 1970

Dupont Circle
Dupont Memorial Fountain
Dedicated 17 May 1921
Daniel Chester French, Sculptor
Henry Bacon, Architect
CFA photo
Alexander 1971

2118 Massachusetts Avenue, Northwest
Archway into entrance court
Completed 1905
Little and Browne, Architects
Dunlop Studios, Photographers

Sheridan Circle
Gen. Philip H. Sheridan Statue
Unveiled 25 November 1908
Gutzon Borglum, Sculptor
CFA photo
Alexander 1971